Living under Austerity

Living under Austerity

Greek Society in Crisis

Edited by
Evdoxios Doxiadis and Aimee Placas

berghahn
NEW YORK · OXFORD
www.berghahnbooks.com

First published in 2018 by

Berghahn Books

www.berghahnbooks.com

Library of Congress Cataloging-in-Publication Data

Names: Doxiadis, Evdoxios, editor. | Placas, Aimee, editor.
Title: Living under Austerity: Greek Society in Crisis / edited by Evdoxios
　　Doxiadis and Aimee Placas.
Description: New York: Berghahn Books, 2018. | Includes bibliographical
　　references and index.
Identifiers: LCCN 2018015953 (print) | LCCN 2018021106 (ebook) | ISBN
　　9781785339349 (eBook) | ISBN 9781785339332 (hardback: alk. paper)
Subjects: LCSH: Greece—Economic conditions—21st century. | Greece—Social
　　conditions—21st century. | Financial crises—Social aspects—Greece.
Classification: LCC HC295 (ebook) | LCC HC295 .L588 2018 (print) |
　　DDC 330.9495—dc23
LC record available at https://lccn.loc.gov/2018015953

British Library Cataloguing in Publication Data

A catalogue record for this book is available from the British Library

ISBN 978-1-78533-933-2 hardback
ISBN 978-1-78920-832-0 paperback
ISBN 978-1-78533-934-9 ebook

Thanks to Jen and John for their support and patience.

Contents

Part II. State Functions, the Welfare State, and the Economic Crisis

Part III. Changes in Greek Society and Culture

Tables and Figures

Tables

Figures

Note on Transliteration

One of the difficult decisions we faced in this volume was to decide how to render Greek words and terms in English. These are several transliteration techniques that we could have used but each presented its own set of problems. After much deliberation, we decided to apply the rules suggested by the *Journal of Modern Greek Studies* and used by the Library of Congress (see http://www.loc.gov/catdir/cpso/romanization/greek.pdf), with some modifications.

We rendered place names in the customary English or foreign form whenever possible (e.g., Athens, not Athena). We retained established anglicizations, and we tried to honor the way the person being cited normally renders his or her name, even if it does not fully match our transliteration system. When this rendering was unknown we opted for a phonetic transliteration (as is commonly used by most Greeks) unless the person in question is known to have used a different form (thus we use Karamanlis rather than Karamanles).

In the case of newspapers and periodicals that already use a transliterated form of their name we selected to follow the form each has chosen (thus *To Vima* and not *To Vema*, and *E Kathimerini* and not *E Kathemerine*).

Proper names in non-English alphabets other than Greek employ the transliteration scheme most common in English.

For simplicity's sake and to avoid confusing readers who do not read Greek we decided against the use of Greek characters and rendered all Greek words in transliteration including in the bibliographies of each chapter. We also avoided the use of accents.

All transliterated Greek words or short phrases in the following chapters follow these rules and appear in italics.

Abbreviations

ADEDY	Civil Servants' Confederation
ANEL	Independent Greeks
ANTARSYA	Front of the Greek Anticapitalist Left
COSCO	China Ocean Shipping Company
CSDH	Commission on Social Determinants of Health
DIMAR	Democratic Left
DT	Public Television (Greek broadcaster)
EBU	European Broadcasting Union
ECB	European Central Bank
EEC	European Economic Community
EIR	National Institute of Radio
EK	Union of Centrists
ELSTAT	Hellenic Statistical Authority
ENEK	United Nationalist Movement
EOPYY	National Organization for Provision of Health Care Services
ERT	Hellenic Broadcasting Company
ESM	European Stability Mechanism
ESY	National Health System
EU	European Union
EU ICS	European Crime and Safety Survey
Frontex	European Border and Coast Guard Agency
GD	Golden Dawn
GDP	gross domestic product
GMI	guaranteed minimum income
GSEE	General Confederation of Greek Workers
IFC	International Financial Commission

IKA	Social Insurance Institute
IMF	International Monetary Fund
IU	United Left
KEA	Social Solidarity Grant
KKE	Communist Party of Greece
KOINSEP	Social Cooperative Enterprise
LAE	Popular Unity
LAOS	Popular Orthodox Rally
LETS	local exchange trading systems
LMU	Latin Monetary Union
LPEs	large protest events
MCCH	Metropolitan Community Clinic of Hellenikon
MoU	memorandum of understanding
MPs	members of parliament
NBG	National Bank of Greece
NCHR	National Commission for Human Rights
NCRT	National Council of Radio-Television
ND	New Democracy
NERIT	New Hellenic Radio, Internet, and Television
NGO	nongovernmental organization
OECD	Organisation for Economic Co-operation and Development
PAME	All-Workers Militant Front
PASOK	Panhellenic Socialist Movement
PEDY	National Primary Healthcare Network
PHC	primary health care
PP	People's Party
PSOE	Spanish Socialist Workers' Party
SAPs	Structural Adjustment Programmes
SYRIZA	Coalition of the Radical Left
TED	Television of the Armed Forces
ToMYs	local health units
Troika	International Monetary Fund, European Central Bank, and European Union
UNHCR	United Nations High Commissioner for Refugees
VAT	value added tax
WHO	World Health Organization
YENED	Information Service of the Armed Forces

Introduction

Crisis and Austerity

Aimee Placas and Evdoxios Doxiadis

It has been a number of years now that Greece has been under the restruc-turing project known as austerity. Dictated by the International Mone-tary Fund (IMF), the European Central Bank, and the European Union (EU), known collectively as the Troika (though not always in consensus)—significant changes have been wrought, in return for the largest bailout in the IMF's history. The extent and lasting impact of this project (for Greece, and for the Troika) we are only just beginning to comprehend. This period, from the start of Greece's sovereign debt crisis up to this writing, has been written about extensively and broadly, popularly and academically. In this literature we find moral tales of corruption and comeuppance, explora-tions of resistance and defiance, and stories of desperation and victimhood. We find macroanalyses of local and global structures, both economic and political. We find detailed and thoughtful depictions from the perspective on the ground, and sweeping orientalist declarations on the South.

What this volume aims to contribute to these varied and competing voices is longitudinal and comparative scholarly research that sets aside the prereceived truths about this period in Greece's history; the authors examine multiple sectors of Greek society on their own terms. The con-tributors span several disciplines: from history to anthropology, criminol-ogy, psychology, political science, sociology, international relations, and cultural studies. We hope that this disciplinary breadth will provide the reader with distinctive and varied approaches and viewpoints to what are, after all, multifaceted problems in Greek society. We also try to cover as many aspects of society as the space of one volume allows, again to demonstrate the impact of these past years on society, state, institutions, and—above all—people.

Additionally, we want to avoid, as much as possible, discussions about causation related to what has come to be called Greece's "crisis." This book pursues neither simple reasons for this "crisis" nor does it propose solutions. Rather, we chose to focus on the impact these years have had on Greece and the people who live there, and to understand the responses. Two crucial elements that these scholars do have in common are (1) their expertise in their field or topic of research specifically predating 2009 and the subsequent economic depression, and (2) a research agenda that extends through this period (with the exception of two authors whose field of research exceeds the Greek crisis geographically rather than temporally). This expertise is significant for several reasons. First, as Janet Roitman has influentially argued, evoking a crisis instigates particular narratives that start by asking a very limited, moralizing version of, "What went wrong?," which compels immediate, Band-Aid type solutions to larger historical problems. This particular causal question has been posed and argued exhaustively elsewhere, and so we hope to offer here narratives that escape crisis-mode and crisis-thinking. Second, evoking a crisis automatically creates periodization, an era with a beginning and end, and particularly an era that is set off as exceptional (Roitman 2013: 28). We recognize these frameworks as limiting the understanding of what is happening in Greece today. With deep knowledge based on long-term research, and/or theoretical frameworks that resist crisis discourse, the authors have the ability to give their own genealogies that disrupt some of the assumptions about what "crisis" has brought to Greece, exactly. They often tell tales of social impact that are much longer, or larger, in scope. Although this book and its chapters replicate some of the popular narratives of the Greek crisis that have held sway—and in fact, in analyzing their effects and how people understand them, could not have done otherwise—it also works against many of the chapters.

A popular metaphor in Greece for understanding the condition of living under austerity has been that of being laboratory animals (*peiramatozoa*). Methods for restructuring the society have been attempted, the results hoped for but ultimately unknown. A laboratory animal does not undergo its trials in order to have its ills healed; it undergoes them so that others do not have to, others who might be healed just the same. The term "laboratory animals" speaks strongly to a long-standing cynicism and suspicion with which these reforms are perceived, and a historically entrenched concern with being the victim of foreign interests and interventions. We are aware that we risk mimicking the scientists of this metaphor in posing our own questions here: Austerity was the experiment, and what are its effects? Again, we believe that the broad temporal and contextual scope that these chapters provide moves beyond a narrow, cause-and-effect focus that other case-study accounts of crisis and austerity provide. Studying Greece is not taken here only as a means to understand austerity effects.

Crisis and Austerity

Beyond being a word that evokes specific narratives, the word "crisis" also has the ability to create its condition by naming it so, a power shared by many other performative economic terms, in that it "contributes to the construction of the reality that it describes" (Callon 2007: 316). As we see in the tumbling of events that followed Prime Minister George Papandreou's declaration after the 2009 elections that Greece was in a state of emergency, naming and creating a crisis modality opened the way for a restructuring of Greece that prior to that moment had been politically impossible (Kyriakopoulos 2011). Giorgio Agamben's (2005) writings on states of exception (i.e., a suspension of the democratic process or rule of law as a response to emergency, aspects of which could become normalized and permanent) have been influential in much of the analysis of Greece under the regime of crisis (see Athanasiou 2012), including much of the work in this volume. This discourse on exception should not be confused, however, with presenting Greece as an exceptional case, which is not the position of this text (see Rakopoulos 2014 for further consideration of this point). The Troika-imposed ideologies and goals of austerity, under which Greece becomes the subject through successive governments' attempts to implement them, are not unique to Greece. At the same time, the changes to Greece's political sphere, the state provisions, and the social responses that result must all be interpreted through the history and cultural context into which they unfold. We do not propose this as an argument for Greece's exceptionalism, but rather for particularism. In short, these are local expressions of global forces.

Austerity is the dominant organizing ideology enabled through this state of exception, however controversial and often resisted it is (as evidenced in Greece by the political instability examined in part I of this volume). The most recent iteration of austerity ideology emerges in response to the 2008 global financial crisis, where the legerdemain of austerity transforms what begins as a problem of finance (rescuing and repairing the banking system) into a political problem of cutting state expenditures in multiple EU economies, not just those who would later be identified as dangerously close to default (i.e., Greece, Ireland, Italy, Portugal, and Spain) (Clarke and Newman 2012). While contemporary austerity in the United Kingdom historically echoes a post–World War II austerity period of self-imposed, shared sacrifice (Clarke and Newman 2012: 307), in Greece the historical echo is the German occupation, a period of forced sacrifice, imposed from the outside (see Knight 2015). The difficulty of creating broad-based consent for such programs is hardly unique to Greece, but this framing of austerity as externally directed—and removed from the country's democratic process—brings it more in line with IMF-led austerity programs in Latin America or the global South in the prior decades than with current austerity programs in other EU countries.

But what exactly do we mean by the phrase "the ideology of austerity?" We view it in relationship to our understanding of a number of its goals: the decrease of state debt toward being more attractive to financial markets, the decrease of state spending and the increase of state income as paths toward the former but also as aims in themselves, and the creation of an economic (and political) environment attractive to outside investment. It is a methodology for dealing with economic difficulty that is meant to stimulate confidence and thus growth (Clarke and Newman 2012), but that also comes laden with moral overtones about profligate spending, inefficiency, waste, and occasionally (certainly in Greece's case) corruption. It is an ideology with enough hegemonic power that some would term this era the "age of austerity" (Breu 2014). It is certainly the case that the 2008 financial crisis created the opportunity for austerity to return as a dominant answer for economic restructuring, irrespective of empirical evidence for its effectiveness (Jabko 2013). Why austerity continues to be a compelling economic answer is beyond the scope of this volume, but exploring its outcomes is a main objective.

Some academic disciplines, and/or political viewpoints, see these structural transformations as a liberalizing of the statist character in the governance of the economic sphere in Greece. Others, including some of the authors in this volume, explicitly frame these structural transformations— and the related kinds of subject formation they produce—as instantiations of a neoliberal model of economics and governance. A number of chapters in this volume reference or detail the neoliberal character of austerity's aims and ideologies specific to their field of research, and give evidence for neoliberal subjectivities that result from, or are intensified by, these changes. These chapters add useful data to help us understand the effects of the institutions and expert discourses that enforce this economic ideology on a global scale (see Ostry, Loungani, and Furceri 2016 for a questioning of these policies' successes from within the IMF itself). The deregulations, privatizations, and reduction in welfare provisions identified as the hallmarks of neoliberal restructuring are explored both as a running thread of background context and in case studies: health care, consumption, mass media. The increased attention to security often linked to neoliberalism (and with its failures, see Goldstein 2010) is also explored on multiple fronts: the scapegoating of so-called criminal foreigners, the new crisis of refugees and Greece's borders, the vigilante policing of Golden Dawn, the attempts to monitor and track financial transactions. The effects of these policies on society's most vulnerable members is a consistent theme in this volume.

A critique of the usefulness of neoliberalism as an analytical category has been circulating for some time now (see Ganti 2014), partially due to its broadness and the fact that its implementations and effects are not uniform, at the same time that its expression as a governmentality often aims for standardization (see Hess this volume for a further discussion). The use of the term is both evaluative and political, because its evocation in academic work implies criticism and critique of its ideological practices and its effects. For more than a decade in Greece, however, the word *"neoeleftherismos"* has had a vigorous life outside of strict academic discourse, in everyday political conversation (though to draw a line between academic discourse and the discourse of everyday life is certainly a false distinction). This use in everyday parlance is unique from many other countries not in the global South, at least before the events of 2008 brought economic ideologies under popular scrutiny more broadly. It has been used to understand and criticize the structural changes the country was undergoing as part of belonging to the EU (visible on protest signs, banners, and in op-eds from at least the early 2000s), and then to address the changes required by the Troika. As such, the term "neoliberalism" in Greece is interpreted and understood through an embodied experience that is specific to its local context, as much as it connects that context to similar processes occurring elsewhere. To use some old-fashioned social science language, it has become both an emic and etic category in understanding the forces shaping everyday life in Greece. Its use by authors in this volume cannot be disentangled from its specificity as an on-the-ground and politicized interpretive framework for comprehending the lived experience of Europeanization and austerity processes in Greece. And it is worth noting Stuart Hall's suggestion that the ultimate usefulness of the term could indeed lie in its political force (Hall 2011).

Chapter Overviews

Michael Herzfeld has noted that external financial control and economic dependence have marked Greece's relationship with the West from the state's very inception—a condition he names "crypto-colonialism" —with the continuing effect of political marginality for the nation (Herzfeld 2003). Although the specific lending markets and the Great Powers involved have changed over time, this paradox of dependency and resentment toward foreign intervention continues through to the current moment, and has had a hand in the reshaping the Greek political sphere. Part I of the volume, titled "The Political Dimension of the Crisis," begins our exploration through a series of examinations of the political culture of Greece, its developments, continuities, and breaks.

Evdoxios Doxiadis begins with our first chapter, "The 'Illegitimacy' of Foreign Loans: Greece, the Great Powers, and Foreign Debt in the Nineteenth Century," a historical examination into the origins of the Greek foreign debt and its perception by the Greek government and public in the nineteenth and twentieth centuries, and their effect on modern perceptions of state debt in Greece. The chapter focuses on the role of the Great Powers and how that role has been understood in Greece, and argues that the frequent confrontations between Greece and the Great Powers of the time has colored Greek perceptions regarding foreign debt to this day, with frequent misappropriations of this history in contemporary political rhetoric. This chapter demonstrates that much of both the current popular and political discourse concerning the state debt and the crisis are grounded in a long history of similar discourses. But it also evaluates why this particular threat of bankruptcy, in a long history of such threats, has played out differently.

The second chapter is by Harris Mylonas, "The Political Consequences of the Crisis in Greece: Charismatic Leadership and Its Discontents." It revisits the argument that austerity disrupted the clientelistic political system in Greece, in order to argue not only that the crisis and its management by political elites has led to a political reconfiguration, but also that these consequences on the Greek party system have been deeper than in other European cases because of the succession crises in the two main political parties of the past generation. Both parties had relied on charismatic leaders whose style of governance undermined institution building, thus handicapping the ability of non-charismatic leaders to manage the crisis.

Kostis Karpozilos continues this examination of how current political trends associated with the crisis are in fact grounded in longer historical trends in his analysis of one of the more disturbing phenomena usually blamed on the crisis: the growth of the extreme-right wing Golden Dawn party. In "Golden Dawn: From the Margins of Greece to the Forefront of Europe," he chronicles the transformation of Golden Dawn from an ideological sect into a body with parliamentary representation and mainstreamed policies. Karpozilos positions the Greek extreme right within the contemporary academic debate regarding the transformation of neofascist movements into post-fascist social phenomena in Europe.

The chapter by Kostas Kanellopoulos and Maria Kousis, "Protest, Elections, and Austerity Politics in Greece," examines the impact of the crisis on the political system through the examination of protest events surrounding the austerity policies and the memorandums of understanding (MoUs) that have led to the rapid loss of faith of Greek citizens toward national and European institutions. Approaching the changes in the political sphere from outside of the history of party politics, as opposed to the inside-approach presented by Mylonas, this chapter identifies the links between social movement activities and electoral outcomes. Kanellopoulos and Kousis detail the structure and content of the large protest events that have characterized anti-austerity expression in Greece, showing the role of both old and new players.

The final chapter in part I is by Björn Bremer and Guillem Vidal, "From Boom to Bust: A Comparative Analysis of Greece and Spain under Austerity," a comparative look at the significantly different political consequences of the crisis on two affected countries: Greece and Spain. The authors argue that the crisis in Southern Europe did not simply lead to a political crisis, but that prior political developments also played a role in bringing about the economic crisis in the first place. They argue that the substantial differences in the restructuring of the party systems of both countries should be seen through a combination of preexisting domestic conflicts, and new conflicts that were brought about by the exceptional economic and political situation. This chapter continues much of the conversation introduced by Mylonas's chapter, as well as Kanellopoulos and Kousis's, regarding the reshaping of politics as a result of austerity, but presents the further argument that election results reflect not just dissatisfaction with government actions, but also a greater disillusionment with the political system overall. This offers an interesting parallel to Karpozilos's arguments regarding the rise of Golden Dawn, and aligns with Kanellopoulos and Kousis's conclusions regarding the eventual decline in large protests.

Part II of the volume, "State Functions, the Welfare State, and the Economic Crisis," explores three distinct sites that have undergone severe changes as a result of privatizations, restructuring, budget cuts, and securitization. To begin, Franklin L. Hess contextualizes a discussion of recent shifts and restructurings of the mass media sphere in Greece with a history of mass media in Greece and its past connections to political turmoil, explicating the long relationships between media and state governance, in "Crisis and the Changes in the Mediascape: Greece and the Globe." He examines the closure and reopening of Greece's public broadcasting channel ERT, an unexpected and controversial silencing that brought domestic and international protest, and other recent shifts in distrusted and trusted voices. A combination of legislative actions, new media formats, charismatic voices, changes in the market, and critical and cynical media consumers are shown to have reshaped Greece's mediascape during this era. The complicated relationship between state, media, and public opinion is particularly significant as a backdrop to many of the other issues discussed in this volume, and Hess additionally draws compelling connections to emergent media phenomena in other countries as well, pointing to neoliberal influences (and neoliberal failures) beyond the immediate impact of Greece's austerity.

Sappho Xenakis and Leonidas Cheliotis continue this attention to governance in their chapter "Crime and Criminal Justice Policy in Greece during the Financial Crisis," where the politicization of crime statistics and criminal policy are clearly linked to the state's attempt to direct public attention toward very specific types of criminality (that affecting the most vulnerable) and away from others (those possibly implicating political elites). Xenakis and Cheliotis deconstruct the myths regarding what kinds of crime are influenced by economic downturns, and speak to their enduring narrative in constructing Greece's crime problem. The focus on migrants and foreigners as a source of danger during the crisis (as opposed to types of criminality potentially linked with the crisis's cause) connects significantly to concerns discussed by other chapters in this volume.

Populations made vulnerable is also Noëlle Burgi's theme, in her exploration of the effects of austerity on the Greek health-care system. In "The Downsizing and Commodification of Health Care: The Appalling Greek Experience since 2010," Burgi details the systematic dismantling of healthcare provisions, offering insight from the doctors currently struggling to work within this changing system. Her chapter demonstrates the effects both of the cutbacks in state spending and also the shift away from healthcare access as a right and more toward a market logic in its provisions and structure. Her work highlights the ways in which those persons who are already precarious are made even more so through these changes. She also describes new social responses to these cuts, however, that are meant to address the gaps left in state care, in the form of solidarity health clinics; this attention to precarity and to collective response is continued in the chapters through the volume's third and last part.

Beginning part III of the book, "Changes in Greek Society and Culture," Alexandra Zavos in "Gendering the Crisis: New Values and Agencies beyond Destitution" provides a detailed overview of the scholarship on the gendered effects of Greece's socioeconomic crisis and austerity, giving a feminist reading to many of the structural changes discussed by authors in part II (something underrepresented in scholarship on austerity). She also offers her own research on new social and economic initiatives that have emerged, with three case studies, finding new avenues of action become available to women during this period of time. She asks, however, what here is actually new and what is a return to or reinvention of traditional roles. This attention to new forms of organization echoes many of the other authors' analyses.

Heath Cabot also brings us to a story that is not new, and yet is now undergoing a double crisis, in "From the Twilight Zone to the Limelight: Shifting Terrains of Asylum and Rights in Greece." A longstanding humanitarian issue in the region, asylum and services to refugees undergo a new austeritization, but one that comes on top of long-existing structural inequities, much as Zavos demonstrates relating to gender equality. She explores the withdrawal or absence of state services—framed in a discourse of rights—to both refugees and citizens, and the new formations such as solidarity movements that fill those gaps. Cabot also reflects on how crisis thinking has shaped not just the response to refugees, but also the way the topic has been approached and studied, echoing this volume's concern with crisis as a limiting modality for academics and what it means when an old problem receives the particular attention that is created during periods defined as crises.

Tracey A. Rosen's piece that follows demonstrates the heterogeneity of migration as an issue in Greece, as the introduction of Chinese goods, capital, and people into the country holds a very different place of concern than that described by Cabot, where the Chinese state is the positive example of the government that aids its citizens while at the same time that the devaluation of labor in Greece is understood to be "becoming Chinese." In "*Giname Kinezoi!* ('We've Become Chinese!'): Critical Developments in the Imaginary of Chinese Labor," Rosen explores the moral discourses surrounding labor and goods that are instigated by Chinese migrants and commodities, against a background of declining domestic production and the creation of a consumer society.

This theme is carried into the final piece, "Disrupted and Disrupting Consumption: Transformations in Buying and Borrowing in Greece," where Aimee Placas gives an overview of the development of consumer society in Greece and explores how consumption under austerity has been a site both of government intervention and social experimentation. The chapter shares with Rosen the argument that what economic life should look like has been under public debate for quite some time in Greece, but also that the crisis seems to have strongly shaped the manner and possibility of the critiques that are offered. Placas considers the way that austerity means to shape the economy at the level of everyday practices, a disciplining of the consumer that is part of the neoliberal subject considered in all of the chapters in this part III. Overall, each of these pieces in part III clearly demonstrates the effects of austerity in everyday life, through diminishing government services, increasing impoverishment, and declining infrastructure. However, they also collectively argue that current austerity is just one iteration of a set of forces relating to ideologies of capitalism, Europeanization, and neoliberalism that have been shaping Greek society for years.

Aimee Placas is a faculty member at the International Center for Hellenic and Mediterranean Studies (ΔΙΚΕΜΕΣ), College Year in Athens. She holds a PhD in Anthropology from Rice University and has published and presented on consumer debt and bankruptcy, the effect of the Greek crisis on overindebted households, and everyday economic life in Greece. She is currently writing an ethnography on the story of consumer credit in Greece in the 21st century.

Evdoxios Doxiadis is an Associate Professor at the Department of History at Simon Fraser University. His research is on Greek, Balkan, and Mediterranean history with a focus in the 18th and 19th centuries and a particular interest in questions of gender, law, state formation, and minorities. His publications include *The Shackles of Modernity: Women, Property, and the Transition from the Ottoman Empire to the Modern Greek State 1750–1850* (2011) and *State, Nationalism, and the Jewish Communities of Modern Greece* (2018).

References

Agamben, Giorgio. 2005. *State of Exception,* translated by Kevin Attell. Chicago: University of Chicago Press.

Athanasiou, Athina. 2012. *E Krise os Katastase "Ektates Anagkes."* Athens: Savvalas.

Breu, Christopher. 2014. "Against Austerity: Toward a New Sensuality." *symplokē* 22(1): 23–39.

Callon, Michel. 2007. "What Does It Mean to Say That Economics Is Performative?" In *Do Economists Make Markets?: On the Performativity of Economics,* edited by Donald A. MacKenzie, Fabian Muniesa, and Lucia Siu, 311–56. Princeton, NJ: Princeton University Press.

Clarke, John, and Janet Newman. 2012. "The Alchemy of Austerity." *Critical Social Policy* 32(3): 299–319.

Ganti, Tejaswini. 2014. "Neoliberalism." *Annual Review of Anthropology* 43(1): 89–104.

Goldstein, Daniel M. 2010. "Security and the Culture Expert: Dilemmas of an Engaged Anthropology." *Political and Legal Anthropology Review* 33(s1): 126–42.

Hall, Stuart. 2011. "The Neo-Liberal Revolution." *Cultural Studies* 25(6): 705–28.

Herzfeld, Michael. 2003. "The Absence Presence: Discourses of Crypto-Colonialism." *South Atlantic Quarterly* 101(4): 899–926.

Jabko, Nicolas. 2013. "The Political Appeal of Austerity." *Comparative European Politics* 11(6): 705–12.

Knight, Daniel M. 2015. *History, Time, and Economic Crisis in Central Greece.* New York: Palgrave Macmillan.

Kyriakopoulos, Leandros. 2011. "The State of Exception as Precondition for Crisis." Hot Spots, *Cultural Anthropology* website, 31 October. Retrieved 7 September 2012 from https://culanth.org/fieldsights/255-the-state-of-exception-as-precondition-for-crisis.

Ostry, Jonathan, Prakash Loungani, and Davide Furceri. 2016. "Neoliberalism: Oversold?" *Finance & Development* 53(2). Retrieved 7 January 2017 from http://www.imf.org/exter nal/pubs/ft/fandd/2016/06/ostry.htm.

Rakopoulos, Theodoros. 2014. "Resonance of Solidarity: Meanings of a Local Concept in Anti-Austerity Greece." *Journal of Modern Greek Studies* 32(2): 313–37.

Roitman, Janet. 2013. *Anti-Crisis.* Durham, NC: Duke University Press.

Part I

The Political Dimension
of the Crisis

Chapter 1

The "Illegitimacy" of Foreign Loans
Greece, the Great Powers, and Foreign Debt in the Long Nineteenth Century

Evdoxios Doxiadis

Introduction

In February 2016, during the many protests staged by Greek farmers against the new tax and insurance reform measures promoted by the left Greek government of the political party Coalition of the Radical Left (SYRIZA) under pressure from its lenders, farmers from Crete raised a banner calling for the expulsion of the Rothschilds from Greece, which gained some publicity in the extreme-right-wing press (*Eleftheros Kosmos gr.*, 8 February 2016). A few months earlier, during parliamentary debates over the negotiations for a new memorandum of understanding (MoU), Nikolaos Mihaloliakos (the leader of Golden Dawn, an extreme-right-wing nationalist party) tied the new bailout loans to those of the Greek War of Independence, which were contracted, according to him, with "English loan-shark bankers" (Hellenic Parliament 2015: 3907). In early 2015 at the other end of the political spectrum the newly elected SYRIZA government, under the initiative of the then president of Parliament Zoe Konstantopoulou, launched an investigation on the Greek public debt via a Truth Committee on Public Debt whose preliminary report described the Greek external debt as "illegal, illegitimate, and odious" (Truth Committee on Public Debt 2015: 51), while some other members of the cabinet publicly suggested that Greece should suspend payments to the International Monetary Fund (IMF) (*E Kathimerini*, 5 May 2015). More recently a radical

---

left website also drew analogies between the bailout loans and the robber loans of the nineteenth century (see Fotiadis 2015), while others argued for the colonial origins of the MoUs (Martin 2015), and the newly elected leader of the center-right opposition party New Democracy (ND) referred to the latest agreement between Greece and its creditors as an "unprecedented loss of national sovereignty" (*E Kathimerini*, 20 May 2016). These references are bound to confuse even informed foreign observers since the Rothschilds, English bankers, or the concept of odious debt do not seem relevant to the current Greek bailout, the largest in history (Tomz and Wright 2013: 257). Yet, they explain to a great degree the public perceptions of foreign debt in Greece, and the reaction of the Greek public and large segments of the political class to the policies implemented by successive governments in order to forestall bankruptcy, perceptions that have been cultivated over a period of two centuries and are often seen even in scholarly work (see Mpaloglou 2001: 183–84; Karpozilos this volume).

This paper will argue that perceptions regarding foreign debt and foreign intervention have been linked throughout Greek history but that the current circumstances are in fact rather unique because of the decision of the Greek governments not to default on its debts. Ironically Greek foreign indebtedness was often seen in the past as an acknowledgment of sovereignty but also as a constant threat to the sovereignty of the Greek state. Greek governments habitually responded to fiscal crises in political rather than economic terms and did not hesitate to default on their obligations. Greek governments rarely chose to respond to the fiscal crises with attempts to drastically curtail expenditures to forestall default—an austerity program, if you will—generally preferring the suspension of servicing the foreign loans to radical cutbacks of expenditure or reforms. On the occasions when such attempts were made the outcome was a dismantling of the existing political order, as experienced in 1843 and 1909. Thus, despite the economic cost of defaults, they were rational choices in terms of domestic politics and the dominant nationalist ideology that has endured through the existence of the Greek state, as long as radical transformations of existing economic and political structures could be avoided. The Greek political establishment was hardly threatened in the nineteenth century even though Greece was technically in default for much of this period. The military interventions of the 1920s and 1930s had little to do with the default of 1932, which barely dented the popularity of the prime minister of the time, Eleftherios Venizelos. As I will argue, it is not defaults that delegitimize the political system but rather policies of austerity, especially if those are perceived to be imposed by foreign actors with the collusion of Greek governments and to affect state employment and expenditures.

What I suggest here is that because the management of many past debt crises in Greece was political rather than economic, those crises did not lead to radical political realignments and transformations in the short term, nor did political change lead to drastic structural change. Although commentators enjoy blaming the Ottoman past for the so-called back-ward, clientelist, or premodern policies and attitudes that have resulted in the enormous debts of the Greek state, including the patronage system of Greek politics (see, e.g., Lewis 2010), in an often Orientalist—or Balkanist, as Maria Todorova (2009) would say—narrative, it is instead a modern de-velopment linked to the emergence of the modern Greek state and its en-suing social and national policies, many of which were tied to a powerful irredentist nationalist program. This process linked from the very begin-ning foreign loans with the political aspirations of the Greek state and the political ambitions of the Great Powers: France, Great Britain, and Russia. Although Greek governments needed and actively sought out the inter-vention of the Great Powers in support of their irredentist claims against the Ottoman Empire throughout the first century of Greece's existence, the constant interventions of the Great Powers in Greek domestic and foreign affairs have led many to see Greece in the nineteenth century as a protec-torate that was not completely sovereign (Dontas 1966: 3). Undoubtedly the frequent direct interventions were a challenge to Greece's national sovereignty but they also had the effect of linking sovereignty to the sov-ereign debt. Many recent works on the history of Greek debt and bank-ruptcies uncritically duplicate this narrative, which was very prominent in the work of the highly influential early-twentieth-century historian and occasional government official Andreas Andreades, who is often referred to as a "colossus" (Choumanidis 1990: 387; see also Andreades 1904). They constantly refer to the *"epachtheis"* (odious) terms of the various loans is-sued to the Greek state (Skliraki 2015: 48, 54, 127, 162; Tzokas 2002: 93, 98), use the term *"lestriko"* (robber) to describe such loans (Skliraki 2015: 46, 51, 53, 54, 103, 110, 138, 155, 160–62; Soilentakis 2012: 43) or denounce the "greed" of foreign financiers and their "excessive" demands (Soilen-takis 2012: 93, 101). Furthermore, by elevating the irredentist goals of the state above all other concerns, Greek governments rendered the servicing of foreign loans and the policies associated with it, and even economic development, of secondary importance, giving servicing an antinational character in the contemporary as well as in modern discourse.

The Origins of Greece's Foreign Debt

The origins of the Greek foreign debt dates to the insurrection against the Ottoman Empire that led to the emergence of the Greek state. Fol-lowing the eruption of the revolt in 1821, the rebellious Greeks were able to hold out against the forces of the Ottoman state in southern Greece

and establish provisional governments under a number of liberal constitutions. Although all European governments, acting within the context of
post-Napoleonic reactionary politics, initially denounced the revolt, the
early successes of the Greeks generated widespread sympathy in Europe,
fueled by a hodgepodge of Romantic, Christian, Liberal, and Classicist
ideals. This feeling coalesced in a strong Philhellenic movement particularly prominent in Western Europe. In addition to hundreds of British,
French, German, and Italian volunteers who joined the fight in Greece,
many more contributed financially to the struggle through pro-Greek
committees that emerged throughout Europe.

  Although significant, the funds from these committees were hardly sufficient to bankroll the war, while the new unstable revolutionary Greek
governments proved incapable of creating a functioning taxation system.
The early constitutions envisioned that taxation would express the new
ideas of popular sovereignty and political freedom, but despite the proclamation of sixty-seven laws dealing with taxation, the Greek authorities
never managed a clear account of their income and expenditures (Bozikis
2010: 34–36). The revolutionary governments relied on tax farming and
duties, collecting 16.1 million *grosia* between 1822 and 1827, while other
income (domestic borrowing, sales of lands, donations and so on) accounted for a further 8.5 million. In comparison the income from foreign
loans discussed below was 27.9 million (Bozikis 2010: 41).[1]

  As the war dragged on, new sources of income were desperately needed
to arm and pay the Greek soldiers and sailors, who when left unpaid often
abandoned the cause to return to their towns and villages. Lack of funds
had significant political ramifications in revolutionary Greece (Kostis 2013:
138). It could undermine the influence of warlords whose troops were tied
to them through patronage, and especially could undermine their ability
to pay the troops. Warlords who did not receive sufficient funds could
turn against the civilian population, despoiling entire provinces or islands, and even reach agreements with the Ottomans and switch sides
(Koliopoulos 1984: 171, 175). At the same time peasants often refused the
authority of the government-appointed tax agents (Harisis 1996: No 1767,
16 July 1826, 15). In response to these challenges, the Greek revolutionary
governments frequently relied on warlords, landowners, and notables for
tax-gathering purposes, in a system of exploitation that was similar to the
previous Ottoman regime (Bozikis 2010: 40, 52; Levandis 1944: 3).

  In these circumstances the idea of resorting to foreign borrowing found
eager supporters in Greece when it was first suggested. Some attempts
to find foreign funding had been undertaken as early as 1821, targeting
wealthy Greek merchants living abroad, while in 1822 the National Assembly authorized the floating of a loan in Italy; that came to naught,

however, due to the hostility of the Austrian authorities (Levandis 1944: 6). Although many fanciful schemes of foreign borrowing were proposed to the Greek authorities by certain disreputable individuals immediately following the revolt (Levandis 1944: 6, 7), the serious proposals were originally conceived in Britain by philhellenic circles and by Greek merchants living in Europe. The Greek revolutionary government embraced the idea and a committee was dispatched to Britain to secure a loan through the good offices of British philhellenes.

One must keep in mind that money markets were still in their infancy, and the emergence of a host of new states in the first decades of the nineteenth century, mostly in Latin America, had introduced new lending opportunities to borrowers with no prior credit history. Britain was at the time already the largest money market in the world and the only one with experience of extensive foreign lending. It was also fortuitous for the Greek government that their quest for a British loan coincided with recent developments that made investors willing to consider supplying funds to a government that was as yet unrecognized by any state in the world.

The conclusion of the Napoleonic Wars had robbed investors of their single best client, the British government, which in the ensuing years steadily reduced the interest rates that it was willing to pay to the investors in British debt from 5 percent to 3.5 percent (Levandis 1944: 10). At roughly the same time Baron Rothschild introduced the concept of foreign securities issued in Britain in pounds sterling, an innovation that significantly reduced the cost of foreign lending that was previously governed by fluctuating interest rates, and other political and economic risks (Levandis 1944: 11; Tomz 2007: 47). These changes created a demand in Britain for lending opportunities that would provide higher returns than the British government was willing to consider, while also creating the tools that would make the risk of foreign lending more palatable. The lending boom in Britain began in 1817 with a Baring Brothers negotiated loan to France and by the mid 1820s most European and Latin American countries had raised debt in London, which would remain the center of international finance over the next century (Tomz 2007: 47).

The fiscal needs of the Greek government, however, was only one aspect of the mission sent to Britain. Alexander Mavrokordatos, who was the leading liberal political figure of the revolution, president of the *Ektelestiko* (executive branch of the government) in 1822, and the main backer of this mission, also had political goals in mind. The mission was supposed to stress the pro-British sentiments of the Greeks and dispel any concerns regarding the revolutionary nature of the government or its support for Russian ambitions in the region (Levandis 1944: 5). Other revolutionary leaders, including Anastasis Tsamados, were also urging international borrowing in order to exert diplomatic pressure on the European powers (Chatziioannou 2013: 45). With these considerations in mind, the Greek mission was indeed successful in securing a loan, though the terms were understandably quite harsh.

The misconceptions at home regarding foreign loans start with this first loan. For the Greeks the conclusion of this loan was heralded as Britain's tacit recognition of the Greek cause and its revolutionary government, a recognition that inexorably led to British intervention in favor of Greece in 1827 (Levandis 1944: 15; Polyzoidis 2011: 32), a belief that continues to be accepted in modern Greek scholarship (Chatziioannou 2013: 33). The British government, on the other hand, saw the loans as a purely speculative investment on the part of private individuals that in no way involved or constrained the government. The Greek misconception is understandable considering that most other European states would not have allowed such a loan if it contradicted their foreign policy objectives. This, however, was not the case with the London money market, which had been quite willing to finance even dubious countries and hostile powers despite poor investment data and information, until a specialized financial press emerged in the 1840s (Tomz 2007: 49). Loans were extended to the revolutionary Cortes government in Spain, for instance, even after the Congress of Verona gave France a mandate to intervene and restore the absolute monarchy, which immediately repudiated the "odious" Cortes debts (Flandreau and Flores 2009: 658). Greece, at least, was a real place unlike the supposedly newly independent Latin American country of Poyais, which in 1822 was able to issue a bond at rates equal to those of real countries like Chile, Colombia, and Peru before the discovery that it was a fictitious entity devised to defraud gullible investors (Tomz 2007: 51; Waibel 2011: 10).

Although at the time considered a success (Trikoupis 1978a: 245), the first Greek loan has been heavily criticized in historiography for its onerous terms (Skliraki 2015: 19; Soilentakis 2012: 43), but that was to be expected for a loan to a government no other recognized as legitimate. Even in the eighteenth century, investors clearly distinguished between new and established state entities, demanding significant premiums from the former (Tomz 2007: 45, 50). Greece, of course, paid a further premium for being unrecognized as a legitimate state, its rates exceeding those of any other state in the 1820s (Tomz 2007: 49) and had to pledge its "national lands" as collateral (Andreades 1904: 17). The condemnation of the loan also concerns the manner in which the proceeds were mismanaged, in part because of the chaotic circumstances of the Greek revolutionary government and political infighting. The bonds were contracted at the same time when the Greek executive branch of the *Ektelestiko* was engaged in a struggle for dominance with the *Vouleftiko* (legislative branch), a struggle that led to two brief civil wars. The loan was partly used to buy support for the executive and ensure its victory in the political conflict, and partly to pacify restless warlords and refugees (Andreades 1904: 19; Choumanidis 1990: 195; Kofas 1981: 9).

Nevertheless, the conclusion of the loan was seen in Greece as a singular political success and the Greek government sought a second loan the next year. An initial attempt to float a loan in Paris failed, in part due to the hostility of the French government toward the Greek revolt, as well as to the smaller size and more cautious attitude of the French money market, so Greece turned to London again (Levandis 1944: 17). Once more the terms were onerous and once again the loan was mismanaged, though in this case it is possible to lay much of the blame on the British and American contractors commissioned to construct warships and provide other war materiel for the Greek government. Even the English press of the time made serious accusations against the British agents and entrepreneurs who managed the loans and contracts (Andreades 1904: 25; Levandis 1944: 22).

The growing indebtedness of Greece was not of immediate concern to the revolutionary government. Although the loans allowed the government to assert its authority and begin a more systematic approach to military affairs (Kostis 2013: 139, 157), the fratricide conflict of 1825–26 and the almost concurrent Egyptian intervention of 1827 nearly succeeded in suppressing the Greek revolt. The Greek government was in complete disarray and unable to defend its earlier gains, let alone service its debts, and in 1826 the revolutionary authorities suspended the servicing of the debt, defaulting on the bonds at a time when Egyptian troops were systematically restoring Ottoman control in Greece.[2] Ironically, the default took place at the moment when France, Great Britain, and Russia were changing policies. In 1827 the three Great Powers dispatched squadrons to Greece that destroyed the Ottoman–Egyptian fleet at the naval battle of Navarino. The ensuing Russo–Ottoman War, and the dispatch of French troops to the Peloponnese, ensured the emergence of the Greek state.

This beneficial outcome for the Greeks, however, came about at a time of near complete political collapse in Greece itself. Following years of bitter disputes and facing military disaster, the Greek revolutionary authorities had appointed as governor Ioannis Kapodistrias, a seasoned and conservative diplomat who had served the Russian czar as foreign minister and been involved in the early post-Napoleonic settlement of Europe. His attempts to establish order, alongside his authoritarian tendencies, led to his assassination in 1831 and yet another complete collapse of Greek political authority. Thus, the political institutions of the new state were created by the three Great Powers with no input from any Greek factions or political figures. The new polity was designed as an absolute monarchy whose king was chosen by the three Great Powers and whose institutional role with regard to the affairs of the new state was enshrined in the convention of London in 1832.

The significance of that document cannot be overstated with regard to the discussion in question. The 1832 convention signed by the representatives of the three Great Powers and representatives of the king of Bavaria, whose second son Otto was chosen as the new king of Greece, did not simply stipulate the terms under which the new king would assume his throne, but also described the continued role of France, Great Britain, and Russia in the affairs of the new kingdom (Convention 1918: Art. IV, 70). Furthermore, many clauses involved a new loan of 60 million francs to be distributed in three installments to facilitate the establishment of the monarchy in Greece and to help create the institutions of the new state. The three Great Powers stood as surety to the new loan that was subsequently contracted by the Rothschild Bank, in part due to the refusal of other banking houses to lend to the Greek state (Andreades 1904: 83; Mpaloglou 2001: 185, 186; Tomz 2007: 55, 228), and in return imposed onerous terms, chiefly among them the contractual obligation of the Greek government to give precedence to the repayment of said loan over any other state expenditure (Convention 1918: Art. XII, 72–73). Thus Greece, because of the political considerations by the Great Powers, became the exception to the general rule that countries in default are unable to contract foreign loans (Tomz and Wright 2013: 260), a process that would be repeated in the future, and is still being repeated today.

The 1832 convention thus introduced the right of the Great Powers to intervene in the finances of the new state as well as to its politics, without even consulting any representatives of the Greek nation or governments, or even the imposed government of young King Otto and his regents. Greece was provided with a necessary loan but under conditions that infringed on concepts of national sovereignty. The supervision of the fulfillment of the Greeks obligations regarding the repayment of the loan was assigned to the diplomatic representatives of the Powers who thus assumed authority beyond those normally assigned to diplomatic personnel in sovereign states (Convention 1918: Art. XII, 73). Furthermore, the convention burdened the Greek state with heavy expenditures in the form of Bavarian troops (Dertilis 2016: 37) and a Bavarian regency for the underage king, again a necessary measure considering the chaotic circumstances of the Greek territories but one that had been imposed without any consideration of Greek sentiment (Convention 1918: Art. 14–15, 73–74). Greece contracted some further small loans and grants from the governments of Russia (1 million rubles) and France (500,000 francs) prior to

1832 (Trikoupis 1978b: 344, 365), and contracted one more loan in Munich in 1832 through the intervention of the Bavarian king Ludwig. This 1.8 million gulden loan was meant to help the Bavarian regency establish its authority in Greece while the details of the loan of 60 million francs were being settled; a further Bavarian loan was contracted in 1835 (Kofas 1981: 29; Mpaloglou 2001: 187).

By this time most of the original bondholders of the two revolutionary loans had offloaded them to speculators who over the next half century would try to recoup their investments. Although the Greek state more or less recognized these obligations, it serviced them only intermittently. An early attempt by the bondholders to get an allotment out of the 1832 loan was refused by the Great Powers, the Earl of Aberdeen expressing the British government's position that although it was not indifferent to the plight of the individuals involved, his government did not engage in speculation of this kind that was a purely private affair, a position reiterated two years later by Lord Palmerston (Levandis 1944: 25–26; Tomz 2007: 55). This stance by the British government was not unique to Greece. In 1828, following the defaults of nearly all new Latin American states, bondholders had sought the aid of the British authorities to recoup their investment only to be rebuffed, being pointedly reminded that they had sought very high returns and that they thus understood there was a proportionate risk involved in their investments (Tomz 2007: 50, 51).

Building a State and a Nation

The Bavarian regency of 1832–35 managed to impose some semblance of order in much of the territory of the Greek kingdom and more impressively was able to lay the foundations of a modern state including a judicial system, a bureaucracy, and an educational system. Despite the political opposition they encountered and the hostility they generated among the Greek population, a hostility remembered to this day, their ultimate goal—to create a modern European state and society—was widely shared in Greece and thus most of their policies were continued by succeeding governments. In the economic arena the Bavarian regency aimed to control expenditures; restore law and order to allow the resumption of agricultural activity and trade; create a framework to control tax evasion and the abuses and corruption of tax collectors, which often resulted in tax revolts (Kostis 2013: 209, 210); and above all secure the allocation of the tranches of the 1832 loan (Mpaloglou 2001: 181).

The Bavarian regency and the first governments of King Otto were quite aware of the constraints of the Greek finances that they had inherited. Even before the Greek revolt, the economy of the region had been in crisis following the end of the Napoleonic wars (Kremmydas 1976–77: 23, 27). A decade of war and years of anarchy had resulted in the economic collapse of the region, to which one must add the cost of creating a state out of practically nothing as well as the cost of the foreign troops that held these regimes in power, and the cost of accommodating the requests of war veterans, widows, orphans, and refugees, a legacy of the fight for independence. In addition, these governments had to pay an indemnity of 11 million francs to the Ottoman Empire for the Muslim properties confiscated in Greece (Mpaloglou 2001: 179; Patouna 2011: 37). They also inherited the liabilities of the defaulted bonds of 1824 and 1825 that had bestowed Greece an indebtedness of over 100 percent of GDP (Reinhart and Trebesch 2015: 5), and of course the new loan of 1832. The fiscal burden was therefore tremendous and the state could not yet count on taxation to alleviate its circumstances since much of the land was technically in its own hands.

The Greek state was also constrained in its ability to use even the resources it possessed, such as the monastic land expropriated from the Greek Orthodox Church or the land of the former Muslim inhabitants of the region. Used as collateral to the financial obligations of the Greek state, the disposition of such lands was not entirely at the discretion of the Greek governments, who would have preferred to distribute them to the landless Greeks in order to stimulate the economy as well as to eliminate the threat posed by a destitute, armed peasantry following the Greek War of Independence. Attempts to settle this question from the 1835 Law of Dotation onward would flounder under domestic and foreign political pressure until the issue was finally resolved in the 1870s (see McGrew 1985). Kapodistrias tried to increase income and was partly successful, raising it by 51 percent between February 1828 and April 1829 before tax receipts collapsed again after his assassination. Even so, expenditures were three times the income collected (Choumanidis 1990: 200) and Greece continued to run substantial budget deficits throughout the regency (Kofas 1981: 26).

When Otto assumed direct rule, he tried to shake free the constraints of the revolutionary loans, refusing to recognize them on the grounds that they were contracted on behalf of all Greeks and not just the small part that had eventually formed the Greek kingdom (Bikelas 1868: 285). Being utterly dependent on France, Britain, and Russia in financial as well as political matters, however, his attempt was futile and instead he was forced to undertake the first austerity program of modern Greece (Kostis 2013: 195, 196). The Greek government tried to reduce its expenditures, cut wages, and fired thousands of state employees and military personnel.

The government even closed all its embassies abroad to save money, including those to the Great Powers. Such savings had a small effect on the budget however, 82 percent of which was devoted to three items: military spending, the servicing of public debt, and the expenses of the monarch (Kostis 2013: 291). Thus, Greece was forced to stop servicing its debt first in 1837 and then definitively in 1843, its first official default.

The year 1843 was a year of tremendous political upheaval in Greece, culminating in a coup that forced Otto to accept a constitution. The Greeks had indicated their preference for representative government from the years of the Greek War of Independence when they produced three increasingly liberal constitutions. The imposition of an absolute monarchy by the Great Powers had always been resented by the Greek public and politicians alike so the 1843 revolt cannot be seen as purely motivated by economic reasons, but the addition of extreme fiscal tightening on an already dissatisfied nation robbed the monarchy of its few supporters, including the army. This was one lesson that future Greek governments would keep in mind when faced with similar fiscal challenges and would avoid Otto's radical cost-cutting or austerity measures, which had not averted default in any case.

The constitutional period of King Otto's reign (1844–63) saw some transformations in Greece. In addition to the new constitution of 1844, the Greek government was purged of foreign nationals, a political act that contributed some fiscal savings. Though Otto continued to meddle in politics, Greece would have uninterrupted parliamentary representation from 1844 until 1909. Though undoubtedly corrupt, clientelist, and full of shenanigans, Greek politics were not much different from those of the rest of Europe and in some respects, as for instance through the participation of nearly the entire male citizenry, they were arguably more democratic. Two closely related issues, however, caused great difficulties for the Greek state and helped undermine the development of its institutions: first, the irredentist nationalism that gripped the country from 1844 onward, and second, the woeful fiscal policies of successive Greek governments.

The former was first explicitly articulated during the debates regarding the constitution of 1844 by the prime minister Ioannis Kolettis; it became known as the *Megali Idea* (Great Idea). Though always left rather vague, the Megali Idea demanded that the primary goal of the Greek state should be territorial expansion to incorporate within its borders all Greeks who remained under Ottoman rule. Although there was never full agreement regarding the exact territorial claims and even the definition of who constituted the Greek nation, the concept itself was unchallenged by any political force in Greece well into the twentieth century, and it became the dominant ideological imperative of the Greek state. The only debates regarding the Megali Idea were on which policies would best lead to its fulfillment: an aggressive foreign policy and confrontation with the Ottoman Empire, and later Bulgaria, or a focus on economic development as a prelude to expansion. The power of this nationalism was such that even economic considerations and debates were couched in nationalist rhetoric skewing objective economic analysis and policies (Dertilis 1989: 63–64).

Unfortunately for Greece, the emergence of the Megali Idea coincided with the eruption of the Eastern Question regarding the fate of the Ottoman Empire and the Greek claims went counter to the interests of most, if not all, Great Powers including the three patrons of the Greek state. The latter had consistently played a significant role in the internal affairs and politics of Greece, supporting or undermining one government after another (Dontas 1966: 18–22). Attempts by the Greek governments to undermine Ottoman rule in Crete, Epirus, Thessaly, and Macedonia brought about condemnation and intervention by the Great Powers, including blockades of Greek ports and, during the Crimean War, a three-year blockade and occupation of Piraeus by British and French troops (1854–57).

Greeks of course resented such blatant interventions as well as the unabashedly contradictory policies of some of the Great Powers. In response to a Greek protest that France's stance regarding the claims of Greece in Crete was at odds with the principle of nationality promoted by France in its Italian policy, the French ambassador the Marquis de Moustier responded that Greece, unlike Piedmont, had not managed to reach the standards of progress, prosperity, and security to allow it to have such aspirations, directly linking Greece's economic shortcomings to its lack of political clout (Dontas 1966: 77). Greek claims remained unfulfilled throughout the nineteenth century with the exception of the two small additions. In 1864 Britain ceded the Ionian islands as a gesture to the new king of Greece George I who succeeded the deposed Otto who lost his throne in 1862 in part as a result of the economic difficulties of the country (Psalidopoulos and Syrmaloglou 2005: 384). The second addition was Thessaly in 1881, a sop by the Great Powers to pacify the Greeks following the emergence of Bulgaria and the independence of Serbia, Romania, and Montenegro in the aftermath of the Congress of Berlin in 1878.[3]

The pursuit of the Megali Idea necessitated significant military spending, vastly disproportionate to the size and economic capabilities of Greece (Sakellaropoulos 2003: 60), which might have had a negative effect on growth, as recent research for the twentieth century has shown (see Antonakis 1997). Even without extraordinary expenditures following mobilizations or procurements of material in times of crises (Kostis 2013: 368, 373), the military budget of Greece was large: it was over 50 percent of total expenditures in 1846 (Kofas 1981: 35) and still 33 percent of total expenditures of the government in 1868 (Bikelas 1868: 297). The naval component was even more out of proportion for the size of the country, with occasional vast expenditures for the construction of warships, as for example a 4.5 million drachma extraordinary charge for the construction of two ironclads in 1867, in addition to another 4 million drachmas of extraordinary military related expenditure at a time when Greece had just initiated negotiations for resuming the servicing of its loans (Bikelas 1868: 271–72, 288; Dontas 1966: 118). Greek military expenditures throughout the nineteenth century ranged from a 4.3 percent to 16.9 percent of GDP, despite the absence of significant conflicts apart from the 1897 war with the Ottomans (Dertilis 2016: 60). Such expenditures led Ioannes Soutsos, the most prominent Greek economist and a strong proponent of fiscal discipline, to oppose the Megali Idea, though his voice was certainly in the minority and more often than not ignored (Psalidopoulos and Stassinopoulos 2009: 508). Again, this willingness to maintain high military spending despite the woeful finances of the Greek state has been a constant theme in Greek modern history to the current crisis. Military spending is more often criticized for being too low, even in times of economic crisis, rather than the opposite, and few governments after Otto in 1843 took the step to reduce military expenditures dramatically, including all governments in the current crisis regardless of their political orientation.

With regard to the economic policies of the state it is significant to note that there was a near consensus among the political class to support the agricultural sector and the peasantry, which formed the bulk of the electorate (Bikelas 1868: 276). Greece's early tax system was in essence a continuation of the Ottoman one (Petmezas 2003: 58). The Greek treasury relied on tariffs for most of its income rather than direct taxation, and politicians, even those who accepted the benefits of trade liberalization, were reluctant to shift the fiscal burden to direct taxation for reasons of social justice, as they repeatedly stated (Psalidopoulos 2005: 386, 393). In fact, from 1843 onward the tax burden of the countryside started to be lightened, a process intensified after 1862 (Dertilis 1993: 26, 38). This is a significant point considering that the period from the 1840s onward is seen as one of great worldwide trade liberalization (Accominotti and Flandreau 2008: 175). While resisting trade liberalization on grounds of social fairness, however, the political class was willing to tolerate a complex, arbitrary, and markedly unfair taxation system that did not even tax personal income (Lazaretou 1995: 32). Instead, Greece required all those employed to procure a certificate from their municipality and levied an occupations tax based on seven categories of professions (Sakkis 2001: 354). The inefficiency of tax collection forced the government to use indirect taxation extensively, collecting nearly 60 percent of its tax receipts through indirect

taxes (Lazaretou 2005a: 209). More research in this area is needed, however, since Greece appears to be at odds with general trends regarding
taxation in the nineteenth century where governments become increasingly more effective in tax collection, increasing their revenues rather than
tax rates, a process that took place even in states like the Ottoman Empire
(Pamuk 2006: 818). The inefficiency of tax collecting and the unfairness of
taxation, especially in times of crisis, is of course another constant in modern Greek history widely lamented during the current crisis.

Compounding these difficulties was a large bureaucracy that in 1861
employed 3,553 people, with the municipal authorities employing a further 5,199, excluding teachers, professors, or military personnel out of a
total working population of slightly more than 300,000 (Bikelas 1868: 272
292). Contemporaries justified this enormous, for the time, number of civil
servants to foreign observers as an outcome of the clientelist Greek political system that could be resolved by the granting of tenure to public servants (Bikelas 1868: 272) and they might have been correct linking politics
to the large bureaucracy. Recent research has shown that Greece consistently followed the spend-tax hypothesis where spending is determined
by the political elites, often for electoral purposes; once the expenditure
had been determined based upon political expediency, the government
sought the required revenue sources and taxes (Richter and Paparas 2013:
13). These expenditures had to be covered by an economy that at the time
of independence was almost entirely based on subsistence farming with
little use of money (Mpaloglou 2001: 178).

Admittedly Greece experienced significant population and territorial
growth in the nineteenth century and early twentieth centuries, that might
have necessitated a large state sector. Following a dramatic drop due to
the ravages of the Greek War of Independence from an estimated 983,765
people in 1821 to 753,400 in 1828, the population had risen to slightly more
than 1 million by 1861, almost 1.5 million by 1870, more than 2 million by
1889, and more than 2.5 million by 1907, by which time both the Ionian
islands and Thessaly had been added. The Balkan Wars and World War
I brought significant new territories to Greece, raising the population to
more than 5 million by 1920 while the influx of refugees after the Asia Minor campaign brought the total to 6,204,684 people by 1928 (Kiochos and
Mavridoglou 2001: 17–18).

To finance the politically motivated expenditures and large public
sector in the absence of reliable foreign lending the Greek governments
proved quite inventive. First of all, the governments frequently restricted
the convertibility of the drachma, as for instance in 1868 during the crisis
over the Cretan Revolution or during the Russo–Ottoman War of 1877–78,
in order to cover increased military spending through paper money using

inflation to finance its military preparations (Lazaretou 2005a: 211, 213). By restricting the convertibility of the drachma, essentially imposing currency controls, Greek governments could use the captive domestic market for borrowing, which they did extensively. Although successful, increasingly the Greek lenders requested high returns for their investment since the use of inflation to relieve its domestic debt burden had damaged the Greek state's reputation as a debtor in the domestic capital market as well (Lazaretou 2005a: 211, 213). It should be noted, however, that at the time domestic debt did not impact the perceptions of the international community since it was assumed that governments had legal and fiscal tools to deal with such obligations, such as the printing of notes or the unilateral restructuring of the debt via legislative action (Gelpern and Setser 2004: 799). The Greek government made some use of seignorage to finance its budgets (see Lazaretou 1995), and relied on increasing remittances from abroad, Greek migrants having some of the highest levels of remittances recorded (Esteves and Khoudour-Casteras 2011: 451).

Another tool in the arsenal of the Greek governments was the use of the National Bank of Greece (NBG), from which it continuously sought loans. Founded in 1841 as a private bank with issuing rights, from 1863 onward the NBG became indispensable to the state to cover public expenditures. The NBG charged a hefty premium over the lending rates in international markets and received various rights to collect public revenues, thus ensuring a healthy profit (Dertilis 1989: 2; Lazaretou 2005b: 334, 335). Occasionally the ambassadors of the Great Powers protested such loans in view of the outstanding obligations of the Greek state to foreign creditors but they did not press the issue due to the fragility of the Greek governments (Dontas 1966: 189). By 1890 the Greek government owed more than 135 million to the NBG (Patouna 2011: 54). Of secondary importance were other local banks such as the banks of Epeirothessalias, Viomechanikes Pisteos, and Konstantinoupoleos that also provided loans to the Greek government to plug holes in the budget through the 1880s (Tricha 2016: 449).

All of these policies allowed the Greek state to run perpetual budget deficits that even contemporaries, including Finance Minister Kehayas, recognized were unsustainable (Bikelas 1868: 288) and led Soutsos to suggest that fiscal restraint should be made a constitutional requirement (Psalidopoulos and Stassinopoulos 2009: 505). They also convinced many foreign observers that Greece was unwilling, rather than unable, to fulfill its obligations to foreign bondholders (Kofas 1981: 38; Tomz 2007: 100), particularly since governments were able to find additional income streams when political circumstances required it, especially when events in the Balkans necessitated increased military spending (Dertilis 1993: 56–57; Kostis 2013: 368, 373).

Fiscal Difficulties in Greece

The Greek state throughout the nineteenth century staggered from one economic crisis to another, but it is noteworthy that these crises did not immediately undermine the established political system with the exception of 1843. The revolt of that year delayed the discussions over the resolution of the outstanding debt obligations, and further delays followed through the deliberate foot dragging of the government of Prime Minister Ioannis Kolettis. The latter's attitude, coupled with his pro-French policies, outraged the British government. Lord Aberdeen and Lord Palmerston, both foreign secretaries and later prime ministers, declared that Britain had the right to intervene over the issue of noncompliance with the 1832 loan; Palmerston dispatched in 1847 three warships to Greek waters as a demonstration (Levandis 1944: 47–48). No resolution ensued, and although Greece was placed under a financial embargo, the guarantor Great Powers did not use their right according to the 1832 convention to take control of the finances of Greece. Instead they resorted to periodic complaints until the Crimean War in 1856, when France and Britain occupied parts of the country—including its capital port—to prevent Greece from assisting Russia (Andreades 1904: 93; Pepelasis-Minoglou 1996: 4). Before withdrawing those troops after the conclusion of the war, France and Britain insisted on the establishment of an International Financial Commission of Inquiry, which from 1857 to 1859 investigated the capacity of Greece to make debt payments and implement fiscal reforms (Levandis 1944: 51). Among other recommendations, they recommended the creation of a national land register,[4] the modification of the land tax, and the restructuring of the entire tax system (Levandis 1944: 52). The Greek state had no choice but to agree to these recommendations in an 1860 agreement, but a mere four years later the Greek government requested a moratorium on the implementation of the reforms and payments stipulated by the agreement. The Powers refused to condone a decrease in payments though they agreed to an extension of the timeframe. To avoid yet another default they also obliged the Greek government to assign one third of the customs revenues of the port of Hermoupolis for the service of the annual debt payments (Levandis 1944: 53). It should be noted that some Greeks like Soutsos also supported the resumption of payments on the foreign loans in order to restore the convertibility of the drachma, which would in turn facilitate trade (Psalidopoulos and Stassinopoulos 2009: 508), but the general Greek public appears to have held dim views of such policies, if contemporary theatrical plays like "The Economist's Duck" are any indication (see Psalidopoulos and Theocarakis 2015).

The settlement of the 1832 loan allowed the Greek government to seek a similar accommodation for the two revolutionary loans. The fiscal difficulties faced by the Greek government due to Greece's exclusion from international money markets during the Cretan Revolution of 1866, when it attempted to support the Cretan rebels, convinced the Greek government of the need to restore confidence in Greece. Early attempts in 1866 were not successful, but in 1878 an agreement was finally reached with those who held the Greek bonds, in part through the services of Greek diaspora financiers (Pepelasis-Minoglou 2002: 42). The outstanding obligations, which over half a century of nonpayment had ballooned to more than £10 million, were slashed to £1.2 million, to be covered by new bonds with a 5 percent interest, while the revenue from the customs house of Cephalonia and part of the stamp duty were assigned to the payment of the bonds (Levandis 1944: 28). In 1880 the final outstanding external obligations of the Greek state, the Bavarian loans, were also settled (Patouna 2011: 42), and Greece was finally able to access the international money markets again.

The debt negotiations of the late 1860s had an additional objective: the entry of Greece into the Latin Monetary Union (LMU) founded in 1865 by Belgium, France, Italy, and Switzerland. The Greek governments hoped that accession to the LMU would ensure monetary stability, reduce exchange rate fluctuations, increase access to the money markets in Paris, and restore the fiscal reputation of the country (Lazaretou 2005a: 212; Lazaretou 2005b: 338). This belief was not entirely misplaced, since countries that adhered to gold standard rules saw positive benefits with regard to the markets' perceptions of their sovereign debt (see Obstfeld and Taylor 2003), and the LMU was as close as Greece could get to such rules. However, although Greece was formally accepted to the LMU in 1867, it was unable to fully participate until 1885, and even then only for nine months (Lazaretou 2005b: 341).

Greece was not well placed economically in the 1870s to exploit the opportunities presented by access to foreign money markets and membership in the LMU. Although Greece attracted considerable capital from diaspora Greeks, much of the investment was of speculative nature that led to accusations of fraud and corruption (see Chatziioannou 2008). Not only was Greece still an overwhelmingly agrarian economy, but it also faced a severe problem of peasant indebtedness (Levandis 1944: 61). At the same time the state was saddled with significant military expenditures that exceeded the capacities of the state, a situation exacerbated by the frequent nationalist adventures and mobilizations. These resulted in Ottoman boycotts of Greek products, thus robbing Greek business of their second-largest trade partner (Britain was the largest; Bikelas 1868: 294). At the same time political instability, war scares, intermittent access to the Ottoman market, and general uncertainty regarding foreign affairs made Greece an unattractive prospect for foreign investment (Lazaretou 2005b: 337; see also Dincecco 2009). As a result of all these factors, coupled with the worldwide economic downturn at the end of the nineteenth century, Greece experienced a significant drop in GDP per capita during the period 1886–94 (Prontzas 2001: 128) or at best static growth (see Dadakas and Varelas 2009).

Foreign borrowing was seen as a possible solution that could spur the economic development of Greece and compensate for the spending spikes due to the perennial spats with the Ottoman Empire. Thus the external debt of Greece rapidly expanded in the 1880s and new loans were contracted to pay the growing domestic and foreign debt obligations, as well as to pay for ambitious infrastructure projects (Lazaretou 2005a: 222; Lazaretou 2005b: 339, 341). Most loans were naturally contracted at high interest rates (5–8 percent) (Levandis 1944: 66). Increasing difficulty in contracting new loans led in 1887 to assigning the revenues of the state monopolies on salt, petroleum, matches, playing cards, cigarette paper, and Naxian emery to the repayment of a new loan which became known as the Monopoly Loan (Levandis 1944: 68). In total, from 1879 to 1890 Greece contracted six loans worth more than 450 million gold francs (Levandis 1944: 71). Over the same period (1883–91), the Greek state continued to run budget deficits worth in total more than 200 million drachmas (Levandis 1944: 72). Although able to raise loans, Greece was widely perceived as a risk due to its past credit history and had to pay the corresponding premiums. As a matter of fact, no other country in the late nineteenth century had to pay as high a yield, even other proven serial defaulters like Ecuador, Mexico, or Venezuela (Tomz 2007: 59–60). To cover these obligations, the Greek state dramatically increased its tax receipts (the per capita tax burden grew from 15.22 in 1869 to 37.63 by 1893) yet was unable to stem the rising debt burden that rose from 94.5 to 363.2 per capita between 1869 and 1893 (Levandis 1944: 73). Significantly the governments did not drastically curtail expenditure during the same period.

The inevitable occurred in 1893, a year of financial panic when half the U.S. railroads were in bankruptcy and several countries were forced to reduce their interest payments (Feis 1930: 12), and one year after the dramatic fall in demand for currants, the main export crop of Greece (Pizanias 1988: 95). With the service of the external debt swallowing up 33 percent of the budget, the Greek government had no choice but to default on its debts again, despite arranging a last-minute funding loan by Hambro (Greece's main underwriter) earlier that year (Flores 2012: 991; Levandis 1944: 75). Foreign bondholders were naturally outraged. The British, French, and German governments officially remonstrated with the Greek government, while the foreign press viciously attacked the Greek government of Prime Minister Charilaos Trikoupis (Levandis 1944: 79). Attempting to pacify the foreign bondholders and their governments, Theodoros Diliyiannis,

Trikoupis's successor, proposed the creation of a Public Debt Commission consisting of Greek ministers, judges, and bankers that would supervise the collection of ceded revenues for the exclusive servicing of the external debt (Levandis 1944: 84). The terms insisted by the foreign creditors, however, were too exacting for the Greek government and the attempted compromise came to naught, especially since Diliyiannis also doubled expenditures despite the default (Dertilis 2016: 63).

The fiscal difficulties of the Greek government did not lead it to try to control expenditures, apart from the 1885–86 period when again Greece was forced to close its embassies[5] abroad because of a disastrously costly eight-month mobilization by the Diliyiannis government in a stand-off with the Ottoman empire.[6] While sympathetic foreign experts like Edouard Law suggested increasing taxes, improving tax collection, restructuring the financial services of the state, and gradually tightening the money supply, his suggestions were rejected by Trikoupis, who feared a rise in unemployment and emigration (Soilentakis 2012: 90, 92). Trikoupis expanded government spending instead, including military expenditures, and resumed infrastructure investment financed primarily through borrowing from domestic banks (Tricha 2016: 448, 449). Even after the default, politicians like Dimitrios Rallis and the Greek press fed public intransigence toward a compromise with the foreign creditors, and thus Diliyiannis suspended negotiations in 1895 (Soilentakis 2012: 111).

The Greek–Ottoman War of 1897 naturally deteriorated the condition of the Greek finances further, not only due to the costs of mobilization and ensuing fighting, but also because Greece, soundly defeated in the war, had to pay 4 million Ottoman pounds as a war indemnity (Levandis 1944: 92). Unable to access the international money markets, Greece needed a guarantee from the Great Powers to raise a new loan for the indemnity. A commission appraised Greek revenue capacity as well as the expenditure obligations of the Greek state and suggested the creation of a commission to manage the state monopolies, tobacco duties, stamp taxes, and the custom duties of the port of Piraeus, allocating 40 percent of these revenues to the Greek treasury and the remainder 60 percent for the servicing of Greece's external debt (Levandis 1944: 104, 107). In 26 February 1898 the Greek Law of Control recognized the International Financial Commission (IFC) that was to supervise and, to a significant degree, control Greek finances over the ensuing decades. These restrictions did not allow Greece to exploit the thawing of the financial markets that begun that same year and would endure till the eruption of World War I (Flores 2012: 980).

Under the constraints of the IFC, Greek governments were forced to adapt their policies, and Greek finances improved markedly. In 1910, following a dozen years of austerity during which Greece cut expenditures, reduced seignorage, and raised taxes, Greece was able to adopt the gold standard (Lazaretou 1995: 35; Lazaretou 2005a: 208; Lazaretou 2005b: 345). That austerity, however, had once more alienated great segments of the Greek public and the army, and had resulted in a military coup in 1909 that led to the radical transformation of Greek politics with the arrival of Eleftherios Venizelos. The improved finances allowed the Greek government to finance the cost of the Balkan Wars (1912–13) and World War I (1917–18) through domestic and foreign loans without impacting the fixed exchange rate of the drachma (Lazaretou 2005b: 346; Patouna 2011: 63–64). This was partly due to a collaboration with France since many of these loans were contracted in France and were used to buy French military equipment while French interests acquired railroad and banking assets in Greece (Feis 1930: 127, 128, 287, 288). However, the continuing military spending during the Greek–Turkish War in Anatolia (1919–22) forced the government once more to print money recklessly, undermining the fiscal and monetary stability that had been achieved (Lazaretou 2005b: 347, 348).

Placing Greece in an International Context

Greece was not the only state in this period to be plagued by severe financial difficulties, just like the current crisis that has also engulfed several European states. In the 1820s many of the newly independent Latin American states had issued bonds promising high returns. A few years later over 90 percent of Latin American bonds were in default and it took four decades to settle them (Waibel 2011: 10). Nor was this limited to Latin America: between 1840 and 1870 fifteen U.S. states defaulted on their loans in circumstances that have been compared to the EU difficulties of 2010 (Roberts 2010: 197). These defaults severely impacted the fiscal reputation of U.S. states, who resisted raising taxes despite their defaults. The defaults impacted even the U.S. federal government to the point that an attempt to float a federal loan in Europe failed while the United States deliberately discriminated against foreign bondholders (Gelpern 2012: 898; Roberts 2010: 199; Sylla and Wallis 1998: 269; Waibel 2011: 3, 6, 7). From the 1820s to the 1840s almost half of the countries in the world were in default in one of several cycles of defaults, a pattern Greece matches well (see Reinhart and Rogoff 2009).

Greece was also not unique in allocating specific revenue streams to service loans or having those supervised by a foreign commission. In the late nineteenth and early twentieth centuries creditors frequently assumed some control over revenue streams in debtor states to recover their investments. The role played by the IFC in Greece was played by the Caisse de la Dette in Egypt until 1940, while a similar function was exercised by the Ottoman Debt Council in the Ottoman Empire from 1876 onward. In a somewhat similar fashion, the United States also assumed control over the finances of debtor countries such as Haiti, Honduras, Nicaragua, and the Dominican Republic (Waibel 2011: 42).

This control over income streams has often been seen in conjunction with or as a direct consequence of direct military intervention by the Great Powers. The idea that creditors and their respective governments resorted to gunboat diplomacy in the nineteenth century to recoup their loans, however, must be taken with caution. New scholarship does not seem to support the idea that the Great Powers used military force to collect debts of other states when other causes such as territorial disputes, civil wars, ethnic conflict, or political aims are also considered (Flores 2012: 983; Tomz 2007: 126, 132, 153, 232). Even in the most famous examples—the intervention of Britain, France, and Spain in Mexico in 1861, or the intervention of Britain and Germany in Venezuela in 1902—the needs of the bondholders in both cases were secondary considerations (Tomz 2007: 132, 143). The use of gunboat diplomacy is not disputed, but the link to the enforcement of debt obligations is quite tenuous, especially since most military interventions were conducted by the United States while the main market for sovereign debt was London (Flandreau and Flores 2009: 649).

Yet it was precisely the foreign interventions that grated the Greek public and elites, who did not distinguish between political and economic aims. Greece was intimately involved in Great Power politics from the moment of its insurrection; for many, the very intervention of 1827 was directly tied to the 1824–25 loans, despite the fact that Prime Minister George Canning (British prime minister from 12 April to 8 August 1827) had expressly rejected intervention in Latin American states over their defaults, and even forbade British diplomats to bring pressure on those states (Flandreau and Flores 2009: 649). While Greece was repeatedly pressured by the Great Powers—as for instance in 1847 with the British naval demonstration or in 1850 when Britain blockaded several Greek ports in the so-called Don Pacifico affair—these and subsequent interventions had political roots, but for the Greek public the links to foreign indebtedness were unquestionable. In fact, those links are still a common theme in Greek historiography (Kostis 2013: 264, 266, 270; Skliraki 2012: 86; Soilentakis 2012: 74) that often dismisses other aspects, such as the anti-Semitic elements of the riots during a visit by Baron Rothschild to discuss the outstanding debt obligations of Greece, which destroyed the property of the British subject Don Pacifico who gives his name to the ensuing incident (see Whitten 1986).[7] Even the most notorious foreign intervention in Greek history—the blockade and occupation of Piraeus during the course of the Crimean War

(1854–57), which was clearly due to Greek agitation in Ottoman territories—is seen in the prism of Greece's foreign indebtedness (Soilentakis 2012: 75), because, prior to withdrawing, France and Britain insisted that Greece accept a commission to investigate the resumption of its debt servicing. Even the 1897 war is blamed on foreign creditors, especially Germany, and is tied to the imposition of the IFC the next year (Skliraki 2015: 131–33; Soilentakis 2012: 108).

Greeks were not wrong in assuming that foreign debt could be used as a pretext for intervention or as a political lever. Creditor countries did not automatically send in the gunboats in cases of default but, as Palmerstone stated in a memorandum, though the British government was not obliged to intervene diplomatically on behalf of British holders of foreign bonds it could do so if it so chose. Even though the British government showed no zeal toward doing so, it did use defaults as pretexts for intervention when it suited political needs. For instance, the 1876 Ottoman and Egyptian defaults led to the military intervention by Britain and France, with the British assuming virtual control of the latter country because of the strategic significance of the Suez Canal (Waibel 2011: 23–24). Britain, France, and Spain intervened in Mexico in 1862 using Mexican defaults as a pretext, imposing in the process Emperor Maximillian of Habsburg on the Mexican throne (Waibel 2011: 30). The most active interventionist power was the United States, which intervened in several countries like Haiti, Honduras, Nicaragua, and the Dominican Republic to control revenue streams for debt servicing (Reinhart and Rogoff 2009: 83). These interventions, however, were instigated by U.S. companies involved in primary production in the region, and were aimed to secure markets for American goods and protect American agricultural and extraction investments, rather than to ensure the repayment of U.S. bondholders (Frieden 1989: 64, 67; see also Frieden 1994). In these cases, the paramount concerns were political rather than financial, and the Great Powers were willing to tolerate long periods of sovereign defaults without coming to the aid of bondholders. Greece is a perfect example of this since, despite the constant interventions, the servicing of the Greek debt did not resume until the Greek government voluntarily and without overt pressure decided to do so in 1879.

The End of Financial Control

In the first three decades of the twentieth century the Greek government was in frequent disputes with the IFC. Greece's use of the printing press to finance its obligations stemming from the wars from 1912 to 1923 led to high inflation and arguments with the IFC that were resolved only through international arbitration (Waibel 2011: 45). Greece was also subjected to economic coercion following the conclusion of World War I when in 1920 the deposed king Constantine, widely seen as pro-German, was reinstated to the throne. A financial embargo was immediately imposed on Greece by its former allies (Pepelasis-Minoglou 1993: 53, 68; Pepelasis-Minoglou 1996: 20), exacerbating the fragile finances of the state already adversely effected by a military campaign in Asia Minor. The ensuing defeat there in 1923 led to an increase of the risk premium of Greek debt, necessitating a loan brokered under the auspices of the League of Nations for the settlement of the 1.5 million refugees from the war (Christodoulaki, Cho, and Fryzlewicz 2012: 562, 565).

The 1920s were a period of rapid growth for Greece due to a combination of high tariffs and a sharp drop of real wages because of the arrival of the refugees from Asia Minor. Loans had to be contracted to resettle the refugees (Choumanidis 1990: 318) while the Greek government continued its policy of loose monetary policy (Tzokas 2002: 36). In 1927 the government introduced a stabilization program and a simultaneous effective devaluation of the drachma that allowed Greece to rejoin the gold standard in 1928 (Lazaretou 2005b: 249–350), despite a U.S. ban on Greek securities (Pepelasis-Minoglou 1993: 339). Greece became one of the main customers of the British Hambros Bank regarding foreign loan flotations (Pepelasis-Minoglou 2002: 47), but the depression of the 1930s presented the Greek government with the unpleasant options of reducing its expenditures or defaulting on its obligations. In 1932 it chose again the latter, despite pressure from the IFC (see Mazower 1991). In April of that year it ended the convertibility of the drachma and abandoned the gold standard. A month later it ceased servicing its foreign debt (Lazaretou 2005b: 351). Unlike much of Europe and the United States, the Greek government pursued a loose fiscal policy that limited the impact of the depression yet managed to keep inflation moderate through modest increases in banknote circulation (Lazaretou 2005b: 351). The eruption of World War II again transformed the economic environment of Europe yet, surprisingly, financial considerations continued to compete with political and military needs. Despite calls in Britain for a more open trade policy with regard to the Balkan states in order to reverse the German stranglehold over their economies (see Fisher 1939), the Chancellor of the Exchequer stated to a 1940 Greek mission that, although he would like to help Greek trade, he could not support easier access unless a settlement on the Greek debt was first achieved (see Eichengreen 1989).

Greece was devastated by World War II and the ensuing Greek Civil War. The latter, however, placed Greece at the front lines of the emerging Cold War and led to massive U.S. aid both through the Marshall Plan and through military aid under the Truman Doctrine (Lazaretou 2005b: 354). From the 1950s, Greece was an economic success story. A devaluation of the drachma by 50 percent against the dollar before Greece joined the Bretton Woods system in 1953, with a simultaneous reduction in government consumption, increase in infrastructure spending, and a balanced budget, contributed to some of the highest rates of growth (an average of 7 percent) until the late 1960s (Lazaretou 2005b: 355). From having been a country where food aid was necessary in the 1950s, Greece was able to become a member of the European Economic Community in 1981, and join the European Union (EU) common currency when it was physically launched in 2002. Despite these achievements, Greek finances were often in a precarious state, such as with high levels of borrowing and expenditure in the 1980s, this time primarily due to social spending, though military expenditures remained high despite the abandonment of irredentist dreams.

When the most recent crisis erupted, Greece chose not to follow the same path it had followed so often in the past and default on its debts, but instead decided to try to implement an austerity program as suggested by the Troika (the European Central Bank, the European Commission, and the IMF are known as the Troika). This had been seriously attempted only twice in similar circumstances, and both times it had resulted in the overthrow of the political system, first in 1843 and again in 1909. There were reasons, however, why the government of George Papandreou thought that this time things would be different. Greece was far more prosperous in 2009 than it had ever been, and more integrated and dependent on the world and Europeans economies, making a default immeasurably more damaging than was the case in the nineteenth or twentieth centuries. More importantly, unlike other periods in its history, Greece had access to the necessary funds to avoid an official default, thanks to the largest bailout in history by its partners in the EU. This funding probably led Greek governments to hope that they could avoid a default and probable ejection from the European common currency, while also avoiding radical reforms, massive layoffs of state employees, or severe cuts in state expenditure or the military.

The signing of the first (and subsequent) MoUs, however, introduced a form of foreign supervision to Greek finances that, even though it lacked the authority exercised by the IFC, brought clear associations to a bygone era of Great Power domination of Greece. In the first couple of years following the first MoU, mass protests and the rise of radical parties and movements on both the right and the left of the political spectrum (examined in subsequent chapters in this volume) threatened a repeat of the political collapses of 1843 and 1909. Indeed, the party most associated with the first MoU, the Panhellenic Socialist Movement (PASOK), was nearly wiped out electorally and has not recovered. Essentially, however, the calculations of George Papandreou proved correct. Although many commentators on the Greek crisis, including many in this volume, often describe the implemented reforms and effects as radical, and certainly Greece has seen dramatically increased taxation, severe cutbacks in services, a rise in unemployment, and a great contraction of the economy, I would argue that based on past experiences the Greek political system survived in part because it effectively avoided truly radical political and structural reforms, mass layoffs of state employees, or even drastic cutbacks in expenditures including military ones. Although the rhetoric from both ends of the political spectrum indicate the continuing widespread acceptance of the idea that foreign loans are contracted for political rather than economic reasons and are vehicles for foreign control over Greece,[8] the ability of the governments throughout the crisis to shelter to a significant degree the public sector has allowed them to portray themselves as resisting the demands of foreigners rather than colluding with them. This was not achieved only by the current leftist SYRIZA government, but also by the previous center-right ND government. Only the original signatory to the MoUs, the center-left PASOK, was tarred by its collaboration with the Troika and saw its electoral power permanently dissipate. Having observed this, subsequent governments reacted by trying to disassociate themselves with the policies of austerity, assigning sole ownership to foreign institutions and actively resisting structural reforms, while continuing to employ an antiforeign rhetoric, especially with regard to foreign debt. This rhetoric was particularly prominent in the first SYRIZA government, some of whose senior figures attempted to brand the external debt as odious, but could also be seen in the earlier ND government that SYRIZA replaced. All governments during the crisis have tried to shield domestic debtors and creditors from the effects of the crisis, something frequently seen in similar circumstances (Hatchondo and Martinez 2010: 3; Tomz and Wright 2013: 264), but the rare attempt to brand the Greek foreign debt as odious is indicative of the perceptions of Greece regarding foreign borrowing.[9]

Greek governments, and by extension the Greek public, have historically seen foreign loans in political rather than economic terms and have sought political, rather than economic, solutions, as Prime Minister Tsipras famously stated (Antoniou 2015; *E Avge Online,* 29 April 2016; Gkantona 2016; Sverkos, 12 March 2016). Tsipras's attitude toward fiscal policy is not too different from the attitude of Venizelos in the 1930s (see Pepelasis-Minoglou 1993: 176, 218, 350; Pepelasis-Minoglou 1996: 34–35). This deep belief in the absolute link of finances with geopolitical goals that is often shared by those in government can be traced back to Alexander

Mavrokordatos and other leaders of the Greek War of Independence who saw foreign loans as a tool to involve foreign states in the Greek cause. This attitude was reinforced by the frequent foreign interventions in Greece, from the gunboat diplomacy of the nineteenth century to modern interventions by the United States during the Greek Civil War or the Greek dictatorship of 1967–74, blurring distinctions between political and financial. Although both foreign interventions and excessive foreign borrowing have been constants in modern Greek history, it is often ignored that—with the exception of U.S. aid after World War II and the recent EU bailouts—most foreign lending to Greece was done by private interests and not by governments. If anything, foreign governments often came reluctantly to the aid of Greece, since a pattern of extensive borrowing, inability to constrain expenditures, or inability to implement structural reforms, followed by default, and ending with the arrangement of rescue loans by foreign governments is clearly evident from the 1820–1830s, 1880–1890s, 1920–1930s, to the present (Reinhart and Trebesch 2015: 8, 14). Although the decision of Greek governments not to default this time and the subsequent rise of extremist parties like Golden Dawn (discussed in an ensuing chapter by Kostis Karpozilos) would point to a departure similar to those attempted prior to 1843 and 1909, I would argue instead that the current crisis is unique in Greek history, solely because of the existence of EU funding that allowed Greek governments to avoid both default and drastic structural reforms that in the past have led to the violent overthrow of the political order.

Evdoxios Doxiadis is an Associate Professor at the Department of History at Simon Fraser University. His research is on Greek, Balkan, and Mediterranean history with a focus in the 18th and 19th centuries and a particular interest in questions of gender, law, state formation, and minorities. His publications include *The Shackles of Modernity: Women, Property, and the Transition from the Ottoman Empire to the Modern Greek State 1750–1850* (2011) and *State, Nationalism, and the Jewish Communities of Modern Greece* (2018).

Notes

1. The currency in Greece during the Ottoman period and the Greek War of Independence was the *grosi* (singular), or *grosia* (plural).
2. In this and subsequent mentions of default I am referring to partial defaults in the sense that Greece never repudiated its debts, although it came close to doing so in 1843. Such repudiation has been remarkably rare historically (see Grossman and Huyck 1988).

3. The annexation of Thessaly was not without costs, not only in terms of administration but also because Greece had to compensate the Ottoman government. Greece had to contract two significant loans to cover these costs (Choumanidis 1990: 286).
4. The same need was stressed by Greek economists in the nineteenth century (Psalido-poulos and Stassinopoulos 2009: 507) but has yet to be implemented fully. The latest efforts floundered in early 2016 (Lialios 2016).
5. Greece reopened its embassies in 1850 only to disband them again in 1863 again due to economic difficulties (Tricha 2016: 100, 123).
6. Diliyiannis tried to cover the increased cost through a domestic, interest-free, so-called patriotic loan, but only a quarter of what was expected was covered (Choumanidis 1990: 289).
7. Significantly, many Greek historians prefer to refer to the events as *Parkerika* after the commander of the British squadron that effected the blockade rather than the victim of the riot.
8. Surveys show that over 30 percent of the population is convinced that the EU attempted to subjugate Greece in the recent crisis (DiaNEOsis 2015: A21).
9. Odious debt involves the ability of governments to renounce obligations stemming from loans that lenders knowingly gave to a corrupt and illegitimate government (Lavdas 2013: 104; Reinhart and Rogoff 2009: 63). Though first mentioned by Grotius, the current understanding emerged from the decision of Chief Justice Taft of the US Supreme Court, who, acting as an arbitrator, ruled that Costa Rica did not have to repay the loans contracted by the dictatorship of Federico Tinoco Granados from the Royal Bank of Canada following the collapse of the dictatorship in 1919, since these loans were meant for Tinoco's personal use and the bank was aware of this (Waibel 2011: 137). Greece of course does not fit any of the prerequisites stated (Lavdas 2013: 106, 110) and it is used for political purposes to imply corruption in prior governments and to link the Greek case to the discourse regarding debt forgiveness in developing economies, including those emerging from authoritarian regimes.

References

Accominotti, Olivier, and Marc Flandreau. 2008. "Bilateral Treaties and the Most-Favored-Nation Clause: The Myth of Trade Liberalization in the Nineteenth Century." *World Politics* 60(2): 147–88.

Andreades, Andr. Mich. 1904. *Istoria Ton Ethnikon Daneion*. Athens: Estia.

Antonakis, Nicholas. 1997. "Military Expenditure and Economic Growth in Greece, 1960–1990." *Journal of Peace Research* 34(1): 89–100.

Antoniou, D. 2015. "Zeteitai Politike Lyse gia Daneia." *E Kathimerini*, 5 November. Retrieved 29 April 2016 from http://www.kathimerini.gr/837431/article/epikairothta/politikh/zhteitai-politikh-lysh-gia-daneia.

Bikelas, Demetrius. 1868. "Statistics of the Kingdom of Greece." *Journal of Statistical Society of London* 31(3): 265–98.

Bozikis, Simos. 2010. "Dynamikes Kai Adraneies Ste Phorologia Kai Sto Forologiko Mechanismo Kata Ten Epanastase Tou 1821." *Mnemon* 31: 31–68.

Chatziioannou, Maria Christina. 2008. "Relations between the State and the Private Sphere: Speculation and Corruption in Nineteenth-Century Greece." *Mediterranean Historical Review* 23(1): 1–14.

———. 2013. "War, Crisis, and Sovereign Loans: The Greek War of Independence and the British Economic Expansion in the 1820s." *Historical Review* 10X: 33–55.

Choumanidis, L. Th. 1990. *Oikonomike Istoria tes Ellados*. Vol. II. Athens: Ekdoseis Papazisi.

Christodoulaki, Olga, Haeran Cho, and Piotr Fryzlewicz. 2012. "A Reflection of History: Fluctuations in Greek Sovereign Risk between 1914 and 1929." *European Review of Economic History* 16: 550–71.

"Convention between Great Britain, France, and Russia, on the One Part, and Bavaria on the Other, Relative to the Sovereignty of Greece." 1918. *American Journal of International Law* 12(2): 68–74.

Dadakas, Dimitrios, and Erotokritos Varelas. 2009. "The Decomposition of Greek Real GDP (1858–1938)." *International Review of Economics* 56(2): 189–202.

Dertilis, G. B. 1989. *To Zetema Ton Trapezon (1871–1873)*. Athens: Morfotiko Idryma Ethnikis Trapezis.

———. 1993. *Atelesforoi E Telesforoi? Foroi Kai Exousia Sto Neoelleniko Kratos*. Athens: Alexandreia.

———. 2016. *Epta Polemoi, Tesseris Emfylioi, Epta Ptochevseis 1821–2016*. Athens : Polis.

DiaNEOsis. 2015. Ti Pistevoun oi Ellenes. Panelladike Erevna – Ekthese Apotelesmaton. Vol. A. Retrieved 29 April 2016 from http://www.dianeosis.org/wp-content/uploads/2016/02/ti_pistevoun_oi_ellines_spreads_A.pdf.

Dincecco, Mark. 2009. "Political Regimes and Sovereign Credit Risk in Europe 1750–1913." *European Review of Economic History* 13(1): 31–63.

Dontas, Domna N. 1966. *Greece and the Great Powers 1863–1875*. Thessaloniki, Greece: Institute for Balkan Studies.

Eichengreen, Barry, and Richard Portes. 1989. "After the Deluge: Default Negotiation and Readjustment During the Interwar Years." In *The International Debt Crisis in Historical Perspective*, edited by Peter H. Lindert and Barry Eichengreen, 12–47. Cambridge, MA: MIT Press.

Esteves, Rui, and David Khoudour-Casteras. 2011. "Remittances, Capital Flows and Financial Development during the Mass Migration Period, 1870–1913." *European Review of Economic History* 15: 443–74.

Feis, Herbert. 1930. *Europe the World's Banker 1870–1914*. New Haven, CT: Yale University Press.

Fisher, Allan G. B. 1939. "The German Trade Drive in Southeastern Europe." *International Affairs* 18(2): 143–70.

Flandreau, Marc, and Juan H. Flores. 2009. "Bonds and Brands: Foundations of Sovereign Debt Markets, 1820–1830." *Journal of Economic History* 69(3): 646–84.

Flores, Juan H. 2012. "Crying on Lombard Street: Fixing Sovereign Defaults in the 1890s." *European Review of History* 19(6): 979–97.

Fotiadis, D. 2015. "Ta Lestrika Daneia tou 1824–1825–1832. E Ptochevse tes Elladas to 1843!" *iskra*, 8 March. Retrieved 29 April 2016 from http://iskra.gr/archive/index.php?option=com_content&view=article&id=894:-1824-1825-1832-1843&catid=55:an-oikonomia&Itemid=283.

Frieden, Jeffrey A. 1989. "The Economics of Intervention: American Overseas Investments and Relations with Underdeveloped Areas 1890–1950." *Comparative Studies in Society and History* 31(1): 55–80.

———. 1994. "International Investment and Colonial Control: A New Interpretation." *International Organization* 48(4): 559–93.

Gelpern, Anna. 2012. "Bankruptcy, Backwards: The Problem of Quasi-Sovereign Debt." *Yale Law Journal* 121(4): 888–942.

Gelpern, Anna, and Brad Setser. 2004. "Domestic and External Debt: The Doomed Quest for Equal Treatment." *Georgetown Journal of International Law* 35(4): 795–814.

Gkantona, S. "O Tsipras Psachnei Politike Lyse, gia na Apofygei… ta Vrachia." *iefimerida*, 15 February. Retrieved 29 April 2016 from http://iefimerida.gr/news/251027/o-tsipras-psahnei-politiki-lysi-gia-na-apofygei-ta-vrahia.

Grossman, Herschel I., and John B. Van Huyck. 1988. "Sovereign Debt as a Contingent Claim: Excusable Default, Repudiation, and Reputation." *American Economic Review* 78(5): 1088–97.

Harisis, Apostolos, ed. 1996. *Archeion Strategou Georgiou Karaiskaki (1826–1827)*. Athens: A Harisis.

Hatchondo, Juan Carlos, and Leonardo Martinez. 2010. "The Politics of Sovereign Defaults." *Economic Quarterly* 96(3): 1–13.

Hellenic Parliament. 2015. *Praktika Voules*. 16th Period, Session 65, 27 June, 3907. Retrieved 29 April 2016 from www.hellenicparliament.gr/UserFiles/a08fc2dd-61a9-4a83-b09a-09f4c564609d/es20150627.pdf.

Kiochos, Petros, and Georgios Mavridoglou. 2001. "Parelthon—Paron Kai Mellon Tou Ellenikou Plethysmou." *Archeion Oikonomikes Istorias* 12(1–2): 17–26.

Kofas, Jon V. 1981. *Financial Relations of Greece and the Great Powers, 1832–1862*. Boulder: East European Monographs.

Koliopoulos, John S. 1984. "Military Entrepreneurship in Central Greece During the Greek War of National Liberation (1821–1830)." *Journal of Modern Greek Studies* 2(2): 163–87.

Kostis, Kostas. 2013. *"Ta Kakomathemena Paidia Tes Istorias" E Diamorphose Tou Neoellenikou Kratous, 18os–21os Aionas*. Athens: Polis.

Kremmydas, Vasilis. 1976–77. "E Oikonomike Krise Ston Elladiko Choro Stis Arches Tou 19ou Aiona Kai Oi Epiptoseis Tes Sten Epanastase Tou 1821." *Mnemon* 6: 16–33.

Lavdas, K. A., et al. 2013. *Stateness and Sovereign Debt, Greece in the European Conundrum*. Lantham: Lexington Books.

Lavdas, Kostas A., Spyridon N. Litsas, and Dimitrios V. Skiadas. 2013. *Stateness and Sovereign Debt, Greece in the European Conundrum*. Lantham, MD: Lexington Books.

Lazaretou, Sophia. 1995. "Government Spending, Monetary Policies, and Exchange Rate Regime Switches: The Drachma in the Gold Standard Period." *Explorations in Economic History* 32: 28–50.

———. 2005a. "The Drachma, Foreign Creditors, and the International Monetary System: Tales of a Currency During the 19th and the Early 20th Centuries." *Explorations in Economic History* 42(2): 202–36.

———. 2005b. "Greek Monetary Economics in Retrospect: The Adventures of the Drachma." *Economic Notes* 34(3): 331–70.

Levandis, John A. 1944. *The Greek Foreign Debt and the Great Powers*. New York: Columbia University Press.

Lewis, M. 2010. "Beware of Greeks Bearing Bonds." *Vanity Fair* 52(10), 1 October. Retrieved 20 July 2015 from https://www.vanityfair.com/news/2010/10/greeks-bearing-bonds-201010.

Lialios, Giorgos. 2016. "Akyrotheke O Teleutaios Diagonismos Gia to Ktematologio." *E Kathimerini*, 17 March. Retrieved 17 March 2016 from www.kathimerini.gr/853322.

Martin, J. 2015. "E Apoikiake Proelevse tou Ellenikou Mnemoniou." Nomadic Universality, 29 April. Retrieved 29 July 2015 from nomadicuniversality.worldpress.com.

Mazower, Mark. 1991. *Greece and the Inter-War Economic Crisis*. New York: Clarendon Press.

McGrew, William W. 1985. *Land and Revolution in Modern Greece, 1800–1881: The Transition in the Tenure and Exploitation of Land from Ottoman Rule to Independence*. Kent, OH: Kent State University Press.

Mpaloglou, Christos P. 2001. "Kateuthynseis Kai Prooptikes Tes Oikonomikes Politikes Tes Antivasileias." *Archeion Oikonomikes Istorias* 12(1–2): 177–216.

Obstfeld, Maurice, and Alan M Taylor. 2003. "Sovereign Risk, Credibility and the Gold Standard 1870–1913 Versus 1925–31." *Economic Journal* 113(487): 241–75.

Pamuk, Sevket. 2006. "Estimating Economic Growth in the Middle East since 1820." *Journal of Economic History* 66(3): 809–28.

Patouna, Dionysia. 2011. *E Diachronike Exelixe Tou Demosiou Daneismou Sten Ellada Kata Ten Periodo 1824–1932 Kai Oi Procheuseis Tou Ellenikou Kratous.* Athens: Perifereiake Dioikese Athenas, Ethnike Schole Demosias Dioikeses.

Pepelasis-Minoglou, Ioanna. 1993. "The Greek State and the International Financial Community, 1922–1932: Demystifying the 'Foreign Factor.'" University of London, London.

———. 1996. *Transplanting Economic Ideas: International Coercion and Native Policy.* London School of Economics & Political Science Working Papers in Economic History, London.

———. 2002. "Between Informal Networks and Formal Contracts: International Investment in Greece During the 1920s." *Business History* 44(2): 40–64.

Petmezas, Socratis. 2003. *E Ellenike Agrotike Oikonomia Kata Ton 19o Aiona. E Periphereiake Diastase.* Herakleio, Greece: Panepistimiakes Ekdoseis Kritis.

Pizanias, Petros. 1988. *Oikonomike Istoria Tes Ellenikes Staphidas 1851–1912.* Athens: Idryma Ereunas kai Paideias tes Emporikes Trapezas tes Ellados.

Polyzoidis, Anastasios. 2011. *Keimena Gia Te Demokratia 1824–1825.* Edited by Filimon Paionidis and Elpida Vogli. Athens: Ekdoseis Okto.

Prontzas, Evaggelos D. 2001. "E Phorodotike Epivarynse Kai Ikanoteta Tou Ellenikou Kratous (1830–1939)." *Archeion Oikonomikes Istorias* 12(1–2): 121–46.

Psalidopoulos, Michalis. 2005. "The Greek 'Society for the Freedoms of Trade' (1865–67): Rise, Activities, Decline." *Journal of the History of Economic Thought* 27(4): 383–98.

Psalidopoulos, Michalis M., and Yorgos Stassinopoulos. 2009. "A Liberal Economist and Economic Policy Reform in Nineteenth-Century Greece: The Case of Ioannes Soutsos." *History of Political Economy* 41(3): 491–517.

Psalidopoulos, Michalis, and Adamantios Syrmaloglou. 2005. "Economists in the Greek Parliament (1862–1910): The Men and Their Views on Fiscal and Monetary Policy." In *Economists in Parliament in the Liberal Age (1848–1920),* edited by Marco E. L. Guidi and Massimo M. Augello, 229–58. Burlington, VT: Ashgate.

Psalidopoulos, Michalis, and Nicholas J. Theocarakis. 2015. "Disparaging Liberal Economics in Nineteenth-Century Greece: The Case of 'The Economist's Duck.'" *European Journal of the History of Economic Thought* 22(6): 949–77.

Reinhart, Carmen M., and Kenneth S. Rogoff. 2009. *This Time Is Different: Eight Centuries of Financial Folly.* Princeton, NJ: Princeton University Press.

Reinhart, Carmen M., and Christoph Trebesch. 2015. "The Pitfalls of External Dependence: Greece, 1829–2015." Working Paper 21664, National Bureau of Economic Research, Cambridge, MA.

Richter, Christian, and Dimitrios Paparas. 2013. "Tax and Spend, Spend and Tax, Fiscal Synchronisation or Institutional Separation? Examining the Case of Greece." *Romanian Journal of Fiscal Policy* 4(2): 1–17.

Roberts, Alasdair. 2010. "An Ungovernable Anarchy: The United States' Response to Depression and Default, 1837–1848." *Intereconomics* 45(4): 196–202.

Sakellaropoulos, Theodoros. 2003. *Keimena Oikonomikes Kai Koinonikes Istorias.* Athens: Dionikos.

Sakkis, Dimitris A. 2001. "The Professional Categories and Social Structure of the Free Greek State." *Archeion Oikonomikes Istorias* 12(1–2): 353–76.

Skliraki, Evi D. 2015. *Ta Daneia Tes Exarteses Kai Tes Chreokopias 1824–1940.* Athens: Smili.

Soilentakis, N. 2012. *Dystychos Eptochevsamen: Oi Staseis Pleromon 1827, 1893, 1932.* Athens: Ekdoseis Papazisi.

Sverkos, N. 2016. "Anazeteitai Politike Lyse." *E Efemerida ton Syntakton,* 12 March. Retrieved 29 April 2016 from www.efsyn.gr/arthro/anazeteitai-politiki-lysi-0.

Sylla, Richard, and John Joseph Wallis. 1998. "The Anatomy of Sovereign Debt Crises: Lessons from the American State Defaults of the 1840s." *Japan and the World Economy* 10: 267–93.

Todorova, Maria. 2009. *Imagining the Balkans.* Oxford, UK: Oxford University Press.

Tomz, Michael. 2007. *Reputation and International Cooperation, Sovereign Debt across Three Centuries.* Princeton, NJ: Princeton University Press.

Tomz, Michael, and Mark L. J. Wright. 2013. "Empirical Research on Sovereign Debt and Default." *Annual Revue of Economics* 5: 247–72.

Tricha, Lydia. 2016. *Charilaos Trikoupis, O Politikos tou "Tis Ptaiei;" kai tou "Dystychos Eptocheusamen."* Athens: Polis.

Trikoupis, Spyridon. 1978a. *Istoria Tes Ellenikes Epanastaseos.* 4 vols. Vol. C. Athens: Chr. Giovanis.

———. 1978b. *Istoria Tes Ellenikes Epanastaseos.* 4 vols. Vol. D, Athens: Chr. Giovanis.

Truth Committee on Public Debt. 2015. Preliminary Report. Athens. Retrieved 25 July 2017 from www.cadtm.org/IMG/pdf/Report.pdf.

Tzokas, S. 2002. *O Eleftherios Venizelos kai to Egcheirema tou Astikou Eksygchronismou 1928–1932: E Oikodomese tou Astikou Kratous.* Athens: Themelio.

Waibel, Michael. 2011. *Sovereign Defaults before International Courts and Tribunals.* Cambridge, UK: Cambridge University Press.

Whitten, Dolphus Jr. 1986. "The Don Pacifico Affair." *Historian* 48(2): 255–67.

Chapter 2

The Political Consequences of the Crisis in Greece
Charismatic Leadership and Its Discontents

Harris Mylonas

Introduction

At this writing, eight years have passed since 2010, when the first memorandum of understanding (MoU) was signed between Greece and its creditors. Seven years of forced reform, seven years of economic recession. Today, having signed a third MoU, unemployment rates in Greece still hover above 20 percent and youth unemployment just below 50 percent, the emigration of highly skilled Greeks has dramatically intensified, and the country's GDP has shrunk by 25 percent since 2009 (Eurostat 2016). The other European economies that faced similar hardships seem to be well on the path to recovery, and all but Greece have exited from the oversight of the European Stability Mechanism (ESM) and participate in the European Central Bank's (ECB's) quantitative easing program (ECB 2017; ESM 2017).

Why did Greece experience such a strong blow to its party system relative to other eurozone countries that also signed loan agreements and implemented stringent austerity measures? The consensus in the literature is that the political equilibrium, involving electoral cycles by cartel parties capturing the state (Katz and Mair 2009) and engaging in machine politics (Mavrogordatos 1997), that existed prior to the crisis could only be sustained by large budget deficits and an exorbitant debt (Mitsopoulos and Pelagidis 2012; Pappas 2013). Thus, when the political establishment could no longer finance its scheme from the international capital markets, it had to negotiate a loan agreement with the ECB, the European Commission, and the International Monetary Fund (IMF) (collectively known as the Troika), which led to a series of forced reforms (Pagoulatos 2013). That, in turn, unsettled the party system, which had sustained the political equilibrium of the post-junta period. In other words, the patronage contract—the party-dominated patron–client networks that reproduced the political and economic system (Mylonas 2012, 2014a) which had existed since independence but was bureaucratized during the post-junta period—gradually deteriorated after 2010 as a result of stipulations in the MoU signed with the country's creditors—for example, freezes in public sector employment.

While these explanations can help us account for the electoral decline of the former ruling parties in Greece, and maybe even the rage of large segments of the Greek population whose vested interests came under attack, they are still underspecified if we want to understand the particular form that the political system has taken as a result of the crisis. In this chapter, I argue that in order to explain the severity of the political transformation in Greece, relative to other crisis-stricken countries of the eurozone, we need to consider the interminable succession crises that ensued within the two dominant parties following the departure of the two charismatic leaders that molded post-junta Greece,[1] Constantine Karamanlis (1907–98) and Andreas Papandreou (1919–96).[2] In particular, my argument is that the personalistic governance style pioneered by these two charismatic leaders habituated Greeks to this type of leadership; undermined the development of internal party democracy; blurred the division of the legislative, executive, and judicial functions of government; and ensured internal opposition against all successors. Moreover, both Constantine Karamanlis and Andreas Papandreou encouraged a state-led type of capitalism. Andreas's rule, in particular, habituated the voters to populist discourse and practices (Pappas 2008, 2015) and a state-led corporatist development of civil society (Mavrogordatos 1993, 1997). After all, charisma and bureaucracy are interdependent (Weber 1978: xciii).

The institutionalization of charisma in party structures failed in the cases of both Karamanlis's New Democracy (ND) and of Papandreou's Panhellenic Socialist Movement (PASOK).[3] When the global financial crisis of 2008 hit Greece, biological successors of these two charismatic leaders were in power, but charisma is not hereditary and their legacy was still palpable. Since the once dominant parties could no longer uphold their side of the patronage contract a legitimation crisis ensued,[4] which partially manifested itself in violent protests (Kalyvas 2010; Mylonas 2011a), low voter turnout, and the earthquake parliamentary elections of 2012 and 2015 (Teperoglou and Tsatsanis 2014; Mylonas 2016).

The Financial Crisis and Democratic Politics
in the European Periphery

Multiple articles and books have been written to describe, analyze, chronicle, or even explain the financial crisis that shook the United States in 2008 and many European countries soon thereafter. At the onset of the crisis, Greece was a country where employment in the public sector was the dream of a large section of the population and the political parties used it as a currency in exchange for votes (Pappas and Assimakopoulou 2013); the tax collecting capacity of the state was weak (Liaras and Mylonas 2011)[5]; and a largely state-dependent private sector and—mainly retail focused—small businesses dominated the real economy (Tsoucalas 1986). For forty years Greece had experienced strong electoral cycles of populist spending, which have increased deficits and built up an enormous state debt over time (Kalyvas, Pagoulatos, and Tsoukas 2012). Doing business in Greece has been hindered by cumbersome bureaucratic structures, inconsistent taxation policy (World Bank Group 2017), and corrupt practices (Transparency International 2017). Moreover, taxpayers have been receiving suboptimal services from the state. As a result, Greece was quickly identified as the weakest link in the eurozone by investors, credit rating agencies (that until then had treated Greek bonds similarly to German ones), so-called speculators, and the global financial institutions. Thus, credit was initially expensive and later unavailable.

Political economists, analysts, journalists, and pundits alike have made a convincing case that the blame for this situation does not lie solely in Greek corners, and that there is definitely a broader European and global context that is to blame as well (Blyth 2015). The eurozone was far from what economists described as an optimum currency area and did not have any emergency plan in place for a situation like the one experienced by Greece (Feldstein 2011; Frieden 1998; Matthijs 2014). Implied in this critique is the responsibility of the European Union (EU) and its monitoring agencies that blithely overlooked the emergence and perpetuation of these practices by member-states (Mylonas 2011b). Finally, given the set-up of the euro, once the sovereign debt crisis hit Greece and other relatively weak eurozone countries (Cyprus, Ireland, Portugal, Spain), their democratically elected governments were left with two rather suboptimal options: default or austerity—in other words, internal devaluation (Mylonas 2014a: 436).

To combat this crisis the Greek government turned hesitantly to international institutions like the European Commission, the European Central Bank (ECB), and the IMF. The policy mix, decided upon by the creditors in consultation with Greek government officials, ultimately punished the countries that failed to converge in terms of competitiveness and fiscal balances, instead of hurting French and German banks as well as risk-seeking bond investors (Blyth 2013). In particular, the policy mix involved internal devaluation through higher taxes as well as lower wages and pensions, because Greek governments did not prioritize structural reforms. Soon the financial crisis in Greece turned into a solvency crisis and ultimately into a crisis in the real economy.

This recipe was followed more or less by the other European econo-mies—especially in Southern Europe—that faced similar problems, al-though the initial conditions were not the same across all cases (Mylonas 2011b). In the middle of the crisis, both Greece and Italy ended up with technocratic governments, something that many observers identified as a clear sign of the democratic legitimacy problem faced by the European pe-riphery (Macartney 2013: 67; Schmidt 2012: 102–14). Left- and right-wing Euroscepticism gained momentum all over the EU since everyone was reminded of the democratic deficit problem that has long existed within the EU—in other words, that nonelected EU institutions, like the ECB and the European Commission, trump the authority of democratically elected governments (Schmidt 2013; Serricchio, Tsakatika, and Quaglia 2013; Tor-reblanca and Leonard 2013).

But then again, despite the economic hardships that they faced, Cyprus, Ireland, Portugal, and even Italy and Spain did not experience the same level of opposition to austerity measures and related reforms or the dras-tic reconfiguration of the Greek political system. Granted, party systems in both Italy and Spain were transformed from two-party into tripolar sys-tems (Morlino and Raniolo 2017). More importantly, Spain experienced the electoral surge of an anti-austerity left-wing movement, Podemos, and Italy experienced the rise of Pepe Grillo's Five Stars, a Eurosceptic populist movement. Only in Greece, however, did anti-austerity parties—Coalition of the Radical Left (SYRIZA) and Independent Greeks (ANEL, which is a party formed during the crisis)—come to power (Della Porta, Kouki, and Mosca 2017).

Moreover, while such parties emerged in Spain and Italy, they did not alter the party system by demolishing longstanding cartel parties (Katz and Mair 2009), like PASOK in the case of Greece. In Italy, for instance, the two dominant parties together received over 84 percent in 2008 and their percentage dropped just under 60 percent in 2013 (Albertazzi and Mc-Donnell 2015: fig. 5.16). In contrast, the two parties that dominated Greek politics for four decades, ND and PASOK, received 77.4 percent in Octo-ber 2009 and 32.1 percent in May 2012 (Mylonas 2013).[6] All in all, although the vote share of dominant parties in Cyprus, Ireland, Italy, Portugal, and Spain has declined, these parties are still the ones forming governmental majorities. Not in Greece.

Documenting Party System Change[7]

The Demise of Greece's Two-Party System

When the global financial crisis hit Greece in 2009, kin to Constantine Karamanlis and Andreas Papandreou were leading the two main parties in the Greek party system, ND and PASOK, respectively.[8] Kostas Karamanlis (born in 1956), nephew of Constantine Karamanlis, was prime minister since 2004 and held early elections in October 2009 due to mounting economic problems. George Papandreou (born in 1952), son of Andreas Papandreou, won the elections with 43.92 percent of the vote. At this critical juncture, on the one hand, the biological successor of Constantine Karamanlis was not able to tame the budget deficit (in fact it became exorbitant under his rule), and on the other hand the biological successor of Andreas Papandreou was not able to navigate the extraordinary conditions he inherited. At first George Papandreou acted as if the situation was manageable. A few months later, however, he signed an MoU with the Troika and then, following an awkward attempt to share responsibility with the Greek people by holding a referendum, he had to concede defeat, resign from prime minister, and turn his power to Lucas Papademos (a technocrat who had served as governor of the Bank of Greece and as vice president of the ECB).

Papademos's government, which lasted for six months, was backed by three parties: center-left PASOK, center-right ND, and the nationalist right-wing Popular Orthodox Rally (LAOS). This government had a special task: to ratify a haircut on 80 percent of Greece's privately held debt and conclude a new loan agreement of €130 billion with the country's creditors. Following this tumultuous period, ND and PASOK, which garnered more than 80 percent of the vote for decades, diminished to a mere 32 percent in May 2012 (see table 2.1). PASOK's vote share was reduced to 13.2 percent and ND's to 18.9 percent. Within just a couple of years, the two-party system put in place by the two charismatic leaders of the post-junta period had been replaced by a volatile party system.

Government Volatility: Seven Prime Ministers in Seven Years

Both Kostas Karamanlis and George Papandreou had been replaced as party leaders by the May 2012 elections—the first parliamentary elections since the initial MoU was signed on 6 May 2010. The parties elected to parliament did not manage to form a government, and this deadlock led to a caretaker government headed by the judge and president of the council of state Panagiotis Pikramenos, which lasted until June 2012 when new elections took place. Antonis Samaras, who had been elected President of ND following its 2009 electoral defeat, became the prime minister with the sup-

Table 2.1. Electoral Results in National-Level Elections, 2009–15

Party	Sept 2015	Jan 2015	May 2014 European Parliament	June 2012	May 2012	Oct. 2009
SYRIZA	35.46	36.34	26.57	26.9	16.8	4.6
ND	28.1	27.81	22.72	29.7	18.9	33.47
Golden Dawn	6.99	6.28	9.39	6.9	7.0	0.29
PASOK	6.28[a]	4.68	8.02[b]	12.3	13.2	43.92
KKE	5.55	5.47	6.11	4.5	8.5	7.54
The River [d]	4.09	6.5	6.6	—	—	—
ANEL [c]	3.69	4.75	3.46	7.5	10.6	—
EK	3.43	1.79	0.65	0.28	0.61	0.27
DIMAR[c]	—	0.48	1.2	6.2	6.1	—
LAOS	—	1.03	2.69	1.58	2.9	5.63
LAE[e]	2.86	—	—	—	—	—
ANTARSYA-M.AR.S	0.85	0.64	0.72	0.33	1.19	0.36

ANTARSYA-M.AR.S = Anticapitalist Left Cooperation for the Overthrow-M.AR.S; DIMAR = Democratic Left; EK = Union of Centrists; KKE = Communist Party of Greece; LAE = Popular Unity.
a. Demokratike Symparataxe—Democratic Coalition: PASOK and DIMAR.
b. Elia—Olive Tree-Democratic Alignment (formed by PASOK and smaller parties).
c. New Party in 2012.
d. New Party in 2014.
e. New Party in 2015.
Sources: Mavrogordatos and Marantzidis 2010; Mylonas 2013, 2015b, 2016.

port of PASOK and Democratic Left (DIMAR—SYRIZA's splinter founded by Fotis Kouvelis in 2010). Last, Alexis Tsipras, head of SYRIZA,[9] was elected prime minister in January 2015 and then again in September 2015 with the support of ANEL (ND's splinter founded by Panos Kammenos in 2012). In between, Vassiliki Thanou-Christophilou became the first woman prime minister for less than a month in August 2015 heading the caretaker government prior to the September 2015 elections. Thus, Greece had four elected prime ministers, one prime minister who was an appointed technocrat, and two caretaker prime ministers within 7 years (see table 2.2).

A Novel Political Cleavage: pro-MoU vs. anti-MoU

George Papandreou negotiated the first loan agreement with the European Commission on behalf of the Eurogroup, the European Central Bank (ECB), and the International Monetary Fund (IMF), and the Greek government was granted its first bailout package (€110 billion) in May 2010 on the

Table 2.2. Prime Ministers since the Onset of the Global Financial Crisis

Kostas Karamanlis, ND	16 September 2007 – 6 October 2009
George Papandreou, PASOK	6 October 2009 – 11 November 2011
Lucas Papademos, PASOK-ND-LAOS[a]	11 November 2011 – 16 May 2012
Panagiotis Pikramenos	16 May 2012 – 20 June 2012
Antonis Samaras, ND-PASOK-DIMAR[b]	20 June 2012 – 26 January 2015
Alexis Tsipras, SYRIZA-ANEL	26 January 2015 – 27 August 2015
Vassiliki Thanou-Christophilou	27 August 2015 – 21 September 2015
Alexis Tsipras, SYRIZA-ANEL	21 September 2015 – today

Note: Italics indicate prime ministers of caretaker governments.
a. LAOS remained in the coalition until February 2012.
b. DIMAR remained in the coalition until June 2013.
Sources: Mavrogordatos and Marantzidis 2010; Mavrogordatos and Mylonas 2011; Mylonas 2012, 2013, 2016.

condition it would implement austerity measures and structural reforms listed in an MoU. From that moment onward a new political cleavage emerged and persisted at least until August 2015. Greek society was divided between pro-MoU and anti-MoU forces (Georgakellos and Mylonas 2013). The former comprised those who believed that austerity measures and reforms were necessary; the latter saw these austerity measures stipulated in the loan agreement as akin to treason and an example of complete surrender of national sovereignty. It was also at this juncture that the three creditors that held Greek governments accountable for complying with the loan agreement were baptized the Troika by the anti-MoU political forces.

Looking at the ratification vote of each consecutive bailout agreement by the Greek parliament reveals the polarization but also captures the volatility in the party system. In the first vote, which took place in May 2010, only four members of parliament (MPs) voted against party lines. All of them were booted out from their respective parties and became either independent MPs or formed (or joined) new parties.[10] In each consequent bailout agreement vote (as well as during votes on medium-term plans) dozens of MPs changed parties, resigned, or formed new political parties. The parliamentary vote on Law 3845/2010 was the first institutional manifestation of the novel political cleavage between pro- and anti-MoU forces. Within the parliament, PASOK and LAOS represented the pro-MoU bloc and ND, KKE, and SYRIZA the anti-MoU bloc. Soon the composition of these blocs changed.

By February 2012 ND and LAOS had switched sides. This switch devastated LAOS electorally but helped ND to position itself as a representative of the pro-MoU bloc in the upcoming May and June double elections of 2012. Despite the bitter rhetoric and the polarization along this cleavage that Greeks experienced in the summer of 2015 (Mylonas 2015a), by August 2015 SYRIZA, ND, PASOK, ANEL, and The River were all part of the pro-MoU bloc. The only parties that never changed sides and remained firmly in the anti-MoU bloc were the Communist Party of Greece (KKE) and Golden Dawn.[11] The once sharp division between the pro- and anti-MoU camps dampened, when most of SYRIZA MPs and all of ANEL MPs voted in favor of the third MoU adding the ESM to the country's list of creditors (see table 2.3). As the results of the September 2015 elections demonstrated, this policy cleavage that dominated Greek politics for almost six years had largely been dissolved. Despite Tsipras's major turnaround during August 2015, SYRIZA won the election and continued to govern with ANEL as a minor coalition partner. The few parties that remained in the anti-MoU camp did not do as well in the elections.

Table 2.3. Parliamentary Votes for the Three Bailout Packages

Bailout Agreement	Present out of 300	"Yes" Vote	"No" Vote	Abstentions	Defections
MoU I 6 May 2010 (Law 3845/ 2010)[a]	296	172 (PASOK, LAOS, & 1 from ND)	121 (ND, KKE, & SYRIZA)	3 PASOK	3 PASOK 1 ND
MoU II 12 February 2012 (Law 4046/ 2012)[b]	278	199 (PASOK, ND, Democratic Alliance)	74 (SYRIZA, KKE, DIMAR, & LAOS)	4 PASOK 1 Democratic Alliance	22 PASOK 21 ND 2 LAOS
MoU III 14 August 2015 (Law 4336/ 2015)[c]	297	222 (SYRIZA, ND, PASOK, ANEL, The River)	64 (32 SYRIZA, KKE & Golden Dawn)	11 SYRIZA	43 SYRIZA[d]

a. Measures for implementing the support mechanism of the Greece economy by the member-states of the eurozone and the IMF.
b. Approval of Plans of Financial Facilitation between the European Financial Stability Facility (EFSF), the Greek Republic and the Bank of Greece, the Plan of Memorandum of Understanding between the Greek Republic, the European Commission, the Bank of Greece, and other urgent measures to reduce the public debt and rescue the national economy.
c. Ratification of the Financial Assistance Draft Contract by the ESM and provisions for the implementation of the Financing Agreement.
d. One SYRIZA MP was absent and three differentiated themselves by voting "yes" in principle and "abstain" for individual articles. If we include these as defections, then the number goes to 47.
Sources: Mavrogordatos and Mylonas 2011: 986; Mylonas 2013: 88; Mylonas 2016: 115.

New Parties in Parliament and New Leadership for Old Parties

In 2012 three parties entered parliament for the first time: Democratic Left, ANEL, and Golden Dawn.[12] In 2015 two parties entered parliament for the first time: The River[13] and the Union of Centrists (EK).[14] Thus, the Greek parliament, which had four parties in 2004 and five parties in both 2007 and 2009, ultimately reached eight parties by 2015. This is a significant change for a system with a 3 percent threshold to enter parliament and a reinforced proportionality electoral system in which the first party receives a bonus of fifty seats in a three-hundred-seat parliament.

Since 2009, most parties represented in the Greek parliament changed leadership. In particular, ND, PASOK, KKE, and DIMAR all went through leadership changes (see table 2.4). In fact, ND has experienced two caretaker presidents and two elected ones, PASOK has also had two elected presidents, KKE has a new general secretary since 2013, and DIMAR—a party founded in 2010—changed its founding leader and has been folded into a coalition with PASOK since 2015. In fact, at the time of writing, this political family, which is temporarily calling itself the Center-Left, is holding internal elections for a new leader who will decide on the name for the coalition (Mylonas 2017b). The only political leaders who have remained at the helm of their parties since 2009 are Prime Minister Alexis Tsipras of SYRIZA and Golden Dawn's Nikolaos Michaloliakos.

Charismatic Leadership and Its Discontents

The cataclysmic changes in Greece's party system described above were triggered by the financial crisis. Greece's political elites could no longer finance the patronage contract between voters and parties because cheap credit was no longer available. This was the case in other problem children of the eurozone, but why did Greece experience such a strong blow to its party system relative to other European countries that also signed loan agreements and implemented stringent austerity measures? I hold that the political consequences of the financial crisis for the Greek party system were deeper than in other European cases partly because of prolonged succession crises of charismatic leaders in both ND and PASOK—the two parties that dominated post-junta Greek politics.

To be sure, weak institutions and dependency on capital inflows were not features specific to the post-junta period. The Greek economy has been weak and dependent on foreign loans since its independence (see Doxiadis this volume). Moreover, from the mid nineteenth century, securing a position in the public sector was considered a path to financial stability. Nationwide party-dominated patron–client networks decided these

Table 2.4. Changes in Party Leadership

	ND	PASOK	KKE	DIMAR
2009	Antonis Samaras defeated Dora Bacoyannis in internal party elections and replaced Kostas Karamanlis (29 November)	—	—	—
2012	—	Evangelos Venizelos was elected unopposed to replace George Papandreou (18 March)	—	—
2013	—	—	Dimitris Koutsoumbas was appointed general secretary by the party's central committee replacing Aleka Papariga (14 April)	—
2015	Antonis Samaras resigned following the 5 July 2015 referendum, and Evangelos Meimarakis became interim president of ND	Evangelos Venizelos resigned during the Party's 10th Congress (6 June). Fofi Gennimata defeated Andreas Loverdos and Odysseas Konstantinopoulos in internal party elections and was elected president (14 June)	—	Fotis Kouvelis resigned in March. Thanasis Theocharopoulos defeated Maria Giannakakis and was elected president (7 June)
2016	Kyriakos Mitsotakis defeated Evangelos Meimarakis in internal party elections and became President of ND (10 January)	—	—	—

Sources: Mavrogordatos and Marantzidis 2010; Mylonas 2013, 2014b, 2016, 2017a.

positions. These networks were vying for the control of the central administration of the state (Pappas 2015: 89–102; Sotiropoulos 1993; Tsoucalas 1986). This formed the foundation for the party–voter patronage contract in Greece. In addition, there was a party–businesses contract since a large number of private companies relied on government contracts, loans, and protection to survive (Mitsopoulos and Pelagidis 2012). Of course, this support by the state often returned in the form of financial support for the very same political parties that allocated these government contracts. As Tsoucalas (2013) put it, the liberal public–private distinction was blurred in Greece.

In post-junta Greece, the chronic features discussed above interacted with two charismatic leaders, Constantine Karamanlis and Andreas Papandreou (Draenos 2012; Mavrogordatos 1984).[15] Upon their return to Greece in 1974, Karamanlis founded ND and Papandreou founded PASOK. Karamanlis governed from 1974 to 1980 and served two terms as president of the republic (1980–85 and 1990–95). While prime minister, Karamanlis organized free and fair parliamentary elections (for the first time in almost ten years), a referendum on the question of the monarchy, legalized the Communist Party of Greece, drafted a new constitution, and signed the treaty for Greece's accession to the European Economic Community (EEC). As Lyrintzis and Nikolakopoulos put it, "The third Greek Republic was born and Karamanlis handled the transition to democracy with remarkable calm and determination and there can be little doubt that political developments during the seventies bear his seal" (2007: 89). Andreas Papandreou governed from 1981 to 1989 and again from 1993 to 1996 (see fig. 2.1). Andreas's rule brought about important reforms in family law, a national health-care system, the recognition of the national resistance (almost forty years after the fratricidal Greek Civil War), and a constitutional revision that reduced presidential prerogatives.

Karamanlis and Papandreou both exercised charismatic authority.[16] By definition a charismatic leader cannot be bound by the institutions of the state or a political party. As Sotiropoulos put it, "ND was a personalist party, founded and managed by Karamanlis, the whole process was effectively a one-man show" (2010: 456). Similarly, Magone wrote about PASOK that it "is a more evident case of a 'charismatic organization' . . . dominated by the political leader and . . . able to achieve a high degree of cohesion and to minimize factionalism" (1995: 97).[17] But this very quality of charismatic leadership is what leaves their political organizations vulnerable after such leaders have departed. A CIA intelligence assessment written in 1983 discussed extensively the problems ND faced after Karamanlis stepped down as president of the party in 1980: "President and former premier Constantine Karamanlis—New Democracy's founder and elder statesman—may be both the party's greatest strength and its biggest liability. He continues to hold the party together, but his moral dominance may be delaying the fundamental changes the party probably must make before it will be able to make another serious run at power. . . . Until Karamanlis does give his successors a bit more room to operate on their own, we believe he runs the risk of stunting the party's development as a political movement independent of his own considerable popularity." (Central Intelligence Agency [CIA] 1983: 1,10).

The style of governance adopted by the two charismatic leaders that molded post-junta Greece, Constantine Karamanlis and Andreas Papandreou, in particular, habituated the voters to personalistic parties, undermined the constitutional separation of powers, and ultimately resulted in a state-led protectionist economy. By the time Andreas's PASOK won the elections in 1981, "half of the economy was state controlled" (Central Intelligence Agency [CIA] 1983: 1) as a result of Karamanlis's policies. Andreas Papandreou intensified this trend. Moreover, PASOK and Andreas Papandreou transformed traditional political patronage, primarily practiced by the dominant right up until 1981, into what Mavrogordatos (1997) called machine politics. The main difference between the two systems being that in the latter patronage is channeled through the impersonal party organization rather than individual politicians. ND quickly followed suit.

Following Greece's accession to the EEC, structural and cohesion funds that were supposed to promote the creation of a land registry, improvement of public sector services, vocational training, modernization of the agricultural sector, and so forth were instead mismanaged and often ended up in bank accounts of various cronies of the two dominant parties. These poorly managed and monitored EEC funds generated perverse incentives in society and exacerbated preexisting trends.[18] Parallels of such practices can also be found in many European societies and especially in the rest of Southern Europe (Pujas and Rhodes 1999: 46).

PASOK and ND dominated the party system and colluded to employ the resources of the state to ensure their own electoral survival (Pappas 2015). The two parties controlled the state and passed legislation that reproduced their dominance (e.g., state funding of parties, reinforced proportional representation, parliamentary immunities, statute of limitations for crimes committed by ministers). And Greek voters continued to return them to office. Both cartel parties led to the development of myriad vested interests, corrupt practices, an emaciated and largely state-dependent private sector, an inefficient public sector, and a culture of reliance on the state. These vested interests, once introduced, were passionately guarded by various trade unions (Mavrogordatos 1988; 2001).

This patronage contract generated substantial deficits, kept resources from being invested in productive activities that could lead to sustainable growth, and accumulated an exorbitant public debt. While this situation was initially legitimated as an attempt to consolidate democracy and to prevent the return to military rule following the junta, it soon became an end in itself.

The succession crises that occurred in the early 1980s in ND and in the mid 1990s in PASOK were not detrimental to the continuity of these dominant parties—despite the fact that the immediate successors of the two charismatic leaders failed to institutionalize charisma in the party.[19] Max Weber would have probably predicted the collapse of these parties, but for a while it looked like both had averted this grave scenario. The resilience of the two parties was largely dependent on loans from the international capital markets and EEC (and later EU) funds. The continuation of the patronage contract was the institutional form that routinization of charisma took in the Greek context. Electoral cycles continued and so did tax evasion.

Two of the successors who succeeded in becoming prime ministers, Konstantinos Mitsotakis and Kostas Simitis, in ND and PASOK respectively, attempted to move their parties and state institutions into the realm of rational–legal authority and escape the shadows of the founders during their terms in office, but to no avail (Gerth and Mills 1958: 1–11). Whenever the electoral base felt that its vested interests were threatened by these attempts, the voters would just point to all the ways that their respective charismatic leader would have done things better and trade unions would go on strike. Moreover, both Mitsotakis and Simitis faced strong internal opposition from party factions loyal to the two founders of their respective parties.[20] The routinization of charisma within party structures had failed in both parties (Weber 1978: 246–54).[21]

In an attempt to counter factionalism and recover the aura of the founding fathers of each party, a biological successor was elected president of ND in 1998 and of PASOK in 2004–the nephew of Constantine Karamanlis and the son of Andreas Papandreou, respectively (see fig. 2.1). Thus, both parties attempted to rely on hereditary charisma. As Weber put it, "The most frequent case of a depersonalization of charisma is the belief in its transfer ability through blood ties" (1978: 1136). Charismatic authority is

C. Karamanlis	A. Papandreou	K. Mitsotakis	K. Simitis	G. Papandreou	A. Samaras
(1974–80)	(1981–89)	(1990–93)	(1996–2004)	(2009–11)	(2012–15)
G. Rallis	Zolotas/	A. Papandreou	K. Karamanlis	L. Papademos	A. Tsipras
(1980–81)	Tzanetakis (1989–1990)	(1993–96)	(2004–09)	(2011–12)	(2015–today)

Figure 2.1. Prime Ministers in Greece since 1974

transitory in nature: "It cannot remain stable, but becomes either tradi-tionalized or rationalized, or a combination of both" (Weber 1978: 246).

With Kostas Karamanlis at its helm, ND succeeded in defeating Simi-tis's PASOK in 2004 and ruled based on traditional forms of authority that relied very much on the same patronage contract described above (for more, see Mylonas 2014a). Kostas Karamanlis governed until September 2009, when he faced mounting financial problems and called early elec-tions. At that juncture, Andreas's son, George Papandreou won the elec-tions. Thus, when the financial crisis hit Greece the biological successors of the two charismatic leaders were in power. As a result of the financial crisis, the political equilibrium of the post-junta period was challenged. By 2010 the forced reforms flowing from Greece's obligations outlined in the bailout agreement with its creditors precluded the continuation of the car-tel-party system and the related patronage contract. Charisma, however, is not hereditary and as soon as the institutionalized economic advantages of the party followers were threatened, a crisis of political representation was unavoidable. In the May 2012 elections the two parties that domi-nated Greek politics for four decades, ND and PASOK, received together a mere 32.1 percent (Mylonas 2013).[22]

A legitimation crisis ensued, manifesting itself in lack of trust for parties, the national government and even democracy (Teperoglou and Tsatsanis 2014). It is in this light that we can make sense of the volatility among both political elites and voters that I described above. It is also only from this vantage point that we can grasp both the (in certain cases mete-oric) rise of very different anti-MoU parties—SYRIZA, KKE, ANEL, and Golden Dawn—and the electoral success of The River and the EK, since the voters were steering their votes away from the systemic parties that betrayed them by breaking the contract or no longer having the resources to maintain it. Finally, the historically low voter turnout in recent elections can be understood as yet another sign of the Greek voters' disenchantment with their party system (Mylonas 2013, 2016).

Conclusion

The political landscape in Greece is the most volatile it has been since the dictatorship fell in 1974 (Kostis 2013). Although the Greek developments are connected to broader trajectories in the European and global commons (Balibar 2002), the Greek case merits specialized study since it clearly il-lustrates the challenges of democratic politics in a member-state of an incomplete monetary union (Tsoucalas 2013). In times of austerity, demo-cratically elected governments in countries that are members of monetary unions without provisions for fiscal transfers do not have financial sovereignty. Thus, the policies of elected officials are constrained by both financial market forces (e.g., credit rating agencies) and the decisions of the Central Bank of the monetary union as well as institutional creditors (e.g., IMF). When the electorate votes for politicians whose political platforms contradict the logic of the market and/or the decisions of the creditors, this ultimately leads to a legitimation crisis.

Political developments in Spain and Italy during 2016 indicate that the Greek case could serve as a window to the future of other European states. In Spain, the Indignados (also known as Movimiento 15-M) anti-austerity movement ultimately led to the establishment of Podemos, a left-wing populist party that managed to upset Spain's two-party system. In Italy, Pepe Grillo's Five Stars Movement managed to shake up Italy's party system. As a result, party systems in Italy and Spain were transformed from two-party systems into tripolar systems (Morlino and Raniolo 2017). But, even compared to Italy and Spain, Greece's experience has been unparalleled. In Greece the parties that dominated the two-party system for three decades were defeated by SYRIZA, a radical left party that won in two elections during 2015 and governs with the support of right-wing ANEL. These parties won on the basis of an anti-MoU platform that did not align with the wishes of the country's creditors. Alexis Tsipras called a referendum on the lenders' draft proposals for the third bailout agreement for Greece in early July and despite the resounding "no" by more than 60% of the voters, the agreement was ratified by the Greek parliament a month later (Mylonas 2016). This was the culmination of a legitimation crisis in Greece.

All in all, austerity politics have affected both the old and the new parties. Politicians are constrained by the politics of austerity in what they can promise and, more importantly, in what they can deliver. Many observers rushed to identify Alexis Tsipras as the next charismatic leader for Greece. He has been accused of mimicking Andreas Papandreou by some and has been perceived as his symbolic successor by many. Others have emphasized the need to move beyond the search of charismatic leaders who will save the country and build strong rational–legal forms of authority through strong institutions instead. So, what is the future for Greece? Charismatic, rational–legal, or traditional authority will prevail? One thing is clear, a return to the patronage contract would be suicidal given the pressures coming from economic globalization and the EU (Morlino and Raniolo 2017: 116). It remains to be seen whether the mentality of the Greek voters and politicians has changed enough for the rational–legal form of authority to take root in the country.

Harris Mylonas is Associate Professor of Political Science and International Affairs at The George Washington University. After completing his PhD at Yale University (2008), he spent two years as academy scholar at the Harvard Academy for International and Area Studies. During 2017–18, he served as Associate Dean for Research at The George Washington University's Elliott School of International Affairs. His research focuses on nationalism, state- and nation-building, diaspora politics, and qualitative research methods. His book *The Politics of Nation-Building: Making Co-Nationals, Refugees, and Minorities* (Cambridge University Press, 2012) won the 2014 European Studies Book Award and the 2013 Peter Katzenstein Book Prize. Professor Mylonas writes the annual report on Greece for the *Political Data Yearbook* published by the *European Journal of Political Research*.

Notes

The author would like to thank Akis Georgakellos, George Th. Mavrogordatos, the reviewers, and the editors of this volume for their helpful comments; as well as Georgios Anagnostopoulos and Lucy Hale for being excellent research assistants. The author expresses appreciation to the Schoff Fund at the University Seminars at Columbia University for their help in publication. The ideas presented here have benefited from discussions in the University Seminar on Modern Greece.

 1. In this chapter, I use the term "charismatic" in a Weberian sense (Weber 1978: 241–45, 1111–57). Weber secularized Rudolf Sohm's (1892) notion of charisma. Sohm described the Christian church not as a legal but rather as a charismatic organization—meaning, an organization established by virtue of divine inspiration, not human law.
 2. In fact, one could argue that these leaders continued a governance style familiar to Greeks. For more on the limitations of charismatic leadership and the problems of institutionalizing charisma focusing on the case of Eleftherios Venizelos, see Mavrogordatos 2010.
 3. Movements or parties led by a charismatic leader are temporary due to biological limitations and if they are to survive at all they must find a routine basis of organization.
 4. As Weber put it, "The routinization of charisma also takes the form of the appropriation of powers and of economic advantages by the followers or disciples, and of regulating recruitment" (1978: 249). For a more elaborate discussion, see Weber (1978: 1121–57). When these economic advantages dry up, the organization falters.
 5. In the years after Greece adopted the euro, Greek public spending and debt crept up and government revenue fell or remained constant. Between 2001 and 2007, Greece's average government revenues totaled 39.4 percent of GDP, whereas the EU average was 44.4 percent.
 6. For more on the comparison between Greece and Spain, see chapter 6 in this volume by Bremer and Vidal.

7. The narrative and the tables of this section build on material from Mavrogordatos and Marantzidis 2010; Mavrogordatos and Mylonas 2011, 2012; Mylonas 2013, 2014b, 2015b, 2016, and 2017a.
8. A two-party system had emerged soon after the fall of the junta in 1974 (Nicolaco-poulos 2005). Constantine Karamanlis founded ND and Andreas Papandreou founded PASOK.
9. SYRIZA was officially transformed into a unified party in 2012 under the leadership of Alexis Tsipras.
10. In November 2010, Dora Bacoyannis founded the Democratic Alliance, after she was expelled from ND because she voted in favor of the first bailout agreement while ND had chosen to oppose the bailout agreement. Four more ND MPs joined the new party after their expulsion from ND. All later returned to ND.
11. Popular Unity (LAE), which was founded on 21 August 2015 by Panagiotis Lafazanis, head of SYRIZA's left platform and minister in the first Tsipras cabinet, and Course of Freedom, which was founded by former president of parliament Zoe Konstantopoulou on 19 April 2016 also represent the anti-MoU bloc, but have not made it in parliament.
12. Concerning the rise of Golden Dawn, see chapter 3 in this volume, by Karpolizos.
13. The River is a centrist and Pro-European party founded on 26 February 2014. It contested in the May 2014 elections for the European Parliament and joined the Progressive Alliance of Socialists and Democrats (S&D), the political group in the European Parliament of the Party of European Socialists (PES).
14. This is not counting the Democratic Coalition, an electoral alliance between PASOK and DIMAR, which was formed on 30 August 2015 in order to contest in the September elections.
15. Constantine Karamanlis founded the National Radical Union in the 1950s and served as prime minister of Greece from 1955 to 1963. Andreas Papandreou, an economics professor at Berkeley and a naturalized U.S. citizen, was elected as an MP with the Center Union in 1964 and served as a Minister in his father's cabinet in the mid-1960s. Here I focus on their post-dictatorship political action.
16. According to Weber, there are three pure types of legitimate domination: rational, traditional, and charismatic (Weber 1978: 215). Charismatic authority is "sharply opposed both to rational . . . and to traditional authority" and it exists when people follow a leader on the basis of a belief in his or her supernatural powers. Thus, it is not respect for rational principles or tradition that motivate them into action but rather their complete devotion "to the extraordinary and unheard-of, to what is alien to all regulation and tradition and therefore is viewed as divine" (Weber 1978: 1115).
17. For more see, Pappas 2008: 259.
18. These funds include the European Regional Development Fund (ERDF), the European Social Fund (ESF), the Cohesion Fund (CF), European Agricultural Fund for Rural Development (EAFRD), and the European Maritime and Fisheries fund (EMFF). For more, see Ederveen, Groot, and Nahuis (2006) and European Commission (2017).
19. As Pappas and Dinas (2006) put it for ND, "From the time the charismatic Constantine Karamanlis departed from the party leadership until the mid-1990s, when his nephew, Kostas Karamanlis, rose to occupy this same post, the party had a succession of four leaders. Of these, none managed to keep the party together, to provide it with an unambiguous and appealing ideological profile, or, of course, to surpass in popularity PASOK's leader Andreas Papandreou. During this long period, ND was harmed by frequent internal dissension and splits, suffered ideological confusion, and lost many elections to a party that lacked a clear ideology or coherent programme but was led by a strong leader" (Pappas and Dinas 2006: 478).
20. As Weber put it, "Under genuinely charismatic domination, parties are necessarily schismatic sects. Their conflict is essentially over questions of faith and, as such, is basi-

cally irreconcilable" (1978: 287). For a more recent analysis of how internal opposition affects political competition, see Pappas 2008: 246–52.
21. Weber writes, "As a rule, routinization is not free of conflict. In the early stages personal claims on the charisma of the chief are not easily forgotten and the conflict between the charisma of the office or of hereditary status with personal charisma is a typical process" (1978: 252). For the case of PASOK, see Pappas 2008: 236.
22. For more on the comparison between Greece and Spain, see chapter 5 in this volume by Bremer and Vidal.

References

Albertazzi, Daniele, and Duncan McDonnell. 2015. *Populists in Power.* London: Routledge.

Balibar, Etienne. 2002. *Politics and the Other Scene,* translated by Christine Jones, James Swenson, and Chris Turner. London: Verso.

Blyth, Mark. 2013. "The Austerity Delusion: Why a Bad Idea Won Over the West." *Foreign Affairs* 92(3): 41–56.

———. 2015. *Austerity: The History of a Dangerous Idea.* New York: Oxford University Press.

Central Intelligence Agency (CIA). 1983. "Greece's New Democracy Party: The Old Guard Fades." An Intelligence Assessment. Retrieved from https://www.cia.gov/library/read ingroom/docs/CIA-RDP84S00895R000100070004-9.pdf.

Della Porta, Donatella, Hara Kouki, and Lorenzo Mosca. 2017. *Movement Parties against Austerity.* Malden, MA: Polity Press.

Draenos, Stan. 2012. *Andreas Papandreou: The Making of a Greek Democrat and Political Maverick.* London: I. B. Tauris.

Ederveen, Sjef, Henri LF Groot, and Richard Nahuis. 2006. "Fertile Soil for Structural Funds? A Panel Data Analysis of the Conditional Effectiveness of European Cohesion Policy." *Kyklos* 59(1): 17–42.

European Commission. 2017. "European Structural and Investment Funds." Retrieved 7 January 2017 from https://ec.europa.eu/info/funding-tenders/european-structural-and-investment-funds_en.

European Central Bank (ECB). 2017. "How Quantitative Easing Works." European Central Bank. Retrieved 7 January 2017 from https://www.ecb.europa.eu/explainers/show-me/html/app_infographic.en.html.

European Stability Mechanism (ESM). 2017. European Stability Mechanism, Luxembourg. Retrieved 7 January 2017 from https://www.esm.europa.eu/financial-assistance.

Eurostat. 2016. "February 2016: Euro Area Unemployment Rate at 10.3 Percent, EU28 at 8.9 Percent." *Press Release/Euroindicators 63/2016,* 4 April. Retrieved 7 January 2017 from http://europa.eu/rapid/press-release_STAT-16-1210_en.htm.

Feldstein, Martin. 2011. "The Failure of the Euro." *Foreign Affairs,* 13 December. Retrieved 7 January 2017 from https://www.foreignaffairs.com/articles/europe/2011-12-13/failure-euro.

Frieden, Jeffrey. 1998. "The Euro: Who Wins? Who Loses?" *Foreign Policy* 112: 24–40.

Georgakellos, Akis, and Harris Mylonas. 2013. "Sand Dunes in the Greek Landscape: Party Politics and Political Coalitions in Times of Crisis." *The Monkey Cage,* June 11. Retrieved 7 January 2017 from http://themonkeycage.org/2013/06/sand-dunes-in-the-greek-land scape-party-politics-and-political-coalitions-in-times-of-crisis/.

Gerth, Hans, and C. Wright Mills, eds. 1958. *From Max Weber Essays in Sociology.* New York: Oxford University Press.

Kalyvas, Andreas. 2010. "An Anomaly? Some Reflections on the Greek December 2008." *Constellations* 17(2): 351–65.

Kalyvas, Stathis, George Pagoulatos, and Haridimos Tsoukas, eds. 2012. *From Stagnation to Forced Adjustment: Reforms in Greece, 1974–2010.* London: C. Hurst & Co.

Katz, Richard S., and Peter Mair. 2009. "The Cartel Party Thesis: A Restatement." *Perspectives on Politics* 7(4): 753–66.

Kostis, Kostas. 2013. *Ta Kakomathemena Paidia tes Estorias: E Diamorfose tou Neoellenikou Kratous 18os–21os Aionas.* Athens: Polis.

Liaras, Evan and Harris Mylonas. 2011. "What Really Went Wrong in Greece?" CNN.com, November 20. Retrieved 7 January 2017 from http://globalpublicsquare.blogs.cnn .com/2011/11/20/what-really-went-wrong-in-greece/.

Lyrintzis, Christos, and Elias Nikolakopoulos. 2007. "Political System and Elections in Greece." In *About Greece,* edited by J. Metaxas, 87–100. Athens: General Secretariat of Communication-General Secretariat of Information.

Macartney, Huw. 2013. *The Debt Crisis and European Democratic Legitimacy.* New York: Palgrave Macmillan.

Magone, José M. 1995. "Party Factionalism in New Small Southern European Democracies: Some Comparative Findings from the Portuguese and Greek experiences (1974–82)." *Democratization* 2(1): 90–101.

Matthijs, Matthias. 2014. "Mediterranean Blues: The Crisis in Southern Europe." *Journal of Democracy* 25(1): 101–15.

Mavrogordatos, George Th. 1984. "The Greek Party System: A Case of Limited but Polarized Pluralism?" *West European Politics* 7(4): 156–69.

———. 1988. *Metaxy Pityokampte kai Prokrouste: Oi Epangelmatikes Organoseis ste Semerine Ellada.* Athens: Odysseas.

———. 1993. "Civil Society under Populism." In *Greece, 1981–89: The Populist Decade,* edited by Richard Clogg, 47–64. New York: St. Martin's Press.

———. 1997. "From Traditional Clientelism to Machine Politics: The Impact of PASOK Populism in Greece." *South European Society and Politics* 2(3): 1–26.

———. 2010. "Limitations of Charismatic Leadership." In *Eleftherios Venizelos: Unknown Aspects of the Man,* edited by Hariclea Zengos, 37–44. Conference Proceedings May 2007. Athens: American College of Greece.

Mavrogordatos, George Th., and Nikos Marantzidis. 2010. "Greece." *European Journal of Political Research* 49(7–8): 991–1000.

Mavrogordatos, George Th., and Harris Mylonas. 2011. "Greece." *European Journal of Political Research* 50(7–8): 985–90.

———. 2012. "Greece." *European Journal of Political Research* 51(1): 122–28.

Mitsopoulos, Michael, and Theodore Pelagidis. 2012. *Understanding the Crisis in Greece: From Boom to Bust.* New York: Palgrave Macmillan.

Morlino, Leonardo, and Francesco Raniolo. 2017. *The Impact of the Economic Crisis on South European Democracies.* Heidelberg: Springer.

Mylonas, Harris. 2011a. "The End of Peaceful Protest?" *E Kathimerini,* July 5. Retrieved 7 January 2017 from http://www.ekathimerini.com/134542/article/ekathimerini/comment/ the-end-of-peaceful-protest.

———. 2011b. "Is Greece a Failing Developed State?" In *The Konstantinos Karamanlis Institute for Democracy Yearbook: The Global Economic Crisis and the Case of Greece,* edited by Konstantina Botsiou and Antonis Klapsis, 77–88. Heidelberg, Germany: Springer.

———. 2012. "2012 Greek Parliamentary Elections: Post-Election Report." *The Monkey Cage,* May 7. Retrieved 7 January 2017 from http://themonkeycage.org/2012/05/2012-greek-parliamentary-elections-post-election-report/.

———. 2013. "Greece." *European Journal of Political Research Political Data Yearbook* 52(1): 87–95.

———. 2014a. "Democratic Politics in Times of Austerity: The Limits of Forced Reform in Greece." *Perspectives on Politics* 12(2): 435–43.

———. 2014b. "Greece." *European Journal of Political Research Political Data Yearbook* 53(1): 140–47.

———. 2015a. "The Agreekment That Could Break Europe: Euroskeptics, Eurocritics, and Life After the Bailout." *Foreign Affairs*, July 14. Retrieved from https://www.foreignaffairs.com/articles/greece/2015-07-14/agreekment-could-break-europe.

———. 2015b. "Greece," *European Journal of Political Research, Political Data Yearbook* 54(1): 125–32.

———. 2016. "Greece." *European Journal of Political Research, Political Data Yearbook,* 55(1): 113–23.

———. 2017a. "Greece." *European Journal of Political Research, Political Data Yearbook* 56(1).

———. 2017b. "The Volatile State of Greek Politics: Syriza's Struggles and the Risk of a Snap Election." *Foreign Affairs,* 27 September. Retrieved from https://www.foreignaffairs.com/articles/greece/2017-09-27/volatile-state-greek-politics

Nicolacopoulos, Ilias. 2005. "Elections and Voters, 1974–2004: Old Cleavages and New Issues." *West European Politics* 28(2): 260–78.

Pagoulatos, George. 2013. "The Political Economy of Forced Reform and the 2010 Greek Economic Adjustment Programme." In *From Stagnation to Forced Adjustment: Reforms in Greece, 1974–2010,* eds. Stathis N Kalyvas, George Pagoulatos, and Haridimos Tsoukas, 247–274. London: Hurst.

Pappas, Takis. 2008. *To Charismatiko Komma: PASOK, Papandreou, Exousia.* Athens: Patakis.

———. 2013. "Why Greece Failed." *Journal of Democracy* 24(2): 31–45.

———. 2015. *Laikismos kai Krise sten Ellada.* Athens: Ikaros.

Pappas, Takis, and Zena Assimakopoulou. 2013. "Political Entrepreneurship in a Party Patronage Democracy: Greece." In *Party Patronage and Party Government: Public Appointments and Political Control in European Democracies,* edited by Petr Kopecký, Peter Mair, and Maria Spirova, 144–62. Oxford: Oxford University Press.

Pappas, Takis, and Elias Dinas. 2006. "From Opposition to Power: Greek Conservatism Reinvented." *South European Society and Politics* 11(3–4): 477–95.

Pujas, Véronique, and Martin Rhodes. 1999. "Party Finance and Political Scandal in Italy, Spain and France." *West European Politics* 22(3): 41–63.

Schmidt, Vivien A. 2012. "The Eurozone Crisis and the Challenges for Democracy" In *The State of the Union(s): The Eurozone Crisis, Comparative Regional Integration and the EU Model,* edited by Joaquín Roy, 102–14. Miami: Miami–Florida European Union Center/Jean Monnet Chair.

———. 2013. "Democracy and Legitimacy in the European Union Revisited: Input, Output and 'Throughput.'" *Political Studies* 61: 2–22.

Serricchio, Fabio, Myrto Tsakatika, and Lucia Quaglia. 2013. "Euroscepticism and the Global Financial Crisis." *Journal of Common Market Studies* 51(1): 51–64.

Sohm, Rudolf. 1892. *Kirchenrecht,* Vol. 1. Leipzig, Germany: Verlag von Duncker and Humblot.

Sotiropoulos, Dimitrios A. 1993. "A Colossus with Feet of Clay: The State in Postauthoritarian Greece," In *Greece, the New Europe, and the Changing International Order,* edited by Harry J. Psomiades and Stavros B. Thomadakis, 43–56. New York: Pella.

Sotiropoulos, Dimitrios A. 2010. "The Authoritarian Past and Contemporary Greek Democracy." *South European Society and Politics* 15(3): 449–465.

Teperoglou, Eftichia, and Emmanouil Tsatsanis. 2014. "Dealignment, De-legitimation and the Implosion of the Two-Party System in Greece: The Earthquake Election of 6 May 2012." *Journal of Elections, Public Opinion and Parties* 24(2): 222–42.

Teperoglou, Eftichia, Emmanouil Tsatsanis, and Elias Nicolacopoulos. 2015. "Habituating to the New Normal in a Post-earthquake Party System: The 2014 European Election in Greece." *South European Society and Politics* 20(3): 333–55.

Torreblanca, Jose Ignacio, and Mark Leonard. 2013. "The Continent-Wide Rise of Euroscepticism." Policy Memo, European Council on Foreign Relations.

Transparency International. 2017. "Corruption Perceptions Index 2016." Transparency International. Retrieved 7 January 2017 from https://www.transparency.org/news/feature/corruption_perceptions_index_2016.

Tsoucalas, Constantine. 1986. *Social Development and the State. The Composition of the Public Sphere in Greece.* Athens: Themelio.

———. 2013. *Morphes Synecheias kai Asynecheias: Apo ten Istorike Ethnegersia sten Oikoumenike Dysphoria.* Athens: Themelio.

Weber, Max. 1978. *Economy and Society,* edited by Guenther Roth and Claus Wittich, translated by Ephraim Fischoff. New York: Bedminster Press.

World Bank Group. 2017. "Ease of Doing Business in Greece." Washington, DC. Retrieved 7 January 2017 from http://www.doingbusiness.org/data/exploreeconomies/greece.

Chapter 3

Golden Dawn

From the Margins of Greece to the Forefront of Europe

Kostis Karpozilos

Introduction

Since 2009 Greece has acquired a seminal position in the ongoing discussion on the future of the common European project. The Greek crisis
became a commonplace theme and generated considerable public and
scholarly analysis that focused on the transformative powers of financial
instability and the multiple ways it intertwined with social, political, and
cultural changes. Nonetheless, the crisis label has often led to a misguided
perception of Greek realities: focusing exclusively on the cataclysmic post-
2009 developments it blurs the importance of historical legacies and preexisting conditions.

The case of Golden Dawn offers an indicative example of this tendency.
The meteoric rise of a marginal extreme-right group into the forefront of
political developments has been portrayed as indisputable proof of the
rapidly shifting conditions amid the crisis. Electoral results confirmed this
line of analysis: in the 2009 national elections, Golden Dawn had gained a
mere 0.29 percent; in May 2012 it received 6.97 percent, becoming thus the
fifth-biggest political party, with twenty-one members in parliament. Despite revelations linking the party to criminal activities and a prolonged
persecution targeting its leadership, Golden Dawn gained 6.9 percent in
the January 2015 elections and ranked third leaving center-left, liberal, and
communist alternatives behind. Nor was the visibility of Golden Dawn
confined to the ballot box. Alongside its electoral gains the party launched
a crusade aiming to transform itself into a social and political movement.
Therefore, Golden Dawn initiated solidarity drives exclusively for Greek

citizens, established a number of front organizations, and promoted a rhetoric in which extreme nationalism was seen as the counterbalance to the challenges of the financial and social crisis. These activities went hand in hand with violent attacks against immigrants, a growing practice of street activism targeting the so-called enemies of the nation, and a conscious effort to create enclaves within the urban landscape under the absolute power of the party. In this context, the dynamics of Golden Dawn can operate as a synonym to the transformative power of the Greek crisis.

Understanding the success of Golden Dawn as an unprecedented phenomenon exclusively associated with the financial crisis can be misleading, however. The steadfast appeal of Golden Dawn suggests a more nuanced interpretation. The aim of this chapter is threefold: The first is to illustrate the historical continuities of the Greek extreme right and to follow its transformations over time. This overview highlights a lengthy history that challenges the idea that Golden Dawn appeared suddenly, while it illustrates the links and dialogue between the extreme right and Greek nationalism as a whole. The second is to position Golden Dawn within broader social and political movements that reflected the dynamics and predominance of Greek nationalism. The third is to highlight the links between events in Greece and concurrent shifts across the European continent, proposing that the rise of Golden Dawn should be associated with the overall appeal of extreme-right parties across Europe.

My main argument is that Golden Dawn has been a visible component of Greek nationalism. It underwent a significant transformation in the early 1990s and has been proven capable of adjusting itself to shifting conditions, paying particular attention to be part of broader movements with nationalistic agendas. Golden Dawn has been at the same time sectarian and opportunistic: it strived to disassociate itself from political coalitions with other extreme-right groups (with some noticeable exceptions) and to establish a visible presence in mass demonstrations, adjusting its agenda accordingly. This blend proved to be especially powerful in the shifting realities of the post-2009 crumbling political order because it portrayed the crisis as a national one that required a nationalistic solution (Vasilopoulou and Halikiopoulou 2015).

According to the party's international newsroom, "Golden Dawn Is a Social and Nationalist Movement" (Golden Dawn International Newsroom, "Our Identity" n.d.). Twelve statements that sketch the ideological foundations and vision of its members follow this initial proposition: the Social Nationalist state is the expression of the will of the organic nation ("in contrast to the transient and fleeting majority of parliamentary voting") and aims to enhance and develop the nation-race against "all forms of destructive 'equalizing' policies." The rhetoric, publications, and practices of Golden Dawn leave no room for interpretation: it is a party of the extreme right rejecting both "the fundamental values, procedures and institutions of the democratic constitutional state" and "the principle of fundamental human equality" (Carter 2005: 17).

The classification of Golden Dawn in the extreme-right camp does not denote the group's neo-Nazi roots and their echoes in its contemporary program. Moving beyond the neo-Nazi label is necessary, though. Golden Dawn has undergone successive transformations that have shifted its emphasis from neo-Nazi symbolisms to a political program of the extreme right that addresses contemporary challenges and issues. Moreover, the insistence on its neo-Nazi features blurs another critical feature: the normalization of its political agenda and the ways it is in dialogue with mainstream politics on certain issues—immigration being the most apparent. Publishing an article on the Greek extreme right in 2012, Antonis Ellinas, a well-informed analyst of the subject, speculated on the future of the Greek extreme right without making a sole reference to Golden Dawn (Ellinas 2012: 136–37). This underestimation of Golden Dawn, evident in the lack of studies on the matter before 2012, to a large extent reflected an underlying consensus that the group was "not something to be taken seriously" (Sportiche 2012). This deep-rooted belief that a neo-Nazi group would never thrive in Greece did not take into account that Golden Dawn since the late 1990s was transforming into a visible force of the extreme right that was in dialogue with broader ideological and political currents.

A World Apart

The origins of Golden Dawn date back to the early 1980s. Being an introvert organization with obscurity surrounding its internal life, very little is known for the period between December 1980, when for the first time a journal titled *Chryse Avge* (Golden Dawn) was published, and February 1986 when the organization People's Association–Golden Dawn was founded in the city of Athens (Psarras 2012: 41–53). The circumstances that propelled its foundation related to the inner strife and internal crisis of the Greek far right in the post-1974 era. The downfall of the 1967–74 military dictatorship and the proclamation of the Third Republic signified a decisive breach in the Greek political and social setting. Despite numerous shortcomings, a major aim of the republic was the end of the division that had defined modern Greek politics since the end of the Greek Civil War (1946–49). The republic proclaimed the end of the postwar division between the triumphant right and the defeated left, legitimized the Communist Party, abolished the monarchy, and declared the country's will to join the common European project. New Democracy (ND) was the governing party of the mainstream right that promoted these reforms, challenging in practice the legacy of the postwar anticommunist state and demolishing the core policies of the recent military dictatorship.

The reconciliatory policies of ND generated dissatisfaction among a diverse world of militant anticommunists, supporters of the military junta, loyal royalists (Union of Royalists) and small-scale groups that had neo-fascist inklings (United Nationalist Movement, or ENEK). In this context, a number of successive parties appeared. The National Democratic Union (1974: 1.1 percent), the National Party (1977: 6.82 percent), the Party of the Progressives (1981: 1.7 percent) and the National Political Union (1984: 2.29 percent) shared a common feeling of betrayal and expressed resentment against the republic. Despite their mediocre results (with the exception of the temporary success of 1977 when the National Party elected five members of parliament [MPs]) their continuous presence highlights the consistent appeal of authoritarianism and the dissatisfaction of conservative, anticommunist voters with the policies of ND.

On the other hand, these postauthoritarian far-right parties rallied around nostalgia for the past rather than a political program for the day after. They defended the legacy of the military dictatorship, they demanded the release of the imprisoned leaders of the 1967 coup, they referred to the past as a period of social stability and financial prosperity, and they propagated the restoration of postwar anticommunism. As commentators have already pinpointed, the Greek postauthoritarian far right tried to rally "nationally minded" citizens without offering a positive identification with the nation and a political project for the future (Ellinas 2013: 545). Complicating things further, the internal world of the far right was marked by stark differences and contests for power. Questions of political tactics interplayed with recent feuds (as in the case of the clash between the junta and the king in 1970), generating splits and intensifying an overriding sense of historical defeat. It was within this crisis that a rising generation of younger activists aimed for a new beginning.

Nikolaos Michaloliakos, the uncontested Golden Dawn leader to this day, was among the main actors of this generation. In 1978, when he was twenty-one years old, he was arrested for taking part in a terrorist network that had organized a series of arsons and bombings in Athens on the fourth anniversary (23 July 1978) of the junta's downfall (Katsimardos and Roubanis 2013: 59–79). The aim of the terrorists was to ignite instability and to underline the shaky foundations of the newborn republic. Targeting cinemas, bookstores, and public spaces, the attacks demonstrated an affinity to the methods of contemporary Italian neo-fascist groups. The links between the Greek and Italian far right dated back to the late

1960s. Italian neo-fascists had frequently visited Greece to seek material assistance from the military dictatorship (Patterson, Miller, and Van Hook 2012: 699–700). On the other hand, a number of Greek students in Italy were active in far-right groups, clashing frequently with leftists—Greek and Italians alike. These exchanges created a space of neo-fascist transnational activism that influenced the subsequent formation of Golden Dawn. While serving his time, Michaloliakos met the imprisoned leaders of the 1967 coup; after his release he initiated, in December 1980, the publication of a periodical entitled *Golden Dawn.*

Published irregularly, *Golden Dawn* reflected the ideological pursuits of a small group of true believers. The editorial of the first issue called for a "Golden Dawn that will signify the passage into the novel civilization of the White Race" (Chasapopoulos 2013: 17). The journal's pages contained selective references to paganism, esotericism, and National Socialism combined with racial theories proving the supremacy of the Greek nation. Explicit references to Nazism hailed the heroism of Adolf Hitler, and racial theories described an apocalyptical future that would fulfill the historical destiny of the white race. "The Mythological Continuity of Land and Blood," an article signed by Michaloliakos, illustrated this transplantation of Nazi theories into a Greek context: the author referred to the Greek traditional folk songs and myths in order to describe his vision of a world governed by "War, Movement, Will, and Power" (Michaloliakos 1982: 27).

The group formed around the journal *Golden Dawn* was not interested as much in claiming the legacy of the recent junta as it was in propagating and educating militant activists for an upcoming battle. The coincidence between the publication of *Golden Dawn* and the rise of Panhellenic Socialist Movement (PASOK) to power in October 1981 illustrates the sense of urgency saturating the minds and actions of the young activists. This shift from the postauthoritarian far right was a common theme across small and local groupings of the extreme right. Makis Voridis, today an ND member of parliament (MP) who was instrumental in the formation of student groupings of the extreme right in the 1980s, has described this discontinuity with the politics of the postauthoritarian right: "All these [the demands of the National Political Union] smelled like mothballs to me! . . . Our demands were historical, not social. . . . The demands about the past blocked our future" (Ellinas 2012: 128).

Golden Dawn championed in this revolt against the traditional far right. The outspoken ideological affinities to Nazism were seminal in this distinction. In World War II Greece had suffered immensely. The occupying German and Italian forces (1941–44) devastated the economy, raided towns and villages, killed thousands of civilians, and orchestrated the deportation of Jewish communities to the death camps of Central and

Eastern Europe. At the same time, a collaborationist government in Athens organized military units to combat the rising, often communist-led, resistance forces. The postwar anticommunist state had subtly recognized the importance of the collaborationist governments, but even so, the reincorporation of their activities in the postwar national narrative did not extend into a positive account of the ideological premises and practices of the German armed forces. Wartime atrocities, the country's postwar position in the Free World camp and the overall denunciation of Nazism as an un-Greek ideology had defined the development of the traditional far right.

Golden Dawn promoted a distinct version of historical interpretation that correlated to its quest for a positive paradigm in the rising neo-Nazi and extreme-right groups across Europe. The group emphasized the seminal role of Greek antiquity in the development of Nazism, portrayed the activities of German armed forces as a response to British imperialism and communist provocations, defended the policies of the collaborationist governments, and, finally, strived to rebrand National Socialism as a Greek ideology. This outlook represented the radicalization of the far-right militant activists amid a changing political atmosphere. The rise of PASOK to power signaled the recognition of the communist-led resistance groups of the 1940s, the implementation of policies promoting gender equality and individual rights, and the promotion of a national consensus on the country's troubled past. For the activists of the extreme right these developments proved the terminal failure of traditional far-right politics and the necessity of a radical response.

The appearance of extreme-right groups in Western Europe offered an example for Golden Dawn. Not coincidentally the group's leadership established contacts with the Spanish Círculo Español de Amigos de Europa (CEDADE), as the two countries shared the transition from an authoritarian past to a republic and the concurrent rise of socialist parties in power. According to Dimitris Psarras, the early Golden Dawn "was modeled on the CEDADE" example (Psarras 2012: 45); at the same time, however, leading figures of Golden Dawn traveled to Spain and took part in a conference of the New European Order, which was a network of neo-Nazi groups across Europe. The result was the transformation of Golden Dawn into an independent political organization. This step coincided with the end of a short-lived period in which Michaloliakos was named leader of the National Political Union youth section. By the mid-1980s Golden Dawn was established as a distinct version within the constellation of the Greek far and extreme right. A significant factor for this was the promotion of a white skinhead subculture. The public demonstration of Nazi paraphernalia, white power music, hooliganism, and a growing sense of comradeship allowed Golden Dawn to establish itself as a dynamic, militant version of extreme-right politics.

Golden Dawn: Becoming Greek and Orthodox

In the early 1990s Golden Dawn turned from a small Athens-based group of militant extremists into a marginal, yet visible, political party of the extreme right. This transformation is interrelated with the ability of Golden Dawn to establish links with the prevailing nationalistic atmosphere in Greece. The downfall of the socialist regimes across Eastern Europe, the Yugoslav Civil War, and the ensuing population movements in the region signaled a rise of nationalistic sentiments in Greece. This development was interwoven with significant social and political transformations, while the country was entering the core of the European Union (EU; then European Economic Community) project. From the early 1990s until the early 2000s three successive issues illustrated the predominance of national concerns in the Greek social and political setting: (1) the diplomatic dispute between Greece and the Former Yugoslav Republic of Macedonia generated an explosion of nationalism that fueled the revival of Greek irredentism, (2) discriminatory practices against immigrant workers were intertwined with concerns on the degenerating effects of immigration, and (3) the strife between the Orthodox Church and the Greek government on the question of new identity cards brought forth a right-wing ethnocentrism and Euroscepticism that challenged the country's integration in the EU.

The rise of Greek nationalism was marked by a stark paradox: the Greek nation was portrayed to be in danger, while Greece was enjoying an unprecedented privileged status of social security and economic growth. The expansion of Greek capital in the Balkans and the cheap immigrant labor propelled a story of financial success that transformed Greek society. In spite of this reality, mainstream media, major political figures, and influential intellectuals underlined that the nation was under threat facing social and geopolitical challenges. In this context, Golden Dawn succeeded in positioning itself within the dominant nationalistic paradigm. Even though this development required a gradual rebranding of Golden Dawn characteristics (mainly the downplaying of its neo-Nazi features), its core policies were in dialogue with basic premises of Greek national identity and concerns. The perception of Greekness is an indicative, and seminal, example of this interplay. Since the nineteenth century, Greek national identity became identical with ethnic identity. This scheme was founded on the idea of the uninterrupted historical continuity of the Greek race from antiquity to the present. Therefore, the Greek nationality law in the twentieth century was based on the principle of *jus sanguinis* and state policies targeted ethnic minorities (and political dissidents in the post-1949 setting) as non-Greeks (Christopoulos 2013). The ethnocentric rhetoric of Golden Dawn appeared to be in harmony with the racially defined understandings of Greekness that emerged and saturated the public scene of the turbulent 1990s.

The Macedonian question became the springboard for Golden Dawn's entrance into mainstream politics. The diplomatic clash between Greece and the newborn Republic of Macedonia regarding the use of the name "Macedonia" became a seminal issue in Greece, leading to huge demonstrations in 1992. The rallying slogan "Macedonia is Greek" reflected a crusade of national awareness across the political spectrum, with the only dissenting voices coming from segments of the left. These popular manifestations of national pride provided a fertile ground for the appearance of Golden Dawn that presented itself as a dynamic version of nationalism within the broader movement. Soon, the Macedonian question became the top priority in Golden Dawn's program: it illustrated the traitorous past of the communist left, it proved that Greece was in danger and, finally, given the efforts of the mainstream right to reach an agreement, it warned against compromises with the enemies of the nation.

The simplistic, uncompromising, and militant rhetoric of Golden Dawn attracted attention, and soon it witnessed a noticeable organizational growth. In April 1992, two months after the first Macedonian rally, Golden Dawn held a public event in Athens leading to its second national conference. The next step, in January 1993, was the regular publication of a biweekly newspaper (*Chryse Avge*) and participation, for the first time, in an electoral contest (1994 Euro-elections: 7.264 votes and 0.07 percent). The party's platform focused primarily on the Macedonian question (the headline of the first issue of *Chryse Avge* was, "No Compromise for Our Macedonia"), with immigration coming second, and accusations of the corrupt political and social elites coming third. At the same time, Nikolaos Michaloliakos, as the group's leader, was becoming a recognizable figure of Greek nationalism and the extreme right. His appearances in mainstream talk shows contributed to this end. In 1995, for instance, he appeared on the second biggest Greek television channel to discuss the question of contemporary fascism with the then-foreign minister Theodoros Pangalos (Pretenderes 2013). Such instances accentuated the visibility of Golden Dawn; the group was becoming more and more the dominant force of the Greek extreme right.

This process went hand in hand with the conscious effort of Golden Dawn to distance itself from its recent neo-Nazi past. Even though explicit references to National Socialism did not disappear entirely, Golden

Dawn strived to present itself as "a Greek nationalist party" (Psarras 2012: 250–51). Greek antiquity and history provided Golden Dawn with a usable past. The notion of the eternal struggle between the nation and its enemies, the racialization of Greek identity, and the belief in a common European future of free white nations remained constant point of references. At the same time, though, Golden Dawn attempted to circumvent the questions regarding the National–Socialism project by turning to the original source of neo-Nazi symbolisms: ancient Greece. In this context, Sparta, the swastika, and hygienic and racial theories were disassociated from their historical enactments in the twentieth century and were presented as mere points of inspiration from the glorious era of the Greek nation: antiquity.

The slogan "For a Greater Greece in a Free Europe" epitomized the political vision of Golden Dawn in the 1990s. It was based on the revival of Greek irredentist claims and got traction during the mass rallies on the Macedonian question. The Greek extreme right was seminal in its popularization by distributing maps with the country's historical claims in the Balkans and by contrasting this version of dynamic nationalism to the conciliatory and "traitorous"—according to Golden Dawn—diplomatic maneuvers of the established political elite. Given the rise of minority issues in the post-1989 Balkans, the presence of a large Greek Orthodox community in southern Albania fueled plans of a border realignment that would incorporate the so-called Northern Epirus. At the same time, a growing concern on the rise of a Muslim axis in the region intensified plans for a dynamic Greek response in the shifting Balkan realities. Segments of the Orthodox Church, enclaves of nationalists in the armed forces, Golden Dawn, and a small number of conservative and right-wing politicians were involved in this debate.

The established alliance between Greece and Serbia, a partnership to a large extent based on the common Orthodox heritage, became a fertile ground for the popularity of this regenerated irredentism. Even though it never materialized into a concrete plan, the irredentist fantasy entailed a joint military operation leading to a Greek–Serbian borderline. On a more realistic level, though, Greece was becoming a safe haven for leading members of Serbian armed forces, while the Orthodox Church, leading politicians, and mainstream media were focused on expressing their support for Serbia in every possible way. Golden Dawn took this atmosphere of cordial alliance further. As recent revelations have confirmed, a number of Golden Dawn activists joined Serbian paramilitary groupings and participated in the Srebrenica massacre. The activities of the Greek Volunteer Guard were well received in Greece. "They are flying now [the four flags: Serb, Greek, Vergina, and that of Byzantium] side by side . . . , a living proof of the love and solidarity of the two peoples" reported a center-left daily supporting PASOK following the fall of the city (Michas 2002: 17–18).

The growing militancy of Golden Dawn members was also evident in the streets of Athens and other cities. Violent attacks against Balkan immigrants illustrated the attempt of Golden Dawn to transform organizational gains into trained groups of direct action. The attacks against immigrants of the 1990s remained to a large extent undocumented as victims were reluctant to report to authorities and the country lacked an institutional structure for the documentation of hate crimes. The anti-immigrant campaign of Golden Dawn reflected its racist premises: it perceived foreigners as a threat to the nation's cohesion and the country's national security. More importantly, though, as in the case of the Macedonian question, the Golden Dawn rhetoric ascribed to a broader development. Xenophobia was on the rise during the 1990s because Greece was becoming for the first time the recipient of a significant flow of immigration. In this context, the low-scale attacks against immigrant communities and individuals organized by Golden Dawn were not isolated incidents—they were expressions of a general upsurge of hate crimes. In October 1999 a twenty-three-year-old Greek killed two immigrants in downtown Athens and left seven wounded. His prosecution revealed close ties to Golden Dawn, but no direct links could be established. On October 22, 1999, the party's newspaper front matter carried the title "Death of a Nation" referring to immigrant presence in Athens. This event illustrates the blurred line between the rhetoric of Golden Dawn, the hate crimes committed in the same period, and the missing links between the party's leadership and the activities of its sympathizers and members.

On the other hand, the vicious attack of an elite Golden Dawn squad against three leading figures of the student movement in June 1998 manifested the orchestrated nature of these attacks. Because one of the victims, Dimitris Kousouris, barely escaped death, the attack provoked public outcry and the first investigation of the group's activities. The results were mediocre. On the one hand, the investigation revealed that Golden Dawn had organized a paramilitary squad named Golden Eagle that carried out attacks against immigrant workers and leftist students. This fact brought into question the legal status of Golden Dawn, and at some point the prospect of a prosecution against its leadership seemed imminent. This never materialized. Periandros Androutsopoulos, the head of the Golden Eagle squad and identified instigator of the attack against Kousouris, escaped prosecution and trial, and disappeared into Latin America (Psarras 2015: 18–23). This development brought the trial to a halt and intensified accusations of extreme-right enclaves in the police force. In addition to this, the liberal nature of the Greek constitution safeguarded the legitimate status of Golden Dawn: contrary to other countries, there was no provision for the prohibition of its political activities.

Nonetheless the 1998 attack had significant repercussions in the cohesion and dynamics of Golden Dawn. A number of prominent members withdrew from its activities either to escape persecution or to express their dissatisfaction with tactical choices in the handling of this internal crisis (Kousoumvris 2004). Moreover, the attack signified the rise of anti-fascist awareness; militant demonstrations called for the banning of Golden Dawn, and for a thorough investigation of its activities. Confronted with multiple challenges, the leadership of Golden Dawn sought a way out in the creation of a political coalition of the extreme right. This was the first, and only, instance where Golden Dawn engaged in dialogue with prominent figures and small groups of the extreme right. The result was *Prote Gramme* (First Line), an electorate front that participated in the 1999 elections to the European Parliament (0.75 percent) and in the 2000 national elections (0.18 percent).

The formation of First Line occurred at a time when the reappearance of a far-right party in mainstream politics was becoming a probable scenario. The causes for this prospect were multifaceted: the successful incorporation of Greece in the core eurozone family intensified concerns on national sovereignty and brought forth a version of Euroscepticism that expressed the concerns of traditional right-wing voters; the shift of ND to the center right alienated those representing a populist right; and finally, in late 1999 the influential Orthodox Church, under the leadership of Archbishop Christodoulos of Athens, initiated a campaign against the implementation of new identity cards that soon transformed into a popular movement defending the premises of Greek nationalism.

The controversy over the identity cards encompasses the consolidation of nationalistic concerns during the time that Greece was entering the core of the common European project. The new bilingual identity cards would omit the requirement to declare the cardholder's religion. The Holy Synod reacted forcefully, cautioning that this was a step toward the de-Hellenization of the nation. The underlying reasoning ascribed to the basic feature of Greek nationalism was that the Orthodox faith and national consciousness were inseparable. Mass demonstrations followed, while the Church claimed that it had collected more than 1 million signatures on its side. Even though there was a long history of the Orthodox Church intervening in the political debate, the intensity and magnitude of this campaign was of a different order. More importantly, the rhetoric of the archbishop of Athens became increasingly identifiable with the far right: his anti-Western rhetoric entailed an attack against the Enlightenment as the root of atheism and materialism, while the future of a federalist Europe was portrayed as an apocalyptical plan demolishing national traditions. A peculiar blend of nationalism, populism, and subtle anti-Semitism saturated the atmosphere and gave rise to scenarios of a new nationalist party on the far-right edge of the political spectrum.

Once again, as had happened in the case of the Macedonian question, Golden Dawn became an active participant in the mass demonstrations. This development illustrated the efforts of its leadership to realign itself with the popular nationalistic sentiment. In the 1980s Golden Dawn had demonstrated strong apocryphal and pagan influences, rejecting Christianity as a degenerated, and Jewish, faith (Zoumboulakis 2013). By the end of the 1990s, such references had become marginal as the party aligned itself with the dominant and mainstream theories of the eternal bond between Hellenism and Christianity. This shift was reflected in the use of Byzantine emblems in the party's public appearances and in the creation of ties between the Golden Dawn leadership and a small number of leading figures of the Orthodox Church with outspoken anti-Semitic and socially reactionary views.

The inherent sectarianism and recent legal accusations prevented Golden Dawn from participating in the formation of a populist and far-right party. In September 2000 Georgos Karatzaferis, an expelled MP of ND, announced the launch of Popular Orthodox Rally (LAOS), a political party that wished to defend the values of Greek nationalism (Psarras 2010). The full name of the new party illustrated the impact of the recent rallies on the identity cards. LAOS operated as a meeting point of figures of the far and extreme right, such as the author of popular anti-Semitic books Konstantinos Plevris, and Makis Voridis of the Greek version of the Front Nationale, with religious-minded people having split off from ND. Their rallying point was a sense of national betrayal and the necessity of defending the Greek nation against the EU policies. This was a novel development because anti-EU politics in Greece were traditionally associated with the communist left.

The emergence of LAOS signified the crystallization of trends and ideas that up to that point had remained scattered across the political spectrum and mainly in the extremes of ND. LAOS developed into a successful political party: the party succeeded in entering the European parliament in 2004 (4.12 percent) and the Greek parliament in 2007 (3.80 percent). These percentages illustrate the growing concern for the financial and social policies of an era marked by the dynamics of Greek capitalism: entry into the eurozone, high development rates, the staging of the Olympic games, and economic expansion to the Balkan countries.

Golden Dawn in Parliament

The post-2008 financial crisis and the ensuing collapse of the existing political order signified the entrance of Golden Dawn into mainstream politics. The electoral successes of the party and its visible presence in the Greek social setting in the early years of the crisis has generated an unprecedented academic interest on the politics of the Greek extreme right, up to that point understudied. The underlying question related to the factors that propelled the meteoric rise of a marginal group into parliament as Golden Dawn gained 6.97 percent and 6.92 percent in the two electoral contests of May and June 2012. The overall realignment of the Greek political landscape suggests an interpretative framework. In 2009, when the prospect of the financial crisis seemed distant, results in the national elections reflected the persistence of the traditional center-left and center-right competition for power. Almost eight in ten voters had chosen the two dominant parties: PASOK and ND. In three years' time their combined strength had shrunk to 32.03 percent, leaving ample space for the rise of challenges either on the left or the right of the political spectrum.

In this context, there was also a concurrent shift in the balance of forces between the Greek far right and the extreme right. Golden Dawn succeeded in becoming the primary choice of voters who had already associated themselves with the right-wing populist LAOS. This tendency was evident in the 2010 municipal elections. The elections were marked by the unprecedented success of Nikolaos Michaloliakos, who as the Golden Dawn candidate for mayor of Athens gained 10,000 votes (5.26 percent). Up to a point this result was the outcome of a systematic anti-immigrant and antipolitical campaign waged by Golden Dawn since early 2009. On a broader level, though, in the 2010 contest the LAOS party did not have a ticket in Athens and therefore it is plausible to suggest that Golden Dawn attracted a significant share of its voters. In Thessaloniki, the second-biggest city, the situation was different. The LAOS candidate gained 3.6 percent whereas the Golden Dawn ticket followed with 1 percent. Subsequent results confirm this trend. In the 2012 national elections, LAOS lost more than 50 percent of its electoral strength (2009: 5.63 percent, May 2012: 2.9 percent, June 2012: 1.58 percent), while Golden Dawn was on the ascend (2009: 0.29 percent, May 2012: 6.97 percent, June 2012: 6.92 percent).

Nonetheless it would be simplistic to suggest that this was just a story of shifting allegiances within the inner world of the far and extreme rights. The electoral rise of Golden Dawn went hand in hand with the growing visibility of its activities across the country, the popularization of its message, and the rise of political violence in the streets of Athens. The success of Golden Dawn reflected the transforming power of the financial crisis, but also the radicalization and dynamics of the nationalistic sentiments that had emerged in the 1990s. Since the onset of the crisis, Golden Dawn intensified its efforts for a rebranding that would eradicate or marginalize its neo-Nazi past. This conscious effort encompassed its ideological manifestations and extended to its everyday practices. The party's main slogan, "On our own, against all," became a metaphor for the material conditions of the Greek population. The party created an image of Greeks being left alone fighting to survive against the overwhelming powers of foreigners—either as financial elites, the EU, or the documented and undocumented immigrants. It was a powerful slogan, allowing Golden Dawn to present itself as the metonym for the state of the nation.

Golden Dawn portrayed the crisis as a byproduct of "traitorous" policies, emphasizing that the only way out necessitated a "catharsis" that would lead to "the Golden Dawn of Hellenism" (Golden Dawn, "Politikes Theseis" n.d.). More specifically the party had promoted a platform that appeared to be in line with a popular interpretation of the crisis: The existing political order had for years established a regime of corruption and self-interest, thus destroying the Greek economy. This political elite was subordinated to the policies of the EU and therefore promoted the de-Hellenization of Greece. And, in the critical moment of the crisis the political elite was accepting orders from the EU and implemented austerity measures that aimed to the further colonization of the country and the promotion of foreign interests. "Greece under Occupation" was the headline of *Chryse Avge* (28 April 2010) following the revelation of George Papandreou that the country was indebted and his government would request an International Monetary Fund (IMF) intervention. On the same page, Nikolaos Michaloliakos promoted the party's new slogan: "Fighting for nationalism against the international usurers." (See Doxiadis this volume for the history of similar political rhetoric.)

This statement encompassed the main themes of the party's development over the next few years. Nationalism was promoted as the sole alternative against the straightjacket of austerity politics imposed by institutions and mechanisms that, according to Golden Dawn, were foreign. Here an interesting point concerns the depiction of the IMF as an internationalist project. According to Golden Dawn, the institutions and bodies created in the aftermath of World War II, such as the United Nations, were expressions of an internationalist order that echoed the desire of liberals and Marxists alike for a global order. In this context, resistance to austerity became the synonym for a national response to a threat imposed by forces outside Greece. This line of reasoning was not unique in the far right of the political spectrum. It was equally promoted by segments of the left. The opening lines of the Golden Dawn manifesto echoed similarities to the 1980s nationalist politics of the leftist PASOK: "Greece belongs to Greeks." The anti-imperialist slogan of the 1980s referred to the long-lasting presence of U.S. military structures in Greece; in the context of the crisis, this was transformed into a slogan against the austerity policies of the IMF and the European Central Bank. Finally, Michaloliakos's reference to international usurers echoed the prevailing anti-Semitism of the far right, but more importantly the effort to position Golden Dawn within a growing tide of conspiracy theories that flourished in Greece during the early stages of the crisis.

Therefore, as Greece entered a spiral of economic and social collapse, Golden Dawn succeeded, as it had done in the past, to align itself with broader concerns. In the summer of 2011 thousands took the streets imitating the Spanish paradigm of the Indignados. For weeks the Syntagma square in Athens became a meeting point of diverse viewpoints. Gradually two distinct and geographically defined poles emerged: the lower part of the square became the rallying point of the left, while the upper side in front of the parliament a hub for the flourishing of right-wing populist and antipolitical slogans. Golden Dawn was not active in the Greek Indignados movement; after all, one of the basic premises of the movement was the denial of entry to organized political entities. On the other hand, though, it was becoming more and more apparent that segments of the demonstrators were adopting slogans, interpretations, and understandings of the crisis that were in dialogue with the political baggage of the Greek far and extreme right. The massive demonstrations reflected popular disagreement with austerity politics and the breach of confidence between traditional parties and the wider public.

The reshuffling of political representation affected the LAOS party. In November 2011, in the immediate aftermath of the massive anti-austerity demonstrations, the party's leadership decided to enter a coalition government bringing together for the first time ND and PASOK under the technocrat Lucas Papademos. This was a necessary step for the implementation of the austerity measures package, the infamous memorandum of understanding (MoU). The LAOS decision had two, seemingly antithetical, results. First it led to its crisis as the party was discredited for supporting the MoU and it propelled the rise of Golden Dawn and Independent Greeks (ANEL) as representatives of the populist, right-wing, antipolitical rejection of the austerity measures. Golden Dawn benefited from this development. From the late months of 2011 Golden Dawn organized a series of events in localities across Greece, often with the help of disenchanted ex-LAOS functionaries. Second, the participation in government of a party with a lengthy and heavy record of racist, anti-Semitic, and nationalistic statements offered a bizarre legitimization of the Greek far right. Its acceptance by the established political order marked the entrance of extremism into mainstream politics. This development contributed to the further normalization of the Golden Dawn message.

The perception of the crisis through a nationalistic lens and hostility against recent immigrants from Africa and Asia are two main domains in which the lines appear to blur. The ethnocentric interpretation of the crisis became a commonplace theme generating accusations of traitorous politics and an overwhelming atmosphere of distrust directed against the country's political and social elite. At the same time, the question of immigration, because Greece was increasingly becoming the point of entry for newcomers from the Middle East and South Asia, led to a visible nationalistic and anti-immigrant rhetoric across the political spectrum. The case of ND illustrated this shift. The statement of Antonis Samaras, the party's leader and prime minister, "Our cities have been taken over by illegal immigrants [and] we have to reclaim them" expressed the emerging dynamics of xenophobia and nationalism (Malkoutzis 2012). In this context, prominent members of the right-wing government established unofficial links with the leadership of Golden Dawn aiming to a potential collaboration. Even though the revelation of these links caused an internal crisis in ND, their existence highlighted that Golden Dawn was increasingly becoming a legitimate player in mainstream politics.

The meteoric rise of Golden Dawn underlines the significance of nationalist responses in the interpretation of the crisis. More importantly it highlights how the financial crisis and the immigrant question created a perception of the nation being under attack. Golden Dawn portrayed austerity politics as the byproduct of foreign imposition and local political elites that were serving foreign interests. This reasoning was not only widespread across the political spectrum, but also related to a lengthy tradition, associated with left, of understanding Greek history as a protracted struggle between national sovereignty and foreign control (see Doxiadis this volume). Contrary to other political parties, though, the Greek extreme right coupled this idea with the question of immigration. In the nationalistic rhetoric of Golden Dawn, the Troika (the name given to the authorities supervising the Greek austerity program: the European Central Bank, the European Commission, and the IMF) and the immigrants were two sides of the same coin: the threat against the Greek nation.

Electorate results reveal the importance of xenophobia in the establishment of Golden Dawn in mainstream politics. Since 2008 Golden Dawn has succeeded in creating local enclaves of support in the sixth regional department of Athens, an area of formerly middle-class neighborhoods currently being infused with immigrants. In the 2010 elections Golden

Dawn received its highest percentage (8.38 percent) in the sixth regional department. This was the outcome of a systematic presence of Golden Dawn members in the region, because they were active in frequent protests against the so-called ghettoization of the area, blaming immigrants for rising crime rates and presenting them as a threat to social cohesion (Kandylis and Kavoulakos 2011: 157–76).

On the other hand, support for Golden Dawn was also visible in neighborhoods with minimal or marginal immigrant presence. This pattern was repeated in later years. When in May 2012 Golden Dawn entered parliament for the first time it was impossible to draw a direct correlation between immigration and the party's electoral strength. The three prefectures with the highest Golden Dawn percentages (Corinth, Lakonia, and Argolida) did not fit at all the theoretical principles of direct association between immigration and the rise of the far right. These agrarian prefectures shared a history of right-wing predominance and noticeable far-right presence. In the case of Lakonia, the appeal of nationalism and far-right politics reveals the significant historical continuities of the authoritarian far right in Greece. During World War II the area was the bastion of paramilitary units fighting the communist-led national resistance, and in the postwar era it was the stronghold of Greek far-right politics. Golden Dawn was the only political party that openly endorsed the legacy of these collaborationist armed groups.

The role of historical legacies, though, was not confined to Lakonia. Golden Dawn capitalized existing far-right sympathies and consistently promoted a narrative that encompassed the continuities of political authoritarianism from the dictatorship of Ioannis Metaxas (1936–40) to postwar anticommunism and the military junta of 1967–74. The genealogy of the authoritarian right appealed to conservative, antipolitical, and national-minded voters who shared nostalgia for a past of national sovereignty, stability, and prosperity. The Metaxas dictatorship provided the prototype of the Social Nationalist state that Golden Dawn envisioned as the road out of the national crisis. Historical analogies had an important role in this association, because the Metaxas regime implemented corporatist social policies, criminalized the rising communist left, and offered a Greek version of national reconstruction from the perils of the interwar financial crisis. More importantly, though, the case of Ioannis Metaxas allowed Golden Dawn to counter accusations of being a neo-fascist and neo-Nazi group. Despite its ideological leanings to fascism, the Metaxas government had declared war against Italy in October 1940 and had fought against the German army in the early months of 1941. Claiming this legacy allowed Golden Dawn to present itself as a solely Greek nationalist movement.

This effort was intertwined with the systematic creation of an alternative social and political space "exclusively for Greeks" (Golden Dawn 2013). Food and blood drives, excursions to mountains, physical activities, history remembrance days, and social events underpinned the idea that Golden Dawn offered an immediate response to the social challenges confronting the nation. The wide array of nationalist social activities reflected the ability of the extreme right to take part in broader shifts. The onset of the crisis and the collapse of the welfare state had generated a dynamic constellation of local mutual-aid initiatives that were transforming Greek society. Theories and practices of self-organization flourished, ranging from social medical units to soup kitchens and small-scale cooperatives. Golden Dawn provided an alternative version: one focusing exclusively on Greeks and prioritizing notions of national cohesion over class antagonism and transnational solidarity. In a telling episode, the party created a medical unit called Médecins Avec Frontières in sharp contrast with the well-known Médecins Sans Frontières organization.

In a similar context, Golden Dawn created an environmental (Green Front) and women's (Women Front) organization. Their program and activities reflected a strategy of bringing a traditional nationalist agenda in dialogue with contemporary challenges. In the first case the interest in environmental issues was in interplay with the nineteenth century *blood und boden* theory and the idea of the inherent link between nation and soil. A similar pattern is evident in the discussion about gender. The creation of the White Women Front underlined the effort of Golden Dawn to counter its male-dominated image and to promote a renewed nationalist gender agenda that focused on women as "mothers of the nation [who] ought to safeguard our Race and the future of our children" (Metopo Gynaikon 2013). Amid a selective blend of eugenics and racism, women in the Golden Dawn rhetoric are designated to carry and foster healthy and nation-minded children who in turn will fulfill the nation's historical destiny. On a more practical level, the party strived to attract women in its ranks, and incorporated a small number in its higher echelons.

In general, Golden Dawn proved to be extremely successful in promoting itself as a social and political force that defended the vulnerable against the powerful. What is important here is the construction of a consistent narrative elevating the ordinary Greek to a martyr suffering from austerity policies and the combined practices of corrupt elites and dangerous immigrants. Mainstream newspapers reported that Golden Dawn members accompanied elder women to ATMs, the party consistently advertised its food and blood drives, while its members in parliament claimed that they donated a significant part of their earnings to the party's humanitarian activities. In many cases these activities never materialized. Taking into account the rising unemployment rates, Golden Dawn more than once announced the creation of employment centers that would be solely for Greeks. According to initial statements, these centers would operate as meeting points between employers and potential employees, thus creating a nationalistic job market against immigrant labor. Even though this plan never materialized, Golden Dawn continued referring to the necessity of a regulated labor market that would provide decent jobs to Greeks, and circulated rumors that this indeed was happening under its auspices. All these initiatives contributed to a growing appeal of Golden Dawn as a dynamic force that not only talked about resistance to austerity politics, but also had a blueprint for action in the present.

The popularity of Golden Dawn was illustrated in the development of links to influential members of the Greek Orthodox Church. This relation dated back to the years of the popular movement against the new identity cards, but the radicalization and politicization of the Church during the crisis created new opportunities for interaction. In October 2012 Golden Dawn members of parliament participated in an attack against the premiere of Terrence McNally's play "Corpus Christi" in Athens. Following the attack, Amvrosios, the metropolitan bishop of Kalavryta, expressed the opinion that Golden Dawn could represent a "sweet hope for the depressed Citizen and a gentle force against this corrupt political system" (Metropolites Kalavryton kai Aigialeias 2012).

Such statements demonstrated the gradual acceptance of Golden Dawn in the public sphere. Celebrities, religious leaders, and a small number of public commentators portrayed Golden Dawn as a novel political force that was speaking the language of truth, and was primarily concerned with the everyday problems of the average Greek. This populist rhetoric expressed dissatisfaction with the existing political order and at the same time presented the rising SYRIZA party as an anti-Greek force, given its pro-immigrant agenda.

For many Golden Dawn activists, all these were signals that the time had come. The party leadership often proclaimed that soon Golden Dawn would be in power, and at the same time orchestrated or allowed violent incidents against the perceived enemies of the nation. As had happened in the mid-1990s, immigrants were the primary targets. This time, though, it was not immigrants from Eastern Europe, but newcomers from Asia and Africa. The language of racial hatred, the success of the party's activities in downtown Athens, and the vulnerable status of the newcomers underpinned the confidence of Golden Dawn members in launching low-scale attacks and organizing local pogroms. According to the Racist Violence Recording Network (2013) there were 154 such incidents for 2012. Among those incidents the most well-known was the assassination of Shehzad Luqman, a Pakistani immigrant, as he was heading to work on his bicycle. In more than one case Golden Dawn members identified for violent attacks were not prosecuted. The party enjoyed considerable support among the police force (according to some reports, one out of two police officers voted for Golden Dawn) and the everyday ties between activists and police officers created conditions favorable for immunity (Christopoulos 2014: 20–41).

Golden Dawn did not assume responsibility for these actions. According to the party's statement, though, these incidents were legitimized expressions of anger and despair. The racial rhetoric of Golden Dawn was not far from the dominant political language of the time. At the same time, the financial crisis generated everyday tensions between Greek employers and immigrant employees. Violent incidents (as in the case of the shooting of farm laborers in the strawberry fields of Manolada in April 2013 or the inhumane torture of an immigrant worker in Salamina in 2012) illustrated the social context that made Golden Dawn activities possible. The party's activists operated as a law-enforcement group targeting Asian and African immigrants. An interesting dimension to this story was the gradual, and subtle, incorporation of immigrants from Albania into Golden Dawn. Claiming an alleged common Orthodox background, a small number of second-generation immigrants became increasingly active in attacks against newcomers. This exemplified a renewed version of racialized xenophobia according to which the Asian and African immigrants were not only non-Greeks, but also non-whites.

The escalation of violence, as it had happened in the mid-1990s, led to a seminal event. In October 2014 members of Golden Dawn under the direct supervision of a party's member in parliament murdered the musician and activist Pavlos Fyssas. This episode took place in Keratsini, a traditional working-class suburb of the Piraeus port. Golden Dawn was active in the region for quite some time and celebrated its electoral successes there as proof that Greek workers were turning their backs on the parties of the left. Violent attacks against Egyptian fishermen and members of the Communist Party in the region had not provoked considerable reactions, but the murder of Fyssas propelled the first state response to the policies and practices of Golden Dawn. A full-fledged investigation revealed the network of Golden Dawn supporters in the highest echelons of Greek police. More importantly, the party's leadership was prosecuted as a criminal group for organizing physical attacks and promoting racial violence (Psarras 2015). The Golden Dawn trial is ongoing as of this writing, and up to this point there has not been much progress in the proceedings. On the other hand, the prosecution had a significant impact because it halted the growing membership of Golden Dawn.

At the same time, though, it did not diminish its electoral strength. In the 2015 elections the party was the third strongest in parliament, while its percentages demonstrated the minimal impact of its persecution. Within this result there were some noticeable developments, mainly the significant rise of its percentages in the Aegean islands that were increasingly receiving large numbers of refugees from Afghanistan, Iraq, and Syria. Nonetheless it would be erroneous to attribute its electoral success to the influx of refugees. After all, in the January 2015 elections, long before the refugee question would become visible in Greece, Golden Dawn had succeeded in gaining 6.28 percent of the popular vote.

Conclusion

The post-2012 electoral stability of Golden Dawn proves the consolidation of a regenerated far right in the Greek political spectrum. Even though the electoral results do not correspond proportionally to membership or participation in its activities, it is evident that Golden Dawn has become a primary point of reference for a wide spectrum of voters. More importantly, key issues that constitute the cornerstones of Golden Dawn's program have increasingly become part of the public debate. The question of immigration is indicative. Even though no other party will use the extreme and racist overtones of Golden Dawn, the language of mainstream politics often demonstrates affinities with the far-right rhetoric. In the 2012 elections the governing ND leadership launched an attack on immigrants and refugees, labeling them as a potential threat and implementing the, now infamous, fence in the Greek–Turkish border of Evros. In a similar fashion, the anti-memorandum discourse before 2015 was also in dialogue with the Golden Dawn policies: understanding the crisis as a national one and portraying the political elite as traitorous became commonplace, allowing the social legitimization of Golden Dawn's platform.

Moreover, the persistent electoral success of Golden Dawn demonstrates the impact of its rebranding process of the late 1990s and early 2000s. In the early stages of its rise many commentators shared the belief that the broad public was ignorant of the historical legacies of Golden Dawn and more particularly its ties to neo-Nazism. It was an erroneous expectation. The continuous flow of revelations possibly hampered the prospects of a further Golden Dawn growth, but it did not lead to its demise. Golden Dawn had eliminated historical references to international fascism, denied its fascist background, and reverted the allegation through its response, "Does love for your country mean that one is a fascist?" The answer to the question was implicit: if so, yes you can call us fascists, but it does not really matter. Taking advantage of a prevailing discourse that portrayed the crisis as a national one, Golden Dawn appeared as a legitimate outcome to social discontent. Recent results suggest that the labeling of Golden Dawn does not suffice to divest it of political legitimacy or power—the language of historical analogies underestimates the distinctive features of different expressions of fascism over time and the fact that the contemporary reactionary phenomena (such as Golden Dawn or even more importantly the French Front Nationale) have less to do with the historical reenactment of a fascist legacy, and more to do with the transformative power of the contemporary financial crisis.

Today, Golden Dawn belongs to the family of the European extreme right and has a leading role in the creation of the Alliance for Peace and Freedom group in the European parliament. Up to this point, the traditional European far-right parties, the ones aligning themselves with the Front Nationale, have been extremely careful not to associate themselves with the overtly xenophobic, anti-Semitic, and antipolitical language and practice of Golden Dawn. To what extent the latter will remain a more or less pariah in the emerging map of the European populist far right is an open question. The continuing transformations of Golden Dawn and the growing radicalization of far-right parties across Europe indicate a possible and alarming convergence. Recent events in Austria, Hungary, Poland, and Slovakia, and the impetus of similar political movements in France, Sweden, and, to a lesser extent, Germany and the United Kingdom, suggest that the far and extreme right are increasingly becoming not expressions of abnormal conditions, but rather permanent and institutionalized political forces.

Kostis Karpozilos is a historian and the director of the Contemporary Social History Archives (ASKI). He is the scriptwriter of the documentary *Greek-American Radicals: The Untold Story* (2013), the author of a book on the Cretan socialist intellectual Stavros Kallergis (Benaki Museum, 2013), and of *Red America: Greek Immigrants and the Quest for a New World, 1900–1950* (Crete University Press, 2017). Dr. Karpozilos was a postdoctoral fellow at Columbia University, Princeton University, and University of Oxford, and has taught at the University of the Peloponnese, at Sciences Po Paris (Campus de Reims), and at Columbia University before joining College Year in Athens.

References

Carter, Elisabeth. 2005. *The Extreme Right in Western Europe.* Manchester, UK: Manchester University Press.
Chasapopoulos, Nikos. 2013. *Chryse Avge: E Istoria, ta Prosopa kai E aletheia.* Athens: Ekdotikos Organismos Livani.

Christopoulos, Dimitris. 2013. *Poios einai Ellenas polites: to kathestos ithageneias apo ten idryse tou ellenikou kratous os tis arches tou 21ou aiona.* Athens: Vivliorama.

———, ed. 2014. *Mapping Ultra-Right Extremism, Xenophobia and Racism within the Greek State Apparatus.* Athens: Rosa Luxemburg Stiftung.

Ellinas, Antonis. 2012. "LAOS and the Greek Far Right since 1974." In *Mapping the Extreme Right in Contemporary Europe: From Local to Transnational,* edited by Andrea Mammone, Emmanuel Godin, and Brian Jenkins, 124–39. London: Routledge.

———. 2013. "The Rise of the Golden Dawn: The New Face of the Far Right in Greece." *South European Society and Politics* 18(4): 543–65.

Golden Dawn. 2013. "Mono gia Ellenes," 10 February. Retrieved 10 June 2017 from http://www.xryshaygh.com/enimerosi/view/mono-gia-ellhnes-to-koinwniko-ergo-ths-chrushs-aughs-mechri-shmera.

———. n.d. "Politikes Theseis." Retrieved 8 April 2018 from http://www.xryshaygh.com/kinima/thesis.

Golden Dawn International Newsroom. n.d. "Our Identity." Retrieved 8 April 2018 from http://golden-dawn-international-newsroom.blogspot.co.uk/p/our-identity.html.

Kandylis George, and I. K. Kavoulakos. 2011. "Framing Urban Inequalities: Racist Mobilization Against Immigrants in Athens." *Greek Review of Social Research* 136: 157–76.

Katsimardos T., and Th., Roubanis. 2013. *E istoria tou Neonazismou sten Ellada.* Athens: Ethnos.

Kousoumvris, Charis. 2004. *Gremizontas ton mytho tes Chryses Avges.* Athens: Erevos.

Malkoutzis, Nick. 2012. "Is Immigration a Bigger Issue for Greece Than the Economy?" *E Kathimerini,* 30 March. Retrieved 8 April 2018 from http://www.ekathimerini.com/140452/article/ekathimerini/comment/is-immigration-a-bigger-issue-for-greece-than-the-economy ().

Metopo Gynaikon. 2013. Blog post, 9 March. Retrieved 10 June 2017 from http://whitewomenfront.blogspot.gr/.

Metropolites Kalavryton kai Aigialeias. 2012. "Apantese ston SYRIZA." Blog post, 27 October. Retrieved 10 June 2017 from http://mkka.blogspot.gr/2012/10/blog-post_4468.html.

Michaloliakos, Nikolaos. 1982. "E Mythologike Synecheia tes Ges kai tou Aimatos." *Chryse Avge,* August–September, 24.

Michas, Takis. 2002. *Unholy Alliance: Greece and Milosevic's Serbia.* College Station: Texas A&M University Press.

Patterson, David S., James E. Miller, and Laurie Van Hook, eds. *Foreign Relations of the United States* (FRUS). 2012. 1969–1976, Vol. 41, *Western Europe: NATO, 1969–1972.* Washington, DC: U.S. Government Printing Office.

Pretenteris, Yannis. 2013. "Telos Epoches." *YouTube,* 29 September. Retrieved 8 April 2018 from https://www.youtube.com/watch?v=RYv863E-lM8

Psarras, Dimitris. 2010. *To krypho cheri tou Karatzaphere: e teleoptike anagennese tes ellenikes akrodexias.* Athens: Alexandreia.

———. 2012. *E Mavre Vivlos tes Chrises Avges: ntokoumenta apo ten istoria kai te drase mias nazistikes omadas.* Athens: Polis.

———. 2015. *Golden Dawn on Trial.* Athens: Rosa Luxemburg Stiftung in Athens.

Racist Violence Recording Network. 2013. "2012 Violence Report." Racist Violence Recording Network, European Union Agency for Fundamental Rights, Vienna, Austria. Retrieved 10 June 2017 from https://www.unhcr.gr/fileadmin/Greece/News/2013/dt/Conclusions Network2012TotalEN.pdf

Sportiche, Sophie. 2012. "Q&A: Greece's Golden Dawn." *Al Jazeera,* 2 May. Retrieved 8 April 2018 from http://www.aljazeera.com/indepth/features/2012/05/20125712325948 2708.html.

Vasilopoulou, Sophia, and Daphne Halikiopoulou. 2015. *The Golden Dawn's "Nationalist Solution": Explaining the Rise of the Far Right in Greece.* London: Palgrave Pivot.

Zoumboulakis, Stavros. 2013. *Chryse Avge kai Ekklesia.* Athens: Polis.

Chapter 4

Protest, Elections, and Austerity Politics in Greece

Kostas Kanellopoulos and Maria Kousis

Introduction

One year after the collapse of Lehman Brothers the aftermaths of the capitalist crisis reached the eurozone countries. In the winter of 2009–10 Greece, a founding member of the eurozone, faced bankruptcy. The cost of lending money in the international capital markets was on the rise and Greece, due to its big budget deficit and its enormous public debt, could no longer borrow money to refinance its debt. Greek bonds were soon characterized by the international rating agencies as junk, and the Greek government, due to the country's membership in the eurozone, was without the monetary and financial means to deal with the crisis. The eurozone was also lacking a bailout mechanism for member-states and a potential Greek default would have threated the existence of the whole monetary union, since most of the Greek bonds were in the hands of German and French banks. Therefore, under these stressful conditions a solution was invented. Going beyond the official European Union (EU) treaties and institutions, the European Commission, the European Central Bank (ECB; the ECB issues the euro) and the International Monetary Fund (IMF) formed a Troika that lent an enormous amount of money to Greece. In return the Greek government had to implement harsh budget cuts in public expenditure and guide a rapid and deep transformation of the Greek economy through extensive privatizations and lowering of wages.

Notes for this chapter begin on page 108.

The effects of this memorandum of understanding (MoU), as it was called, between the Troika and the Greek government were devastating for the Greek economy. In the 2009–13 period Greece lost 25 percent of its GDP, unemployment rose to over 25 percent, and the public debt as a percentage of the GDP increased to over 175 percent. In contrast to the initial aim of the first MoU, Greece could not return to international capital markets for refinancing its debt. Thus, a second MoU followed in 2012 with the same economic policies as conditions for the bailout. Then a third MoU with again the same austerity and countercyclical policies was signed in 2015. In the summer of 2017 Greece was still excluded from the international markets and the Greek government agreed to continue austerity and budget cuts until at least 2020.

The main figures of the Greek economy resemble those of the Great Depression of the 1930s or those of a country in wartime. Consequently, the effects in the Greek society were also devastating, at least for a considerable part of it. The rates of relative and extreme poverty skyrocketed. In 2012 there were over 1 million households where none of the members of the household was employed. Many more households face difficulties in paying their bank loans and/or their mortgages, their taxes, and even their electricity and water bills (Sakellaropoulos 2014).

It is only because of philanthropic organizations, solidarity organizations, nongovernmental organizations (NGOs), public charities organized by the Greek Orthodox Church, and the municipal authorities that phenomena of famine are not apparent in the streets of the Greek cities. Unlike the 1930s, contemporary states are in a better position to deal with the extreme consequences of economic crises. We also have to bear in mind that Greece belonged to—and still belongs to—the cohort of the most advanced economies in the world. The economic crisis has certainly had negative effects, but it neither has equally affected everybody nor has it turned Greece into a failed state.

Many Greek business managed to survive the crisis. The Greek middle class was weakened, but it still represents a sizeable segment of the population. In contrast, those in the lower social strata and the working class endured the most severe losses; they face a continuous threat to their lifestyles and their standards of living. It is these economic and social transformations that have triggered the realignment of the political system we will examine in this chapter.

However, our central argument is that the economic crisis only triggered the changes in the Greek political system, but did not cause them. In our understanding the Greek political system changed drastically because of the massive political and social anti-memorandum protests of the period after 2009. Against the backdrop of a series of mass protest events,

and through the conflicts and the coalitions that occurred inside the protest camp, the contemporary alignment of the Greek political forces has
formed.

Protest and Politics

The severe economic crisis of the Greek state and the spiral of anti-austerity mobilizations that followed have deeply affected the political regime
of the country. Within just a few years, the basic features of the Greek
political arena that had been stable for over three decades have changed
drastically, altering both voting patterns and the status quo of political
actors and their challengers, both inside and outside of parliament.

Although economic factors had been neglected in the contentious politics literature of the past two decades, economic and political contention
has more recently returned in social movement discussions, initially in
regard to defensive protests against neoliberal policies in Latin America
(Almeida 2007, 2010). Economic change and variation affect collective action in one of two ways: either by shaping responses to political threats
and opportunities, or by constituting themselves as significant threats and
opportunities (Kousis and Tilly 2005: 7).

Most scholars of social movements define opportunities either as signals to social or political actors to mobilize (Tarrow 1996: 54) or as the
probability that social protest actions will lead to success in achieving the
desired outcome (Goldstone and Tilly 2001: 182). In Goldstone and Tilly's
conceptualization, threats are not the exact opposite of opportunities but
they are divided into two components: (1) a general threat, or exposure to
a set of harms, and (2) a collective action threat, or the cost a social group
must incur if it gets active or that it expects to suffer if it remains inactive
(Goldstone and Tilly 2001: 183; Kousis and Tilly 2005: 3).

The Greek case is arguably a case witnessing transformation in both
contentious and conventional politics. Transnational economic change, a
deep global recession, and a deep national economic crisis have destabilized the political regime of the country, and they have created opportunities and especially threats that have mobilized various social and political
actors more frequently during the past years. These actors aim either to
ameliorate the impacts of the austerity measures and delay the structural
reforms, or to protect themselves from the burdens of the crisis.

The contention in Greece does not only involve demonstrations, strikes,
and riots but also conventional politics in the form of polarized electoral
campaigns, party splits, and political realignments. Elections and social
movements are the two major forms of political conflict and political par-

ticipation in democratic systems (Goldstone 2003; Meyer and Tarrow 1998) but their interactions have seldom been specified in a systematic way (McAdam and Tarrow 2010, 2013). Most relevant studies either give the party system a key role in determining whether and how social movements mobilize (e.g., Kriesi et al. 1995) or do not mention elections as an important factor of movement activity (e.g., McAdam [1982] 1999; Tilly 1978). However, as McAdam and Tarrow have recently argued, "Few citizens are deeply engaged in the party system as such. For most people, it is the proximate influence of the electoral *campaign*—and not the party system—that provides signals that guide them on public policy issues, that tells them how to judge the political elite, and that identifies potential coalition partners. Conversely, elections are the occasions on which parties are made aware of the presence and strength of social movements and can change course in order to appeal to these constituencies" (emphasis as in original; McAdam and Tarrow 2010: 533).

In short, on the one hand elections could be used as a protest tactic when protest groups engage in proactive and reactive electoral mobilization, and on the other hand, longer-term changes in electoral regimes affect the patterns of protest mobilization and demobilization (McAdam and Tarrow 2013: 328). Kriesi (2014) also links contentious reactions in the direct-democratic and protest arena and the public's electoral reaction, and emphasizes the need to pay equal attention to both.

Especially in times of economic recession when the economy is more likely to dominate other issue concerns (Singer 2011) one of the first signs of popular discontent is drastic shifts in voting patterns (Beissinger and Sasse 2014; Bermeo and Bartels 2014a; Kriesi 2014). Economic voting is more easily traced when the political conjuncture allows voters to clearly attribute responsibility for economic performance to the government and to specific governmental political parties (Duch and Stevenson 2008; Powell and Whitten 1993). In such cases, Kriesi (2014) argues that, depending on the party system, disaffected voters might turn to established opposition parties or opt for new challengers in the party system, who typically adopt populist appeals—in other words, the new populist right in Western Europe. However, in the face of deep recession, austerity cuts, and severe job losses, discontent voters could reinforce the exit hypotheses by (1) rejecting all mainstream parties, the established political elites, or the political class, or (2) turning against all political parties—in other words, abstaining from voting (Kriesi 2014: 300)

A significant point we want to make here is that it is analytically preferable to distinguish between political and social protests on the one side and social movements on the other. Protest is defined by Karl Dieter Opp "as joint (i.e., collective) action of individuals aimed at achieving their goals by influencing decisions of a target" (2009: 38) whereas a protest group is a collectivity of actors who want to achieve their shared goals by influencing decisions of a target (Opp 2009: 41). These definitions are obviously referring to political protests and political protest groups. That means there are several protests—joint action of individuals aimed at achieving their goals—that are not inherently political. They are apolitical not because their claims do not have political implications, but, on the contrary, simply because some protestors do not aim at influencing the decisions of a specific target, either because this is their will or because the target in question is not that specific and personalized. We could label these protests as social protests. It is obvious that every political protest is social too, but every social protest is not necessarily political in the narrow use of the term.

In addition, both political and social protests can lead to or be amplifications of a social movement, but they do not themselves constitute a social movement. According to Tilly (1994) and Diani (1992), a social movement requires some time to grow and develop, some collective identity making, a lot of collective action framing, and a growing sense of solidarity among its adherents. A political or a social protest might possess these qualities but certainly also might not; that is why it is better to distinguish between protests and social movements.

It seems to us that in Greece during the 2010–17 period there were plenty of anti-austerity and anti-memorandum social and political protests, but it is harder to claim that an anti-memorandum social movement as such developed. Rather, especially for the period prior to the January 2015 elections, there was an impressive series of large anti-austerity and anti-memorandum protests that constitute an anti-austerity campaign (Diani and Kousis 2014; Kousis 2016).

Thus, this chapter aims to (1) analyze and discuss large protest events (LPEs) related to the Greek financial crisis and their impact on the political system, and (2) understand and illustrate the diversity of actors and goals inside the Greek anti-austerity campaign. In the following sections we will present our research approach, based mainly on LPE and claim analysis, and then we will analyze the main features and patterns that characterize the Greek anti-austerity campaign.

Research Approach: Large Protest Events and Claims, a National Campaign

This section will analyze and discuss LPEs related to the Greek financial crisis and their impact on the political regime. While protest events depict one level of contention, the data set of forty-nine LPEs found in the 2010–16 period in Greece comprises an anti-austerity campaign. A campaign consists of a higher level of contention involving whole populations engaged in wider struggles; a campaign is defined as "sustained, organized public efforts making collective claims on target authorities," constituting one element (of three) of a social movement (Tarrow 2008: 229; Tilly 2004: 3). As Tilly noted, "Unlike a one-time petition, declaration, or mass meeting, a campaign extends beyond any single event—although social movements often include petitions, declarations, and mass meetings. A campaign always links at least three parties: a group of self-designated claimants, some object(s) of claims, and a public of some kind. The claims may target governmental officials, but the "authorities" in question can also include owners of property, religious functionaries, and others whose actions (or failures to act) significantly affect the welfare of many people" (Tilly 2004: 4).

The study of LPEs is especially significant for periods of *"thickened history* [when] the pace of challenging events quickens to the point that it becomes practically impossible to comprehend them and they come to constitute an increasingly significant part of their own causal structure" (emphasis in original; Beissinger 2002: 27).

Given the focus on the national campaign as well as the high frequency of contentious events during this thickened period, choosing the LPEs as the unit of analysis facilitates the systematic tracing of all key events and synchronized actions at the national level; these events and actions constitute a national anti-memorandum and anti-austerity campaign sparked by neoliberal adjustment and austerity policies in Southern European countries. The campaign mainly involved demonstration marches and national general strikes with claims against the Troika's MoU and state-imposed austerity measures. From February 2010 to February 2016 it encompassed forty-nine LPEs sharing the following features:[1]

1. High numbers of participants (minimum 5,000—maximum 500,000)
2. High number of parallel and synchronized actions
3. Focus on national level claims challenging the Troika MoU and government austerity policies
4. Broad, cross-class coalitions involving a large number of groups and the general public
5. Based in Athens's Constitution Square, addressing the Parliament
6. Paralleled by smaller protests in cities and towns across the country with the same claims

These LPEs were widely covered by national and transnational media, depicting the discursive content of claims-making, the repertoire of related actions, the embeddedness of movement groups in multi-organizational fields, the relations between opportunities and mobilization, as well as other dimensions of public sphere issues (Koopmans 2007; Kousis 1999). The LPE-claims approach created for this analysis draws from protest event, protest-case, as well as political claims analysis and uses national newspaper and alternative electronic media reports to code information on economic and political claims (Koopmans and Statham 1999; Kousis 1998; Rucht et al. 1998; Tilly 1978).

Thus, as in previous periods of thickened history, the best strategy is a blanketing strategy (Beissinger 1998: 290–300) using multiple available sources in order to enrich the data set. Therefore, five major sources were selected: *Eleutherotypia* (quality paper of the center-left), leftist *Rizospastis* (paper of the Communist Party of Greece, or KKE), and *Augi* (paper of the Coalition of the Radical Left, or SYRIZA) as well as the alternative e-media sites Indymedia and realdemocracy.gr (which included minutes of meetings and referenda). They were supplemented by other Greek national news sources, including *To Vima, Ta Nea, E Kathimerini, Epochi,* tvxs.gr, international news sources (the *Guardian,* Reuters, BBC, and blogs such as iskra.gr, as well as the official sites of the unions).

Main Features of the Campaign

Based on the mentions drawn from 520 articles, these are the main features:

- Thirty-two of the forty-nine LPEs were mainly called and organized by the two big confederations of trade unions in Greece (the General Confederation of Greek Workers, or GSEE and the Civil Servants' Confederation, or ADEDY). Most of the times these LPEs were general strikes accompanied by big marches in Athens and other major Greek cities.
- Nine were carried out on dates commemorating the following: (1) Greece's refusal to allow Axis forces to enter Greece on 28 October 1940, beginning the country's participation in World War II; (2) the Polytechnic student uprising against the military dictatorship on 17 November 1973; (3) the unprovoked fatal shooting of fifteen-year-old Alexis Grigoropoulos by a police officer in the center of Athens on 6 December 2008.
- Two were part of transnational action days: one following the Occupy movement on October 15, 2011, and a second on the first anti-austerity strike by European unions across member-states on 14 November 2012.[2]

- Eight were associated with the Greek Indignados (also called the Aganaktismenoi) Constitution Square occupations in the summer of 2011. Two of the Indignados LPEs overlap with general strikes and trade union's demonstrations in the square, which was also the main site of Indignados protest.
- Finally, two were called and organized in early 2016 by groups and associations of lawyers, doctors, other freelance professionals, and farmers.

The above analysis of LPEs clearly demonstrates the crucial role of big trade unions in calling numerous general strikes, and thus providing the space for a sustained anti-austerity mobilization. GSEE and ADEDY are officially recognized social partners that participate in the national dialogue on industrial relations. Since wage-cuts, diminishing labor rights, and privatizations were among the main prerequisites of all bailout packages and the subsequent MoUs between the Troika and all Greek governments (with their effect of worsening working conditions), it was public and private sector labor unions that were among the major organizers of resistance. Besides labor mobilization, our data shows that only the Greek Indignados were capable of calling and coordinating LPEs by themselves. But Indignados mobilization was a short-lived phenomenon in Greece.

A closer look at the data also reveals the importance of the political parties of the Greek left in the mounting of the LPEs. Most of the LPEs were called by GSEE and ADEDY, but numerous other organizations and groups participated, and some of them were actually among the main organizers. These other organizations and groups were mainly the political parties of the left (KKE, SYRIZA, ANTARSYA [Front of the Greek Anticapitalist Left], and later LAE [the Popular Unity party that split from SYRIZA]), groups that were formed during and for the Indignados protest, a coordination of independent primary unions, and a constellation of anarchist groups. In table 4.1 we can see the times and the percentage of appearances of each main organization/group in the forty-nine LPEs.

The presence of the political parties and organizations of the left in the anti-austerity campaign is constant. These parties either coorganized many of the LPEs or actively supported them by mobilizing their members throughout the campaign. The KKE, which enjoys the highest mobilization capacity, was present in all the events except for those initiated by the Indignados in 2011, because the party disagreed ideologically and politically with the Indignados master frame. ANTARSYA was even more present in the LPEs since its members supported and participated in the Indignados events, and it was absent—or, more accurately, it was not recorded as a primary actor—only from a few general strikes in 2013–14.

Table 4.1. Participation of Organizations and Groups in 49 Large Protest Events, 2010–15

Group	Participation in Number of LPEs	Percent Participation in the Total 49 LPEs
GSEE	30	61.2
ADEDY	32	65.3
PAME[a]	31	63.2
Coordination of Primary Unions[b]	16	32.6
KKE	37	75.5
ANTARSYA	38	77.5
SYRIZA	31	63.2
LAE	7	14.2
Indignados	9	18.3
Anarchist groups	18	36.7

a. All-Workers Militant Front (PAME) is KKE's fraction in trade unionism.
b. The Coordination of Primary Unions is an initiative of several sectoral and company unions that mobilize independently from GSEE. They accuse GSEE of governmental unionism, and they are more prone to radical unionism and anticapitalist goals.

SYRIZA was actually the main champion of all protests in Greece and not only of those associated with the LPEs, until the summer of 2015 when SYRIZA's government (which came into power in January 2015) made a compromise with the Troika and eventually became itself the target of anti-austerity protests. After this point in 2015, the newly formed party LAE took SYRIZA's place and continued the mobilization against austerity cuts and neoliberal reforms associated with the new bailout package. Finally, throughout the 2010–16 period the presence of radical unions and anarchist groups was also visible, at least in some LPEs.

In short, private and public sector union confederations (GSEE and ADEDY) called the general strikes, but because of Greek workers' widespread distrust of GSEE and ADEDY, and the accusations toward them for governmental unionism (Vogiatzoglou 2014), it was the active support political parties and groups of the left that helped the campaign to grow in numbers (Kanellopoulos and Kostopoulos 2013) to diffuse across the country (Kousis 2016) and to hold on for a long time (Kousis and Kanellopoulos 2014). Even at the Indignados' protests a closer look reveals the same trend—most of the Indignados organizers due to dual membership belonged at the same time to left-wing political parties and groups, and this dual involvement helped the spreading of protest (Kanellopoulos et al. 2017; Stavrou 2011).

Turning to the political claims of the LPEs, the contenders demanded that the wealthy be taxed, jobs created, and social welfare (health and education) provided. They also demanded the resignation of those politicians responsible for the crisis, the end of privatizations, and the annulment of the externally imposed austerity policies. The major claims of the protesting groups were against the unprecedented austerity laws and measures, which included dramatic wage and pension decreases, tax increases, privatization of public enterprises, and changes in public education, in addition to other neoliberal structural reforms. The protests' demands stress serious concerns about the impacts of these austerity measures, especially those regarding the economy, society, sovereignty, and democracy (Diani and Kousis 2014; Kanellopoulos and Kostopoulos 2014; Kousis 2015).

Protesters viewed the consecutive Greek governments of the 2010–16 period (including the parliament and the police force) as their primary target, followed by the European Commission. The second targeted group in importance included the international organizations—in other words, the Troika, IMF, the European Central Bank, and foreign banks. The third challenged group included financial institutions and credit agencies, the Greek elite, and local government agencies. Less frequently mentioned were capital markets and the G-20/G-8. Finally, in one-fifth of the events Germany was targeted, especially in the second year after June 2011 (Kousis 2014).

Out of this multitude of political and economic claims and demands, the single most common and enduring feature was the continuous and persistent resistance against the austerity cuts and the neoliberal reforms contained in the bailout packages and in the MoUs of consecutive Greek governments with the Troika.

As we can see in figure 4.1 this resistance movement up to the present can be broken into three distinct phases:

1. The first and most spectacular in terms of numbers and outcomes was the period February 2010–February 2012. During this period we observe the most LPEs (twenty-four) and especially the most massive and contentious LPEs. The protest campaign came to a temporary halt at its peak, following the huge demonstration of more than half a million people on 12 February 2012, after which both parliamentary parties of the left (KKE and SYRIZA) prioritized their electoral campaigns for the May 2012 general elections over their participation in street politics.
2. The second phase started in September 2012 after the formation of a coalition government between New Democracy (ND), Panhellenic Socialist Movement (PASOK), and Democratic Left, a split toward

the center from SYRIZA in 2010 (DIMAR), where SYRIZA, after its spectacular electoral growth, became the second-largest party in Greek parliament. LPEs evolved again around GSEE and ADEDY general strikes, but they never reached the numbers and the climax of the first phase. Many activists describe this phase as a period of assignment. The Greek political system had been based on the alteration in power between the two biggest political parties in parliament (consistently ND and PASOK in the past). SYRIZA had become the second-strongest party and had the obvious potential to become the first (Mavris 2012). Thus, a large part of the anti-austerity movement had assigned SYRIZA, the main political champion of the anti-memorandum campaign, the mission of reversing austerity and neoliberal reforms on its expected rise to power (Kouvelakis 2016). The last LPE of this phase occurred in December 2014, just before the early general elections of January 2015 that marked the end of ND and PASOK rule.

3. When SYRIZA along with Independent Greeks (ANEL; an anti-memorandum far-right party that split from ND in 2012) formed a coalition government in January 2015, the anti-austerity LPEs ceased to exist since the government was trying to negotiate with the Troika. But as soon as the SYRIZA government receded from its promises and agreed on a bailout package with new austerity cuts and neoliberal reforms in the summer of 2015, the anti-austerity campaign started again. After the early elections of September 2015, from November 2015 until February 2016 five LPEs were mounted, organized by GSEE and ADEDY, and supported by the KKE and the extra-parliamentary left, with the additional participation of new social groups like middle-class freelance professionals and farmers. This third phase of the campaign could be characterized as the phase of demobilization and frustration. The LPEs were not as massive as those of the first phase and far less diffused geographically. Even when in early summer 2017 the SYRIZA and ANEL government imposed via the parliament new cuts in pensions and new heavy taxation that prolonged the austerity policies until at least 2020, the protests were very weak and the anti-austerity campaign seemed to be fading away.

SYRIZA had advanced throughout the 2010–15 period an easy anti-austerity rhetoric that allowed the party to dominate in the protest campaign. This rhetoric also allowed for coalition building with broad segments of the population across the political spectrum (Kanellopoulos et al. 2017). As a result, the radical-left SYRIZA was able to rise to power and formed a coalitional government with the far-right ANEL. The anti-

Figure 4.1. Number of Participants in Large Protest Events, 2010–16

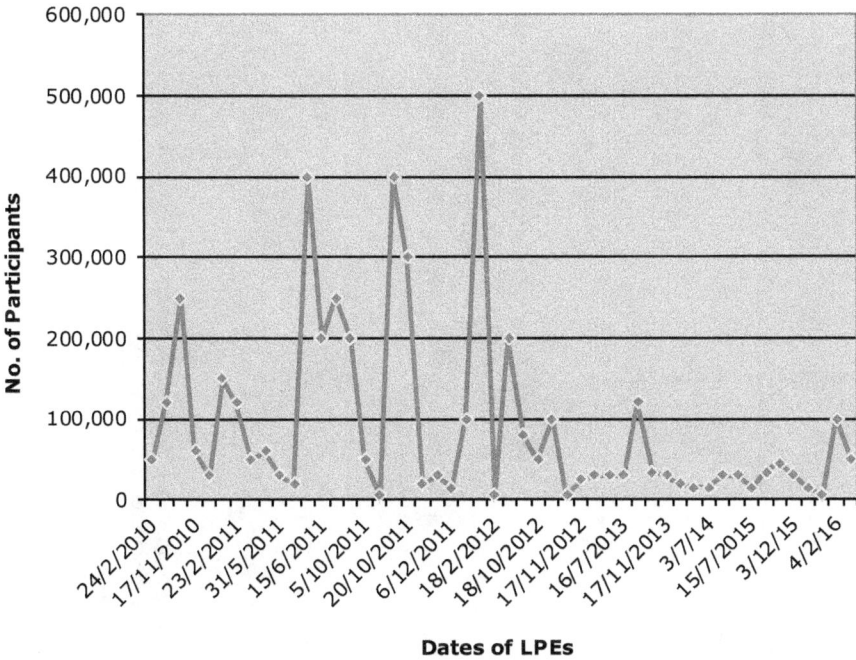

Dates of LPEs

austerity campaign was largely based on the—what proved to be—illusionary rhetoric that SYRIZA's government could tear apart the MoUs and Greece could remain a member of the eurozone, or that SYRIZA's government could unilaterally erase the public debt. Once in power, SYRIZA's political and ideological current inside the anti-austerity campaign remained without proponents and without a central narrative.

The politics of austerity are ineradicably blurred with the politics of protest in all three phases of the campaign, creating a similar pattern that causes and contributes to the inconstancy of the Greek political system. Massive protests had occurred many times in Greece after the transition to democracy in 1974. These protests had caused some minor changes, but they had never destabilized the political system. The combination of the economic crisis, the policies selected to overcome the crisis, and the opposition to this policy selection is what destabilized the Greek political system.

In table 4.2 we try to depict this pattern in numbers. We present the austerity policies and neoliberal reforms imposed by the Troika and consecutive Greek governments year by year 2010–16. In columns 3 and 4 we

Table 4.2. Economic, Political, and Social Aspects of the Greek Crisis

Year	Austerity Policies and Measures	Percent Change of GDP [a]	Percent Unemployed	Percent Trust in Greek Government [b]	Number of MPs Dismissed	Number of New Parties [c]	Number of LPEs
2010	First and second stability packages, first MoU	-5.5	12.7	25	3		3
	Multipurpose Act			21	1	2 DIMAR (DESY)	3
2011	Intermediate program	-9.1	17.9	16	1	1 (Arma Politon)	9
	Multipurpose Act			8	1	1 (Eleutheroi Polites)	7
2012	Multipurpose Act, PSI (Private Sector Involvement), second MoU	-7.3	24.4	6	45	2 (ANEL, Demiourgia Xana)	2
	Intermediate program			7	8		6
2013	Multipurpose Act	-3.2	27.5	9	17		2
	Multipurpose Act			10			4
2014		0.7	26.5	16		1 (Potami)	2
				11			3
2015	Third MoU Multipurpose Act	-0.3	25.0	37	1	1 (KIDESO)	0
				16	44	1 (LAE)	4
2016	Multipurpose Act				2		4

a. Data for changes in the Greek GDP and the rate of unemployment in Greece stems from www.statistics.gr/documents/20181/1518565/greek_economy_19_02_2016.pdf (accessed 26 February 2016) and from www.ec.europa.eu/economy_finance?eu/countries/greece_en.htm (accessed 26 February 2016).

b. Date for the trust in the Greek government stems from the Eurobarometer reports http://ec.europa.eu/public_opinion/archives/eb_arch_en.htm (accessed 24 June 2016).

c. DIMAR is a split of SYRIZA in 2010; Democratic Coalition (DESY) is a split of ND in 2010; Citizen's Chariot (Arma Politon) is a split of PASOK in 2011; Free Citizens (Eleutheroi Polites) is a split of PASOK in 2011; ANEL is a split of ND in 2012; Creation Again (Demiourgia Xana) and River (Potami) are newly found liberal parties; Democratic Socialists (KIDESO) is a split of PASOK in 2014; LAE is a split of SYRIZA in 2015.

observe the evolution of the Greek GDP and the Greek unemployment rate, respectively. The Greek economy was already in deep recession from 2008, which contributed to the de facto bankruptcy in 2010, but the rescue packages that have been implemented since then obviously did not manage to put it back on track. In fact, one could plausibly argue that these exact measures and conditions contained in the rescue packages caused the further deterioration of virtually all the figures of Greek economy (Featherstone 2011; Flassbeck and Lapavitsas 2015; Lapavitsas 2012; Matsaganis 2011; Varoufakis 2015). Although proponents of economic austerity might disagree with the certainty of that assessment, certainly the lived experience of these measures for the average person directly links the MoU passed with the continuing decline of the economy, and this experiential connection was part of the discourse of the protests.

The legislative passage of every austerity package was fiercely opposed in the streets through the LPEs (see column 7). In parallel, opposition was also occurring inside the national parliament where MPs belonging to all governing parties in all three phases broke ranks with their leadership and voted against the austerity measures their parties were supporting (see column 6). Eventually the crisis of political representation led to an overwhelming mistrust in Greek government, and the continuous formation of new political parties (see column 7). The findings of the regular Eurobarometer are devastating (see column 5): trust in the PASOK government fell from 25 percent to 8 percent when it imposed the first MoU, the caretaker Papademos government in early 2011 (PASOK with ND and LAOS) was mistrusted from the beginning, and the coalitional Samaras government (ND, PASOK, and DIMAR) was never trusted by more than 16 percent of Greek citizens. In striking contrast, the trust figures were high for the first Tsipras coalition government (SYRIZA and ANEL) in the first semester of 2015 (37 percent when this government was elected with the promise to stop austerity). These figures dropped sharply when the SYRIZA and ANEL government finally compromised with the Troika and imposed a new austerity and neoliberal reforms package (from 37% to 16 percent) in the autumn of 2015.

The Greek debt crisis drastically changed the political system. However, as this research shows, this was possible only through the active intervention of an impressive series of mass social and political protests. The tense interaction between challenger and challenged groups caused major realignments in the Greek political system, and the successive mobilizations against the austerity packages internally polarized the Greek political parties. As is shown in table 4.2, the pattern of the Greek political crisis is as follows: the government passes a package of austerity measures, strikes and demonstrations occur (often led by the political parties of the left opposing the measures), some governmental MPs do not back the measures, recession ensues, unemployment rates rise, distrust of the wider public toward the political system grows, new austerity measures are proposed, new demonstrations occur, new MP losses result, and so on.

The Greek political system was a predominantly two-party system (when PASOK and ND jointly claimed around 80 percent of the votes in the national elections) with few other parties represented in the parliament until 2009. After the earthquake elections of May 2012, the Greek political system was transformed into an inconstant system with fragile governmental coalitions and many political parties gaining (and losing) parliamentary representation (Mavris 2012; Teperoglou and Tsatsanis 2014; Mylonas this volume). Table 4.3 shows the changes in participation for the national elections before and after the crisis.

The three phases of the Greek anti-austerity campaign analyzed above coincide to a large extent with the electoral cycles of the same period, testifying both for the interaction between protest and elections and for the economic voting hypothesis. A closer look at figure 4.1 reveals the role of elections as crucial intervening factors in the anti-austerity campaign. At the peaks of the campaign (high number of LPEs in continuous months with massive participation) there were no elections (figure 4.2).

To the contrary, the valleys of the campaign coincide perfectly with election periods. As a matter of fact, eight elections have been held in Greece since 2010, with austerity and the positioning toward the MoUs as the main issues in all of them (four national elections, one election for the European parliament, two regional and municipal elections, and one referendum).

Table 4.3. Participation in the Greek National Elections, 2004–15

National Election Years (participation percent)	Percent Change
2004–7 (76.50–74.15%)	−3.00
2007–09 (74.15–70.95 percent)	−4.31
2009–12 May (70.95–65.10 percent)	−8.25
2012 May–2012 June (65.10–62.47 percent)	−4.04
2012–15 January (62.10–63.94 percent)	+1.84
2015 January–2015 September (63.94–56.16 percent)	−7.78

Source: "Results of National Elections," Hellenic Republic Ministry of Interior, http://www.ypes.gr/el/Elections/NationalElections/Results/.

Figure 4.2. Number of Large Protest Events and Elections per Month

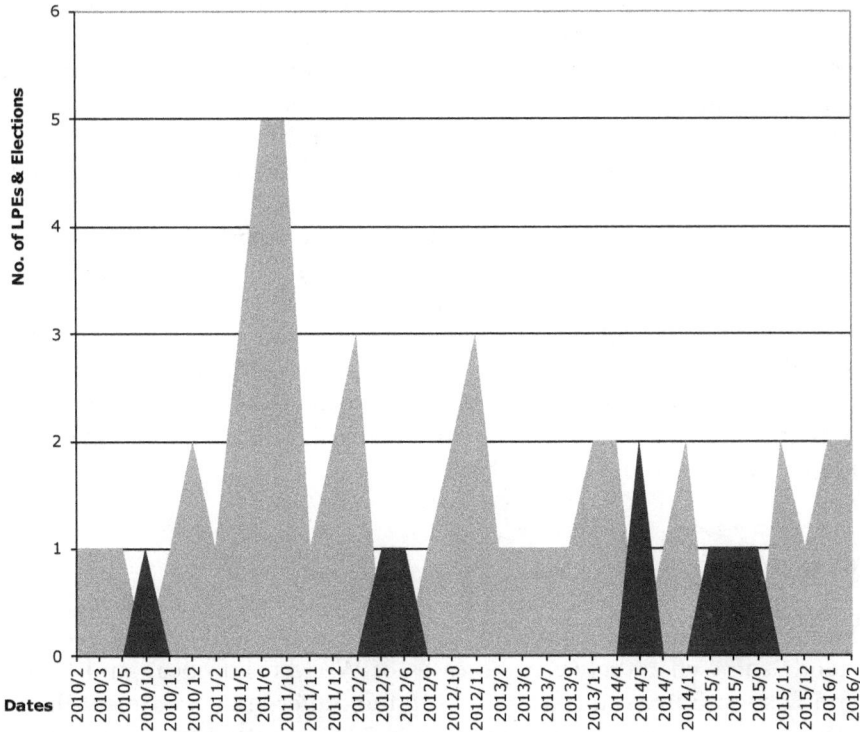

The first phase of the campaign (2010–12) was temporarily interrupted by the regional and municipal elections of October 2010, which were mainly won by the governing PASOK forces (Verney 2012).[3] One year later, in the autumn of 2011 and at the peak of the anti-austerity campaign, George Papandreou attempted to regain legitimacy by calling a referendum. However, many of his party leaders disagreed and Papandreou's government was overthrown, creating a broad crisis of political legitimacy and a new peak of the insurgency in the streets. A caretaker government was formed by PASOK and ND that agreed on a second MoU with the Troika. But this agreement led to the parliamentary disintegration of both PASOK and ND and the eventual call for elections. In effect it took two national elections in a span of forty days in May and June 2012 for the political system to stabilize and the protest movement to demobilize. The old political forces (ND and PASOK) managed to form a coalitional government (along with DIMAR), while at the same time SYRIZA moved to the position of the main oppositional party. LPEs started over again in the autumn of 2012, but with a lower level of tension and less participation, and were again effectively interrupted by the dual elections of May 2014 (regional and municipal as well as European elections). In 2015 the period between the national elections of January and the referendum[4] of July was without anti-austerity LPEs because an anti-memorandum coalition was in office. When this same coalition turned pro-memorandum, protest resumed and it took another early national election in September to tame it.

The new period is characterized by (1) the tremendous rise of SYRIZA from a small left party struggling to retain its parliamentary representation to the biggest oppositional party in 2012 and the biggest Greek party in 2015, though not as big and hegemonic as PASOK used to be (Kouvelakis 2016); (2) the electoral advance of far-right parties, from the overtly neo-Nazi Golden Dawn to the nationalist ANEL;[5] (3) the formation of fragile coalition governments, and (4) the significant drop in the participation rate in elections (see table 4.3).

Conclusion

Based on the analysis above and following Kriesi (2014), the Greek case stands somewhere between the cases of Western European and Central and Eastern European countries. Both the center-left government that attempted to impose austerity measures in 2009 and the center-right government that imposed austerity in 2010–12 faced a severe electoral punishment, as in most Western European cases; unlike in Western Europe, though, the political system changed radically. New political parties—and especially far-right parties—appeared and had an immediate success in the ballots, as in many Central and Eastern European cases. But at the same time, unlike both sets of European cases, the political parties of the left in Greece were significantly empowered. The Greek parliamentary left took advantage of its already established institutional position and, along with the Greek trade unions and many small political organizations of the extra-parliamentary left, played an important role in the mounting of the LPEs against austerity and structural adjustment policies.

Faced with the threat of bankruptcy in early 2010, the country entered the era of the MoUs and the loss of sovereignty under the Troika in a contentious manner. The Troika institutions on the one hand financed the Greek sovereign debt, but on the other dictated a series of deep reforms and rapid structural adjustments in a wide variety of policy areas (Lapavitsas et al. 2010). All the main pillars of the democratic regime were weakened: economic growth was halted, democratic deliberation was largely ignored, and even national sovereignty was called into question. And an unwilling and unprepared party system was left to rapidly reform the state and boost the economy (Kouvelakis 2011). Meanwhile Greece lost one-fifth of its GDP in less than five years, unemployment rose to an EU record of 27.5 percent, and poverty and social exclusion rates also hit record numbers (Sakellaropoulos 2014). Many Greeks started moving abroad in search for employment opportunities and the trust in national and EU political institutions hit zero numbers (Zambarloukou and Kousis 2014).

In an environment where even national independence and popular sovereignty were jeopardized, the massive anti-austerity mobilizations acted as the spark that set in motion the processes of deep transformation of the political system. SYRIZA, a party of Eurocommunist origins, managed in the 2012 general election to become the main oppositional party, boosting the hopes of many protesters that as a future government it would stop austerity. The electoral path was seemingly prioritized and the anti-austerity protest campaign was slowed down. Eventually in January 2015 SYRIZA rose to power but proved incapable to alter austerity policies and soon agreed on a new MoU with the Troika institutions containing a new round of austerity cuts, privatizations, and neoliberal reforms. As an indirect result of SYRIZA's compromise, the anti-austerity campaign was revitalized in the winter of 2015–16, but to a much lesser degree.

Through the consecutive LPEs, responsibility was clearly attributed by the protesters to the ruling political parties that imposed austerity measures and as a result the economic voting hypothesis was confirmed: mainstream parties were punished in elections and parties with populist appeals came to the fore (see also Stavrakakis and Katsambekis 2014). At the same time, Kriesi's (2014) exit hypothesis seems also to be confirmed. The participation rate to elections dropped significantly while many disillusioned citizens turn to new independents or anti-parties.

In times of crisis social movement campaigns and electoral campaigns are in close connection. In Greece, LPEs resisting austerity and neoliberal policies destabilized an already inconstant political system and brought to the fore political forces like SYRIZA. But in the meantime, through the consecutive elections the anti-austerity campaign was gradually demobilized. SYRIZA rose to power due in part to the mass anti-austerity protests of 2010–12, but in the absence of tense protest it soon resumed its institutional role as a parliamentary and governing party. At the same time, the endless electoral rounds eventually increased political apathy.

Kostas Kanellopoulos is adjunct lecturer at the Hellenic Open University, postdoctoral researcher at the University of Crete, and general secretary of the Hellenic Political Science Association. He has taught at the Higher Technological Institutes of Piraeus and Patras, and at the Universities of Athens and Crete. His work on social movements, urban riots, anti-austerity campaigns, and contemporary political sociology has appeared in journals including *Social Movement Studies, Journal of Civil Society, Situations: Project of the Radical Imagination, Greek Sociological Review, Intersections: East European Journal of Society and Politics* and in collective volumes published by Ashgate, Palgrave, and Routledge.

Maria Kousis is professor of sociology and director of the Centre for Research and Studies at the University of Crete. Her research centers on the socioeconomic and political dimensions of the 2008 crisis, especially in the context of the Greek–German Ministries Cooperation (GGCRISI), and the European Commission projects LIVEWHAT (FP7), TransSOL, and EURYKA (H2020). Publications include the editing (2017) of the special section of *Partecipazione e Conflitto*, "Alternative Forms of Resilience Confronting Hard Economic Times: A South European Perspective," and articles in journals including *Mobilization, Politics & Policy, Environmental Politics, American Behavioral Scientist, Theory and Society, Southern European Society and Politics,* and *Humanity & Society.*

Notes

1. It is important to note here that throughout the 2010–16 period countless protest events took place (see Rudig and Kariotis 2013; Serdedakis and Koufidi 2018) and probably some of them were indeed large (more than five thousand participants). But in our data set we include only LPEs that specifically oppose austerity policies and the MoU. These events address the Greek parliament and its members of parliament (MPs) or issues that concern the whole nation-state. Thus, the sitting in the Constitution Square, addressing the authorities at the highest national level, is crucial (Kousis 2016).
2. There were also many transnational solidarity protest events in support of the Greek anti-austerity campaign in various places in Europe and North America, but we have chosen not to include them in our sample because they were not directly addressing the Greek government, they were rather small in number of participants, and they did not coincide with the LPEs in Greece. In many countries the Occupy protests were seen as the continuation of the Indignados protests. In Greece it is difficult to support such an affinity since the Indignados protests in the summer of 2011 involved millions of people across Greece while the Occupy protests in October 2011 involved only five thousand people.
3. The pace of insurgency was also slowed down by the escalation of violence that occurred in the massive LPE of 5 May 2010, at the same day of the voting in parliament of the first MoU, when three people were killed by a Molotov bomb.

4. This constitutionally debatable referendum was called by SYRIZA's leaders in just a week's notice over the agreement of Greek citizens on the bailout package proposed by the European Commission's president Mr. Junker. Mr. Junker withdrew his proposal few days before the referendum but this did not prevent SYRIZA's government from holding the referendum and then interpreting its result.
5. Golden Dawn never called or openly participated in any LPE against austerity. Its electoral rise could be associated with the rise of criminality in big cities and the subsequent evolution of a racist frame (Kandylis and Kavoulakos 2011). However, many people with far-right ideas were present in anti-austerity protests, especially those associated with the Greek Indignados (Petropoulos 2014).

References

Almeida, Paul. 2007. "Defensive Mobilization: Popular Movements against Economic Adjustment Policies in Latin America." *Latin American Perspectives* 34(3): 123–39.
———. 2010. "Social Movement Partyism: Collective Action and Oppositional Political Parties." In *Strategic Alliances: Coalition Building and Social Movements,* edited by N. Van Dyke and H. McCammon, 170–96. Minneapolis: University of Minnesota Press.
Beissinger, Mark. 1998. "Event Analysis in Transitional Societies: Protest Mobilization in the former Soviet Union." In Rucht, Koopmans, and Neidhardt, *Acts of Dissent,* 284–316.
———. 2002. *Nationalist Mobilization and the Collapse of the Soviet State.* Cambridge: Cambridge University Press.
Beissinger, Mark, and Gwendolyn Sasse. 2014. "An End to 'Patience'? The Great Recession and Economic Protest in Eastern Europe." In Bermeo and Bartels, *Mass Politics in Tough Times,* 334–70.
Bermeo, Nancy, and Larry Bartels. 2014a. "Mass Politics in Tough Times." In Bermeo and Bartels, *Mass Politics in Tough Times,* 1–39.
———, eds. 2014b. *Mass Politics in Tough Times: Opinions, Votes, and Protest in the Great Recession.* Oxford: Oxford University Press.
Diani, Mario. 1992. "The Concept of Social Movement." *Sociological Review* 40(1): 1–25.
Diani, Mario, and Maria Kousis. 2014. "The Duality of Claims and Events: The Greek Campaign against Troika's Memoranda and Austerity, 2011–2012." *Mobilization* 19(4): 387–404.
Duch, Raymond, and Randolph Stevenson. 2008. *The Economic Vote: How Political and Economic Institutions Condition Election Results.* Cambridge: Cambridge University Press.
Featherstone, Kevin. 2011. "The Greek Sovereign Debt Crisis and EMU: A Failing State in a Skewed Regime." *Journal of Common Market Studies* 49(2): 193–217.
Flassbeck, Heiner, and Costas Lapavitsas. 2015. *Against the Troika: Crisis and Austerity in the Eurozone.* London: Verso.
Goldstone, Jack. 2003. "Introduction: Bridging Institutionalized and Non-Institutionalized Politics." In *States, Parties, and Social Movements,* edited by Jack A. Goldstone, 1–24. Cambridge: Cambridge University Press.
Goldstone, Jack, and Charles Tilly. 2001. "Threat (and Opportunity): Popular Action and State Response in the Dynamics of Contentious Action." In *Silence and Voice in the Study of Contentious Politics,* edited by Ronald Aminzade, Jack Goldstone, Doug McAdam, Elizabeth Perry, William H. Sewell Jr., Sidney Tarrow, and Charles Tilly, 179–94. Cambridge: Cambridge University Press
Kandylis, George, and Karolos Kavoulakos. 2011. "Framing Urban Inequalities: Racist Mobilization against Immigrants in Athens." *Greek Review of Social Research* (special issue) 136C: 157–76.

Kanellopoulos, Kostas, and Konstantinos Kostopoulos. 2013. "Alliance Building in the Greek Anti-austerity Campaign 2010–2012." Paper presented at the 7th ECPR General Conference, Bordeaux, France, 4–7 September 2013.

———. 2014. "The Major Organizations/groups behind the Greek Anti-austerity Campaign. Repertoires of Action and Political Claims." Paper presented at the 8th ECPR General Conference, Glasgow, Scotland, 3–6 September 2014.

Kanellopoulos, Kostas, Konstantinos Kostopoulos, Dimitris Papanikolopoulos, and Vasileios Rongas. 2017. "Competing Modes of Coordination in the Greek Anti-austerity Campaign 2010–2012." *Social Movement Studies* 16(1): 101–18.

Koopmans, Ruud. 2007. "Who Inhabits the European Public Sphere? Winners and Losers, Supporters and Opponents in Europeanised Political Debates." *European Journal of Political Research* 46(2): 183–210.

Koopmans, Ruud, and Paul Statham. 1999. "Political Claims Analysis: Integrating Protest Event and Political Discourse Approaches." *Mobilization* 4(2): 203–21.

Kousis, Maria. 1998. "Protest-Case Analysis: A Methodological Approach for the Study of Grassroots Environmental Mobilizations." Working Paper Series, No. 570, Center for Research on Social Organization (CRSO). University of Michigan, Ann Arbor, May. Retrieved 18 March 2018 from http://deepblue.lib.umich.edu/bitstream/2027.42/51334/1/570.pdf.

———. 1999. "Environmental Protest Cases: The City, the Countryside, and the Grassroots in Southern Europe." *Mobilization* 4(2): 223–38.

———. 2014. "The Transnational Dimension of the Greek Protest Campaign against Troika Memoranda and Austerity Policies, 2010–2012." In *Spreading Protest: Social Movements in Times of Crisis*, edited by Donatella della Porta and Alice Mattoni, 137–70. Colchester, UK: ECPR Press.

———. 2015. "La campaña panhelénica de los memorandos y de las políticas de austeridad." In special issue "GRECIA Entre la Tragedia y la Rebellion." *Revista ÁBACO* 83/84: 38–44. Retrieved 18 March 2018 from http://www.revista-abaco.es/.

———. 2016. "The Spatial Dimensions of the Greek Protest Campaign against Troika's Memoranda and Austerity Measures, 2010–2013." In *Street Politics in the Age of Austerity: From the Indignados to Occupy*, edited by Markos Ancelovici, Pascale Dufour, and Heloise Nez, 137–70. Amsterdam: Amsterdam University Press.

Kousis, Maria, and Kostas Kanellopoulos. 2014. "Impacts of the Greek Crisis on the Contentious and Conventional Politics, 2012–2012." In Tsobanoglou and Petropoulos, *Social Impacts of the Eurozone Debt Crisis*, 443–62.g

Kousis, Maria, and Charles Tilly. 2005. "Introduction: Economic and Political Contention in Comparative Perspective." In *Economic and Political Contention in Comparative Perspective*, edited by Maria Kousis and Charles Tilly, 1–14. Boulder, CO: Paradigm.

Kouvelakis, Stathis. 2011. "The Greek Cauldron." *New Left Review*, 2nd series 72: 17–32.

———. 2016. "SYRIZA's Rise and Fall." *New Left Review*, 2nd series 97: 45–70.

Kriesi, Hanspeter. 2014. "The Political Consequences of the Economic Crisis in Europe: Electoral Punishment and Popular Protest." In Bermeo and Bartels, *Mass Politics in Tough Times*, 297–333.

Kriesi, Hanspeter, Ruud Koopmans, Jan Willem Duyvendak, and Marco Giugni, eds. 1995. *New Social Movements in Western Europe: A Comparative Analysis*. Minneapolis: University of Minnesota Press.

Lapavitsas, Costas. 2012. *Crisis in the Eurozone*. London: Verso.

Lapavitsas, Costas, Annina Kaltenbrunner, Duncan Lindo, Juan Pablo Michell, Juan Pablo Painceira, Eugenia Pires, Jeff Powell, et al. 2010. "Eurozone Crisis: Beggar Thyself and Thy Neighbour." *Journal of Balkan and Near Eastern Studies* 12(4): 321–72.

Matsaganis, Manos. 2011. "The Welfare State and the Crisis: The Case of Greece." *Journal of European Social Policy* 21(5): 501–12.

Mavris, Yiannis. 2012. "Greece's Austerity Election." *New Left Review* 76: 95–107.

McAdam, Doug. [1982] 1999. *Political Process and the Development of Black Insurgency 1930–1970.* Chicago: University of Chicago Press.

McAdam, Doug, and Sidney Tarrow. 2010. "Ballots and Barricades: On the Reciprocal Relations between Elections and Social Movements." *Perspectives on Politics* 8(2): 529–42.

———. 2013. "Social Movements and Elections: Toward a Broader Understanding of the Political Context of Contention." In *The Future of Social Movement Research,* edited by Jacquelien van Stekelenburg, Conny Roggerband, and Bert Klandermans, 325–46. Minneapolis: University of Minnesota Press.

Meyer, David, and Sidney Tarrow, eds. 1998. *The Social Movement Society: Contentious Politics for a New Century.* Lanham, MD: Rowman & Littlefield.

Opp, Karl-Dieter. 2009. *Theories of Political Protest and Social Movements: A Multidisciplinary Introduction, Critique, and Synthesis.* London: Routledge.

Petropoulos, Nicos. 2014. "A Sociopolitical Profile and The Political Impact of the Greek Indignados: An Exploratory Study." In Tsobanoglou and Petropoulos, *Social Impacts of the Eurozone Debt Crisis,* 463–519.

Powell, G. Bingham, and Guy Whitten. 1993. "A Cross-National Analysis of Economic Voting: Taking Account of the Political Context." *American Journal of Political Science* 37(2): 391–414.

Rucht, Dieter, Ruud Koopmans, and Friedrich Neidhardt, eds. 1998. *Acts of Dissent: New Developments in the Study of Protest.* New York: Rowman & Littlefield.

Rudig, Wolfgang, and Karyotis, Giorgios. 2013. "Beyond the Usual Suspects? New Participants in Anti-Austerity Protests in Greece." *Mobilization* 18(3): 313–30.

Sakellaropoulos, Spyros. 2014. *Krise kai Koinonike Diastromatose sten Ellada tou 21ou Aiona.* Athens: Topos.

Serdedakis, Nicos, and Myrsini Koufidi. 2018. "Sygrousiakos kai eklogikos kyklos stin Ellada tis krisis." *Greek Political Science Review* 44(1): 7–30.

Singer, Matthew M. 2011. "Who Says 'It's the Economy'? Cross-National and Cross-Individual Variation in the Salience of Economic Performance." *Comparative Political Studies* 44(3): 284–312.

Stavrakakis, Yiannis, and Giorgos Katsambekis. 2014. "Left-wing Populism in the European Periphery: The Case of SYRIZA." *Journal of Political Ideologies* 19(22): 119–42.

Stavrou, Achilleas. 2011. "E 'Pano Plateia' e Otan Milane oi Mazes 'Oe, oe, oe, Sekothekame ap'ton Kanape" . . . " In *Demokratia Under Construction: Apo tous dromous stes Plateies,* edited by Christos Giovanopoulos and Dimitris Mitropoulos, 31–40. Athens: Synecheia.

Tarrow, Sidney. 1996. "States and Opportunities: The Political Structuring of Social Movements." In *Comparative Perspectives on Social Movements: Political Opportunities, Mobilizing Structures and Cultural Framings,* edited by Doug McAdam, John D. McCarthy, and Mayer N. Zald, 41–61. Cambridge: Cambridge University Press.

———. 2008. "Charles Tilly and the Practice of Contentious Politics." *Social Movement Studies* 7(3): 225–46.

Teperoglou Eftichia, and Emmanouil Tsatsanis. 2014. "Dealignment, De-legitimation and the Implosion of the Two-Party System in Greece: The Earthquake Election of 6 May 2012." *Journal of Elections, Public Opinion and Parties* 24(2): 222–42.

Tilly, Charles. 1978. *From Mobilization to Revolution.* New York: Random House.

———. 1994. "Social Movements as Historically Specific Clusters of Political Performances." *Berkeley Journal of Sociology* 38: 1–29.

———. 2004. *Social Movements, 1768–2004.* London: Paradigm.

Tsobanoglou, George, and Nicholas Petropoulos, eds. 2014. *The Social Impacts of the Eurozone Debt Crisis.* Athens: Gordios Books.

Varoufakis, Yanis. 2015. *Europe after the Minotaur: Greece and the Future of Global Economy.* London: Zed Books.

Verney, Susannah. 2012. "The Eurozone's First Post-bailout Election: The 2010 Local Govern-
    ment Contest in Greece." *South European Society and Politics* 17(2): 195–216.
Vogiatzoglou, M. 2014. "Die griechische Gewerkschaftsbewegung: Protest- und Sozialbewe-
    gungen im Kontext der Austeritätspolitik." *WSI-Mitteilungen* 5: 361–68.
Zambarloukou, Stella, and Maria Kousis, eds. 2014. *Koinonikes Opseis tes Krises sten Ellada.*
    Athens: Pedio.

Chapter 5

From Boom to Bust

A Comparative Analysis of Greece and Spain
under Austerity

Björn Bremer and Guillem Vidal

Introduction

The economic crisis in Greece has been mirrored by a crisis of the political
system: not only has Greece experienced five elections in six years, but in
addition a technocratic government was installed for six months and the
traditionally bipartisan party system underwent a major transformation.
Although the economic crisis has been the deepest in Greece, it has also
reshaped political competition in other crisis-ridden countries. In Italy a
technocratic government under the leadership of Mario Monti replaced
the Berlusconi government in November 2011 and the political establishment has been undermined by the rise of the populist Five Star Movement
in the past few years. In Portugal, the Left Block obtained an unprecedented 10 percent of the vote-share in the 2015 elections and anti-austerity
parties were able to form a coalition government.[1] Even in Ireland, which
is often viewed as a poster child for austerity, the populist party Sinn Fein
dramatically gained in popularity and led large protests in 2014 and 2015
against new municipal water charges. Finally, in Spain, large-scale protests have also swept across the country in response to the economic crisis. Two new parties, Podemos and Ciudadanos, have dramatically gained
popular support, uprooting the previously stable bipartisan party system.

However, in the context of the economic turmoil in the eurozone, the
political transformations in Greece and the other crisis-ridden countries
are still ill understood (Hopkin 2015: 163).

To analyze these transformations more rigorously, we compare the experiences of living under austerity in Greece and in Spain because of the many similarities between the two countries. In both Greece and Spain, the introduction of the euro caused a large inflow of foreign credit, which left both countries vulnerable to external forces when the financial crisis created a sudden stop of liquidity. The economic conditions for the crisis, however, were mediated by the political context. Importantly, both countries suffered from institutional degradation (Royo 2014) in the precrisis years and governments and regulators failed to prevent the precrisis boom. Because clientelism and corruption allowed the Greek and Spanish elites to benefit disproportionately from the boom, these same elites had no incentive to lean against the wind and prevent economic imbalances. The windfalls from European integration tempered the political dysfunctionalities in Greece and Spain, but the drying up of foreign resources meant that the state could no longer buy off its citizens with high economic growth. Consequently, a collapse of the political order followed the collapse of the economic order. Widespread dissatisfaction with the political system and a decline in support for traditional parties presented an opportunity for new challengers. Yet, the new challengers that emerged in both countries, and the resulting changes in the party system, were different. We compare Greece and Spain according to the logic of the most similar system design to shed light on these differences.

We argue that the political transformations cannot be understood independently of the social and political dynamics behind the crisis. In other words, we attempt to link the consequences of the crisis to the political context of the countries in question and argue that these political contexts before the crisis not only contributed to the economic crisis, but also structured the political consequences. Moreover, we show that the imposition of austerity from the Troika (the International Monetary Fund [IMF], the European Commission, and the European Central Bank [ECB]) was a lot harsher and more closely monitored in Greece than in Spain. As a result, the conflict between Greece and its creditors over austerity overshadowed all other political conflicts. This allowed traditional political forces to remain at the heart of the political crisis in Greece: while New Democracy (ND) remained the right-wing pillar of the bipolar party system, Coalition of the Radical Left (SYRIZA), the main challenger party, eventually became an ideological purifier on the left that replaced the former center-left Panhellenic Socialist Movement (PASOK). In contrast, in Spain the new challenger parties also tapped into the opposition to austerity and dissatisfaction with the functioning of national democracy, but less so toward the European Union (EU). Most importantly, however, these challenger parties have recurrently emphasized their distinctiveness from the previous political order. Although the pro- versus anti-austerity conflict came to dominate politics in Greece, we argue that the division between old and new politics is key for understanding the evolution of political contestation in Spain.

The chapter proceeds in four steps. In the first section we analyze the economic and political context out of which the crisis emerged in Greece and Spain. For this purpose, we review the dominant economic explanation for the crisis and show how the political and economic context contributed to unsustainable economic developments in both countries. Next, we compare the crisis dynamics in both countries. For this purpose, we analyze the austerity measures that have been implemented in response to the crisis in Greece and Spain, and assess the economic consequences. We show that Greece had to endure a lot more austerity than Spain, which is important in order to understand the diverging political consequences. In the third section, we build on this insight to analyze these political consequences of the economic crisis. Distinguishing between a behavioral and attitudinal dimension of the political crisis, we show that there are important similarities in Greece and Spain but that the consequences of economic meltdown have been conditioned by the domestic political context and the crisis dynamics in both countries. In the final section we outline the implications of our argument.

The Origins of the Crisis in Greece and Spain

The Economic Origins of the Crisis

The economic origins of the crisis in Southern Europe have been analyzed in-depth. The story usually starts with the adoption of the euro; the euro was criticized at its inception for forcing diverse national economies into a currency union, thus making economic management difficult (e.g., Bayoumi and Eichengreen 1997; for reviews see De Grauwe 2012; Jonung et al. 2009). These problems became obvious at the turn of the century when the German economy was struggling and the *Economist* (1999) famously called Germany the "sick man of the Euro," while other countries in the eurozone were booming. In response to this asymmetry of European business cycles, the ECB conducted a monetary policy that was appropriate neither for the German core nor for the booming periphery (De Grauwe and Ji 2014). It created pressures for divergence within the eurozone and helped to build up large current account imbalances. Large export surpluses in the North were offset by deficits in the South, which were financed by credit that the North granted to the South (Hall 2012). The result was a large inflow of credit into both Greece and Spain, which increased the liabilities of both countries vis-à-vis nonresidents (as represented by the financial account in figure 5.1).

In Greece the government mostly used this inflow of credit as an opportunity to expand government expenditure by borrowing from domestic and foreign banks. This was possible because financial markets had repriced Southern European sovereign bonds and, hence, it became a lot cheaper for the Greek government to issue debt. For several consecutive years the government ran large fiscal deficits, increasing the amount of sovereign debt to 117.5 percent of GDP in 2009. But contrary to popular perceptions, this did not happen in Spain, where government debt remained relatively low. Instead, the ready availability of credit allowed the private sector to go on a spending binge: domestic banks leveraged their balance sheets by borrowing money from Northern European banks to finance a mix of real estate development and consumption in the early 2000s. This led to a huge boom in the Spanish construction sector similar to that in Ireland (Eichengreen 2012), which was also evident in employment figures: more than a fifth of all Greek employees worked in the public sector, but the Spanish construction sector employed nearly every fourth male employee (Fernández-Villaverde, Garicano, and Santos 2013).

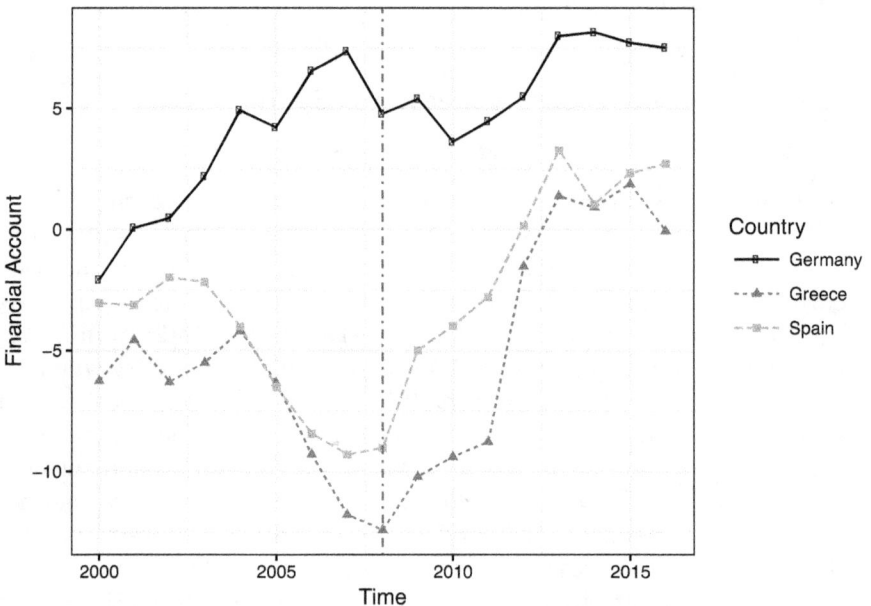

Figure 5.1. Financial Account as a Percentage of GDP of Germany, Greece, and Spain, 2000–16
Source: IMF 2017.

In other words, unlike the Greek growth model, which was built on an expansion of the public sector, the Spanish growth model was built on an expansion of the construction sector.

Nevertheless, the consequences were similar. The large inflow of foreign capital left both countries exposed to an external shock. This external shock came in September 2008, when the financial conglomerate Lehman Brothers collapsed in the US. The global credit crunch led to a flight to safety and a sudden stop of liquidity in Greece and Spain, which resulted in a balance-of-payments crisis (Copelovitch, Frieden, and Walter 2016; Wolf 2011). Consequently, the bubble in the construction sector in Spain burst and Greece struggled to finance its deficit on the capital markets. As investors lost trust in the ability of the Greek government to service its debt, the country had to turn to the EU and the IMF for bailouts in 2010, 2012, and 2015. Similarly, eventually the Spanish government could not control the crisis and, on behalf of its banks, it also applied for a bailout in 2012.

The Political Origins of the Economic Crisis in Spain and Greece

The comparison between Spain and Greece shows that the economic origins of the crisis in Greece were, indeed, systemic. Although the details are different, the economic crisis played out in a similar manner in both countries. With the benefit of hindsight, it is, therefore, easy to argue that there were structural problems with the eurozone (Eichengreen 2012). Yet, this begs the question why politicians and regulators allowed the structural problems to persist in the run-up to the crisis. Much of the existing literature focuses on the economic and financial origins of the crisis and largely ignores the political and social foundation of markets (Polanyi 2001 [1944]). But in order to understand the consequences of the economic meltdown, we need a comprehensive understanding of the crisis, which includes the social and political dynamics behind it.

Matthijs and Blyth (2015) have come a long way in addressing this shortcoming of the literature. They focus on the transnational bargains that are at the heart of the euro and argue effectively that the euro's lack of embeddedness in proper European institutions is at the heart of the current crisis: not only did the euro lack a proper financial and fiscal union, but it also lacked a political union that could create democratic legitimacy. However, on the domestic levels these institutions existed. For example, the member-states of the eurozone possessed the necessary tools to regulate the banking sector, as Hansen and Gordon (2014) point out. Why did they not use them?

In the absence of effective European institutions, the burden to counteract the growing imbalances in Europe was on domestic institutions. Yet, this burden was placed largely on the shoulders of countries that were least able to do it. First, Greece and Spain both have a weakly institutionalized party system. As democratic latecomers, the party systems were formed when the level of socioeconomic development had already been relatively high (Hopkin 2001); consequently, the party systems are weakly anchored in civil society. As a response, parties formed a cartel to obtain resources from the state (Katz and Mair 1995, 2009), which they did "either through mass party clientelism and corrupt use of public office to raise money, or through the state funding of parties" (Hopkin 2002: 10). This weakened the patterns of partisanship even further and contributed to the prevalence of informal politics in Southern Europe.

In Greece two parties dominated the political system before the electoral crisis: ND and PASOK. ND governed Greece's young democracy in the 1970s, until PASOK came to power with a landslide victory in 1981. Initially PASOK supported radical left-wing policies, including an exit from the European Economic Community, but quickly the party renounced its most extreme positions and shifted toward the center. In programmatic terms, some differences between ND and PASOK continued to exist, but they paled in comparison to the way these two parties conducted themselves when they were in power: both parties used the state resources to give out favors in return for electoral support (Featherstone 2011). As a result, both parties welcomed the cheap access to credit following eurozone membership. Real government consumption increased by nearly 30 percent from 1995 to 2003, when PASOK was in power, and increased by 17 percent from 2004 to 2009, when ND was in power. Consequently, it was not in the interest of Greek politicians to prevent the increasing imbalances in the Greek economy in the early 2000s. Rather, they fed off them and used them to entrench their position in society.

In Spain the government did not play the same role and the situation is less clear-cut. In fact, the notion of a clientelistic Southern model should be treated with caution. For instance, Hopkin (2001) finds little evidence of extensive clientelistic mobilization in Spain, whereas Lyrintzis (2007: 101) argues that "clientelism was the major characteristic of Greek political parties."[2] Still, there is clear evidence of crony capitalism in Spain, much of which was revealed after the outburst of the crisis (Royo 2014: 1574). Contrary to the situation in Greece, where the clientelistic networks were mostly centralized at the national level, the regional and local authorities played a more important role in the case of Spain after the administrative and political decentralization in the early 2000s (Hopkin 2012). Eventually, the political decentralization "led to the emergence of regional, local elites that took over the local and regional institutions. This included the *cajas*, whose boards were quickly filled with political appointees who used their position for their own personal gain and/or as a clientelist instrument to finance their projects" (Royo 2014: 1574).[3] The rapid expansion of the construction sector facilitated by privatization processes increased the opportunities for favoritism, mostly at the regional and local levels.[4] Most importantly, the distribution of public contracts for infrastructure projects allowed politicians to generate financial and public resources.

Although initially parties tried to blame individual politicians for this behavior, the problem was more endemic. Molinas (2012, 2013) argues that an extractive political class had developed in Spain due to institutional arrangements that had been agreed to during the transition to democracy. For instance, proportional representation and blocked party lists consolidated a weakly institutionalized party system, which the political class used to collude with economic elites to extract resources from society. As in Greece, they formed a powerful set of interests that could resist reforms that would have prevented the increasing economic problems.

As Royo (2014) argues, however, the problem was not one of extractive elites only. Instead, other vested interests prevented the government from pursuing reforms that would have reduced the dependency of Greece and Spain on foreign credit. Importantly, the benefits of the welfare state across most of Southern Europe are geared toward providing benefits to particular political constituencies (Ferrera 1996, 2005; Rhodes 1997). As Beramendi et al. (2015: 395) show, the Southern European welfare states are characterized by weak social investment policies and "particularistic, often residual and regressive social policies of consumption." In particular, the pension systems are expensive due to high replacement rates, and high employment protection legislation has contributed to a dualized labor market pitting organized insiders against an increasing amount of outsiders, who do not benefit from this legislation (Rueda 2007). Before the crisis this created an institutional bias against reform: vested interests had captured the welfare state and were unwilling to forgo these benefits.

The protection of insiders came at the expense of the outsiders, but the economic windfalls from European integration helped to taper the tensions and insulated elites from political pressures for reforms. In other words, there was a vicious cycle: the existing institutional power structure created unsustainable economic growth, which in turn entrenched the institutional power structure further. This power structure not only contributed to the crisis, but also determined how the economic crisis played out in the two countries. Despite the similarities in the economic and political origins of the crisis, we argue in the next sections that the diverging political outcomes of these two countries are rooted in the way the dynamics of the crisis interplayed with preexisting structures, thus allowing for a better understanding of the diverging fates of both countries.

Crisis Dynamics in Greece and Spain

The Economic Response to the Crisis in Spain and Greece

Although the symptoms of the crisis were different in both countries, international policymakers prescribed the same medicine. Building on the idea of expansionary fiscal contraction (Alesina and Ardagna 2010; Alesina and Perotti 1997), the creditors insisted on structural reforms combined with a sharp reduction of government spending. With respect to Spain, this was a fundamental misdiagnosis of the crisis because the Spanish crisis was not caused by government profligacy (De Grauwe 2013). However, creditors viewed Spain through the prism of Greece and condemned both countries to austerity.[5]

A detailed analysis of the memorandums of understanding (MoU) in Greece and Spain is beyond the scope of this chapter, but it is useful to briefly compare them on a number of dimensions in order to understand their impact. In both countries, the international creditors pushed for austerity and structural reforms. Still, the Greek and Spanish governments had already implemented reforms before they signed the MoUs. Greece came under pressure after the newly elected prime minister, Papandreou, revealed in October 2009 that the budget deficit would be a lot higher than previously predicted. Hence, financial markets became nervous and the credit rating agency Fitch Ratings first downgraded Greece on 8 December 2009 from A– to BBB+ (Oakley 2009).[6] Bowing to the pressure of the markets, Greece announced a first set of austerity measurements in February and March 2010 even before the government signed the MoU on 3 May 2010. In the hope of regaining the confidence of investors, these measures included, for instance, an increase of the value-added tax (VAT), a recruitment freeze in the public sector, and cuts to government expenditure. In the absence of a credible commitment from a lender of last resort, however, these measures could not restore the confidence of investors.

Similarly, Spain reacted to the pressure of financial markets before the official bailout. In response to the 2008 financial crisis, the government had initially pursued a stimulus program; in 2011 the worst seemed over, when the Spanish economy grew again. However, the domestic banks were crippled by many nonperforming loans on their balance sheets, which forced the government to bail them out. In combination with the costs of the initial stimulus program, this increased the government's deficit and debt burden. In the context of the Greek crisis, international financial markets became increasingly worried about the size of the government's budget deficit and, starting in May 2010, Fitch downgraded Spain six times until the country lost its A rating in June 2012. Spain introduced austerity mea sures in 2010 and 2011 to regain the trust of financial markets well before the government agreed to the MoU on 27 July 2012. In 2011, the Spanish Socialist Workers' Party (PSOE) and the conservative People's Party (PP) even amended the Spanish constitution requiring governments to cap deficits at 0.4 percent of GDP from 2020 onward (Tremlett 2011).

The contents of the programs introduced to combat the crisis were also similar in both countries. In Greece, for example, the terms of the first bailout included cuts in public sector pay, additional increases in VAT and other taxes, as well as a limit on public investment and expenditure. In 2010 alone the aim was to generate savings for a total amount of 2.5 percent of GDP, and by 2014 the fiscal deficit was supposed to be reduced from 13.6 to below 3 percent of GDP (IMF 2010). Similarly, in Spain, in June 2012 Prime Minister Rajoy announced spending cuts and tax increases worth 65 billion euro (Tremlett 2012); as in Greece, these measures included areas like health care and education. The government also committed itself to increasing taxes and reducing government investment and expenditure, for example by a freeze on the pay of government employees. Moreover, in both countries, austerity measures were combined with structural adjustment programs. The Greek government committed itself to liberalizing closed professions and reducing employment protection; over the years the creditors demanded that the Greek government intensify this program by abandoning the central wage bargaining system, dismissing 15,000 government employees, and introducing a large privatization program. The Spanish government also implemented a labor reform in February 2012 that made it easier to lay off workers and weakened the collective bargaining system. Additionally, the government pursued other reforms that resembled those in Greece, including cuts in social benefits, a rise in the retirement age, and a privatization program to increase government revenue.

Despite these similarities between the austerity programs in Greece and Spain, there are also important differences. First, Spain's austerity program was shorter. Greece has remained in the spotlight of the crisis ever since October 2009 and it first implemented austerity measures in spring 2010. As the economic recession worsened, Greece was forced to pursue several additional reform programs. In 2012 and 2015 it promised reforms in return for new bailouts; even in between the MoUs, the Greek government implemented additional austerity packages to satisfy the demands of the creditors. Spain also pursued initial reforms in 2010 and 2011, but most measures were announced only in 2012, after the economy had slid back into recession. Most importantly, Spain became the second country in the eurozone to exit the bailout program again in January 2014, while an end to the Greek program is not in sight.

Second, international creditors arguably put a lot more pressure on Greece to pursue austerity than on Spain. On the insistence of the German government, the IMF was closely involved in the negotiations of the Greek bail-out and its implementation. Officials from the IMF joined policymakers from the European Commission and the ECB to form the Troika, and delegates from the three institutions set up camp in Athens and became regular visitors in Greek ministries. Their presence there increasingly constrained consecutive governments, while they were a lot less influential and visible in Madrid. Moreover, the ECB was reluctant to act as a lender of last resort in response to the Greek crisis in 2010. Only when the crisis had fully reached Spain (and Italy) in 2012 did the ECB change its approach. Fearing an implosion of the euro, ECB president Mario Draghi famously promised to do whatever it takes to preserve the euro in July 2012. This change of course was more successful in regaining the confidence of investors than any set of austerity measures could have been: within days, the borrowing costs of Spain and Greece decreased. Hence, Draghi's announcement came just in time to take some pressure off the Spanish government by reducing the borrowing costs of the crisis countries and by supporting their ailing banking sectors.

Third, the austerity program pursued by the Spanish government was less severe than the program pursued by Greece. Although a comparison between the size of different austerity packages is difficult, the structural balance can be used as a proxy because it excludes the impact of the economic cycle (e.g., through automatic stabilizers) and one-off measures (e.g., the sale of mobile phone licenses) on the government's budget balance. Using this measurement as a basis for comparison, Greece's balance improved by 20.3 percentage points from 2009 to 2014, while the structural balance in Spain improved by 8.6 percentage points over the same period. This indicates that Greece pursued a great deal more austerity than Spain—in fact, Greece had to endure the deepest austerity package of all crisis-ridden countries according to this measurement. Although austerity programs created large economic dislocations in both countries, the consequences of the economic crisis were particularly harsh in Greece, reaching an unprecedented severity in modern times.

The Economic Consequences of the Crisis in Spain and Greece

Greece experienced by far the deepest economic downturn of all countries in Europe. It was in recession from 2008 to 2013, when real GDP fell by 26.0 percent. In contrast, Spain had a relatively strong recovery after the global financial meltdown had dragged it into an economic slump from 2008 to 2010. In 2012, however, Spain slipped back into recession, and overall Spanish real GDP fell by 7.3 percent from 2008 to 2013. This fall in economic activity in Greece and Spain created similar levels of unemployment in both countries (figure 5.2a) but unemployment before the crisis was higher in Spain than in Greece. In Greece unemployment increased from 7.2 percent in July 2008 to its peak of 27.9 percent in January 2014. In Spain, it increased from 11.2 percent to 25.9 percent over the same period. These levels of unemployment not only were dramatically higher than in Northern Europe, but they were also a lot higher than in the rest of the crisis-ridden South. Still, the true damage of unemployment is evident from the high levels of youth unemployment: in both countries, the share of unemployed under the age of twenty-five tripled between 2007 and 2013 (figure 5.2b), reaching 60 percent in Greece and 56.9 percent in Spain.

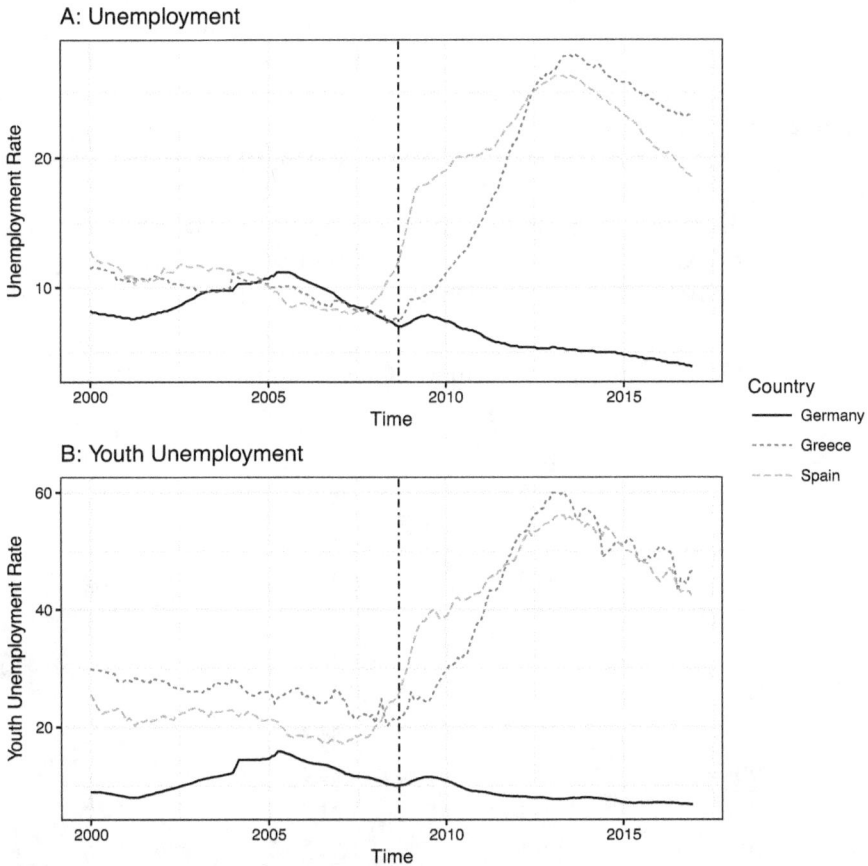

Figure 5.2. Unemployment Rate in Germany, Greece, and Spain, 2000–16
Source: Eurostat 2017a.

Consequently, the crisis hit some of the most vulnerable people in society because young labor market participants and low-skilled workers were the first ones to lose their jobs.

However, even many people who retained their jobs were a lot worse off because of the crisis. On average, the wages of employees fell in both Greece and Spain. In Greece this fall was particularly steep: from 2009 to 2014, the average real wage fell by nearly 24 percent in Greece, while the average annual real wage fell by 7 percent in Spain. This contributed to a low level of domestic consumption, but it also increased poverty and social exclusion. In 2014, 36 percent and 29 percent of the entire population was at risk of poverty or social exclusion in Greece and Spain, respectively. Compared to 2007 this figure increased by more than 25 percent in both countries and, consequently, inequality also increased during the crisis according to various measures. While the Gini coefficient rose from 33.4 in 2008 to 34.5 in 2014 in Greece, it rose from 31.9 in 2008 to 34.7 in 2014 in Spain (table 5.1). Similarly, the income of workers at the ninetieth percentile (individuals earning more than the bottom 90% of the population) compared to the earning of workers at the tenth percentile (individuals earning higher than the bottom 10 percent) increased in Greece and Spain by 20 and 18 percent, respectively.

Hence, the social dislocations of the crisis have been large in both countries and the pains of the economic adjustment were not shared equally across society. The crisis produced a large group of people who were left

Table 5.1. Gini Coefficient in Germany, Greece, and Spain, 2005–16

Year	Germany	Greece	Spain
2005	26.1	33.2	32.2
2006	26.8	34.3	31.9
2007	30.4	34.3	31.9
2008	30.2	33.4	31.9
2009	29.1	33.1	32.9
2010	29.3	32.9	33.5
2011	29.0	33.5	34.0
2012	28.3	34.3	34.2
2013	29.7	34.4	33.7
2014	30.7	34.5	34.7
2015	30.1	34.2	34.6
2016		34.3	34.5

Source: Eurostat 2017b.

unemployed, received few social benefits, and suffered from the decreasing quality of public services in health and education (Matthijs 2014). At the same time, austerity policies have not even had the desired effect on government finances. In both countries the government debt in 2015 was significantly larger than at the beginning of the crisis, and the deficits remained outside the 3 percent limit specified by the Stability and Growth Pact.

The data for Greece and Spain support this conclusion. Even though the fall in GDP was a lot farther in Greece compared to Spain and any other European country, Greece is no exception when it comes to results of the attempted economic reforms. While Spain has fared better than Greece during the crisis, it is no poster child for austerity either.[7] In fact, a comparison with Greece needs to consider not only that the original crisis in Greece was a lot deeper than the crisis in Spain, but also that the path of adjustment was a lot more difficult for Greece due to a more ambitious reform program, as shown above. Moreover, politicians and commentators have consistently and deliberately overstated the positive trajectory of Spain,[8] but the average citizen still feels the hangover after the party, as we show below.

The Political Consequences of the Economic Crisis

The Attitudinal Dimension: A Widespread Political Malaise?

It is no surprise that an economic shock with such social repercussions triggered extraordinary political reactions. These reactions were expressed in both attitudinal (lack of confidence in political institutions and the political system) and behavioral (protests, electoral volatility and collapse of party systems) dimensions (Kriesi 2015; see also Kanellopoulos and Kousis this volume, and Mylonas this volume). For the first dimension, indicators of political trust toward the key representative national and European political institutions, as well as those of the levels of satisfaction with democracy, are particularly revealing. Since the beginning of the economic crisis in September 2008, as marked by the vertical dotted line in our figures, these indicators followed a remarkably similar pattern in both countries. The average of satisfaction with the way democracy works in the national country and in the EU (figure 5.3) decreased substantially after 2008 in both Greece and Spain, reaching some of the lowest levels recorded since the transition to democracy in both countries.[9]

Mistrust toward the national government, parliament, and political parties (figure 5.4), followed an almost identical trend.[10] Although in both countries mistrust toward political parties had been considerably lower

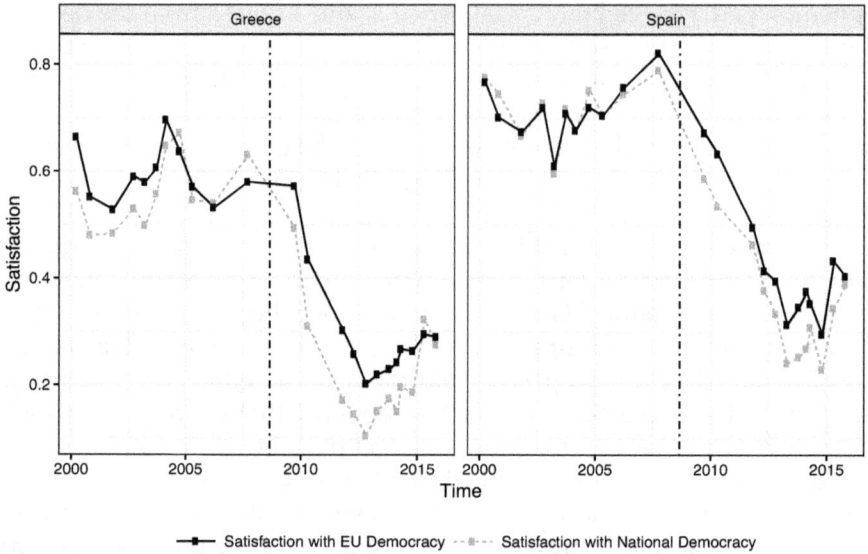

Figure 5.3. Satisfaction with the European Union and National Democracy, 2000–16

Source: European Commission 2016.

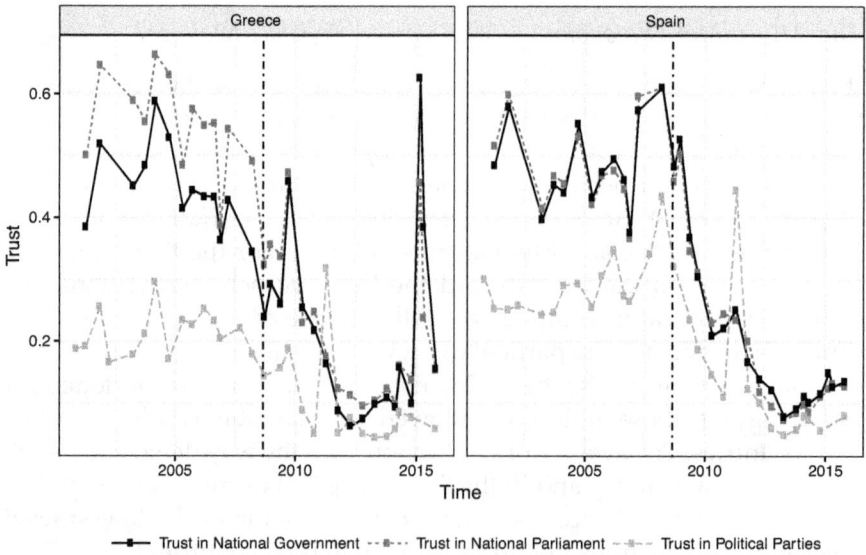

Figure 5.4. Trust in National Institutions, 2000–16

Source: European Commission 2016.

than toward parliament and government before the crisis, we observe that the levels converged to another historical low during the crisis. Compared to the levels of trust toward government and parliament prior to 2008, the decrease is nothing less than spectacular: while more than 50 percent of respondents trusted the national parliament before the crisis, less than 10 percent of respondents trusted the national parliament at the height of the crisis.[11] European political institutions also did not go unpunished: figure 5.5 illustrates that European institutions suffered the largest average drop in trust in Greece and Spain compared to all other institutions. In 2015 there was a slight recovery in these attitudes, but the average levels in both countries remain far from the averages prior to the crisis.

Although some studies have shown a strong correlation between the drop in trust in political institutions and macroeconomic indicators, particularly with unemployment (Roth, Nowak-Lehmann, and Otter 2013), the widespread political malaise can hardly be attributed solely to economic explanations. Applying the classic literature of economic voting whereby voters punish or reward incumbent governments depending on the economic performance, we would expect that levels of trust toward the incumbent government would have decreased because citizens would blame it for its bad management of the economy. If this were the case, however, trust should recover after citizens are given the opportunity to

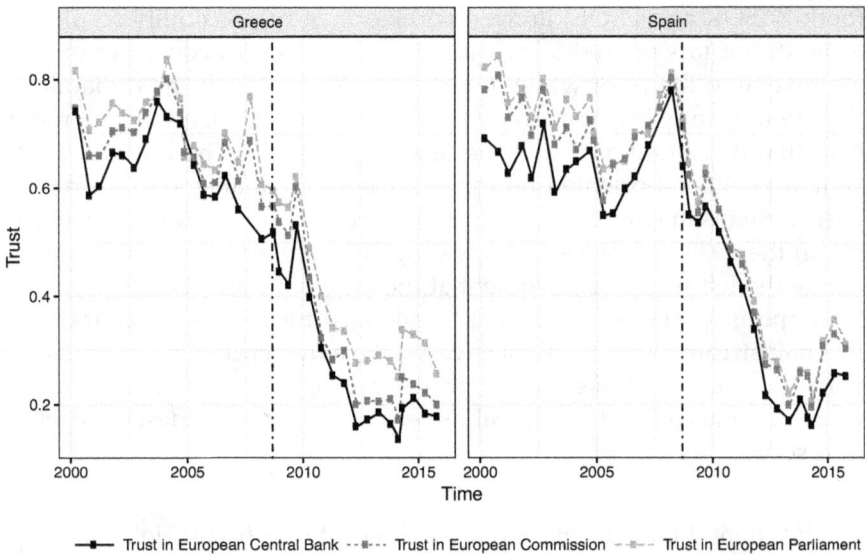

Figure 5.5. Trust in European Institutions, 2000–16
Source: European Commission 2016.

reward or punish political parties for their performance in government (Key and Cummings 1966). However, this is not what we observe. Instead, "the cumulated effect of the Great Recession, goes far beyond the short-term punishment of incumbents" (Hernández and Kriesi 2016: 221) and mistrust is indiscriminately projected toward both national and European political institutions, regardless of elections and changes of governments. This suggests that both Greece and Spain suffered a far deeper political malaise than simply discontent with the incumbent's performance that led to the collapse of their respective party systems. We argue that, beyond the economy, the political consequences of the crisis were related to a feeling of widespread discontent linked to the perception of a democracy without choices (Bosco and Verney 2012), in which mainstream parties were perceived as lacking a differentiated policy program.

The diagnosis is the following: mainstream parties, regardless of their ideology, were strongly constrained in economic policy, leading to a situation where voters could not perceive any significant programmatic differences between them. In other words, the lack of political alternatives that accompanied the austerity programs and reforms triggered widespread disenchantment with the political systems of Greece and Spain. As a result, large sections of society did not feel politically represented and stopped trusting political institutions. More specifically, the neoliberal reforms and welfare cuts implemented by the mainstream left parties (both PASOK and PSOE) under the rhetoric of responsibility resulted in a significant loss of credibility insofar as these parties could not offer an alternative to the right while in government. Although the dynamics of this situation are described in detail later in this section, it is worth noting here that this situation is not the first to take place. The introduction of similar neoliberal-oriented reforms produced an analogous distortion of party systems in Latin America during the era of the Washington Consensus in the 1980 and 1990s (Mainwaring 2006; Roberts 2013): in countries where the left was in government at the time of implementing cuts, new left populist parties emerged that challenged the true leftist character of the mainstream party. In all these cases, the emergence of the populist left parties was closely linked to the protest arena, the other crucial—and intrinsically intertwined—political dimension of the crisis described in the next section.

The Behavioral Dimension: From the Streets to the Institutions

The attitudinal expressions of the political crisis in both Greece and Spain eventually translated into a behavioral dimension, which manifested itself in both contentious (protests) and conventional (electoral punishment and new parties) politics. In the electoral arena, this took the form of a two-step process in both countries, as shown in tables 5.2 and 5.3. In the first elections during the crisis, the incumbent lost to the mainstream challenger party (ND to PASOK in 2009 and PSOE to PP in 2011). In a second step, new challenger parties gained a significant share of the votes (2012 and 2015 in Greece and 2015 in Spain).

However, while this two-step electoral process was similar in the two countries, there are significant differences in the protest dimension of the crisis that are worth stressing. In Spain, the mass demonstrations that would give the name to the 15-M movement—and that would later trigger similar protest in the United States under the "We are the 99 percent" banner (Castañeda 2012)—were initially convened by a small online platform called Democracia Real Ya! (Real Democracy Now!) in May 2011. With a

Table 5.2. Spain General Elections Results, 2008–16

Party	2008	2011	2015	2016
PP	39.9 (154)	44.6 (186)	28.7 (123)	33.0 (137)
PSOE	43.9 (169)	28.7 (110)	22 (90)	22.6 (85)
IU	3.8 (2)	6.9 (11)	3.7 (2)	—
Podemos	—	—	20.7 (69)	21.2 (71)
Ciudadanos	—	—	13.9 (40)	13.1 (32)
Turnout (percent)	73.4	68.9	69.7	66.5

Note: Number of seats in parentheses. IU = United Left.
Source: Spanish ministry of interior 2017.

Table 5.3. Greece General Elections Results, 2009–15

Party	2009	2012		2015	
		May	June	January	September
ND	33.5 (91)	18.8 (108)	29.6 (129)	27.8 (76)	28.1 (75)
PASOK	43.9 (160)	13.2 (41)	12.3 (33)	4.7 (13)	6.3 (17)
SYRIZA	4.6 (13)	16.8 (52)	26.9 (71)	36.3 (149)	35.5 (145)
KKE	7.5 (21)	8.5 (26)	4.5 (12)	5.5 (15)	5.5 (15)
XA	0.3 (0)	7 (21)	6.9 (18)	6.3 (17)	7 (18)
ANEL	—	10.6 (33)	7.5 (20)	4.7 (13)	3.7 (10)
Turnout (Percent)	70.9	65.1	62.5	63.6	56.6

Note: Number of seats in parentheses. KKE = Communist Party of Greece; XA = Golden Dawn; ANEL = Independent Greeks.
Source: Greek ministry of interior 2017.

simple, direct and nonpartisan message, Spanish people mobilized both inside and outside Spain. "We want more democracy!," "We are not commodities of bankers and politicians!," or "They do not represent us!" were some of the slogans that were coined by the movement. The so-called Indignados movement could connect with large sections of the population despite (or perhaps because of) the fact that they refused any involvement with traditionally politicized organizations such as labor unions or youth organizations of parties. More than just anti-austerity protests, the movement had to do with providing "time and space for every participant to express themselves and take an active part in the camp and movement organization, notably through long group discussions and the creation of commissions and working groups around specific issues" (Kaldor and Selchow 2015: 206).

The causes of contention that sparked the movement were rooted in the perception that an extractive and corrupt elite had governed unaccountably and made the citizens pay for a crisis that they had not caused. Whereas austerity was an important mobilizing factor for the protests, the movement also repeatedly identified the political structure of the country as one of the main problems (Calvo, Gómez-Pastrana, and Mena 2011). The idea of new politics grew as an alternative to old or traditional politics, which, to the movement, was represented by the extractive economic and political elites. At the core of this idea were participatory mechanisms and claims for more direct democracy, with the use of the internet and social media being its main driver (Hughes 2011). The Indignados movement was, therefore, not solely an anti-austerity protest movement, but also a much wider expression of the dissatisfaction with the Spanish political system. In fact, it was the inception of this new conflict in Spanish politics that would later be expressed with the emergence of new parties like Podemos and even Ciudadanos, as explained below.

Although the so-called Greek Indignados also played a role in the anti-austerity protests from 2010 to 2012, they were neither the only actor nor the most important one. In fact, anarchists, social justice groups, educational groups, youth organizations, but especially political parties and labor unions (from the private and public sector), were equally if not more important—depending on the individual protest—in participating and organizing the protests. For instance, the two large trade union confederations, the General Confederation of Greek Workers (GSEE) and the Civil Servants' Confederation (ADEDY), as well as the youth organizations of the Communist Party of Greece (KKE), SYRIZA, and ANTARSYA, played a key role in the organization of several major protests in the country (Kanellopoulos and Kostopoulos 2014; Kanellopoulos and Kousis this volume). One of the main differences between the way in which anti-austerity protests were organized and developed in Spain and Greece—which is particularly important to understand the political consequences and the characteristics of new parties—is precisely that the Indignados in Spain "mainly involved young and highly educated people not connected with 'old' political actors like trade unions and political parties" (Karyotis and Rüdig 2015: 496). This difference is central for explaining how these movements translated into the conventional political arena and the nature of the new challengers.

The New Challengers: A Populist Left?

The strong dissatisfaction with traditional parties and the mobilization in the contentious arena opened an exceptional opportunity for new political entrepreneurs to capitalize on the political crisis. Social democratic parties in both countries faced an irreconcilable dilemma that would ease the emergence of new parties on the left. This dilemma, framed by Mair (2009) as responsibility versus responsiveness, describes the situation confronted by both PSOE and PASOK. Both had to introduce measures contrary to their ideology—whether through changes in the constitution or through the implementation of cuts on welfare—in order to behave responsibly and satisfy the demands of the international creditors (Bremer 2018). This came at the cost of responsiveness to the ideological foundations of these parties.

In Greece this implied the near disappearance of PASOK, going from 43.9 percent of the vote in 2009 to 4.7 percent in 2015. By implementing austerity after its election in 2009, the party not only had committed an ideological somersault, but by depleting the resources available to distribute, it had also undermined the clientelistic linkages that the party depended on (Afonso, Zartaloudis, and Papadopoulos 2014; Mylonas this volume). SYRIZA benefited the most from this decline of PASOK, going from 4.6 percent in 2009 to winning both elections in 2015 with over 35 percent of the votes. Not only did most of SYRIZA's votes came from PASOK, but in addition even some politicians changed affiliation to the new party. As PASOK lost the credibility to stand up to the European creditors and to implement a leftist program, SYRIZA became PASOK's ideological purifier, a type of challenger party that is successful when established parties are forced to change their position with regard to salient lines of conflict (Lucardie 2000). With a radical leftist and anti-austerity agenda, the party promised to be responsive toward the electorate by standing up to the international creditors' demands and putting an end to austerity, while at the same time combating the domestic oligarchy. Thus, SYRIZA confronted both the domestic and the European elites, dubbed as the internal and the external Troika.

Similarly, in Spain the initial challenger party that emerged from the In-dignados movement was Podemos, which became the third-largest party in the 2015 election winning nearly 21 percent of the vote. Although both SYRIZA and Podemos have been labeled as parties of the new populist left in Southern Europe, and despite the visible links between both parties,[12] there are significant differences that suggest that they are two different an-imals. Most visibly, SYRIZA was presented as a clear alternative from the left and had a long political tradition, despite its weak parliamentary rep-resentation in the past. In contrast, Podemos was a completely new party, which, in line with the ideas of inclusiveness of the 15-M movement, shed traditional left-right ideological labels. A more analogous situation would have been for the United Left (IU) in Spain, a traditional leftist party with a clear anti-austerity message, to "purify" PSOE, just as SYRIZA did with PASOK. Why did this not happen? Why did it take a new party such as Podemos to capitalize on the emerging protest vote?

The electoral arenas of politics in Greece and Spain were closely in-fluenced by developments in the arena of contentious politics. Whereas in Greece the anti-austerity discourse was one of the key issues in all the demonstrations (i.e., demands that the rich are taxed, social welfare pro-vided, ceasing of privatizations, etc., see Kanelloupulous and Kousis this volume), which was the political territory of the left, this was not so clear in the case of Spain. As explained above, the Indignados emerged as an all-encompassing movement that persistently claimed to be inclusive to all citizens regardless of their ideology, pursuing the idea of new politics. Thus, the issue of new politics, including corruption and the opposition to the domestic political system, became salient in Spain in both the conten-tious and conventional arena of politics, while the intervention of external European actors in domestic politics did not play a determining role as much in Spain as it did in Greece. In fact, Calvo, Gómez-Pastrana, and Mena (2011) show that the most important objectives of the 15-M move-ment were the fight against corruption and the reform of the electoral system. As explained in the previous section, this was because the inter-vention of these external actors became much more pronounced in the case of Greece. Therefore, Europe and the enforcement of austerity played a smaller role in reshaping the Spanish political system than that of Greece (see also Hutter, Kriesi, and Vidal 2018).

The greater importance of domestic renewal over European anti-austerity issues also explains the strong rise of a new politics right-wing party in Spain, Ciudadanos, which has gained rapid electoral support since the last regional elections in 2015.[13] Despite being a pro-austerity party, it entered the conventional political arena as the right-wing equiva-lent of Podemos, which also challenged the domestic elites but had little to say about Europe. Although Ciudadanos self-identifies as a liberal party with a very different program from that of Podemos, their voters share a set of characteristics that place both parties in direct competition with each other on this new dimension of conflict despite being on different sides of the ideological spectrum. Compared to the voters of PP and PSOE, voters for both parties are more concerned with the political situation and are more likely to be young and from urban areas (Vidal 2017), indicating a new dimension of political conflict in Spain.

This new dimension of conflict in Spain also explains why it would take a new party such as Podemos to capitalize on the emerging protest vote. Although the traditional left party IU had long campaigned against austerity, it did not correspond with the idea conveyed in the contentious political arena about the necessity of new politics and was, thus, not able to capitalize on the emerging protest vote. Being perceived as part of the old politics weighted heavily among young and urban voters, who were demanding a change in political culture. Conversely, the dominance of the new dimension of conflict in Spanish politics can also account for failure of Podemos to purify PSOE. While the difference in the depth of austerity (and, thus, the degree of ideological betrayal) that the social democratic parties were forced to implement is also important for explaining the extent that voters and politicians switched, it is only one part of the story. Importantly, many old political forces, including the trade unions, remained loyal to PSOE because they also felt threatened by the rise of the new challenger parties in Spain. In contrast, as pointed out by Kanellopoulos and Kousis (this volume), one of the important characteristics of the Greek case was SYRIZA's capacity to mobilize the mass demonstrations with the participation of major unions. Thus, while in Greece old actors (i.e., major unions) and new actors (i.e., Greek Indignados) joined forces under the same banner, the division between old and new actors weighted heavily and defined the dividing lines of Spanish politics during the crisis.

The political developments of Greece and Spain on the eve of the Great Recession resemble each other, but there are important differences that explain the diverging patterns in the shaping of the new structure of conflict. The restructuring of the party systems in both countries was different because the main challenger in each country responded to different patterns in the contentious arena, which led to a different institutionalization of conflicts.[14] Due to the intensity of the crisis, the conflict about austerity dominated in Greece, while a conflict between old and new politics became more prominent in Spain. In other words, the domestic dimension prevailed in Spain, whereas in Greece the European dimension became more important. Naturally, these new conflicts are deeply intertwined with other idiosyncratic conflicts in each country. For instance, the rise and success of Ciudadanos cannot be understood without the territorial conflict in Spain because the issue of independence for Catalonia is key to Ciudadanos's program (Rodríguez Teruel and Barrio 2015). Although a full discussion of these issues is beyond the scope of this chapter, it is important to note that the domestic political culture of countries is essential for understanding the new political conflicts in Greece and Spain.

Conclusion

The response to the economic crisis in Europe has been driven by neoclassical economic theory. Policymakers have attempted to turn the South into the North in order to create the optimal currency area that Europe has never been. However, in this chapter we have argued that the introduction of the euro is not exclusively to blame for the crisis and the resulting imbalances in Europe. Instead, prior political dynamics also played an important role. The cases of Spain and Greece are tellingly similar in that respect: both countries suffered a period of institutional degradation (Royo 2014), where governments and regulators failed to prevent the precrisis boom. Clientelism and corruption, in its different levels and forms, allowed the Greek and Spanish elites to extract resources and benefit from the precrisis boom disproportionality. In combination with the support from entrenched interests that benefited from the dualized welfare system, this disincentivized regulation that would have controlled the excesses in the public sector (in the case of Greece) and the private sector (in the case of Spain).

In the precrisis era the economic windfalls of European integration were large enough to shield the political system from domestic opposition, but the political dysfunctionalities of Greece and Spain were exposed in the past few years. In the wake of the crisis, the trust toward national and European political institutions dropped dramatically as citizens became increasingly dissatisfied with the political system. This dissatisfaction was rooted not only in the declining performance of the economy, but also in the political context—that is, the clarity of responsibility and the availability of alternatives. The result was an attitudinal crisis that was similar in Greece and Spain, but that evolved into two distinct behavioral patterns in the two countries.

In Greece the austerity programs were so harsh and comprehensive that they overshadowed every other political issue. Thus, the international creditors, personified by German politicians and bureaucrats of the Troika, were quickly regarded as the main culprit for the economic situation in Greece and, as a result, the main conflict in Greek politics became one that posed domestic political actors against international actors (and their domestic allies). In Spain, in contrast, the political crisis played out differently. The austerity program in Spain not only was less deep, but also the European institutions did not have the same (perceived) involvement in its design. While the austerity policies were also politically divisive, the main political conflict in Spain became an internal one: political forces, who stood for old or traditional politics, were attacked by new protest movements and political parties, which were supporting a form of new politics centered around claims for participatory mechanisms and more direct democracy.

The new political parties that have emerged out of these conflicts are representative of these patterns and, despite their common stance against austerity, SYRIZA and Podemos are different political animals. These differences are best explained by the developments in the contentious arena of both countries, which created the political opportunities for the new challengers. Whereas in Greece it was the traditional left that capitalized on the emerging discontent, it took a new party that shunned ideological labels in Spain to do so, at least initially. Therefore, the behavioral consequences of the crisis were different because of a combination of preexisting domestic grievances and new conflicts that were brought about by an exceptional economic and political situation.

Our comparison of Greece and Spain shows what an encompassing effect the economic crisis and the austerity policies had on the Greek political system and society. Although other European countries like Spain also suffered heavily during crisis, the shackles of austerity in Greece were unprecedented. The Greek political system underwent radical transformations, which other chapters in volume help us to understand better (e.g., Mylonas this volume; Kaprozilos this volume; Kanellopoulus and Kousis this volume). Importantly, these transformations are far from over. The transformations of the Greek political system have been that of a punctuated equilibrium: it is once again dominated by two political parties: the conservative ND on the right and the governing party SYRIZA on the left. In 2015 SYRIZA signed a third MoU including further austerity and reforms without the guarantee of much-needed debt relief. Because SYRIZA is struggling to live up to its political promises to end the austerity regime, the political situation is still subject to further changes. Overall, the political consequences of the crisis in Greece have already been colossal, but they might have only been the prelude of what is still to come.

Björn Bremer is a doctoral researcher in the Department of Social and Political Sciences at the European University Institute in Florence, where he is a member of the ERC project "Political Conflict in the Shadow of the Great Recession." He holds a bachelor of arts in philosophy, politics, and economics from the University of Oxford, and a master of arts in International Relations and International Economics from the School of Advanced International Studies at Johns Hopkins University. His main research interests focus on the politics of macroeconomic policies and on social democratic parties in the context of the Great Recession.

Guillem Vidal is a doctoral researcher in the Department of Social and Political Sciences at the European University Institute in Florence, where he is part of the ERC project "Political Conflict in the Shadow of the Great Recession." He holds a bachelor of science in political economy from the Utrecht University, and a master of arts in international relations from the Barcelona Institute of International Studies. His main research focuses on the crisis of political representation and new political parties in Southern Europe.

Notes

The authors gratefully acknowledge funding from the European Research Council project Political Conflict in Europe in the Shadow of the Great Recession (Project ID: 338875).

1. Austerity is defined as the reduction in government spending during hard economic times.
2. See Mylonas in this volume for a further discussion of clientelism in Greece.
3. *Cajas* are Spanish savings banks. Many of them were involved in financing the real estate booms and, as a consequence of the crisis, had to be rescued by government bailouts.
4. This process was even supported by the benefits of membership in the European Monetary Union. Funds from the EU's Convergence and Cohesion Funds allowed the public sector to finance new railway stations, highways and airports across the country (Hopkin 2012). It is also important to note that while the construction sector also experienced some growth in Greece, the value added of the construction sector paled in comparison to that of Ireland and Spain (see Giavazi and Spaventa, 2011: 213).
5. For an account of the origins of austerity as an idea, see Blyth (2013).
6. This was the first time in a decade that Greece did not have an A rating and reflected the worry in the financial markets about the sustainability of the Greek debt.
7. In the wake of the Greek referendum, many commentators have claimed that austerity has worked elsewhere. For example, the Council of Economic Experts in Germany claimed, "Ireland, Portugal, and Spain all successfully completed their program [and that] the economic situation has markedly improved" (Bofinger et al. 2015: 1).
8. Fearing punishment from voters and capital markets, politicians have done this deliberately. For instance, Prime Minister Rajoy claimed in a state of the union address, "Spain has passed from being a country on the brink of bankruptcy to a model of recovery that provides an example to other countries in the EU" (Buck 2015).
9. Respondents were asked the following two questions: "On the whole, are you very satisfied, fairly satisfied, not very satisfied or not at all satisfied with the way democracy

works in (OUR COUNTRY)?" and "How about the way democracy works in the EU?" We recoded the answer categories, which now range from four to one: 4 = "Very satisfied"; 3 = "Fairly satisfied"; 2 = "Not very satisfied"; 1 = "Not at all satisfied."

10. Respondents were asked the following question: "I would like to ask you a question about how much trust you have in certain institutions. For each of the following institutions, please tell me if you tend to trust it or tend not to trust it." We recoded the answer categories, which now range from zero to one: 1 = "Tend to trust"; 2 = "Tend not to trust."

11. The recovery of trust in 2015 in the case of Greece is likely due to the victory of SYRIZA in the January legislative elections of 2015. As part of the classic reward-punish mechanisms in democracies, elections tend to momentarily increase trust towards institutions.

12. On 22 January 2015, for instance, Alexis Tsipras symbolically invited Pablo Iglesias, the leader of Podemos, to the end-of-campaign meeting before the elections.

13. Although there is a similar new party in Greece, To Potami (The River), it obtained only 4 percent of the votes in September 2015 and 6 percent in January 2015.

14. Although the leaders of Podemos speak of overcoming the left–right spectrum in order to attract voters regardless of their ideological position, studies have shown that citizens persistently place the party on the very left of the ideological scale (Fernández-Albertos 2015).

References

Afonso, Alexandre, Sotirios Zartaloudis, and Yannis Papadopoulos. 2014. "How Party Linkages Shape Austerity Politics: Clientelism and Fiscal Adjustment in Greece and Portugal during the Eurozone Crisis." *Journal of European Public Policy* 22(3): 315–34.

Alesina, Alberto, and Silvia Ardagna. 2010. "Large Changes in Fiscal Policy: Taxes versus Spending." *Tax Policy and the Economy* 24(1): 35–68.

Alesina, Alberto, and Roberto Perotti. 1997. "Fiscal Adjustments in OECD Countries: Composition and Macroeconomic Effects." *Staff Papers (International Monetary Fund)* 44(2): 210–48.

Bayoumi, Tamim, and Barry Eichengreen. 1997. "Ever Closer to Heaven? An Optimum-Currency-Area Index for European Countries." *European Economic Review*, Paper and Proceedings of the 11th Annual Congress of the European Economic Association, 41(3–5): 761–70.

Beramendi, Pablo, Silja Häusermann, Herbert Kitschelt, and Hanspeter Kriesi, eds. 2015. *The Politics of Advanced Capitalism*. Cambridge: Cambridge University Press.

Blyth, Mark. 2013. *Austerity: The History of a Dangerous Idea*. New York: Oxford University Press.

Bofinger, Peter, Lars Feld, Christoph Schmidt, Isabel Schnabel, and Volker Wieland. 2015. *Consequences of the Greek Crisis for a More Stable Euro Area*. Wiesbaden, Germany: German Council of Economic Experts.

Bosco, Anna, and Susannah Verney. 2012. "Electoral Epidemic: The Political Cost of Economic Crisis in Southern Europe, 2010–11." *South European Society and Politics* 17(2): 129–54.

Bremer, Björn. 2018. "The Missing Left? Economic Crisis and the Programmatic Response of Social Democratic Parties in Europe." *Party Politics* 24(1): 23–38.

Buck, Tobias. 2015. "Rajoy Promises Jobs and Growth as Fringe Parties Gain Ground." *Financial Times*, 24 February. Retrieved 15 July 2017 from http://www.ft.com/intl/cms/s/0/5876fd4c-bc30-11e4-b6ec-00144feab7de.html#axzz3pHeBhojo.

Calvo, Kerman, Teresa Gómez-Pastrana, and Luis Mena. 2011. "Movimiento 15M: ¿Quiénes son y qué Reivindican?" *Zoom Político* (special issue) 15-M(4): 4–17.

Castañeda, Ernesto. 2012. "The Indignados of Spain: A Precedent to Occupy Wall Street." *Social Movement Studies* 11(3–4): 309–19.

Copelovitch, Mark, Jeffry Frieden, and Stefanie Walter. 2016. "The Political Economy of the Euro Crisis." *Comparative Political Studies* 49(7): 811–40.

De Grauwe, Paul. 2012. *Economics of Monetary Union*, 9th ed. Oxford: Oxford University Press.

———. 2013. "The Political Economy of the Euro." *Annual Review of Political Science* 16(1): 153–70.

De Grauwe, Paul, and Yuemei Ji. 2014. "The Future of the Eurozone." *Manchester School* 82: 15–34.

Draghi, Mario. 2012. "Speech by Mario Draghi, President of the European Central Bank at the Global Investment Conference." London, 26 July. Retrieved 7 July 2017 from https://www.ecb.europa.eu/press/key/date/2012/html/sp120726.en.html.

The Economist. 1999. "The Sick Man of the Euro." 3 June. Retrieved 7 July 2017 from http://www.economist.com/node/209559.

Eichengreen, Barry. 2012. "European Monetary Integration with Benefit of Hindsight." *Journal of Common Market Studies* 50(s1): 123–36.

European Commission. 2016. Pooled biyearly Eurobarometers 53-83.1 2000-16. TNS Opinion & Social, Brussels [Producer]; GESIS Data Archive.

Eurostat. 2017a. Unemployment rates by sex, age and citizenship (lfsq_urgan). Retrieved 7 July 2017 from http://appsso.eurostat.ec.europa.eu/nui/show.do?dataset=lfsq_urgan&lang=en.

Eurostat. 2017b. Gini coefficient of equivalised disposable income - EU-SILC survey (ilc_di12). Retrieved from 7 July 2017 http://appsso.eurostat.ec.europa.eu/nui/show.do?dataset=ilc_di12.

Featherstone, Kevin. 2011. "The JCMS Annual Lecture: The Greek Sovereign Debt Crisis and EMU: A Failing State in a Skewed Regime." *Journal of Common Market Studies* 49(2): 193–217.

Fernández-Albertos, José. 2015. *Los Votantes de Podemos: Del Partido de Los Indignados Al Partido de Los Excluidos.* Madrid: Catarata.

Fernández-Villaverde, Jesús, Luis Garicano, and Tano Santos. 2013. "Political Credit Cycles: The Case of the Eurozone." *Journal of Economic Perspectives* 27(3): 145–66.

Ferrera, Maurizio. 1996. "The 'Southern Model' of Welfare in Social Europe." *Journal of European Social Policy* 6(1): 17–37.

———, ed. 2005. *Welfare State Reform in Southern Europe: Fighting Poverty and Social Exclusion in Italy, Spain, Portugal and Greece.* Routledge/EUI Studies in the Political Economy of Welfare 6. New York: Routledge.

Giavazzi, Francesco, and Spaventa, Luigi. 2011. "Why the Current Account May Matter in a Monetary Union: Lessons from the Financial Crisis in the Euro Area." In *The Euro Area and the Financial Crisis,* edited by Miroslav Beblavý, David Cobham, and L'udovít Ódor, 199–221. Cambridge: Cambridge University Press.

Hall, Peter A. 2012. "The Economics and Politics of the Euro Crisis." *German Politics* 21(4): 355–71.

Hansen, Randall, and Joshua C. Gordon. 2014. "Deficits, Democracy, and Demographics: Europe's Three Crises." *West European Politics* 37(6): 1199–222.

Hernández, Enrique, and Hanspeter Kriesi. 2016. "The Electoral Consequences of the Financial and Economic Crisis in Europe." *European Journal of Political Research* 55(2): 203–24.

Hopkin, Jonathan. 2001. "A 'Southern Model' of Electoral Mobilisation? Clientelism and Electoral Politics in Spain." *West European Politics* 24(1): 115–36.

———. 2002. "The Emergence and Convergence of the Cartel Party: Parties, State and Economy in Southern Europe." Paper presented at the 13th Conference of Europeanists, Chicago, 14–16 March 2002.

———. 2012. "Clientelism, Corruption and Political Cartels: Southern Europe." In *International Handbook on Informal Governance,* edited by Thomas Christiansen and Christine Neuhold, 198–215. Cheltenham, UK: Edward Elgar.

———. 2015. "The Troubled Southern Periphery: The Euro Experience in Italy and Spain." In Matthijs and Blyth, *Future of the Euro,* 161–84.

Hughes, Neil. 2011. "'Young People Took to the Streets and All of a Sudden All of the Political Parties Got Old': The 15M Movement in Spain." *Social Movement Studies* 10(4): 407–13.

Hutter, Swen, Hanspeter Kriesi, and Guillem Vidal. 2018. "Old versus New Politics: The Political Spaces in Southern Europe in Times of Crises." *Party Politics* 24(1): 10–22.

International Monetary Fund (IMF). 2010. *Greece - Memorandum of Economic and Financial Policies 2010.* Retrieved 8 April 2018 from https://www.imf.org/external/np/loi/2010/grc/080610.pdf.

———. 2017. *Balance of Payment and International Investment Positions Statistics* (BOP/IIP). Retrieved 7 July 2017 from http://data.imf.org/?sk=7A51304B-6426-40C0-83DD-CA473 CA1FD52.

Jonung, Lars, Eoin Drea, European Commission, and Directorate-General for Economic and Financial Affairs. 2009. *The Euro—It Can't Happen, It's a Bad Idea, It Won't Last U.S. Economists on the EMU, 1989–2002.* Brussels: European Commission, Directorate-General for Economic and Financial Affairs. Retrieved 7 July 2017 from http://ec.europa.eu/economy_finance/publications/publication16345_en.pdf.

Kaldor, Mary, and Sabine Selchow. 2015. *Subterranean Politics in Europe.* New York: Palgrave Macmillan.

Kanellopoulos, Kostas, and Konstantinos Kostopoulos. 2014. "The Major Organizations/groups behind the Greek Anti-Austerity Campaign. Repertoires of Action and Political Claims." Retrieved 15 July 2017 from http://ecpr.eu/Filestore/PaperProposal/ff897920-1ba0-49c7-947b-562c8ee29448.pdf.

Karyotis, Georgios, and Wolfgang Rüdig. 2015. "Blame and Punishment? The Electoral Politics of Extreme Austerity in Greece." *Political Studies* 63(1): 2–24.

Katz, Richard S., and Peter Mair. 1995. "Changing Models of Party Organization and Party Democracy the Emergence of the Cartel Party." *Party Politics* 1(1): 5–28.

———. 2009. "The Cartel Party Thesis: A Restatement." *Perspectives on Politics* 7(4): 753–66.

Key, Valdimer Orlando, and Milton C Cummings. 1966. *The Responsible Electorate.* Cambridge: Belknap Press of Harvard University Press.

Kriesi, Hanspeter. 2015. "Political Mobilization in Times of Crises: The Relationship between Economic and Political Crises." In *Austerity and Protest: Popular Contention in Times of Economic Crisis,* edited by Marco Giugni and Maria Grasso, 19–34. Burlington, VT: Ashgate.

Lucardie, Paul. 2000. "Prophets, Purifiers and Prolocutors Toward a Theory on the Emergence of New Parties." *Party Politics* 6(2): 175–85.

Lyrintzis, Christos. 2007. "Political Parties in Post-Junta Greece: A Case of 'Bureaucratic Clientelism'?" *West European Politics* 7(2): 99–118.

Mainwaring, Scott. 2006. "The Crisis of Representation in the Andes." *Journal of Democracy* 17(3): 13–27.

Mair, Peter. 2009. "Representative versus Responsible Government." Working Paper. Max Planck Institute for the Study of Societies, Cologne. Retrieved 15 July 2017 from http://cadmus.eui.eu/handle/1814/12533.

Matthijs, Matthias. 2014. "Mediterranean Blues: The Crisis in Southern Europe." *Journal of Democracy* 25(1): 101–15.

Matthijs, Matthias, and Mark Blyth, eds. 2015. *The Future of the Euro.* New York: Oxford University Press.

Molinas, César. 2012. "Theory of Spain's Political Class." *El País,* 12 September. Retrieved 15 July 2017 from http://elpais.com/elpais/2012/09/12/inenglish/1347449744_053124.html.

———. 2013. *Qué Hacer Con España: Del Capitalismo Castizo a La Refundación de Un País.* Madrid: Ediciones Destino.

Oakley, David. 2009. "Greece Downgraded over High Debt." *Financial Times,* 8 December. Retrieved 7 July 2017 from http://www.ft.com/intl/cms/s/0/2763a1d6-e3fc-11de-b2a9-00144feab49a.html#axzz3pHeBhojo.

Polanyi, Karl. 2001. *The Great Transformation: The Political and Economic Origins of Our Time.* Boston: Beacon Press. First published 1944.

Rhodes, Martin, ed. 1997. *Southern European Welfare States: Between Crisis and Reform.* London: Frank Cass.

Roberts, Kenneth. 2013. "Market Reform, Programmatic (De)alignment, and Party System Stability in Latin America." *Comparative Political Studies* 46(11): 1422–52.

Rodríguez Teruel, Juan, and Astrid Barrio. 2015. "Going National: Ciudadanos from Catalonia to Spain." *South European Society and Politics,* December: 1–21.

Roth, Felix, Felicitas Nowak-Lehmann D., and Thomas Otter. 2013. "Crisis and Trust in National and European Union Institutions: Panel Evidence for the EU, 1999 to 2012." EUI Working Paper RSCAS 2013/31, Robert Schuman Centre for Advanced Studies, San Domenico di Fiesole, Italy. Retrieved 15 July 2017 from http://cadmus.eui.eu/handle/1814/26975.

Royo, Sebastián. 2014. "Institutional Degeneration and the Economic Crisis in Spain." *American Behavioral Scientist* 58(12): 1568–91.

Rueda, David. 2007. *Social Democracy inside out: Partisanship and Labor Market Policy in Industrialized Democracies.* Oxford: Oxford University Press.

Spanish Ministry of Interior. 2018. Website. Retrieved 21 March 2018 from http://www.infoelectoral.mir.es accessed.

Tremlett, Giles. 2011. "Spain Changes Constitution to Cap Budget Deficit." *The Guardian,* 26 August. Retrieved 15 July 2017 from http://www.theguardian.com/business/2011/aug/26/spain-constitutional-cap-deficit.

———. 2012. "Mariano Rajoy Announces €65bn in Austerity Measures for Spain." *The Guardian,* 11 July. Retrieved 15 July 2017 from http://www.theguardian.com/business/2012/jul/11/mariano-rajoy-spain-65bn-cuts.

Vidal, Guillem. 2017. "Challenging Business as Usual? The Rise of New Parties in Spain in Times of Economic Crisis." *West European Politics.* Advance online publication.

Wolf, Martin. 2011. "Merkozy Failed to Save the Eurozone." *Financial Times,* 6 December. Retrieved 7 July 2017 from http://www.ft.com/intl/cms/s/0/396ff020-1ffd-11e1-8662-00144feabdc0.html#axzz3p05Sd600.

Part II

State Functions, the Welfare State, and the Economic Crisis

Chapter 6

Crisis and Changes in the Mediascape
Greece and the Globe

Franklin L. Hess

Introduction

The arrival of new mass media seems to coincide historically with periods
of political turmoil and extremism in Greece. Cinema is a prime example. Cinema exhibition arrived in Greece in November of 1896 and was,
from that point forward, a regular feature of Athenian life (Delveroudi
1999: 388–89). Indigenous, commercially oriented productions, however,
did not begin to appear until 1912,[1] when the Hungarian cameraman Joseph Hepp, who had settled permanently in Greece and would become
a fixture of Greek cinema, produced a newsreel titled "Little Princes in
the Garden of the Palace" ("Mikroi Prigkepes ston Kepo ton Anaktoron"),
which documented the everyday life of Greece's royal family. A second
newsreel, "The Entrance of the Greek Army in Thessaloniki" ("Eisodos
tou Ellenikou Stratou ste Thessaloniki"), which prominently featured
King Constantine I on horseback, followed later that year (Soldatos 2001:
19). The expansion of indigenous production capacities that followed, occurring in fits and starts from 1912 through the mid-1930s, coincided with
the great opposition between the republicans of Eleftherios Venizelos's
Liberal Party and the royalists of the People's Party, which began with the
Goudi Coup of 1909 and lasted through the end of the Second Republic
in 1935. Indeed, the topic matter of Hepp's first films and his reputation
as a royalist suggest that commercial cinema production in Greece was
politicized from its inception.

Notes for this chapter begin on page 174.

An intimate relationship between the introduction of new mass media and political turmoil is also evident in the histories of radio and television. Though radio buffs had begun broadcasting experimentally on a local scale much earlier, the first step toward the creation of a national radio network, the creation of a national radio station in Athens, took place in 1938 during Metaxas's dictatorship. Likewise, the creation of the national broadcaster, the National Institute of Radio (EIR), took place in 1945, immediately after the end of World War II as the Greek Civil War was beginning to take shape. Similarly, television's rise to prominence was intimately linked to the turbulent years of the 1960s, which saw first the rise to power of Georgios Papandreou's center-left party, the Center Union, and then its suppression by first the royal family and then the junta of the colonels, which ruled Greece from 1967 to 1974.

Today, once again, political instability and dramatic changes in Greece's mediascape are happening simultaneously. Politically, since the onset of the eurozone's sovereign debt crisis in 2010, Greece has seen a number of dramatic changes. The first is the weakening of the political center. The crisis has contributed to the marginalization of the most powerful political party of the post-junta era, the Panhellenic Socialist Movement (PASOK), and the weakening of its traditional rival, the center-right New Democracy (ND). Second, the crisis has weakened Greek democracy by dramatically increasing the influence of foreign politicians and external organizations (the so-called Troika of lenders: the International Monetary Fund, the European Commission, and the European Central Bank) over domestic policy decisions. The crisis even led to a breakdown in the parliamentary system and the appointment of an unelected technocrat, Lucas Papademos, as prime minister. Additionally, the crisis has elevated formerly marginal political movements to positions of prominence such as the far-right, neo-Nazi party Golden Dawn, which became the third-largest party in parliament after the January 2015 elections. Last, the crisis has brought about mass popular unrest and extensive political protest. This is but a partial list of the incidents of political instability that the country has experienced. Greece's mediascape has also changed radically in multiple ways. First, prominent newspapers have closed or struggled to keep their doors open. Second, the national broadcaster, the Hellenic Broadcasting Company (ERT), was unexpectedly shuttered in 2013 and its 3,500 employees summarily fired. Third, the influence of print and television journalism over public opinion has weakened and the influence of internet bloggers, aggregators, and alternative news sources has grown. Additionally, a comedian, Lakis Lazopoulos, has become one of the most influential political opinion makers in the country through his weekly television show "Al Tsantiri News," and last the Coalition of the Radical

Left (SYRIZA)–led government attempted a major reorganization of the sphere of television.

This chapter will explore the transformation of Greece's mediascape—exclusive of cinema, which is beyond the scope of this study and deserving of separate analysis—since the onset of the sovereign debt crisis in 2010. Simultaneously, it will attempt to document the relationship between mediascape transformation and the political change that the country has experienced. At first glance, the historical coincidence of changes in the mediascape and the occurrence of political turmoil might appear to be happenstance. Greek history has known its fair share of instability, political extremism, and military rule. It is only logical that there would be a significant amount of overlap with transformations of the mediascape. A close examination of the present moment, however, suggests that relationship is not merely aleatory, but multicausal. New mass media regimes change the way that the public accesses information, create spaces for alternative perspectives and for manipulating public opinion, and thereby destabilize the economic and political status quo. The destabilizing effects of mass media regime change, I will suggest, are often felt earlier and more strongly in the periphery, as opposed to the core, since political and economic power in the periphery is often more concentrated in the hands of a few and therefore frequently less elastic in its response to change. I will also suggest that the relationship between mass media regime change and political instability is not unidirectional. Political instability, in turn, leads citizens to distrust the veracity of information sources that are vetted by the status quo, prompting a turn to alternative media, alternative news sources, and alternative perspectives. A vicious circle is thus created that undermines the smooth functioning of democracy.

Theoretical Framework

The political power of the mass media has long been a focus of the field of media studies. In the 1970s and 1980s debates raged between techno-optimists (most prominently, Marshall McLuhan), and techno-pessimists (like Friedrich Kittler, Guy Debord, and Jean Baudrillard). McLuhan, the master of the aphorism, famously dubbed the media "extensions of man" (McLuhan 1994: 3) and claimed that "the medium is the message" (McLuhan 1994: 7). By the former he meant that the mass media grow out of the fundamental human desires such as the desire to expand our ability to communicate with others and the desire to mediate our mortality. Through the latter he suggests that the media, by altering our perception, also alter our social and political lives together. In other words, media become vehicles for political communication and, by extension, both liberation and oppression.

McLuhan's insights have been foundational for the field of media studies. They have not, however been without controversy. In particular, the humanistic tendencies in his thought created a backlash. Kittler is perhaps paradigmatic of McLuhan's critics. He begins *Gramophone-Film-Typewriter,* for instance, by declaring that "media determine our situation" (Kittler 1999: xxxix), by which he means that media determine both our consciousness and the subsequent development of media technologies. Whereas McLuhan viewed new media technologies as being founded on the content of old media technologies and thus part of a historical trajectory over which humans exert continued influence, Kittler argued that media technologies break with the human and acquire a trajectory of their own. He thus declares that "understanding media [the title of McLuhan's influential book] . . . remains an impossibility precisely because the dominant information technologies of the day control all understanding and its illusions" (Kittler 1999: xl). The forefront of this self-sustaining technological evolution, for Kittler, is the military industrial complex, which drives innovation. Communication technologies, for him, have become so central to our existence that traditional notions of war and power no longer apply: "real wars are not fought for people or fatherlands, but take place between different media, information technologies, data flows" (Kittler 1999: xli). Though they may have appeared hyperbolic until very recently to many readers, these words have acquired new significance in the age of Assange, Snowden, Wikileaks, American cyber-attacks on Iranian uranium processing facilities, and Russian election meddling.[2]

Subsequent scholarship that addresses the political role of the mass media has generally occupied positions on the spectrum defined by McLuhan and his critics. New media technologies have come and gone. Focuses have narrowed to specific genres or even subgenres of film, television, music, and new media. More attention has been given to audiences and the processes by which the media contribute to the creation of subjectivity. Additionally, the political focus of scholarship has tended to shift from politics in general to the political concerns of the cultural studies movement: race, ethnicity, class, gender, and sexuality. In general, however, McLuhan's fundamental observation about the influence of media over consciousness and hence politics, and the subsequent debate about human influence over this process, remains fundamental. Indeed, one need only think about the role that Twitter has played, on the one hand, in various democratic movements around the world and, on the other hand, in the Trump campaign and the presidency to understand that the debate between techno-optimism and techno-pessimism continues to be relevant.

The present study breaks with much previous scholarship in that it focuses not on the influence of a single media technology but on the mediascape as a whole. I am borrowing the term "mediascape" from Arjun
Appadurai's *Modernity at Large: Cultural Dimensions of Globalization* (1996).
For Appadurai, the term "mediascape" addresses both the media-produc-
tion and media-consumption capacities of a society as well as the content
those media. In other words, it refers both to "the distribution of the electronic capabilities to produce and disseminate information (newspapers,
magazines, television stations, and film-production studios) . . . and to
the images of the world created by these media" (Appadurai 1996: 35).
According to Appadurai, mediascapes are thus intimately linked to the
work of the imagination: "Whether produced by private or state interests, . . . [they provide] narrative-based accounts of strips of reality, and
what they offer to those who experience and transform them is a series of
elements . . . out of which scripts can be formed of imagined lives, their
own as well as those of others living in other places" (Appadurai 1996: 35).
The work of the imagination, for Appadurai, is the mechanism by which
media engage with the political through the structuring of consciousness
and the collective contemplation of shared presents and futures. Focusing on the mediascape as opposed to a single medium or genre lays bare
the process by which different media technologies are imbricated into
our existence and shape both individual consciousness and our collective
lives together. It suggests that subjectivity in general and political subjectivity in particular are structured through an agonistic process in which
various media and media actors are competing to shape the terrain of
consciousness.

Examining the current mediascape thus requires that attention be paid
to the mechanisms by which the mediascape is shaped: media ownership
structures, the legal frameworks within which the media operate, the various channels by which political parties and politicians attempt to exert
influence over the media, the cultures of media content production and
consumption, and so on. In other words, theorization about the political
role of the mass media should be based on a clear assessment of structures
that shape the current moment. The broader framework in which these
changes will be examined is the increasing spread of neoliberal capitalism
in Greece. The term neoliberalism is inherently amorphous and ambiguous. Nonetheless as Springer, Birch, and MacLeavy (2016) have suggested,
most scholars agree that the term describes a set of "new political, economic, and social arrangements within society that emphasize market
relations, re-tasking the role of the state, and individual responsibility"
(Springer, Birch, and MacLeavy 2016: 2). This is not to say, however, that
the principles of neoliberalism are uniform in their application. As Peck

has pointed out, "there are not 'pure' or paradigmatic neoliberal transitions, but a series of institutionally mediated and geopolitically distinct hybrids" (Peck 2004: 395).

There are problems, however, with giving emphasis to the geographical diversity of neoliberalism. First, neoliberalism's principles are designed to bring greater standardization across cultural and political borders by regulating economic and political life. Second, the application of neoliberal principles often occurs through international pressure rather than internal democratic processes. These processes can be more or less coercive, ranging from recommendations by economic advisers and trade agreements to, in cases of financial crisis, memorandums of understanding (MoUs) that require reforms in return for financial support. This second point is particularly germane for Greece, which, since the sovereign debt crisis emerged in 2010, has served as a laboratory for the application of neoliberal principles of its Troika of lenders, who have frequently insisted on reforms and sacrifices that they would not dare to implement in their home countries. A partial list of the reforms that Greece has been asked to implement since 2010 includes the liberalization of markets and the opening of closed professions, the privatization of state-owned businesses, extensive changes in the tax code designed to increase revenue and reduce tax evasion, the contraction of the welfare state and the public sector, multiple reductions of pensions, and the liberalization of labor laws (in order to weaken the influence of organized labor).

These changes, the results of which have been mixed at best for the Greek economy, have not been met with passivity. There has been considerable protest, both active (marches, protests, political organization) and passive (tax evasion and other forms of personal noncompliance). The mass media have been caught in the vortex of this neoliberal change as successive governments have attempted to dramatically alter the mediascape by restructuring television. ND fired the opening salvo here, closing ERT in 2013 and replacing it with a dramatically streamlined public broadcaster. After winning the elections in 2015, the SYRIZA government reinstated ERT and proceeded to attempt a dramatic restructuring of private television in 2016. The mass media have also served as one of the principal means by which debates about the neoliberalism and its consequences have been conducted. The narrative of the mass media's encounter with neoliberalism that follows is largely a story of destabilization and contestation. This narrative will attempt to elucidate the mechanisms by which political change and media-regime change interact. In so doing, it will also attempt to document the processes by which an evolving mediascape allows new channels for both protest and submission to emerge.

The State of the Media before the Crisis

In their book, *Mass Media in Greece: Power, Politics, and Privatization,* Thimios Zaharopoulos and Manny E. Paraschos describe the traditional raison d'etre of the mass media in Greece as "partisan goal advancement" (Zaharopoulos and Paraschos 1993: 2). The Greek mediascape, in fact, has long been shaped by complexly interwoven relationships between three main groups: (1) the political class, which awards government contracts and shapes the business climate; (2) business oligarchs, who profit from government contracts, seek a beneficial regulatory climate for their business interests, and frequently own an interest in major media groups; and (3) journalists, many of whom benefit personally and professionally from their ties to the political class and the business oligarchs. This chapter will explore the changing nature of these relationships under austerity. My focus on these relationships, however, should not be construed to suggest that Greece represents an exceptional case in this regard. Quite the opposite, these types of complexly interwoven, mutually reinforcing networks are becoming increasingly the norm in the Western world. Nor should this statement be interpreted as an argument that independent journalistic voices do not exist in Greece. There are plenty of committed journalists who produce quality journalism that benefits the public good. On this last point, however, I would sound a note of caution: the type of complexly interwoven political and business interests that exist in Greece and elsewhere in the West inevitably influence even the neutral and objective journalistic voices by shaping the discursive and economic terrain on which they function. As documentary filmmaker and former journalist Aris Chatzistefanou has argued, journalists are "minions to power . . . [who are] at their best employees and at their worst shareholders" (Chatzistefanou 2011).

Print Media

By American and Western European standards, Greece's print journalism culture in 2009 was, in many ways, vibrant and diverse. Athens, a city of 5 million people, had nearly thirty daily newspapers with significant circulations as well as a wide variety of weeklies, representing a wide spectrum of political perspectives. Greece had a significant newspaper-buying public prior to the crisis. According to statistics collected by the Union of Daily Athenian Newspaper Owners, 104,000,000 daily newspapers were sold in Greece in 2008 and 92,800,000 were sold in 2009 (roughly 9.5 and 8.4 newspapers per inhabitant per year) ("Oi Treis 'Typhones'" 2013). Major statistical organizations like Eurostat and the Organisation for Economic Co-operation and Development do not collect statistics on newspaper circulation, so it is difficult to establish a point of comparison; but Greece's per capita newspaper sales, even before the crisis, were probably less than many other European Union (EU) countries. In the United Kingdom, for instance, approximately 46 percent and 42 percent of households had a daily newspaper subscription in 2008 and 2009, respectively (Communic@tions Management 2013: 11). The relative paucity of Greek newspaper sales likely reflects the fact that home delivery of newspapers is virtually nonexistent. Newspapers are sold almost exclusively in kiosks and small neighborhood stores.

Print journalism in Greece is less consolidated and more overtly politicized than in the United States and many other Western democracies. This was true before the crisis (Zaharopoulos and Paraschos 1993: 15–34, 67–106), and it continues to be true. Most newspapers have a defined political slant, and many are aligned with specific political parties. Many of these alliances are more or less permanent. *Rizospastis,* for instance, is the mouthpiece of the Communist Party of Greece (KKE). *Avgi* is associated with the parties of the new left: Synaspismos until 2004 and the SYRIZA afterward. *Eleftherotypia, To Vima, Avriani,* and *Ta Nea* were traditionally associated with the center-left PASOK, while *Apogevmatini, Eleftheros Typos, Ethnos,* and *Kathimerini* to varying degrees supported center-right and right-wing positions and ND. Such political alliances, however, are not always permanent, reflecting the fact that political affiliations are often very closely tied to specific business interests of media owners in Greece, which shift over time. Loyalties, in other words, may be redirected as the political winds change direction. Both *Avriani* and *Eleftheros Typos,* for instance, have flirted with the other side of the political spectrum during their recent histories, as reported by the newspaper *Proto Thema* ("Thymetheite Merika" 2014) and on the news website Zougla ("Apo ton Voudouri" 2009).

Ownership structures of newspapers vary greatly. Some are party mouthpieces, and others are comparatively independent. Some are owned by large publishing companies, such as the Lambrakis Journalistic Organization, which owns *Vima* and *Nea,* the newspaper that usually has the largest circulation in Greece. Others are owned by their editors. Still others are owned by economic oligarchs. *Eleftheros Typos,* for instance, was owned by the industrialist Theodore Angelopoulos and his wife Gianna Angelopoulos-Daskalaki until they sold the paper in 2009 ("Pouletheke kai Episema" 2009). Likewise, *Kathimerini* is owned by the Alafouzos family, which made its fortune in shipping and has since diversified into other concerns. Last, *Ethnos* is published by Pegasus Publishing, which is controlled by the Bobolas family, which also owns Ellaktor, Inc., a major construction company that specializes in public works projects, and the television station Mega.

Though the commitment to investigative journalism is strong, newspapers are not always guided by an equally strong code of journalistic ethics; occasionally they resort to innuendo and mudslinging to score political points. The newspaper reading public, however, is by and large aware of the highly politicized nature of print journalism. They often purchase multiple newspapers, particularly on Sundays, in order to get a range of perspectives on the issues of the day.

Television

Television arrived comparatively late in Greece. The first experimental broadcasts took place at the 1960 Thessaloniki International Fair and were organized by the Greek electrical company DEH (Public Power Corporation) in conjunction with the Dutch electronics company Phillips, which provided the broadcasting equipment and placed a hundred television sets at key locations around Thessaloniki (Valoukos 1998: 13). After the Thessaloniki broadcasts, however, plans for a television station lay dormant for five years as government agencies wrangled over control and politicians dragged their feet. Finally, in 1965, during the Georgios Papandreou government, experimental broadcasts began again in Athens under the auspices of EIR and TED (Television of the Armed Forces), which was renamed YENED (Information Service of the Armed Forces) in 1970.[3] The broadcasts of EIR and TED became regularized early in 1966, though the television program was fairly basic. Each channel broadcast approximately three hours a day during the evening hours (Valoukos 1998: 14).

From 1965 through 1989 state television had a monopoly over the airwaves, and governments, whether democratically elected or not, exerted considerable influence over the television program, particularly the news broadcasts. Propaganda, of course, was most pronounced during the junta, but it did not stop after the return to democracy. Both PASOK and ND used the power of patronage to exert influence over television, appointing supporters to key administrative, journalistic, and creative positions after electoral victories.[4] In the summer of 1975 the ND-led government of Constantine Karamanlis passed a law creating a new corporation, ERT. They envisioned the incorporation of YENED into this new broadcaster in 1977. Military control of the second channel, however, did not end until 1982, when control was shifted to civilian government, which at the time was led by Andreas Papandreou's PASOK, and the station was renamed ERT2.

Private television did not arrive in Greece until 1989, when permits were granted to two channels, Mega and New Television. The former became a mainstay of Greek television. The latter never actually broadcast. Subsequently, other private channels were created: ANT1 (also known as Antenna), Alpha, ALTER, SKAI, and Star as well as numerous smaller channels. The principal impetus to create private television channels came from conservative politicians and business oligarchs, but PASOK, increasingly a center-left party in the 1990s and 2000s, quickly adapted to the new media environment. Private channels rapidly outpaced their public counterparts in terms of viewership, but public television remained a vital part of public discourse. The news broadcasts of NET (New Greek Television, the successor of ERT2), in particular, maintained a significant viewing public.

Because television broadcasting is a capital-intensive activity, Greece's major publishers and business oligarchs have played a key role in the creation of private television stations. For instance, major stakeholders in Mega, which traditionally vies with ANT1 and Alpha for the top spot in terms of viewership, include the Vardinogiannis family; the Lambrakis Journalistic Organization, which publishes *Nea* and *Vima*; and Pegasus Publishing, which until recently was controlled by the Bobolas family. Because of financial difficulty, the latter two organizations changed hands in 2017. The Lambrakis Journalistic Organization was purchased by Alter Ego, the media company owned by shipping magnate Evangelos Marinakis, and Pegasus Publishing was acquired by Dimera Media Investments, which is controlled by Russian–Greek businessman Ivan Savvidis. The Antenna Group, which owns ANT1, is controlled by the heirs of the recently deceased ship-owner and industrialist Minos Kyriakou.[5] Alpha, the third of the big three, has a long and complicated ownership history. It began its career as SKAI and was under the control of ship owner Giannis Alafouzos. In the 1990s, when the Alafouzos Group encountered economic problems, it was sold to Dimitris Kontominas, whose principal business interests were in insurance (Interamerican) and banking. In 2008, Kontominas sold a majority stake in the company to the RTL Group (formerly Radio Television Luxembourg), which is controlled by the German publishing giant, the Bertelsmann Group ("RTL Buys into Greek Television Market" 2008). Kontominas, however, continued to be the principal minority shareholder and to serve as the president of the company. When the RTL Group decided to leave the Greek market, Kontominas repurchased their shares through his holding company DEMCO, and is once again the majority shareholder (Sweney 2012). The Alafouzos family returned to the airwaves in 2006, purchasing a small channel, Seven, for its broadcasting permit and reopening SKAI (Nedos 2006). Last, the Vardinogiannis family, whose principal interests are in oil and gas, shipping, and athletics, controls Star as well as the largest stake in Mega.

The legal framework in which private television stations operated is poorly defined and even more poorly enforced. Law 1866/1989, which established private television stations, contained no provisions for the allocation of the frequency spectrum. The law did, however, contain a provision for the granting of licenses and a requirement for returning a certain percentage of the station's profits to the government (Zaharopoulos and Paraschos 1993: 137–38). Neither has never been properly enforced. In 1993, without any sort of competition, the ND-led government granted seven special, seven-year permits for national stations that stretched through the year 2000. The PASOK-led government that followed later that year after elections granted two additional special permits for national stations and three for regional stations. An auction for the next round of permits was announced in 1997 and applications were taken. The applications were never acted on, however, and the competition was invalidated in 2002. The same story was repeated in 2003 and 2004. Since 2000, private stations have been operating without permits and are technically illegal ("E Amartole Istoria" 2015). This state of affairs has benefited the established political parties, PASOK and ND, since political connections play a major role in determining who has been granted de facto permission to broadcast. The political parties have also jockeyed for political control of the National Council of Radio–Television, which is in charge of enforcing regulations.

Radio

The creation of the first national station occurred in 1938 in Athens during the Metaxas regime. This was far from the first radio broadcast that had occurred on Greek territory, however. Thessaloniki, in fact, had had private broadcasts since 1928. These broadcasts, which continued for more than twenty years, were the creation of a local radio enthusiast, Christos Tsingiridis. There were also experimental broadcasts during this period in the Athens area (Heretakis 2014: 1–2).

After the end of the Tripartite Occupation of Greece during World War II, the Greek government took steps to consolidate its control over the airwaves by creating a national broadcasting corporation, EIR, in 1945. Soon afterwards, Tsingiridis's station in Thessaloniki, after an attempt at nationalization, was closed by the government, which in keeping with most European governments sought to maintain public control of broadcasting. The government opened its own station in 1947 in Thessaloniki. The military also began regular radio broadcasts during the Greek Civil War, and rapidly expanded, with the assistance of the U.S. military, a parallel radio network in the years that followed. The military maintained a separate radio broadcasting network until 1982, when their radio stations, along with their television station, were incorporated into the national network (Zaharopoulos and Paraschos 1993: 39–42, 47).

The creation of EIR in 1945 marks the beginning of a state monopoly over radio broadcasting. In practice, however, this monopoly was far from complete. In contradistinction to television broadcasting, which is highly capital intensive, the creation of a small-scale radio station requires very little investment. Accordingly, Greece has a long tradition of unofficial, pirate stations. Beginning in 1987 the state monopoly over radio began to show fissures. Following legislation that allowed municipalities and communities to set up independent stations, the mayor of Athens, ND's Miltiadis Evert, created Athens 9.84 on 31 May. Later that year, Law 1730/1987 established a legal framework for the creation of private radio stations, which began a flood of private radio broadcasting (Zaharopoulos and Paraschos 1993: 49–53, 55).

Radio broadcasters in the years leading up to the crisis were diverse and plentiful. Many political parties maintained their own station. Many newspapers and television stations also maintained radio stations. The state channels, broadcasting higher-quality programs that featured artistic folk music, classical music, culture magazines, and news broadcasts, maintained a significant audience.

Internet

Greece has been comparatively slow to adopt the internet. According to Eurostat, only 31 percent of Greek households had an internet connection in 2008, compared to an EU average of 60 percent. This put Greece at the bottom of the EU-27, slightly above Bulgaria and Romania. Similarly, there were only 38.2 internet users per 100 residents in 2008. By 2010, however, Greece was showing signs of catching up. The number of internet users per capita had grown to 44.4 percent, and the percentage of households with internet had increased to 46 percent (Seybert 2012: 2). The latter represents a 48.3 percent growth rate that far outstripped the EU-27's 16.7 percent growth rate during the same period.

Greece's comparatively slow adoption of the internet prior to 2008 likely reflects cultural biases and bureaucratic rigidity as opposed to economic development. Many poorer European countries including Estonia, Latvia, Lithuania, Hungary, and Poland were much quicker to gravitate to the Web. Greek culture traditionally places a high emphasis on face-to-face interaction in public spaces. Accordingly, the internet and its virtual communities were originally met with a high degree of suspicion.

Critical Events and Phenomena Restructuring the Mediascape

As with the Greek economy as a whole, the Greek mass media have experienced contraction during the crisis. Newspaper circulation has shrunk, and newspapers have closed. Television stations have closed, including for a period of time the national broadcaster, ERT. Other stations have been forced to dramatically reduce or alter their programs and find new investors to survive. The one exception to this trend is the internet, which has expanded its penetration into Greek households and has emerged as an important alternative source of information and entertainment. The crisis has also coincided with significant innovation as content creators have adapted to the new mediascape. New and innovative ownership structures have emerged in the print media. Private television has seen its influence over the voting public wane. Additionally, with public distrust of politicians and journalists at extremely high levels, comedians have emerged as new, trusted voices in the public sphere. Last, the internet has spawned a new class of parajournalistic information sources: news aggregators, blogs, and alternative journalism sites.

Diminishing Newspaper Circulation and Newspaper Closures

Newspaper circulation has fallen precipitously since the onset of the crisis. From 104 million daily newspapers per annum in 2008, circulation dropped to 43 million in 2012 ("The "Oi Treis 'Typhones'"" 2013). This contraction continued a long-term trend of diminishing newspaper sales, a trend that has been evident virtually everywhere in the globe. There is little doubt, however, that the crisis and the accompanying economic problems have accelerated the contraction of newspaper sales in Greece.

The reasons for this contraction are quite simple: expanding access to internet news sources, which include the online portals of the major newspapers, on the one hand, and shrinking disposable income, on the other. Quite simply, spending a euro on a newspaper has become a luxury for many Greeks. The reduced revenue stream that has resulted from the contraction of sales has had negative effects on the diversity of voices in the print media. Several major newspapers have been forced to shutter their doors. *Eleftherotypia,* a newspaper that was created in 1975 after the end of Greece's military dictatorship as an opposition paper to the ND governments that were led by Constantine Karamanlis, began facing economic difficulties in the summer of 2011 as its access to credit withered. By the end of the year, the newspaper was in bankruptcy proceedings and had suspended publications ("Ypevlethe apo ten *Eleftherotypia*" 2011). The paper managed to briefly reorganize and resume publication in 2013

("Aurio Epanakyklophorei" 2013), but ceased publication again in November 2014.

The crisis also saw the closure of a second traditionally left-leaning newspaper, *Avriani*, which used to pride itself as on its masthead as "the newspaper that destroyed the cult of Karamanlis" ("*e ephemerida pou gkremise ton Karamanlismo*"). Created in 1980 by the businessman Giorgos Kouris, ostensibly as a vehicle for establishing influence over Greece's politicians, the newspaper managed to gain traction by undercutting its competition in terms of price and ignoring a general press strike in 1980. Sales skyrocketed in that year because *Avriani* was the only newspaper being published during the strike, and the newspaper continued to maintain its market share once the strike concluded. The purchase of a major stake in the television station, ALTER, followed in the 1990s ("G. Kouris" 2012). The downfall of Kouris and *Avriani* was swift. By 2012 Kouris and his associates allegedly found themselves in difficult economic straits, and both the newspaper and television station were closed. Bankruptcy followed in 2013, as did a series of lawsuits by journalists who accused Kouris of raiding the company's bank accounts and leaving journalists and the Greek state unpaid. Kouris, in turn, blamed two of his associates at ALTER for misappropriating funds and sending them to off-shore companies that were registered in the names of relatives ("Gramma apo ten Phylake" 2013). His son Andreas, who was on the board of directors of ALTER, eventually stood trial for owing the government €2 million in unpaid taxes ("Enas Kouris sten Phylake?" 2013). He was found innocent in late 2014 ("Athoos gia ten Ypothese" 2014). Kouris proceeded to open a new newspaper toward the end of 2013, *Kontra News* ("O Giorgos Kouris Vgazei" 2013).

Newspapers on the political right have also been hit hard by the crisis. *Apogevmatini*, another mainstay of post-junta journalism, closed its doors in early November 2010. Its publisher, the industrialist Kostas Sarantopoulos, claimed economic difficulties, but courts rejected his bankruptcy claims and later sentenced him to three years in jail for failure to pay tax obligations associated with the company ("Tria Chronia me Anastole" 2013). *Eleftheros Typos*, which belonged to the industrialist Theodore Angelopoulos and his wife Yianna Angelopoulos-Daskalaki, who led the Organizing Committee for the 2004 Athens Olympic Games, was also closed briefly in 2009 ("Kleinei o *Eleftheros Typos*" 2009). It reopened, however, later that year following its sale, and continues to be published today (Galanis 2009).

As the above closures demonstrate, the crisis has weakened many of the complex clusters of political and economic interests that have dominated print journalism in Greece. As government spending has diminished and as the political landscape has become unstable, the print media have become less valuable as a vehicle for currying favor and exerting influence. Additionally, the crisis has also weakened the independence of journalists. Journalists at surviving newspapers, because of their economic vulnerability, feel pressure to toe the line and not upset advertisers and ownership. Nonetheless, amid the closures and diminished circulation, there are also some very positive developments that herald the emergence of more independent journalistic voices. Of particular interest here is *Efimerida ton Syntakton* or the *Newspaper of the Editors*. This newspaper was formed in 2010 by former employees of *Eleftherotypia*, about a hundred of whom chipped in to form its starting capital. Its workers are organized as a cooperative, the Cooperative of Workers at Newspapers and Periodicals, and the paper is published by the Independent Mass Informational Media, Inc., a company that is majority owned by the cooperative ("E Istoria tes 'Ef.Syn'" 2016). All the approximately 150 workers receive the same pay, except for the editor in chief, Nicholas Voulelis, who works for free ("We Had No Investors" 2015). Since its inception the paper has quickly gained readership. As of the summer of 2017, it was the second- or third-most popular newspaper in Athens and the fourth- or fifth-most popular nationally. Its journalism initially represented a vital, independent voice within the current political landscape. More recently, however, the paper has been criticized for becoming too closely allied to SYRIZA. Its ownership structure nonetheless constitutes a potential model for journalists and newspaper workers elsewhere in the world as they seek to survive in a rapidly evolving media environment.

The weakened position of traditional print media, as noted previously, is also due to the rising prominence of the internet within Greek society. Newspapers have adapted to this state of affairs; nearly all major newspapers have created electronic portals. The competition, however, has expanded even more rapidly. News aggregators have multiplied. The blogosphere and Twittersphere have exploded, changing the way the political events are organized and understood (Papailias 2012: 5). Most significantly, new types of online media outlets have emerged that fulfill at least some of the journalistic duties of traditional newspapers. Significant among them are Protagon (www.protagon.gr), which occupies the political center and was founded by the journalist turned politician Stavros Theodorakis; tvxs (TV Without Borders, tvxs.gr), which slants to the left and has been associated with the journalist and member of the European Parliament, Stelios Kouloglou; and the Press Project (www.thepressproject.gr), which is left wing in its orientation, but not associated with a particular politician or party. There is also a host of smaller, and often less reputable, online media outlets.

Of particular interest here is the Press Project. The Press Project is the brainchild of BitsnBytes, an internet services company founded by Konstantinos Papadopoulos (pen name Kostas Efimeros) that has been involved in a wide variety of activities, including the production of the Katerina Kitidi and Aris Chatzistefanou's documentary *Debtocracy;* in addition, the Press Project supported the ERT Open campaign's web broadcasts in the aftermath of the closure of ERT (see below). It began as a selective news aggregator but, according to their website, evolved into a self-described "experimental medium that aims for the substantive and in-depth analysis of specific aspects of contemporary events and in its current version functions as a complete information portal" (Press Project 2016). Although their staff is limited in number, the organization strives to provide a full-service news portal that includes radio and video offerings and emphasizes original investigative journalism. To further these aims, the organization embarked in the latter parts of 2015 on a fundraising campaign, titled "the 1101," that attempts to target donors who are willing to donate 5€ a month to help them expand their operations and provide journalism that is truly independent and free from the taint of cronyism. They believe that such journalism is crucial for the future success of democratic governance in Greece. With the untimely death of Efimeros in June 2017, however, the future of these initiatives is uncertain.[6]

The Closure of the Hellenic Broadcasting Corporation and the Fear of a Nationless State

By far the most momentous change in the mediascape that occurred during the crisis was the closure of ERT (the Hellenic Broadcasting Corporation). On Tuesday 11 June 2013, at 4:00 P.M., Greek governmental spokesperson Simos Kedikoglou dropped a bombshell: he announced the government was closing ERT and firing its 2,656 employees. The closure—which was accomplished by ministerial decree and approved by Prime Minister Antonis Samaras—would be effective in eight hours, at 12:00 A.M. of the follow day. By closing ERT, the government would be satisfying in one fell swoop long-standing demands from the Troika to reduce the number of public employees. Kedikoglou, in his statement, described ERT as a particularly glaring example of public sector corruption and waste that could be corrected only through a complete purge. This would not mean, he assured the public, the end of public television and public radio. The government, in the same statement, announced plans to create a smaller, more efficient, more neutral, and more transparent broadcaster, which would be named New Hellenic Radio, Internet, and Television (NERIT) and would emerge in September.[7]

Kedikoglou's statement contained massive inaccuracies. ERT, which housed three domestic television stations, one satellite television station, three radio stations, and an important state orchestra, was not particularly overstaffed. Its staffing levels compared favorably to other European state broadcasters, like Germany's Association of Public Broadcasting Corporations in the Federal Republic of Germany (ARD) and Second German Television (ZWF), and the British Broadcasting Corporation (BBC), in terms of its number of employees and its cost to the taxpayer ("Spiegel" 2013). Its three television stations averaged together between 11 percent and 14 percent of the television audience in any given week, not the 4 percent figure that Kedikoglou cited in his statement ("Ekleisan ten ERT" 2013). While no one would argue that ERT was a model state institution, it was making steady progress in terms of efficiency. Its employees had suffered the same cuts in salary that other public employees had suffered. Additionally, the payrolls had been cut by more than a thousand employees since the start of the crisis. Funded in part by a monthly 4€ tax on the electric bill, ERT had managed in both 2010 and 2011 to actually return substantial funds to the general budget of the Greek state. Closing ERT or making it smaller did not represent a substantial savings to the taxpayers of Greece ("ERT se Arithmous" 2013).

Kedikoglou's statement also conveniently overlooked the fact that that the two major political parties of the post-junta era, ND and PASOK, were largely responsible for whatever inefficiency and corruption existed at ERT. Every change in political leadership brought changes in the leadership and staff at ERT as politicians sought to consolidate control over the message of the state broadcaster and reward their supporters with public sector jobs. Since Greek public employees—particularly those with political connections—are frequently hired for life, the employee rolls swelled, and talented people were often shunted into meaningless jobs. In spite of this decades-long noxious interference of politicians in the day-to-day operations of public broadcasting in Greece, the vast majority of ERT's employees took their responsibilities seriously. The radio and television stations of ERT, as of 11 June 2013, were all functioning as independent journalistic voices and all were contributing substantially to the public sphere. They were the only voice on television that was not economically beholden to Greece's oligarchs. With a weak coalition government in place that had almost no ability to exercise the powers of patronage, they were also increasingly independent of the political class. The ND government's decision to close ERT clearly reflected a desire to neutralize this journalistic voice.

The condemnation of the decision to shutter ERT was swift and broad-based. Virtually all sectors of Greek society were adamant in the rejection of both the decision and the way that it was made. Of the major political parties, only ND and the fascist Golden Dawn stood behind the decision. Governing coalition partners, PASOK and the Democratic Left (DIMAR) claimed that they had been blindsided by the decision, and DIMAR eventually left the coalition government over the closure (Kitsantonis and Donadio 2015). Television journalists went on strike for four days in support of their colleagues at ERT. Greece's two major trade unions also held a general strike to protest the closure, and a diverse crowd of protesters gathered daily in the courtyard of the ERT building to protest the government's decision ("24ore Apergia gia ten ERT" 2013, "Kinetopoieseis kai Apergies" 2013). The Greek Council of State also weighed in on the issue, first in a temporary decision by its president that was then confirmed by a plenary session, stating that ERT must remain open until the new state broadcasting entity has been constituted ("Semasia tes Apophases" 2013). In spite of the decision, the Samaras government proceeded with the closure of ERT and the termination of its employees.

The crisis surrounding the closing of ERT almost became a tipping point in the European sovereign debt crisis, both within Greece and within Europe as a whole. Within Greece, it has exposed the political leadership as never before, confirming their subservience to the Troika and reinforcing suspicions that they were indifferent to not only the average Greek person, but also to the Greek nation as a whole. For other member-states of the EU, the shuttering of ERT not only raised the specter of the loss of polyphony in the public sphere, but also raised the even more alarming possibility that cultural particularity in the new Europe will be sacrificed on the altar of economic efficiency.

Accordingly, the condemnation of Samaras's decision internationally was equally swift and vociferous. Journalists and international media organizations such as the European Broadcasting Union (EBU) expressed shock at the decision and characterized it as antidemocratic. Public broadcasters in Belgium broadcast with the logo of ERT as a show of solidarity, and a variety of European politicians commented negatively on the decision. Ironically, even the European Council and the Troika took pains to distance themselves from the decision of the Samaras government, stating publicly that they had not asked for the closure of ERT ("ERT Shutdown" 2013; "Diapseudei o O. Ren" 2013).

The closing of ERT moved Greece's fellow EU members in ways that the impoverishment, hunger, and economic chaos that everyday Greeks suffer had not. One suspects that, inadvertently, the Samaras government's decision to shutter ERT, by highlighting the very real and multifaceted cultural chaos that austerity was creating, laid bare the logic of the

Troika-imposed cuts in a way that the cuts to health care and education have not. It laid bare, in other words, the prospect that European integration, particularly with Germany at the helm, will result in an assembly of nationless states: states that are nations in name only and that have been evacuated of the traditions, habits, and values that constitute the imagined, but nonetheless very tangible, substance of nationhood.

After the formal closure of ERT and the seizing of its internet addresses and digital transmitters, members of the staff barricaded themselves in ERT headquarters and began producing a pirate broadcast, which was eventually given the name ERT Open. This broadcast that was distributed with the help of the EBU, which provided a satellite feed for the channel and internet addresses and server space for a web TV broadcast ("EBU Continues to Underpin" 2013). The assistance from the EBU lasted until 21 August 2013, when the EBU decided to discontinue assistance after an interim Greek broadcaster, Public Television (DT), which had begun broadcasting on 10 July, started producing a news bulletin ("ERT Streaming to End" 2013). After the EBU's support ended, the ERT Open program continued to be distributed via the internet by other means. These pirate broadcasts were generally well received and struck many as some of the most independent, unbiased reporting that Greece had ever seen. The pirate broadcasters were abetted by a group of sympathetic citizens who occupied the courtyard of ERT and helped keep the police at bay. The government, wary of the potential tinderbox that they had created, was also eager to avoid a heavy-handed takeover of the building. Finally, in the early morning hours of 7 November 2013, Greek SWAT forces broke into ERT headquarters, arrested four staff members who were working there, and temporarily closed the pirate broadcasts down ("Parousia Eisangelea" 2013).

NERIT

DT was a poor replacement for ERT. It employed limited personnel, who were largely inexperienced and had been hired on temporary contracts, and it broadcast only one channel of content, which largely consisted of obscure films including documentaries. The government appointed a board of supervisors for NERIT in August of 2013 ("Oi 'Eklektoi'" 2013), which hired a board of directors in October of the same year ("E NERIT Apektese" 2013). In January 2014 the new organization assumed control of DT and began hiring a permanent staff for NERIT, which was to be capped at five hundred ("E Prokeryxe ASEP" 2014). The station was officially renamed NERIT on 4 May 2014.

The coalition government that closed ERT promised a more stream-lined, more professional, more independent broadcaster that would be modeled on the BBC ("Oloklere e Anakoinose Kedikoglou" 2013). The broadcaster that emerged was certainly more streamlined, but it failed on all other counts. Because they largely hired younger, inexperienced journalists, its news and athletic broadcasts were of very low quality and lacked polish. Additionally, there were allegations that the government, after trumpeting its pledge to create a neutral broadcaster, was actually trying to exert political influence over the station. In August 2014, for instance, parliament passed a resolution streamlining the process for se-lecting members of NERIT's board of supervisors. The EBU criticized this move, arguing that it removes safeguards designed to prevent undue po-litical influence ("EBU Concerned" 2014). Additionally, representatives of the governing coalition appeared to be attempting to influence the sta-tion's hiring practices and journalistic decisions ("Familiar Faces" 2014). In September 2014 charges of political interference in the hiring of 132 journalists for NERIT led to the decision to pursue judicial research on the topic ("Eisangelike Ereuna" 2014). Finally, in October 2014, four mem-bers of the board of supervisors, including the chair and deputy chair, resigned, citing government interference in the hiring procedures and journalistic decisions (Eptakili 2014; Mac Con Uladh 2014).[8]

One of SYRIZA's electoral platforms was the reopening of ERT and the rehiring of its workers, which was accomplished on 11 June 2015. This decision restored much of the status quo ante of July 2013; however, Law 4324/2015, which reopened ERT, met with resistance from POSPERT, the National Federation of Associations of the Personnel of the Workforce of Hellenic Broadcasting Company, the union that traditionally represented the workers of ERT, except the journalists. POSPERT protested many aspects of the law, including the relatively benign treatment of NERIT employees. The central bone of contention, however, seems to be that the law excluded the union's high-level members from serving on the board of directors of the new ERT, which includes two positions for em-ployees, one of which must be filled by a journalist. The law specifically forbids members of the board of directors of a union or other labor or-ganization from holding either of these positions and specifies that the representatives will be determined by a direct, secret, and universal vote. As part of their protest POSPERT continued separate ERT Open radio broadcasts on 106.7 FM in Athens and on the Web even after ERT returned to the air ("Kontra SYRIZA kai POSPERT" 2015; Maniatis 2015b). On 23 September 2015 the president of POSPERT, Panagiotis Kalfagiannis, and Dimitris Kounis, the organization's treasurer, were arrested for illegally broadcasting the ERT Open program ("Erixan Mauro" 2015).

Distrust of Traditional Media and
the Rise of the Comedian as Political Voice

On 28 June 2015 the government of Prime Minister Alexis Tsipras broke off negotiations with the Troika over the terms for receiving the next installment of capital from the second MoU and announced that they would conduct a referendum on 5 July to give the Greek people a voice in determining whether to accept (yes) or reject (no) the bailout terms that the Troika had proposed: a package of debt extension, austerity measures, and structural reforms that were supposed to make the Greek debt manageable and the economy more competitive. As soon as this vote was announced, chaos broke loose. The Eurogroup rejected Greece's request for a week of bridge funding, which they wanted to maintain economic stability in the period leading up to the referendum. Because of the drawn-out negotiations and brinksmanship in the weeks before the announcement of the referendum, Greeks had begun withdrawing their deposits from the banking system. This trickle became a full-blown bank run as the possibilities of a Grexit became more and more tangible. On 30 June, when the ECB refused to grant Greek banks additional liquidity to cover their positions, the Tsipras administration was forced to call a bank holiday. Withdrawals were limited to €60 a day and could be made only from ATMs. The stock market was closed as well.

The Tsipras administration thus went into the referendum with considerable economic headwinds. In the days leading up to the referendum, most analysts believed, based on public opinion research, that the vote would be very close. Many thought that the yes vote, accepting the Troika's terms, would win a slight victory (Panas 2015). The assumption was that the economic uncertainty that the referendum had engendered, in conjunction with the private television channels, who were making an unrestrained push for a yes vote, would push undecided voters into the yes camp.[9]

The results of the vote, however, belied this expectation. The referendum resulted in a resounding victory for the no camp, with 61.3 percent voting against the Troika's offer. This victory is even more impressive when one considers that a majority of voters in all of Greece's thirteen regional administrative districts voted no. Emboldened by this result, SYRIZA returned to the negotiating table. A new round of brinksmanship followed that resulted in the SYRIZA government eventually caving to EU demands as they faced the possibility of an uncontrolled bankruptcy, a demolished banking system, and a return to the drachma. A third MoU was signed on 13 July 2015.

The results of the referendum revealed the extent to which traditional media channels were no longer trusted by the Greek people. ERT was the only broadcaster consistently supporting the no position. According to AGB Nielsen Greece, ERT received a significant bump in viewership during the days leading up to the referendum (Maniatis 2015a). On 28 June it was in fifth place among the evening news broadcasts, yet on the evening of the referendum it was the third-most-watched broadcast (Maniatis 2015c). Its morning news broadcasts were rated as high as second in the week following the referendum, and its news broadcast was the highest-rated news broadcast in the 9:00 p.m. slot during this week, and the second-highest overall (Paschalides 2015a, 2015b).

The bump in ratings that ERT received prior to the referendum is an indication that a certain segment of the population was seeking an anti-memorandum perspective on news broadcasts, but it is not enough to explain the resounding vote against the Troika's offer. This is particularly true when one considers that aggregate data from AGB Nielsen Greece for the period from 26 June to 7 July 2015 does not show a sustained rise in viewership for ERT (Nielsen Audience Measurement Greece 2015). Seemingly, many viewers were continuing to watch pro-memorandum private channels, but were reading their news broadcasts with a high degree of skepticism and decided to vote no.

The skepticism that viewers of news broadcasts and news magazines demonstrated is part of a growing distrust of economic oligarchs and politicians that has manifested itself during the crisis. Political outsiders have emerge as the most trusted political analysts during this period. As Papailias (2012) notes, the phenomenon of Lakis Lazopoulos has been notable in this regard. Lazopoulos is a comedian whose weekly show on Alpha Channel *Al Tsantiri News* has been one of the most highly rated programs during the crisis, routinely attracting 40 percent or more of the viewing audience in his time slot, more than 20 percent of the population ("O ALPHA Kerdise" 2015; Maniatis 2015d; "E Premiera tou *Al Tsantiri*" 2015). Papailias (2012) explains that the show's name plays on Al Jazeera News and the Greek words *"tsantiri,"* which means a Gypsy's tent or, more generally, any sort of humble abode. We might also add the word *"tsantilas,"* which means a hotheaded individual, someone who gets angry easily. The program thus promises (1) alternative, non-Western perspectives on current events, (2) social commentary on the deprivation that the Greek people have experienced, (3) a biting, bottom-up critique of contemporary Greek culture and the failings and cultural pretensions of Greece's economic and political elites, and (4) a good dose of outrage at the treatment that average Greeks have received at the hands of both their political class and its European partners. It delivers on all fronts and, in the process, has transformed Lazopoulos from a very good comedian into a dynamic political player who has the power to shape public opinion in ways that few others in contemporary Greece can.

Though he has steadfastly refused, unlike the Italian comedian Beppe Grillo, to create a political party and run for office, Lazopoulos has not shied away from inserting himself into political debates or from using his broadcast to mercilessly lampoon politicians with whom he disagrees. Though he has tended to focus on politicians from the traditional left and right, members of SYRIZA (now former members), such as Zoe Konstantopoulou, Yanis Varoufakis, and Panagiotis Lafazanis, have not escaped his wrath. He has also called for investigations into the companies who conduct public opinion research on politics that he claims serve as "vehicle for handcuffing public opinion" and are in cahoots with the "television triangle of cronyism: Mega, SKAI, and ANT1" (Lazopoulos 2015). Additionally, he maintains an alternative news website, altsantiri.gr, for which he routinely pens editorials.

Radio as a Space for Creativity and Experimentation

Radio has experienced something of a resurgence during the crisis. Highly prominent television journalists such as Nikos Chatzinikolaou, who for years was Greece's most popular anchorman and a fixture on Mega, and Giorgos Tragkas, a prominent reporter and commentator at a number of outlets, have devoted significant energy to radio. While it is not uncommon for television journalists to also do radio work in Greece, it is uncommon for journalists of the caliber of Chatzinikolaou and Tragkas to establish radio as their principal journalistic vehicle. In 2007 Chatzinikolaou left Mega for ALTER and, at the same time, created a radio station, Real FM, and a Sunday newspaper, *Real News*. After ALTER went bankrupt in late 2011, Real FM, on which he hosts a daily show, and *Real News*, for which he wrote editorials, became his principal journalistic venues. He returned to television in September 2013, when Star signed him to a contract to anchor the evening news, but radio and print have continued to be a large part of his portfolio. Tragkas has likewise made radio the central focus of his journalistic endeavors. He has not been absent from television and the editorial pages of *Real News*, but radio has been his principal vehicle.

Chatzinikolaou is center-right in orientation, and Tragkas is a right-wing nationalist who is against the MoU. Real FM, however, offers a full spectrum of political perspectives. Since 2011 the station has also hosted the highly successful and innovative left-wing call-in show "Hellenophrenia," which was originally on SKAI FM. The show—the title of which is a play on the word schizophrenia and is based on the Greek words Hellene (Greek) and fren (the mind)—features hosts Thimios Kalamoukis and Apostolis Barbayiannis taking calls and riffing on caller comments, spoofing politicians and celebrities, and spinning multilevel cultural and political critiques that frequently feature snippets from Greek popular cinema, music, television shows, and politicians of the past and present. As Papailias (2012) notes, the show also uses a phenomenon that she terms "archival re-collection," the deploying of digital archives in order to critique politicians and other public figures and their record of failures and broken promises (Papailias 2012: 10). The resulting product mobilizes satire to simultaneously affirm Greece's cultural identity as a nation and critique entrenched facets of that culture that have contributed to economic and political stagnation. The pair also have a television show on SKAI, it should be noted, that is neither as powerful nor as profound. Though they lack the stunning mass appeal of Lazopoulos, Kalamoukis and Barbayiannis should also be viewed as representatives of the increasingly significant political role that satire is playing in political discourse.

Chatzinikolaou, Tragkas, Kalamoukis, Barbayiannis, and their audiences all seem to relish in the comparative freedom that radio offers journalists.[10] Radio's lower overhead and lower economic stakes (i.e., the advertising revenue) allow a broader range of topics to be addressed. There is also more room for controversy and provocative opinions. Tragkas, Kalamoukis, and Barbayiannis all take particular delight in voicing extreme positions and provoking the establishment with their critiques. The same is happening on a much smaller scale because the crisis has been accompanied by a flourishing of low-budget, small-audience radio broadcasts, most of which are Web-based. Notable here are Vmedia.gr and Plateia Radio (Town Square Radio, www.plateiaradio.gr) that host broadcasts by a variety of small political movements such as the left-wing, anti-austerity parties the Greek Direct Democracy Movement (Elleniko Kinema Ameses Demokratias) and the I Don't Pay Movement (Kinema den Plerono), which began as a movement to encourage citizens to protest austerity by not paying for government services, such as access to the highway system, that they believe should be provided for free or for a reduced price (particularly those whose costs were raised under austerity).

The Transition from Analog to Digital Broadcasting

The 2009 creation of Digea, a digital broadcasting consortium, began a five-year transition away from analog to digital terrestrial broadcasting. The consortium, which is an equal partnership between seven of Greece's largest private broadcasters—Alpha, ALTER, ANT1, Makedonia TV, Mega, SKAI, and Star—was declared in February 2014 the sole provider of digital terrestrial broadcasting services in Greece after the completion of a bidding process that was overseen by the National Committee for

Telecommunications and Postal Services. Digea was the only company to place a bid, and it had already begun digital broadcasting in much of Greece from 2010 to 2013 ("E Digea Monadike Symmetoche" 2014). Over the course of 2014, the different regions of Greece phased out analog broadcasting, and Digea began broadcasting an exclusively digital signal. According to the terms of the bid, the maximum profit that Digea can make is capped at €291,000,000 over ten years.

Some smaller regional broadcasters have been very vocal about their dissatisfaction with Digea. They resent being forced to pay for the company's service and contend that it constitutes a monopoly. The political left is also dissatisfied with the creation of the company, which they contend extends the influence and control of the oligarchs and their political parties. They argue that the bidding process lacked transparency and that Digea's control of the airwaves will inevitably weaken the plurality of voices on the airwaves ("Erotese 49 Vouleuton" 2014).

Law 4339/2015, Broadcasting Permits, Digea, and a New Digital Carrier

On 24 October 2015 the SYRIZA government passed a law designed to bring order to what they perceived as the chaotic state of affairs in television broadcasting. Although the law was ultimately declared unconstitutional by Greece's highest court, the Council of State, it is worth examining in detail since it reveals much about the evolving political environment within which television operates.

The most significant provisions of the new legal framework proposed by Law 4339/2015 were (1) establishment of a procedure for auctioning off broadcasting permits, (2) establishment of minimum capital requirements and minimum requirements for the number of employees a broadcaster must have, (3) creation of a new digital broadcasting company that would be housed under the umbrella of ERT and capitalized to the tune of €7,000,000 by the state, (4) capping of the number of national high-definition broadcasters that produce general news programs at four, and (5) shifting the responsibility for conducting the auctions from the National Council of Radio-Television (NCRT) to the Ministry of State (Law 4339/2015). The last two provisions were added to the law through Article 2A, which was passed as an addendum to Law 4367/2016 (Law 4367 2016).

According to the law, broadcasting permits were to be issued through open auctions—participants had to certify their financial health—and were to last for a ten-year period. This stipulation was seemingly designed to

simultaneously increase state revenues and strike at the cozy relationship
that had existed between Greek broadcasters and the traditional political
powers, PASOK and ND. The political left has long contended that in-
expensive access to the airwaves and lax enforcement of regulations has
allowed broadcasters to profit unreasonably at the expense of the state
and thus contributed to the creation of a symbiotic relationship between
broadcasters and the traditional political powers (Papaeliou 2015). Television station owners countered these arguments by contending that their
stations make adequate contributions to the common good by paying
taxes and by employing citizens ("Oi Kanalarches" 2015). Conceivably,
the auctions would also allow new players to enter the field, including
those that are more favorably disposed to the SYRIZA government.

The law's second provision set different capital and employee requirements for stations that engage in broadcasting news programs (€8,000,000
and four hundred employees), news entertainment (€5,000,000 and two
hundred employees), and just entertainment (€2,000,000 and fifty employees). There were also different requirements for national as opposed to
regional and local broadcasters. The provision was seemingly designed
to ensure that adequate staff and economic resources would exist for stations that are undertaking journalism as part of their mission. If it had
ultimately been enforced, this provision would have likely raised the cost
of doing business for privately owned channels. The third of the significant provisions of the law was a clear attempt to limit the influence and
profitability of Digea, which is viewed by the political left as a monopoly
that has the potential to limit the plurality of voices on television ("Erotese
49 Vouleuton" 2014).

The fourth provision, the capping of the number of permits, was supposedly based on analysis of the available advertising revenue and the
financial health of existing stations. Opponents saw it as an unnecessary
market regulation and an attempt to limit the influence of the private mass
media. The fifth provision was likely inserted to get rid of bureaucratic
impediments to conducting the auctions and to give the SYRIZA government more control over the process.

The Auctions and Their Aftermath

Almost immediately after the passage of Article 2A, questions were raised
about its constitutionality (Tsiliotis 2016) and the technological and economic necessity of limiting the number of broadcasters to four (Bletsas
2016). Nonetheless, the government proceeded with the auctions, a tor-
tured affair that stretched out over sixty-six hours in late June 2016 and

would have generated €246,000,000 in revenue for the Greek state (Chiotis 2016a). The results, had they been allowed to stand, would have dramatically altered the television landscape. First, Mega, which was facing considerable economic difficulties as were some of its shareholders, was excluded from the auctions for failing to conform to multiple aspects of the financial reporting requirements (Grammeli 2016). Two other applications, one controlled by Cypriot interests and another controlled by the Russian–Greek businessman Ivan Savvidis, were initially excluded for similar, though less extensive, failures (Grammeli 2016). They were eventually allowed to participate in the auctions, however, after amending their applications (Kassimi 2016).

The auctions themselves saw two existing channels, SKAI (€43.6 million) and Antenna (€75.9 million), emerge victorious. The two other permits were won by Alter Ego Mass Media, A. E. (€73.9 million), owned by shipping magnate Evangelos Marinakis, and Ioannis Vladimiros Kalogritsas Television of National Coverage, M. A. E. (€52.6 million), owned by Yiannis Kalogritsas, the son of businessman Christos Kalogritsas (Chiotis 2016a).[11] The latter currently presides over a medium-sized construction company, Toxotis A. E., but in the 1980s and 1990s was involved in newspaper publishing and private television station ownership and had served as the general director and president of the board of directors of ERT under PASOK governments ("Poios Einai o Christos Kalogritsas" 2016). Neither Marinakis nor Yiannis Kalogritsas was an ideal candidate for mass media ownership. Marinakis, who owns both one of Greece's storied athletic teams, the Olympiacos athletic club of Pireaus and the Nottingham Forest Football Club in England, has been under investigation in recent years for crimes including match fixing and running a criminal organization in the sphere of athletics ("Ti Anapherei o Eisangeleas" 2016).[12] Yiannis Kalogritsas, who was the publisher of the leftwing Sunday newspaper *Documento*, saw his organization's candidacy dissolve in a barrage of charges that included dubious documentation of the organization's wealth sources, dubious loans granted under very favorable terms to Toxotis, and tax evasion by family members (Chiotis 2016b, 2016c; Goutzanis 2016). The organization eventually failed to make the initial down payment within the required fifteen-day window, thus forfeiting their permit ("Aposyrtheke Kaken–Kakos" 2016).

Even before the conclusion of the auctions, the established channels had moved to challenge the legality of the process. Their case focused on a number of provisions of the law, including the starting price of the auctions, the minimum employee requirements, the limiting of the number of channels, and the decision to hold the auctions under the auspices of the Ministry of State (Tsimboukis 2016). Ultimately, it was this last provision that was deemed unconstitutional by the Council of the State in their 13 January 2017 ruling, which declared that the NCRT is the sole legal authority for the regulation of the sphere of radio and television (Mandrou 2016). The decision overturned the results of the auctions, though it did leave open the possibility of new auctions being conducted under the auspices of the NCRT. The SYRIZA government has been pushing for this option and would like to see Law 4339/2015 used as the basis for the new auctions ("Oi Protaseis SYRIZA" 2016). ND has opposed proceeding with auctions under the auspices of Law 4339/2015 due to the many aspects of it that have yet to receive a ruling on their constitutionality from the Council of the State ("Mitsotakis pros ESR" 2017).

The uncertainty about when and if new airwave auctions will be held in the future has not impeded those oligarchs who aspire to television ownership from being very active in the sector. In particular, Mega's economic distress has created an opportunity for Marinakis and Savvidis to move aggressively. Marinakis's aforementioned purchase of a controlling stake in the Lambrakis Journalistic Organization also gives him 22.11 percent of the shares of Mega, making him the second-largest shareholder after the Vardinogiannis family, which continues to hold 35 percent of the shares. After losing the airwave auctions, Savvidis acquired a 19.64 percent stake in Mega from the Bobolas family's economically troubled Pegasus Publishing. Pegasus Publishing continues to hold a 13.09 percent stake in Mega, but these shares are pledged as collateral on bank loans. Should the company go into default, these shares would be put up for auction (Manifava 2017; Manifava and Papadogiannis 2017).

In retrospect, Law 4339/2015 and the permit auctions were clearly an attempt by the SYRIZA government to alter the terrain of private broadcasting in their favor. Just as the closure of ERT was an attempt by ND to alter the terrain of public broadcasting and to neutralize an organization that it could no longer use patronage to control, the SYRIZA government used Law 4339 to raise the cost of private television ownership and to promote politically allied stations. This is particularly evident in the case of Ioannis Vladimiros Kalogritsas Television of National Coverage, M. A. E., which had obvious sympathies for SYRIZA. The Kalogritsas application received preferential treatment in the financial-reporting stage of the auction and should have been red-flagged for gaps in its documentation including, most flagrantly, the use of pastureland on the island of Ithaca to meet capitalization requirements (Chiotis 2016b). The government's decision to allow the Marinakis application to move forward was also questionable, given his legal troubles, though political motivations for this decision are not immediately evident.

Conclusion

The preceding portrait of the changing Greek mediascape from 2010 to 2017 reveals a tremendous nexus of economic, political, and technological change. It also reveals the difficulties of exerting human control over the process of change once that process has been set in motion. For instance, attempts by the political parties to control the media have been largely thwarted. The political protest of viewers and organized resistance of workers helped to alter the trajectory of ERT's closure and eventually contributed to its reinstatement once SYRIZA was elected. Similarly, the judicial system helped to undermine SYRIZA's attempts to refashion the terrain of private broadcasting and make it more sympathetic to its political aims. Finally, attempts to use the media to manipulate public opinion, such as the private television stations' campaign for a yes vote on the referendum, have also largely failed.

Yet these observations belie the extent to which the mass media are, at some level, still able to effectively mold public opinion. The media are, in other words, still subject to human control and manipulation. The vote on SYRIZA's referendum, for instance, was largely divided on age lines, which in turn correspond to media preference. The private television stations, in fact, were quite successful in shaping the opinion of older Greeks who rely primarily on television for information. That segment of the population overwhelmingly voted yes on the referendum. Meanwhile, younger Greeks, whose consciousness is shaped increasingly by the internet, largely voted no. This vision of the continued importance of television for shaping public opinion is evidently shared by many of Greece's oligarchs, who were prepared to risk tens of millions of euros for television licenses, which promised very uncertain economic returns but a chance to shape the news flow.

Focusing on the mediascape more broadly instead of an individual medium thus reveals that the media are perhaps best viewed as an agonistic field in which humans interact through various institutions and affinity groups to construct and critique narratives of their shared past, present, and future. The emphasis on agonistic struggle suggests that humans still exert considerable influence over their media futures: as inventors of new media technologies, as owners of media outlets, as producers of media content, as politicians who determine the legal framework in which the media operate, as lawyers and judges who interpret and evaluate that legal framework, and as consumers of media products who interact with other consumers in various ways and who vote with their feet. This statement should not be interpreted, however, as declaration that the media do not exert considerable influence over human consciousness or that they do not, in the process, articulate logics of their own. Rather, it suggests that this influence is always mediated through human actors and shaped by human decisions. Returning to the foregoing discussion of the refer-endum, we thus see that the media still play an important role in deter-mining consciousness, but that the importance of this role is mediated by generational divides. Human actors, in other words, by interacting differ-entially with the mediascape in which they exist, still play a role in deter-mining their collective future.

A focus on agonistic struggle within the mediascape also serves to pre-vent the reification of individual media as good or bad or as inexorably linked to progress and democracy. The internet, for instance, has largely been seen as a force for good. By reinforcing the skills of traditional literacy and giving engaged citizens immediate access to a tremendous amount of information, it has been cast as a bulwark of democracy. This vision is belied, however, by the extent to which, in recent years, forces of darkness and oppression have developed strategies for using the internet to further their own goals. It is also belied by the emergence of a postliterate internet in which users interact with material without using the basic skills of liter-acy: close reading, the evaluation of sources, and critical thinking. Instead of reading and evaluating discourse, they consume simple, aphoristic messages via Twitter. Many have lost their ability to evaluate sources and distinguish between real and fake news. The postliterate internet is being further expanded by the tendency to farm out search functions to personal assistants like Apple's Siri, Amazon's Alexa, and Microsoft's Cortana, who provide information without reference to source.

With the foregoing discussion in mind, I would like to return to the question of the relationship between media regime change and political and economic chaos. As I have argued, the Greek sovereign debt crisis and the political chaos and change that it has engendered have coincided with a significant transformation of Greece's mediascape. Questions of etiology loom large here. The crisis in Greece almost certainly engendered political instability and the diminution of democracy. The extent to which it has engendered changes in the mediascape, however, is not entirely clear. Cer-tain changes such as shrinking newspaper sales and the growing promi-nence of the internet as a source of information clearly predate the crisis. The crisis likely increased the rate of the decline of newspapers and con-tributed to the closure of several newspapers, but it was not the root cause of these changes. The same can be said of the expanding prominence of the internet as a news and information source. On the other hand, certain events are almost certainly directly linked to the crisis. It is difficult, for instance, to imagine the closure of ERT without the crisis and the political instability that it engendered serving as impetuses. Likewise, it is difficult to imagine that public trust in the traditional mass media and the traditional political classes would sink so low if it were not for the crisis.

There is a larger question here as well: Are the phenomena that Greece has experienced since 2010 local or global in nature? Are they specific to Greece or are they indicative of a broader crisis in the relationship of the mass media to governance? I would like to conclude this chapter by arguing that, when viewed from the vantage point of its impact on the mass media, the Greek crisis, though extreme, is not at all unique. Greece is the canary in the coalmine for a broader legitimacy crisis in neoliberal capitalism and its information regimes. We see similar phenomena emerging around the world. Public trust in journalists is at a low ebb in many countries (Morris 2013; Swift 2013). Citizens are seeking out alternative sources of news, which are now much more readily available due to the internet. Even the phenomenon of the satirist becoming an information gatekeeper and political authority is not particularly unique to Greece. Beppe Grillo has channeled political anger in Italy through his comedy and created an anti-establishment party, the Five Star Movement, which placed third with 25.5 percent of the vote in the 2013 general elections. In the United States, Bill Maher's *Politically Incorrect* and Stephen Colbert's *Colbert Report* replaced the evening news for many young people. The comedian Jan Böhmermann is beginning to play a similar role in Germany (Smale 2015, 2016). Likewise, we see the disintegration of the traditional political landscape in many countries in late 2015 and early 2016. In the United States, rank-and-file members of the Republican Party have rejected establishment politicians for outsiders, resulting in the election of Donald Trump. On the left, Bernie Sanders nearly upset Hillary Clinton for the Democratic nomination and continues in his efforts to redefine and legitimize socialism for an American audience. The success that he has had in making socialism acceptable in American political discourse is something that would have been unthinkable a mere ten years ago. In France the National Front is ascendant and both the Socialist Party and the center-right Union for a Popular Movement are in freefall. Similar political patterns are emerging in Austria, Germany, and other European countries.

Neoliberal capitalism's legitimacy crisis is largely of its own making. Deregulation of the banking industry set the tables for a multipronged global economic crisis. The outsourcing of jobs and the liberalization of trade laws has led to the stagnation of wages in Western democracies and the contraction of the middle class. Lobbying and political donations have weakened trust in the political class, and multinational capital's ownership and control of media companies has weakened the public's confidence in journalism. If the Greek example has anything to teach us, it is that the extent to which the resolution of neoliberalism's ongoing legitimacy crisis represents a return to the status quo—versus a turn toward more fully democratic governance—will likely depend on the extent to which citizens and pro-democratic centers of power are able to reassert influence over the flow of information and ideas through the mass media.

Franklin L. Hess is the coordinator of the Modern Greek Program and a senior lecturer in the Institute of European Studies at Indiana University in Bloomington. He has presented and published extensively on Greek popular culture, music, cinema, and literature. He has been heavily engaged with the Modern Greek Studies Association since 2005 and currently is the organization's president.

Notes

1. Identifying the first Greek film production is an exercise fraught with peril. Newsreels, of course, had been shot in Greece by foreign cinema production companies prior to 1912. Additionally, Balkan cinema pioneers the Manaki brothers, who spoke Aromanian as their first language, began filming local life in 1905 in their village, Avdella, which eventually became part of the Greek province of Epirus. I have consciously used the modifier "commercial" to avoid the controversies about the Manaki brothers, their identity, and their place in Greek film history. Hepp, who was from Budapest and arrived in Greece as an employee of the French firm Pathé, is considered to be a Greek film pioneer because he settled permanently in Greece and worked in the Greek film industry until his death in 1968.
2. In fairness to McLuhan, he was not as relentlessly sanguine about mass media technologies as he is often portrayed to be. As Michael McDonald (2006) points out, he actually saw considerable downside to mass media technologies and his criticisms were often echoed by those who defined themselves as his opponents.
3. The armed forces in Greece in the 1950s and 1960s were closely allied with the royal family and conservative political factions. The creation of broadcasting service that were under military control was both a reflection of the political influence that the military exerted during the Cold War and an attempt to maintain this influence, as well as the influence of allied political factions, in a period of increasing political liberalization.
4. There was a brief experiment with more independent control of the entertainment portions of the television program when film director Roviros Manthoulis was the artistic director of ERT from late 1975 to early 1977. During Manthoulis's tenure, however, a political loyalist, Yiannis Lampsas, remained the general director of the ERT and exerted control over the news broadcasts and informational programming. This period is documented by Manthoulis in his book *The State of Television* (1981).
5. Kyriakou died 2 July 2017. The consequences of his death for the future of Antenna are unknown at the time of writing.
6. Efimeros suffered from heart problems that were the result of an earlier heart attack. He was only forty-two years old.

7. Kedikoglou's statement is available in its entirety in *Proto Thema* ("Oloklere e Anakoinose Kedikoglou" 2013).
8. The breaking point appears to have been coverage of the Thessaloniki International Trade Fair. Traditionally, governing and opposition political figures both give a speech and hold a press conference at this event, both of which are broadcast. In 2014 the coalition government gave one speech (Venizelos's PASOK) and one press conference (Samaras's ND), mostly because neither politician was terribly eager for a lot of public exposure. Tsipras, however, kept with tradition of both a speech and a press conference. NERIT had agreed to broadcast both live. In return, Tsipras would take a question from a NERIT reporter, something he had never done, because SYRIZA had not officially recognized the legitimacy of the broadcaster. Unnamed government officials apparently tried to intercede to prevent this from happening. The minister of Communication also publicly claimed this was unfair, giving SYRIZA more public broadcasts than PASOK and ND.
9. Most newspapers were also pushing for a yes vote. The exception here was newspapers that were affiliated with SYRIZA and other anti-austerity parties.
10. Kalamoukis has even acknowledged in an interview that he believes radio is a much freer vehicle for expression than television (Galanis 2010).
11. Technically the ownership structure of these companies differs slightly from the American corporation because they are formed under common law. They are closer in structure to the British Limited Liability Corporation. Alter Ego is an anonymous company. Ioannis Vladimiros Kalogritsas Television of National Coverage is a single-person anonymous company.
12. Marinakis has also been linked, thus far peripherally, to the Noor 1 case in which 2.1 tons of heroin, destined for the Greek market, was seized on an aging oil tanker at the port of Lavrio.

References

"24ore Apergia gia ten ERT." 2013. *Eleftherotypia*, 12 July. Retrieved 15 July 2017 from http://www.enet.gr/?i=news.el.article&id=369426.

"Apo ton Voudouri sten Angelopoulou." 2014. *Zougla*, 22 June. Retrieved 15 July 2017 from http://www.zougla.gr/topstory/article/apo-ton-voudouri-stin-agelopoulou.

"Aposyrtheke Kaken–Kakos o Kalogritsas: Den Katebale ta Chremata gia ten Adeia." 2016. *Proto Thema*, 30 August. Retrieved 15 July 2017 from http://www.protothema.gr/greece/article/613994/aposurthike-kakin-kakos-o-kalogritsas-den-katevale-ta-hrimata-gia-tin-adeia/.

Appadurai, Arjun. 1996. *Modernity at Large: Cultural Dimensions of Globalization*. Minneapolis: University of Minnesota Press.

"Athoos gia ten Ypothese ton Opheilon tou ALTER sto IKA o Andreas Kouris." 2014. *E Kathimerini*, 2 December. Retrieved 14 July 2017 from http://www.kathimerini.gr/753443/article/epikairothta/ellada/a8wos-gia-thn-ypo8esh-twn-ofeilwn-toy-alter-sto-ika-o-andreas-koyrhs.

"Aurio Epanakyklophorei e Efemerida *Eleftherotypia*." 2013. *E Kathimerini*, 9 January. Retrieved 14 July 2017 from http://www.kathimerini.gr/24281/article/oikonomia/epixeir hseis/ayrio-epanakykloforei-h-efhmerida-eley8erotypia.

Bletsas, Michail. 2016. "Oi Sovares Technikes Ateleies tes Apophases ton 4 Kanalion." *Ta Nea*, 19 February. Retrieved 15 July 2017 from http://www.tanea.gr/news/greece/article/5336144/oi-sobares-texnikes-ateleies-ths-kybernhtikhs-apofashs-gia-ta-4-kanalia/.

Chatzistefanou, Aris. 2011. "Apo Rouphianoi, 'Pretenterides'." *Lifo*, 6 April. Retrieved 14 July 2017 from http://www.lifo.gr/mag/columns/3841.

Chiotis, Vasilis. 2016a. "E Demoprasia ton Tessaron Teleoptikon Adeion Vema–Vema." *Proto Thema*, 30 August. Retrieved 15 July 2017 from http://www.protothema.gr/greece/article/606218/i-dimoprasia-ton-tessaron-tileoptikon-adeion-vima-vima-/.

Chiotis, Vasilis. 2016b. "Gelio gia ton Kalogritsa pou Evale 'Daneiko' Voskotopi sto Pothen Esches." *Proto Thema*, 16 September. Retrieved 16 July 2017 from http://www.protothema.gr/greece/article/611153/gelio-gia-ton-kalogritsa-pou-evale-daneiko-voskotopi-sto-pothen-eshes/.

Chiotis, Vasilis. 2016c. "Kai Phorodiafyge 32,8 Ekat. Evro apo ton Kalogritsa." *Proto Thema*, 24 September. Retrieved 16 July 2017 from http://www.protothema.gr/greece/article/613690/kai-forodiafugi-328-ekat-euro-apo-ton-kalogritsa/.

Communic@tions Management Inc. 2013. "Daily Newspaper Circulation Trends, 2000–2013: Canada, United States, United Kingdom." 28 October. Retrieved 14 July 2017 from http://media-cmi.com/downloads/CMI_Discussion_Paper_Circulation_Trends_102813.pdf.

Delveroudi, Eliza-Anna. 1999. "Kinematographos." In *Istoria tes Ellados tou 20ou Aiona*, ed. edited by Hristos Hatziiosif, 389–399. Athens: Vivliorama.

"Diapseudei o O. Ren oti e Troika Zetese na Kleisei e ERT." 2013. *Eleftherotypia*, 12 June. Retrieved 15 July 2017 from http://www.enet.gr/?i=news.el.article&id=369383.

"E Digea Monadike Symmetoche sto Diagonismo gia ten Adeiodotese Diktyon Epigeias Psephiakes Teleorases." 2014. *newmoney*, 30 January. Retrieved 15 July 2017 from http://www.newmoney.gr/palmos-oikonomias/epixeiriseis/item/120648-37974-222-h-digea.

"E Istoria tes 'Ef.Syn'." 2016. *Efimerida ton Syntakton, efsyn.gr*. Athens, Greece. Retrieved 4 January 2016 from http://www.efsyn.gr/h-istoria-tis-efsyn.

"E NERIT Apektese Dioiketiko Symvoulio." 2013. *tvxs*, 3 October. Retrieved 14 July 2017 from http://tvxs.gr/news/internet-mme/i-nerit-apektise-dioikitiko-symboylio.

"E Premiera tou *Al Tsantiri Niouz* Eklepse ten Telethease." 2015. Newsbomb, 24 September. Retrieved 15 July 2017 from http://www.newsbomb.gr/media-agb/story/498843/h-premiera-toy-al-tsantiri-nioyz-eklepse-ti-tiletheasi.

"E Prokeryxe ASEP gia 259 Proslepseis ste NERIT—Deite Theseis kai Prosonta." 2014. *Ta Nea*, 21 January. Retrieved 15 July 2017 from http://www.tanea.gr/news/greece/article/5076564/prokhryksh-asep-gia-259-proslhpseis-sth-nerit-deite-theseis-kai-prosonta/.

"EBU Concerned about NERIT Board Change." 2014. *E Kathimerini*, 25 August. Retrieved 15 July 2017 from http://www.ekathimerini.com/4dcgi/_w_articles_wsite1_1_25/08/2014_542381.

"EBU Continues to Underpin ERT's Public Broadcasting Services." 2013. EBU Member News, 19 June. Retrieved 15 July 2017 from https://www3.ebu.ch/contents/news/2013/06/ebu-continues-to-underpin-erts-p.html.

"Eisangelike Ereuna gia Proslepseis Demosiographon sten NERIT." 2014. *To Vima*, 10 September. Retrieved 15 July 2017 from http://www.tovima.gr/media/article/?aid=629967.

"Ekleisan ten ERT me Athroistiko Pososto Theamatikotetas 13 percent." 2013. Typologies, 31 December. Retrieved 15 July 2017 from http://www.typologies.gr/έκλεισαν-την-ΕΡΤ-με-αθροιστικό-ποσοστ/.

"Enas Kouris sten Phylake?" 2013. *Proto Thema*, 8 April. Retrieved 14 July 2017 from http://www.protothema.gr/greece/article/269900/enas-koyrhs-sth-fylakh/.

Eptakili, Youli. 2014. "NERIT: Oute Demosia oute Teleorase." *E Kathimerini*, 28 September. Retrieved 15 July 2017 from http://www.kathimerini.gr/785361/article/politismos/thleorash/nerit-oyte--dhmosia-oyte-thleorash.

"Erixan Mauro sten ERT Open, Synelavan kai ton Kalfayianni." 2015. *Proto Thema*, 23 September. Retrieved 15 July 2017 from http://www.protothema.gr/greece/article/511758/sunelifthi-o-proedros-tis-pospert/.

"Erotese 49 Vouleuton tou SYRIZA: Pros Exontose oi Perifereiakoi Stathmoi Logo Digea." 2014. *Avgi*, 1 October. Retrieved 15 July 2017 from http://www.avgi.gr/article/10838/ 4249047/erotese-49-bouleuton-tou-syriza-pros-exontose-oi-periphereiakoi-stathmoi-lo.

"ERT se Arithmous—To Prophil." 2013. *news 247*, 12 June. Retrieved 15 July 2017 from http:// news247.gr/eidiseis/psixagogia/media/h-ert-se-arithmous-to-profil.2291961.html.

"ERT Shutdown: EBU Urges EU Leader to Overturn Greek Government Decision." 2013. *Guardian*, 13 June. Retrieved 15 July 2017 from https://www.theguardian.com/media/ 2013/jun/13/ert-shutdown-ebu-urges-eu-overturn.

"ERT Streaming to End as Interim Broadcaster Launches News Bulletin." 2013. EBU News, 19 August. Retrieved 15 July 2017 from http://www.ebu.ch/contents/news/2013/08/ert-streaming-to-end-as-interim.html.

"Familiar Faces among NERIT Appointments." 2014. *ENetEnglish*, 13 August. Retrieved 15 July 2017 from http://www.enetenglish.gr/?i=news.en.article&id=2044.

"G. Kouris: Antisymvatikos, Autodemiourgetos, kai panta Aurianistes." 2012. Newsbomb, 3 February. Retrieved 14 July 2017 from http://www.newsbomb.gr/politikh/news/ story/111647/g-koyris-antisymvatikos—aytodimioyrgitos-kai-panta-ayrianistis.

Galanis, Dimitris. 2009. "Ti tha Allaxei ston *Elefthero Typo*." *To Vima*, 13 September. Retrieved 14 July 2017 from http://www.tovima.gr/culture/article/?aid=288157.

Galanis, Dimitris. 2010. "Ellenophreneia: O Pangalos Einai o Kalyteros Pelates Mas." *To Vima*, 24 April. Retrieved 15 July 2017 from http://www.tovima.gr/culture/article/?aid=327905.

Goutzanis, Spyros. 2016. "Oi 'Amartoles' Scheseis Kalogritsa—Tr. Attikes: Daneia 77,6 ekat. € tous Teleutaious 20 Menes." *Proto Thema*, 20 August. Retrieved 15 July 2017 from http:// www.protothema.gr/economy/article/612206/sto-fos-oi-amartoles-sheseis-kalogritsa-tr-attikis-me-daneia-776-ekat-euro-tous-teleutaious-20-mines/.

"Gramma apo ten Phylake: Ti Graphei o Giorgos Kouris ston Themo Anastasiadi." 2013. *iefimerida*, 15 April. Retrieved 14 July 2017 from http://www.iefimerida.gr/news/100285/ γράμμα-από-τη-φυλακή-τι-γράφει-ο-γιώργος-κούρης-στον-θέμο-αναστασιάδη.

Grammeli, Afroditi. 2016. "Kopekan Mega, Savvidis kai Kyprioi apo tis Teleoptikes Adeies." *To Vima*, 19 July. Retrieved 15 July 2017 from http://www.tovima.gr/media/ article/?aid=816381.

Heretakis, Manolis. 2014. *E Radiophonia sten Ellada, 1930–1950*. Athens: Left Media.

Kassimi, Alexandra. 2016. "Enteka Ypopsephioi gia Tesseris Teleoptikes Adeies." 2016. *E Kathimerini*, 5 July. Retrieved 15 July 2017 from http://www.kathimerini.gr/866169/ article/epikairothta/ellada/enteka-ypoyhfioi-gia-tesseris-thleoptikes-adeies.

"Kinetopoieseis kai Apergies gia to Kleisimo tes ERT." 2013. *E Kathimerini*, 12 June. Retrieved 15 July 2017 from http://www.kathimerini.gr/42731/article/epikairothta/ellada/ kinhtopoihseis-kai-apergies-gia-to-kleisimo-ths-ert.

Kitsantonis, Niki, and Rachel Donadio. 2015. "One Coalition Partner Quits Greek Government." *New York Times*, 21 June. Retrieved 15 July 2017 from http://www.nytimes.com/ 2013/06/22/world/europe/smallest-coalition-partner-quits-greek-government.html?_r=0.

Kittler, Friedrich. 1999. *Gramophone-Film-Typewriter*, trans. translated by Geoffrey Winthrop-Young and Michael Wutz. Stanford, CA: Stanford University Press.

"Kleinei o *Eleftheros Typos*." 2009. *Ta Nea*, 22 June. Retrieved 14 July 2017 from http://www .tanea.gr/news/greece/article/4523109/?iid=2.

"Kontra SYRIZA kai POSPERT gia ten Epanaleitourgia tes ERT." 2015. *Huffington Post* (Greek Version), 12 March. Retrieved 15 July 2017 from http://www.huffingtonpost .gr/2015/03/12/-koinonia-kontra-pospert-SYRIZA_n_6854134.html.

Law No. 4339. 2015. *Efimeris tis Kyverniseos tis Ellinikis Dimokratias*, 19 October: 1371-13–79.

Law No. 4367. 2016. *Efimeris tis Kyverniseos tis Ellinikis Dimokratias*, 15 February: 1371-13–79.

Lazopoulos, Lakis. 2015. "Amese Epemvase tou Eisangelea." *altsantiri.gr*, 21 September. Retrieved 15 July 2017 from http://www.altsantiri.gr/homepage/lakis-lazopoulos-amesi-epemvasi-tou-isangelea/.

Mac Con Uladh, Damian. 2014. "Government Interference Cited as Nerit Chairman and Deputy Resign." *ENetEnglish,* 12 September. Retrieved 15 July 2017 from http://www.enetenglish.gr/?i=news.en.article&id=2055.

MacDonald, Michael. 2006. "Empire and Communication: The Media Wars of Marshall McLuhan." *Media Culture & Society* 28(4): 505–20.

Mandrou, Ioanna. 2016. "STE: Kai Typika Antisyntagmatikos o Nomos gia tis Adeies—To Skeptiko tes Apophases." 2016. *E Kathimerini,* 20 July. Retrieved 20 July 2017 from http://www.kathimerini.gr/899802/article/epikairothta/ellada/ste-antisyntagmatikh-h-synexhs-paratash-paragrafhs-forologikwn-a3iwsewn---sthn-olomeleia-h-telikh-apofash.

Maniatis, Sotiris. 2015a. "Anatropes Semantikes logo tou Demopsephismatos." *Efimerida ton Syntakton,* 30 June. Retrieved 15 July 2017 from http://www.efsyn.gr/arthro/anatropes-simantikes-logo-dimopsifismatos.

Maniatis, Sotiris. 2015b. "Anoikta Themata gia ERT sto Neo Schedio Nomou." *Efimerida ton Syntakton,* 10 March. Retrieved 15 July 2017 from http://www.efsyn.gr/arthro/anoikta-themata-gia-ert-sto-neo-shedio-nomoy.

Maniatis, Sotiris. 2015c. "Proto to Star, alla 'Skarphalose' ki e ERT." *Efimerida ton Syntakton,* 7 July. Retrieved 15 July 2017 from http://www.efsyn.gr/arthro/proto-star-alla-skarfalose-ki-i-ert.

Maniatis, Sotiris. 2015d. "Satira kai Komodia Dinoun ton Rythmo." *Efimerida ton Syntakton,* 27 March. Retrieved 15 July 2017 http://www.efsyn.gr/arthro/satira-kai-komodia-dinoyn-ton-rythmo.

Manifava, Dimitra 2017. "Me 22,89 Ekat. o DOL Pernaei ston Elegcho tou Omilou Marinaki." *E Kathimerini,* 1 June. Retrieved 22 July 2017 from http://www.kathimerini.gr/912079/article/oikonomia/epixeirhseis/me-2289-ekat-o-dol-pernaei-ston-elegxo-toy-omiloy-marinakh.

Manifava, Dimitra, and Yiannis Papadogiannis 2017. "Polese tou 19.63 Percent tou Mega ston Ivan Savvidi apo ton Pegaso." *E Kathimerini,* 23 May. Retrieved 22 July 2017 from http://www.kathimerini.gr/910669/article/oikonomia/epixeirhseis/pwlhsh-toy-1963-toy-mega-ston-ivan-savvidh-apo-ton-phgaso.

Manthoulis, Roviros. 1981. *To Kratos tes Teleorases.* Athens: Themelio.

McLuhan, Marshall. 1994. *Understanding Media: The Extensions of Man.* Cambridge: MIT Press.

"Mitsotakis pros ESR: Na men Prochoresei e Adeiodotese me to Nomo Pappa." 2017. *E Kathimerini,* 21 February. Retrieved 20 July 2017 from http://www.kathimerini.gr/897393/article/epikairothta/politikh/mhtsotakhs-pros-esr-na-mhn-proxwrhsei-h-adeiodothsh-me-to-nomo-pappa.

Morris, Harvey. 2013. "How Much Do You Trust Journalists?" *New York Times,* 16 February. Retrieved 15 July 2017 from https://rendezvous.blogs.nytimes.com/2013/02/16/how-much-do-you-trust-journalists/.

Nedos, Vasilis. 2006. "Apo ton SKAI sto Smart kai apo to Seven sto SKAI." *To Vima,* 9 April. Retrieved 14 July 2017 from http://www.tovima.gr/relatedarticles/article/?aid=172467.

Nielsen Audience Measurement Greece. 2015. "Stoicheia Teletheases 2406-07072015." Personal correspondence, 7 December.

"O ALPHA Kerdise Telethease me to *Al Tsantiri Niouz* kai to Kentriko tou Deltio." 2015. *Newsbomb,* 30 September. Retrieved 15 July 2017 from http://www.newsbomb.gr/media-agb/story/501136/o-alpha-kerdise-tiletheasi-me-to-al-tsantiri-nioyz-kai-to-kentriko-toy-deltio.

"O Giorgos Kouris Vgazei Nea Efemerida, ten *Kontranews.*" 2013. *iefimerida,* 31 October. Retrieved 14 July 2017 from http://www.iefimerida.gr/news/128526/ο-γιώργος-κούρης-βγάζει-νέα-εφημερίδα-την-kontranews.

"Oi 'Eklektoi' gia to Epoptiko Symvoulio tes NERIT. 2013. *tvxs,* 5 August. Retrieved 14 July 2017 from http://tvxs.gr/news/internet-mme/oi-epta-%C2%ABeklektoi%C2%BB-gia-epoptiko-symboylio-tis-nerit.

"Oi Kanalarches Antidroun sto Nomoschedio gia tis Teleoptikes Adeies." 2015. *Efimerida ton Syntakton*, 31 July. Retrieved 15 July 2017 from http://www.efsyn.gr/arthro/oi-kanalarhes-antidroyn-sto-nomoshedio-gia-tis-tileoptikes-adeies.

"Oi Protaseis SYRIZA pros ESR gia tis Teleoptikes Adeies." 2017. *Naftemboriki*, 30 January. Retrieved 20 July 2017 from http://www.naftemporiki.gr/story/1199587/oi-protaseis-syriza-pros-esr-gia-tis-tileoptikes-adeies.

"Oi Treis 'Typhones' pou Apeiloun na Sarosoun ta Entypa MME." 2013. *To Pontiki*, 27 August. Retrieved 14 July 2017 from http://www.topontiki.gr/article/57379/oi-treis-tyfones-poy-apeiloyn-na-sarosoyn-ta-entypa-mme.

"Oloklere e Anakoinose Kedikoglou pou Ekleise ten ERT." 2013. *Proto Thema*, 11 June. Retrieved 14 July 2017 from http://www.protothema.gr/politics/article/285596/oloklhrh-h-anakoinosh-kedikogloy-poy-ekleise-thn-ert/.

Panas, Epameinondas. 2015. "Axiologontas ta Apotelesmata tou Demopsiphismatos." *Huffington Post* (Greek version), 6 July. Retrieved 15 July 2017 from http://www.huffington post.gr/epameinondas-panas/-_671_b_7736846.html.

Papaeliou, Yiorgos. 2015. "Proto Vema sten Antimetopise Diaplokes kai Diaphthoras sta MME." *Avgi*, 28 October. Retrieved 15 July 2017 from http://www.avgi.gr/article/5977 267/proto-bima-stin-antimetopisi-diaplokis-kai-diafthoras-sta-mme.

Papailias, Penelope. 2012. "Reporting as an Act of Citizenship: The Net, the News, and the Greek "Crisis." In Spassov, Orlin, ed. "Citizenship, Activism and Mobilization: Internet Politics in Greece, Turkey and Bulgaria." *Euxeinos - Culture and Governance in the Black Sea Region* 5. Retrieved 6 April 2017 from https://gce.unisg.ch/en/euxeinos/archive/05.

"Parousia Eisangelea ta MAT Ekkenosan to Radiomegaro tes ERT." 2013. *To Vima*, 7 November. Retrieved 15 July 2017 from http://www.tovima.gr/media/article/?aid=538261.

Paschalides, Yiorgos. 2015a. "Poio Deltio Eideseon Vgeke Proto se Mache tes Teletheases?" *tvnea.com*, 15 July. Retrieved 15 July 2017 from http://www.tvnea.com/2015/07/blog-post_909.html.

Paschalides, Yiorgos. 2015b. "Se Prote These o Papadakis Ekplexe e ERT . . . " *tvnea.com*, 9 July. Retrieved 15 July 2017 from http://www.tvnea.com/2015/07/blog-post_227.html.

Peck, Jamie. 2004. "Geography and Public Policy: Constructions of Neoliberalism." *Progress in Human Geography* 28(3): 392–405.

"Poios Einai o Christos Kalogritsas: Apo ten *Proti* to 1986 se Kanali to 2016." 2016. *To Pontiki*, 26 September. Retrieved 16 July 2017 from http://www.topontiki.gr/article/183569/poios-einai-o-hristos-kalogritsas-apo-tin-proti-1986-se-kanali-.

"Pouletheke kai Episema o *Eleftheros Typos*." 2009. *Capital*, 10 September. Retrieved 15 July 2017 from http://www.capital.gr/story/810401.

Press Project. 2016. BitsnBytes, Athens, Greece. Retrieved 4 January 2016 from www.the pressproject.gr.

"RTL Buys into Greek Television Market." 2008. *New York Times*, 23 September. Retrieved 14 July 2017 from http://www.nytimes.com/2008/09/23/technology/23iht-rtl.4.16411995 .html.

"Semasia tes Apophases tou Symvouliou Epikrateias gia ERT." 2013. *E Kathimerini*, 24 June. Retrieved 15 July 2017 from http://www.kathimerini.gr/43876/article/epikairothta/politikh/h-shmasia-ths-apofashs-toy-symvoylioy-epikrateias-gia-ert.

Seybert, Heidi. 2012. "Internet Use in Households and by Individuals in 2012." in *Eurostat: Statistics in Focus* 50: 1–8. Retrieved 14 July 2017 from http://ec.europa.eu/eurostat/documents/3433488/5585460/KS-SF-12-050-EN.PDF/39000dab-e2b7-49b2-bc4b-6aad0bf01279.

Smale, Alison. 2015. "Comic's Task: To Get Young Germans to Log Out, Tune in and Laugh Out Loud." *New York Times*, 4 December. Retrieved 15 July 2017 from https://www .nytimes.com/2015/12/05/world/europe/jan-bohmermann-germany-comic.html.

Smale, Alison. 2016. "Comedian's Takedown of Turkish President Tests Free Speech in Germany." *New York Times*, 11 April. Retrieved 15 July 2017 from https://www.nytimes.com/2016/04/12/world/europe/jan-bohmermann-erdogan-neo-magazin-royale.html.

Soldatos, Yiannis. 2001. *Ellenikos Kinematographos: Enas Aionas*, Volume I. Athens: Kohlias.

"*Spiegel:* Ta Germanika ARD kai ZDF Katarriptoun ton Mytho tes 'Spatales' ERT." 2013. *Ta Nea*, 13 June. Retrieved 15 July 2017 from http://www.tanea.gr/news/greece/article/5023683/spiegel-giati-den-kanoyn-ta-germanika-kanalia-zdf-kai-ard-gia-protypa-ths-ert/.

Springer, Simon, Kean Birch, and Julie MacLeavy. 2016. "An Introduction to Neoliberalism." In *The Handbook of Neoliberalism*, edited by Simon Springer, Kean Birch, and Julie MacLeavy. New York: Routledge.

Sweney, Mark. 2012. "RTL to Exit Greek TV market." *The Guardian*, 6 January. Retrieved 14 July 2017 from https://www.theguardian.com/media/2012/jan/06/rtl-greek-tv-market.

Swift, Art. 2013. "Honesty and Ethics Ranking of Clergy Slides to a New Low." *Gallup*, 16 December. Retrieved 15 July 2017 from http://www.gallup.com/poll/166298/honesty-ethics-rating-clergy-slides-new-low.aspx.

"Thymetheite Merika apo ta 'Istorika' Protoselida tes *Avrianis.*" 2014. *Proto Thema*, 7 August. Retrieved 15 July 2017 from http://www.protothema.gr/politics/article/269427/thymhtheite-merika-apo-ta-istorika-protoselida-ths-ayrianhs/.

"Ti Anapherei o Eisangeleas gia ten Prosorine Kratese Marinaki—E Apantese tou Proedrou tou Olympiakou." 2016. *E Kathimerini*, 6 September. Retrieved 16 July 2017 from http://www.kathimerini.gr/873625/article/epikairothta/ellada/ti-anaferei-o-eisaggeleas-giathn-proswrinh-krathsh-marinakh---h-apanthsh-toy-proedroy-toy-olympiakoy.

"Tria Chronia me Anastole ston Proen Ekdote tes *Apogevmatinis.*" 2013. *E Kathimerini*, 28 November. Retrieved 14 July 2017 from http://www.kathimerini.gr/61044/article/epikairothta/ellada/tria-xronia-me-anastolh-sto-prwhn-ekdoth-ths-apogeymatinhs-ksarantopoylo.

Tsiliotis, Charalambos. 2016. "Antisyntagmatike Symperiphora sto Thema ton Adeion." *E Kathimerini*, 23 March. Retrieved 15 July 2017 from http://www.kathimerini.gr/854085/opinion/epikairothta/politikh/antisyntagmatikh-symperifora-sto-8ema-twn-adeiwn.

Tsimboukis, Panagiotis 2016. "Kanalarches sto StE gia ten Akyrose tou Nomou gia tis Adeies." *Proto Thema*, 10 May. Retrieved 15 July 2017 from http://www.protothema.gr/greece/article/576716/prosefugan-sto-ste-kai-zitoun-akurosi-tou-nomou/.

Valoukos, Stathis. 1998. *Ellenike Teleorase: Odegos Teleoptikon Seiron 1967–1998*. Athens Aigokeros.

"We Had No Investors. We Did It Alone, Believing in our Powers and our Abilities." 2015. *The Guardian*, 19 July. Retrieved 14 July 2017 from https://www.theguardian.com/media/2015/jul/19/greece-newspaper-cooperative-no-investors-journalists.

"Ypevlethe apo ten *Eleftherotypia* e Aitese Ypagoges sto Arthro 99." 2011. *To Vima*, 30 December. Retrieved 14 July 2017 from http://www.tovima.gr/society/article/?aid=436847.

Zaharopoulos, Thimios, and Manny E. Paraschos. 1993. *Mass Media in Greece: Power, Politics, and Privatization*. Westport, CT: Praeger.

Chapter 7

Crime and Criminal Justice Policy in Greece during the Financial Crisis

Sappho Xenakis and Leonidas K. Cheliotis

Introduction

There has naturally been great and widespread interest in the impact of the ongoing international financial crisis on society. As with previous crises, one of the issues to have received particular attention in political, media, and public discourse has been the effect of rising socioeconomic hardship on common crime, with the former typically presumed to have substantially increased the prevalence and severity of the latter. Empirical reality, however, has problematized this presumption. On the one hand, the long-term trend of falling rates of police-recorded crime in Britain and the United States has continued unabated since the onset of the financial crisis, in terms of both property and violent offenses (see, e.g., Campos et al. 2011; Finklea 2011). On the other hand, a comparative study of non-Anglophone countries that experienced an economic downturn in 2008–9 showed that crime rates did not increase everywhere, and that crime growth did not always include serious violent offenses such as robbery or homicide (United Nations Office on Drugs and Crime [UNODC] 2012).

To the extent that such findings convey that the relationship between economic downturn and crime is far from linear or uniform, they are in broad accord with the long tradition of pertinent case studies in Europe and the United States. These studies have generally demonstrated a mild positive link between economic recession and certain types of property crime (e.g., burglary), and have found only little to no correlation between

Notes for this chapter begin on page 210.

economic recession and crimes against the person (e.g., aggravated assault and homicide). In fact, crimes against the person are more likely to increase in times of prosperity (see, inter alia, Cook 2010; Henry and Short 1954; Radzinowicz 1941; Short 1980; Thomas 1927). Research also suggests that downswings in the business cycle bring about a rise in various forms of white-collar crime (see, e.g., Simpson 1986), but this relationship is underprivileged in the public domain compared to the role of white-collar crime in instigating recession (see further Levi 2009; van de Bunt 2010).

There exist various and often tangled explanations as to how economic downturn impacts on levels and patterns of crime. Just as, for example, recessions are thought to strengthen the incentive to engage in property or white-collar crime by causing a reduction of access to employment and other legitimate means of attaining or sustaining desired or basic standards of life, so too they are thought to limit the frequency of opportunities for property crime in that potential burglary victims are more likely to stay at home and thus serve as guardians for their possessions. Similarly, recessions are believed to lead to a decrease in the ability to purchase and consume alcohol that could fuel violence, but they are also associated with drops in public expenditure for criminal justice organizations, which might undermine crime control (Cook 2010; see also Box 1987; Reiner 2007).

Insofar as empirical reality casts doubt on dominant political, media, and public discourse that presumes a strong link between economic downturn and a rise in the quantity and seriousness in crime, the immediate question concerns the reasons underlying the existence—and, indeed, persistence—of this discourse. To solve the puzzle, scholars have often drawn attention to the way in which phantom crime growth has been evoked by political elites to further personal, in-group, and affiliate interests during recessions. Hall et al. (1978), for example, suggested that the moral panic over muggings by young black men in Britain in the early 1970s was in good part an invention of the then-ruling Conservative party, an invention intended to manage the political challenges posed by the ascendancy of free-market policies and the consequent recession in the country at the time. In particular, the so-called mugging moral panic served to legitimate the imposition of intensified policing controls on disaffected black youths living on the margins of society, as well as to redirect mass economic and ontological insecurities against them. Focusing on California during the last quarter of the twentieth century, Gilmore (2007) has similarly argued that political elites sought to manage the reverberations of the financial crises caused by their aggressive capitalist policies through systematically deploying an alarmist discourse about crime and introducing laws that criminalized a wide variety of behaviors and raised sentencing levels. This paved the way to a rapid expansion in the use of imprisonment, which helped to contain the growing and increasingly agitated population of chronically unemployed urban low-wage workers, most of whom were Latino and African American, and simultaneously appealing to depressed regional communities that saw hopes for resuscitation in prison building. (For a similar study, see Hagan 2010.)

As pointed out in a range of other studies, however, the crime problem does not need to be a construct in order to be deployed in the service of given politico-economic imperatives. It might be true that crime as a grounded social reality creates political complications of its own, but these complications are by no means insurmountable (see, e.g., Garland 2001; Hay et al. 1975; Lynch 1988; Pearson 1983; Quinney 1977). In any case, what the literature has not yet addressed in sufficient depth is the political selection of crime over different social problems, or the prioritization of certain types of crime over given others. (For partial exceptions see, e.g., Box 1987; Hollway and Jefferson 1997; Simon 2001.) There is, for example, significant room for analysis of the ways in which violent interpersonal crime is publicly more compelling and thereby politically more useful than global warming or cancer, the reasons why violent interpersonal offenses possess superior political utility compared to grand corruption or industrial manslaughter, and the links that exist between violent interpersonal crime and other forms of lawbreaking both in terms of their actual or perceived occurrence and their representation in the public domain. Indeed, research on the relationship between recession and crime has tended to focus narrowly either on violent and property offenses or, to a lesser degree, on white-collar crime, thereby arguably missing crucial interconnections and their political underpinnings (but see Hagan 2010), not to mention the possible relevance of additional types of lawbreaking.

More generally, systematic research into how politics mediates the relationship between economic downturn and crime has overwhelmingly concerned itself with Anglophone jurisdictions, even though a broader international comparative analysis would seem essential in order to better answer this question. Little is thus known, for instance, about the filtering effect different domestic, transnational, or international political systems and environments has on how recession impacts on levels and patterns of crime, or on how likely crime (real or phantom) is to be exploited by political elites under conditions of financial crisis. Regardless of jurisdictional scope, moreover, there is still no in-depth work on how politics and crime have interacted in the context of the current international economic downturn.

With a view to contributing to scholarship on these themes, this chapter scrutinizes the experience of Greece. Greece constitutes a prime case for examining the way in which politics has mediated the relationship between economic downturn and crime, given the depth of the country's prevailing financial crisis and its socioeconomic ramifications. In 2009 the emerging sovereign debt crisis of eurozone member-states proved to be most severely experienced by Greece; in 2010 Greece was the first country to seek international financial assistance in order to service its public debt (Lynn 2011). Since 2009 Greece has been in deep recession. The austerity measures adopted to meet the conditions of successive bailouts have spanned spending cuts, public sector layoffs, tax rises, and the privatization of public assets. Although the initial barrage of measures was considered progressive by European comparison (Callan et al. 2011), subsequent policies, especially those pertaining to pensions and indirect taxation, have been less so.

Exactly how the combined effects of recession and austerity measures translate into socioeconomic hardship is not a forgone conclusion: economic crises, for example, do not necessarily bring about lower family incomes or higher levels of inequality and poverty (Matsaganis 2012). The data from Greece are complex but show that the impact of the crisis has indeed been asymmetrical, with those least able to access political power suffering the highest rates and increases in levels of poverty (Matsaganis 2012). If the wealthy have contributed most under the austerity measures and have recorded the largest reductions in income, the poor have contributed a greater share of their income and have suffered disproportionately from their loss (Matsaganis and Leventi 2011: 26). Even before the crisis, Greece had manifested one of the highest levels of income inequality and poverty in the European Union (EU) (Cheliotis and Xenakis 2010). Between 2009 and 2011, however, the proportion of the population below the poverty line, as adjusted for inflation, rose from 20.1 percent to 30.3 percent (Matsaganis 2012).

According to the Hellenic Statistical Authority (ELSTAT), unemployment surged from 9.4 percent in April 2009 to 22.6 percent in April 2012 (ELSTAT 2012). At the same time, living standards dropped, falling particularly sharply from late 2010 onward (as evident from surveys of gross disposable household income and material deprivation; European Commission 2012c: 83–84). A dramatic rise in negative health outcomes reflected cuts to health and welfare spending and the consequent reduction in access to medicines and medical care, as well as the intensification of a gamut of socioeconomic pressures on families and individuals. These outcomes have included a steep increase in HIV/AIDS infection report rates (a rise of 57 percent between 2010 and 2011, significantly linked to the suspension of free needle exchange programs for drug users), rising cases of malaria and tuberculosis, and elevated rates of suicide (Hellenic Centre for Disease Control and Prevention [KEEPLNO] 2011, 2012, 4; Kentikelenis et al. 2011, 2012; Paraskevis et al. 2011; *The Guardian,* 15 March 2012).

The financial crisis has seen the case of Greece become a focus of international commentary and analysis from the fields of politics and sociology. The key part played by crime in the politics of the crisis, however, has hitherto been neglected. While by no means unique in this respect, the Greek case offers an example in which the connections between crime, financial crisis, and politics have been particularly prominent and revealing. This chapter seeks to contribute three analytic points to the understanding of the relationship between economic downturn and crime as mediated by politics, including the role of government policy and dominant political discourse in enhancing the actual criminogenic impact of the financial crisis, although the causal mechanisms that directly intervene between financial crisis and crime (e.g., poverty and unemployment) are not our focus.

First, financial crisis is sometimes associated with a broader range of criminal or otherwise deviant behaviors than is typically acknowledged, whether by political elites, the mass media, and public opinion; or by pertinent scholarly literature. In the case of Greece, despite a tendency to construe the relationship between the financial crisis and the so-called problem of crime in the narrow sense of common property and violent offenses, corruption and political violence are also key to grasping the ramifications of the financial crisis in terms of criminal and deviant activities. Second, in contrast to dominant political, media, and public discourse, the criminogenic impact of financial crisis might lack linearity and uniformity—not just in terms of common property and violent crime, as previous research has shown, but also with regard to corruption and political violence. In the Greek case, for instance, burglaries, thefts, and robberies rose substantially after 2009, but homicide rose only slightly and rape decreased. Elite corruption seems to have mounted, whereas the magnitude of petty corruption appears to have dropped significantly. And while organized political violence identified as far-left or anarchist initially rose but then fell, violence perpetrated by far-right groups saw a steady ascent. Third and finally, there could be linkages imbued with politics between a wide variety of criminal and deviant behaviors, which are intensified and thereby rendered all the more discernible in times of financial crisis. In Greece, public concerns about elite corruption across public and private sectors incentivized governments to draw attention instead to common property and violent offenses, and the extent to which immigrants were involved as perpetrators. At the same time, government inaction against elite corruption and the perceived failure of state agencies to satisfactorily address common property and violent offenses were used—whether singly or together—as grounds for a variety of domestic actors to engage in political violence.

To elucidate these points, we begin by briefly discussing the role of corruption in triggering Greece's financial crisis, considering trends in petty and elite corruption and summarizing the three grand corruption scandals that rocked Greek politics around the time that the crisis broke. We also point to the way in which these trends and ongoing practices of elite corruption fueled antagonism between the public and traditional mainstream political parties. The legitimacy of public fear of crime and punitiveness is then explored in conjunction with levels and patterns of common property and violent offenses, shedding light on the role of so-called signal disorders in spurring fear of crime, and exploring the particular emphasis placed on immigrants in associated discourse and policy. The following section examines developments in political violence in terms of the spectrum of actors involved, from substate groups on the far left and the far right, to public mobilizations of protesters, to the police force.

A couple of caveats regarding the chapter's scope are in order at this juncture. The cutoff point of our analysis is roughly the beginning of 2015, when a coalition government led by the left-wing party assumed power against the backdrop of a so-called refugee crisis mounting in various parts of the globe and manifesting itself particularly acutely in Greek border areas. This temporal span was necessary partly due to limitations of space, and partly because at the time of writing the Coalition of the Radical Left (SYRIZA)–led coalition had been in office for too short a period for its policies on matters of crime and criminal justice to be conclusively assessed. As concerns earlier years, our analysis of trends in crime, criminal justice, and associated issues and policy fields is on occasion limited to the early years of the crisis. This is due to a lack of official or other reliable data for more-recent years.

Corruption

A large number of domestic and international commentators have identified patterns of corruption in Greece as a key factor contributing to the emergence of the country's financial crisis, organically related to overexpenditure and mismanagement of public funds (see, e.g., Lewis 2011; Lynn 2011; Manolopoulos 2011; Mitsopoulos and Pelagidis 2011). Although corruption did not cause the crisis, there has been a degree of consensus in recognizing that corruption increased the vulnerability of the Greek economy to collapse. Considerable controversy has remained, however, as to which form of corruption caused greater damage to state finances, and whether the general public or political elites have been primarily responsible in this regard.

Debating Blame

On the one hand, there has been the thesis—exemplified in the immortalized pronouncement of Greece's deputy prime minister Theodoros Pangalos in 2010, "We ate it all together" (*To Vima*, 22 September 2010)—that all levels of Greek society were complicit in, and benefited from, practices of patronage, petty corruption, and tax evasion, and thus shared blame for the growing precariousness of the Greek state's finances before crisis struck.

According to this perspective, a sufficient segment of the public colluded in the clientelist logics that lay behind the repeated political provision of ad hoc exemptions and post hoc legitimation for unfair and illegal practices (such as the regular preelection wave of targeted tax collection laxity and legalizations granted to illegally renovated and constructed properties), and in the routine support for unnecessary and underqualified public sector appointments (see, e.g., Lewis 2011: 48; Skouras and Christodoulakis 2011), contributing to a situation that has been described as "corrupt legality" (Transparency International–Greece 2012: 15). Similarly, the public was said to have connived to a degree in the patronage rationales that underpinned a patchwork of social protection privileges accorded to diverse trades groups but withheld from others (such as the inclusion of hairdressing and cheese-making, but not firefighting or rubbish collecting, within the state category of hazardous and arduous professions that warranted early retirement; see, e.g., *Athens News* 5 December 2011). Moreover, certain interest groups from among the general public—whether regional or trade constituencies—were repeatedly accused of resisting the efforts of politicians to carry out structural reforms that promised to dislodge patron-client relationships. Additionally, the populace has routinely been characterized as systemically lazy and devious, traits alleged to have played a particularly egregious role in simultaneously burdening and depriving state finances (an argument that, when made by foreigners about the Greeks, has drawn critiques of racism; see, e.g., Bratsis 2011).

There has clearly been a high level of recognition by the Greek public that corruption is a major problem in the country (see, e.g., European Commission 2011c; Pew Research Center 2012). This is unsurprising: the extensiveness of tax evasion and the relatively large shadow economy are common knowledge. Tax revenue shortfalls increased steadily in the years preceding the eruption of the financial crisis in 2009, despite the Greek economy enjoying a 4 percent growth rate over the same period (Capó Servera and Moschovis 2008), with tax evasion estimated to account for 48 percent of the country's budget deficit shortfall in 2008 (Skouras and Christodoulakis 2011). Meanwhile, the size of the country's shadow economy is estimated to have stood at around 25 percent of official GDP in the three years that preceded the start of the crisis (2007–9) (Schneider 2012, 5), a situation that was likely to have facilitated corruption (see Buehn and Schneider 2012a). Over the previous decade more generally, Greece displayed one of the largest shadow economies among wealthy Organisation for Economic Co-operation and Development (OECD) member-states (Buehn and Schneider 2012b: 159).

On the other hand, there has been a strong conviction among the public that elite corruption bears overwhelming responsibility for the parlous state of public finances on the eve of the crisis. Many Greeks believe that they have been forced to act as accomplices by a corrupt system that is ultimately structured and perpetuated by elites. More so than being the victim of petty or bureaucratic corruption (providing extra payments, which are unregulated and untaxed, for routine services), it is grand corruption as perpetrated by elites that has most antagonized the public.

From this standpoint, given the brash impunity of corruption perpetrated by the infamously intermeshed privileged political, media, and business circles (the *diaplekomena*), the very invocation of shared guilt for bringing the system to crisis through corruption has been provocative. Tax evasion, for example, has been most common among the top 10 percent of the population in terms of income (Matsaganis and Flevotomou 2010), while more-lucrative professional occupations that display closest ties to members of parliament have been the most tax avoidant (key industry groups in this respect include those from the fields of law, medicine, education, accounting, and the financial services; see Artavanis, Morse, and Tsoutsoura 2012). As pointedly remarked by Nikos Lekkas, the head of the tax inspectorate (Financial and Economic Crime Unit [SDOE]), in 2012, while tax evasion has long been systemic in the country, the elites have played a central role to this effect: in particular, elected officials and politicians have been immune from investigation in practical terms, thanks not least to the parliament's use of delaying tactics to undercut pertinent SDOE enquiries (*Die Welt*, 8 June 2012).

Given not only that the public has believed corrupt practices to be most pervasive among national-level politicians (European Commission 2011c), but also that the public has overwhelmingly held Greek governments to be primarily responsible for the country's current economic problems (Pew Research Center 2012: 18), it is no surprise that the degree of immunity from prosecution enjoyed by Greek politicians has been a key focus of public concerns. According to Article 86 of the Greek constitution, serving or former members of the cabinet or undersecretaries can be prosecuted only with the consent of parliament. Such consent, which requires an absolute majority within parliament, must be provided no later than the end of the second yearly session of parliament following that which began after the offense was committed. Additionally, Law 3126/2003 imposes a short, five-year statute of limitations on the criminal liability of ministers (Transparency International–Greece 2010). These legal conditions were invoked in 2011, when members of parliament absolved themselves of responsibility for two of the three largest cases of corruption to rock Greek political life in recent years: the Vatopedi and Siemens scandals. These scandals implicated members of the two political parties that had dominated government over the decades following the fall of the military dictatorship in 1974 (center-left Panhellenic Socialist Movement, or PASOK, and center-right New Democracy, or ND), and concerned, respectively, a monastery land-swap arrangement, and security systems and telecommunications contracts.

Three Key Grand Corruption Scandals: Vatopedi, Siemens, and Ferrostaal

The Vatopedi scandal emerged when, in 2008, following six years of political lobbying, monks from the Vatopedi monastery of the autonomous monastic state of Mount Athos managed to assert historic ownership rights over a lake that had more recently been designated by the Greek state as a national nature reserve (*Athens News*, 19 September 2008, 24 October 2010). With the support of high-ranking government ministers (including, allegedly, the then prime minister), the monks persuaded the Greek state to agree to an unusual land-swap in which the monks exchanged the lake for a collection of state-owned properties, but simultaneously secured the reclassification of the latter from noncommercial to commercial usage status. As a result, the monks were free to resell to developers the land they had just acquired, all of which was processed remarkably expeditiously. In this endeavor, the monks were also alleged to have spent hundreds of thousands of euros hiring the wife of the then-serving Merchant Marine minister to act as public notary, as well as employing her father and brother to provide other legal services associated with the transactions (*Athens News*, 18 January 2008, 5 December 2008). Further aggravating this unusual exchange was the fact that the Greek state allegedly accepted a significantly inflated price for the lake, while state assessors were accused of having vastly underestimated the value of state land that was exchanged in return (*Athens News*, 19 September 2008; Lewis 2011: 74–77). An opinion based on a preliminary review of the evidence that was issued by Supreme Court Prosecutor George Sanidas estimated the loss the land swap caused to the public purse to be in the region of €100 million to €150 million (see further *Athens News,* 19 September 2008, 5 December 2008; *Athens News Agency,* 20 November 2008). Two ND ministers resigned after the scandal broke (the Merchant Marine minister and the minister of State, who was a close aide of the prime minister), but no senior politician was ever prosecuted. Three other members of the ND government—one minister and two deputy ministers—were indicted by the Greek parliament over their involvement in the scandal, but the cases were dropped due to the passage of time under the statute of limitations (*Athens News,* 12 January 2012; see also Lewis 2011: 65). The highest-profile individual to be arrested and charged with inciting public officials to commit fraud, perjury, and money laundering was the abbot of Vatopedi, who was imprisoned in December 2011 awaiting his trial, only to be released a few months later after paying bail of €300,000 (*E Kathimerini,* 1 April 2012). All defendants were eventually acquitted by the Court of Appeals for Serious Crimes in March 2017.

Meanwhile, grand corruption scandals concerning the awarding of civil and military defense contracts by the Greek state were particularly important given their regular and cumulative expense to the public purse. Two scandals that received particular prominence in the Greek media around the time of the crisis concerned bribery paid by foreign firms—Siemens and Ferrostaal—to secure high-profile defense contracts. In the Siemens affair, Siemens Hellas (a subsidiary of the German industrial conglomerate) paid more than €100 million to Greek politicians and senior officials between 1997 and 2002 in order to secure telecommunications contracts from the state-controlled operator Hellenic Telecom, including for the task of establishing a surveillance system known as C4I in advance of the country's hosting of the Olympic Games in 2004. The highly complex system, whose final cost to the Greek state would exceed €250 million, proved to be operationally dysfunctional from the moment it was due to launch (Samatas 2011). Siemens is alleged to have provided political party financing and to have paid bribes to more than twelve cabinet ministers of PASOK and ND governments. Both parties denied accepting any payments, and only one former minister admitted having received money. He was convicted of failing to declare his assets to the tax authorities, and was given a comparatively small fine and a suspended three-year prison sentence, while other politicians were protected from prosecution by the statute of limitations. Siemens itself had been made to pay a record fine of $1.6 billion to U.S. and European authorities in 2008 to settle charges that the company had routinely used bribery to secure contracts worldwide since the mid-1990s (*New York Times,* 15 December 2008), but Greek authorities were not party to this settlement. In July 2012, however, following a protracted dispute about unpaid bills by Greece and the Greek government's damage claims against Siemens related to bribery allegations, the Greek parliament ratified an out-of-court settlement valued at €270 million between the company and the Greek state. According to this agreement, Siemens would pay compensation of €170 million to the Greek state and would provide a €100 million investment to Siemens Hellas, while waiving outstanding fees of €80 million owed by the Greek state. The Greek state, for its part, would unfreeze a €41 million contract with Siemens in which the company would provide technology for an extension of the metro system in Athens (*E Kathimerini,* 18 July 2012; *Financial Times,* 8 March 2012).

The Ferrostaal scandal involved another German firm that was alleged to routinely use bribery to secure contracts internationally. In late 2011, following an investigation into the company's use of bribes to secure contracts in Greece and Portugal, Ferrostaal agreed to pay a German court a fine of €140 million (Matussek 2011). The case in Greece concerned the alleged payment of an estimated €230 million in bribes by Ferrostaal to members of the PASOK government, as well as to civil servants, military officials, and intermediaries, to secure the sale of four submarines to the country during the early 2000s in a deal worth €1.26 billion, a cost that had risen to almost €3 billion by the next decade, when another PASOK government decided to buy two more submarines. By late 2009, however, Greece had paid around 70 percent of the total bill owed, but not one of the submarines had yet been delivered, after one had been tested and found to be faulty. Unusually for such a scandal, in 2012 the Ferrostaal case led to a high-profile arrest: that of former PASOK minister of Defense Akis Tsochatzopoulos, who left politics in 2009 and was expelled from the party in 2011 following allegations about his involvement in corruption, including accepting a bribe for the submarine deal. Indeed, in 2013 Tsochatzopoulos was sentenced to twenty years imprisonment on charges of money laundering.

Persistent Elite Corruption

Since the financial crisis broke in Greece in 2009, not only did politicians provocatively absolve themselves of legal responsibility for involvement in major corruption scandals, but they also appeared to continue sanctioning corruption carried out by other wealthy elites of the country, by allegedly extending protection from prosecution to those who had engaged in fraud, embezzlement, and tax evasion.

A piece of legislation introduced in 2010 (Law 3904) provides for charges to be dropped against individuals suspected of embezzlement if the funds are returned prior to prosecution. This law proved central in one of the

largest scandals to have emerged since 2009 involving the Greek banking sector. The scandal in question concerned Lavrentis Lavrentiades, a
pharmaceuticals and media magnate who became the president of Proton
Bank in 2009. Along with a cabal of associates, Lavrentiades was alleged
to have embezzled millions of euros, a fraction of which (€51 million) provoked initial official investigations. In July 2011, one day before EU-wide
stress tests on banks, the country's finance minister approved a €100 million transfer of public funds to the bank in order to avert the potential
negative effects on the Greek banking system were the hole in the Proton
Bank's finances to be publicly exposed. Despite some parliamentary resistance and ongoing investigations, and, indeed, in apparent contravention
of a law prohibiting financial assistance to banks under investigation (Law
2362/1995), the transfer went ahead. A new law (4002/2011) was passed,
however, that retroactively permitted public funding to banks to be determined by the need for systemic stability in the banking sector (Vaxevanis
2011). The following month, Lavrentiades returned €51 million to the
bank. The government then effectively nationalized Proton Bank in October that year by mandating the transfer of a further €800 million of public
funds to recapitalize the bank, which was the first use of a rescue fund set
up by the eurozone and the International Monetary Fund (IMF) as part of
their bailout of Greece (*Financial Times*, 21 August 2011; *Reuters*, 12 January 2012; Vaxevanis 2011). Finally, in 2012 Lavrentiades was charged with
fraud in association with accusations that, under his presidency, Proton
Bank had issued bad loans worth approximately €700 million to companies he owned or with which he was associated (*E Kathimerini*, 21 March
2012). He was remanded into custody in 2012, and released on a €500,000
bail in 2014.

The Greek government also introduced a tax amnesty in 2010, con-
tradicting political rhetoric that pledged commitment to countering tax
evasion and money laundering. Although this measure was widely criticized for failing to raise the significant funds promised and for allowing evaders to pay only small fines in order to avoid being subjected to a
tax investigation (*Financial Times*, 30 September 2010; *GR Reporter*, 24 July
2012), a further amnesty scheme was already under consideration by the
government in 2012, only to be dropped due to international pressure in
early 2013. More provocative still was a scandal that erupted in late 2012
after revelations that, between 2010 and 2012, PASOK ministers of Finance
George Papaconstantinou and Evangelos Venizelos had failed to ensure
investigations were undertaken into more than two thousand wealthy
Greeks suspected to have engaged in tax evasion, whose names were on
a list allegedly provided by then minister of Finance in France, Christine
Lagarde, and that was subsequently "lost." More generally, there were to

be very few prosecutions of wealthy tax evaders in the years following the start of the financial crisis, notwithstanding a slow rise in the number of token high-profile arrests carried out with media fanfare. Furthermore, while a significant drop in the reported size of bribes requested in public and private sectors following the onset of the financial crisis in 2009 led to a fall in the overall magnitude of petty corruption (Public Issue 2011), a development that might have also facilitated a notable decline in the estimated size of the country's shadow economy over the same period (Schneider 2012), income underreporting among the wealthiest of the population appears to have increased, contributing to a rise in tax evasion since the advent of the crisis (Matsaganis et al. 2010).

Public Anger and Political Elites

The scale and breadth of impunity for elite corruption has provoked great public resentment. While public frustrations with elite corruption in Greece have long stood at a very high level by European comparison, those frustrations have been aggravated by the widespread socioeconomic costs of the crisis and the freezing of mass political patronage. In past eras, patronage could help to mollify public consternation over elite corruption scandals in the country (see Dobratz and Whitfield 1992: 177). Conditions of austerity have meant that the expensive option of clientelism has been less available to political elites for managing mass dissatisfaction, while foreign and domestic elite demand for political stability in the country has worked against efforts to revoke impunity toward grand corruption.

As illustrated by a large-scale opinion survey carried out in 2011, public anger against the country's political elite became intense: 28.6 percent of respondents stated they would be prepared to attack politicians with eggs and yogurt, 16.1 percent said they would be prepared to beat up political figures, and 12.5 percent said they would be prepared to set fire to the vehicles of parliamentarians and ministers (*To Vima*, 11 March 2012). This anger was vented both physically and politically: low-level assault and intimidation of politicians reportedly became more common (see, e.g., *Ta Nea*, 9 June 2012), and during 2012, in the first elections to be held after the financial crisis broke, voters punished PASOK and ND.[1] Between 2009 and 2012, the party that saw the greatest rise in its votes was SYRIZA. Constrained by their commitment to austerity measures, PASOK and ND avoided competition against SYRIZA on its demands for improved socioeconomic conditions. Instead, they sought to garner support by encouraging and exploiting fear of crime and xenophobic sentiments through keeping the issues of property and violent crime, and immigration, in the public spotlight.

Property and Violent Crime[2]

Since the financial crisis broke, public fear of crime and punitiveness in Greece have stood at very high levels, and seem to have undergone a substantial increase, especially in relation to immigrant populations. This has been in no small part due to political and media discourse citing police-recorded crime statistics showing both an important rise in the prevalence of thefts, burglaries, and robberies over this time span, and a significant overrepresentation of non-Greek individuals among known perpetrators of these offenses. Whether directly or indirectly, this discourse has associated crime with broader social concerns such as unemployment and poverty, but also with the growing presence of poor immigrants, drug use in public places, and homelessness, particularly as these issues have manifested themselves in central urban areas.

A nexus of crime, irregular immigration and urban degradation, for example, was central to the political agenda in the lead-up to the national elections of May and June 2012, with PASOK, ND, and the neo-fascist far-right party Golden Dawn, among other parties, openly linking the issues to one another in a competition for xenophobic votes. PASOK minister of Citizen Protection Michalis Chrysochoidis pointed the finger of blame for a 10 percent increase in muggings and robberies in 2011 on undocumented immigrants, referring to their poor living conditions in central Athens as "a ticking bomb for public health" ("Compulsory Health Checks" 2012). The leader of ND who was subsequently elected prime minister, Antonis Samaras, meanwhile, pledged to reclaim Greek cities from irregular immigrants and their purported criminality and infectious diseases. The most extreme messages came from Golden Dawn, which mainly based its campaign on an anti-immigrant platform under the slogan, "So we can rid this land of filth," and saw its electoral support increase from a meager 0.29 percent of the vote in 2009 to 6.92 percent in June 2011, thus winning 18 out of 300 seats in parliament.[3] Not only did Golden Dawn castigate irregular immigrants for their putative role in spiraling crime rates and falling living standards for the Greek majority, but it also called for cracking down on irregular immigration by laying landmines along the Greek–Turkish borders in Evros and placing special forces in the area with a license to shoot at will. All this discourse was accompanied by government action in the form, for instance, of intensified policing of immigrants and an effort to introduce legislation that would provide for the detention of immigrants and asylum seekers suspected of representing a danger to public health (see further Cheliotis 2017; Human Rights Watch 2012: 35–36; Kosmatopoulos 2012; see also Cabot, this volume).

Whereas police-recorded data might seem to offer some explanation for the level and composition of political and public attitudes toward crime, a deeper look finds the data and the attitudes they helped nurture to be exaggerative and grossly biased.

Crime and Public Attitudes: A First Glance

According to Eurobarometer survey data, although public concern in Greece about crime as an important national issue has been surpassed in the wake of the financial crisis by heightened concern about such matters as the country's economic situation, unemployment, inflation, and government debt, it has stood at high levels by EU comparison. Indeed, public concern about crime more than doubled in Greece between 2008 and 2009, before returning to pre-crisis levels thereafter, whereas the average national rate of concern about crime in the EU concurrently almost halved following a steady gradual decline. Thus, although Greece has been in line with (and has, in fact, led) the broader EU trend toward growing economic concerns among the public within member-states, its extraordinarily stabilized rate of public concern about crime came to exceed the respective EU average (for further discussion, see European Commission 2008, 2009, 2011a, 2012a).

Since the onset of the financial crisis, moreover, rates of fear of criminal victimization have been found by domestic research to be very high in Greece, and appear to have risen substantially in relation to the already elevated rates for earlier years, at least insofar as the data permit comparisons with prior studies. In a nationwide survey by Giannakopoulou (2011) in 2010–11, for instance, 85 percent of respondents thought that crime had increased significantly over the past five years, 66 percent reported that they often or sometimes thought about the possibility of becoming a victim of crime and how to avoid it, and 44 percent reported feeling unsafe or very unsafe, or altogether avoiding, walking alone in their area of domicile after dark. As far as respondents' worry about being a victim of specific offenses, 56 percent reported being very or fairly worried about being mugged or robbed, 48 percent about physical attacks by strangers, 40 percent about having their home broken into and something stolen, and 38.5 percent about being sexually assaulted (see *To Vima*, 27 May 2012, for similar findings from another recent survey).

In the same study by Giannakopoulou (2011), when respondents were asked about the single most important cause behind heightened fear of crime in Greece, 24 percent named the increasing number of immigrants and minorities in the country, while a mere 13 percent named increasing crime. But the most common response, given by 35 percent of respondents, concerned current economic conditions and financial uncertainty. Given that 75 percent of respondents in this study did not think their fear of crime was unnecessary, their attribution of heightened fear of crime in the country primarily to current economic conditions and financial uncertainty seems to be indicative of an underlying belief that poverty and socioeconomic insecurity increases the propensity of those most subjected to them, characteristically immigrants, to engage in crime (see Figgou and Condor 2007 for relevant discussion).

There is some evidence to suggest that, similar to fear of crime, public punitiveness in Greece has stood at very high levels since the onset of the crisis (and also seems to have undergone a substantial increase, again insofar as the data allow for comparisons with previous research). In a large-scale survey with residents of Athens in 2011–12, for instance, respondents were asked to sentence a male offender in a burglary scenario that varied only in terms of the ethnic origin of the offender and his legal status, in the case of non-Greeks. The harshest possible sentence (i.e., imprisonment for more than two years) was chosen by 46 percent of respondents for a documented immigrant from Albania, by 49 percent of respondents for an undocumented immigrant from Afghanistan, and by 52 percent of respondents for an undocumented immigrant from Albania, whereas an impressively smaller 27 percent of respondents chose the harshest sentence in the scenario where the burglar was Greek. While, then, the legal status of the offender was not found to matter significantly, the role of ethnic origin proved to be decisive, confirming earlier studies about the especially punitive attitudes Greeks tend to hold toward foreign offenders and even more so toward Albanians (see further *To Vima*, 27 May 2012).

At first glance, police-recorded crime statistics seem to provide some grounds for the levels and patterns of public fear of crime and punitiveness in Greece since the crisis struck. Between 2009 and 2012, for example, the rate of burglaries and thefts per thousand inhabitants rose by 20.3 percent, from 6.4 to 7.7. During the same period, the rate of robberies per thousand inhabitants increased by 26.8 percent, from 0.41 to 0.52. Among the total number of burglars and thieves known to the police for the years 2009–12, Greeks were the majority (53.1 percent), but non-Greeks were overrepresented in proportion to their estimated one-tenth share of the general population. As concerns robberies, however, non-Greeks were both the majority (52.7 percent) and proportionately overrepresented.

Unfortunately, such data have helped to retrospectively justify what have been longstanding trends of disproportionately high levels of public fear of criminal victimization, but also of public support for the harsh punishment of common offenders, especially of immigrant origin. Indeed, over the three decades that preceded the crisis, Greece became one of the most crime-fearing and punitive nations in Europe and beyond. The results of the European Crime and Safety Survey (EU ICS) of 2005, for instance, showed the public in Greece to be the most fearful of criminal victimization both on the continent and by global comparison (van Dijk, van Kesteren, and Smit 2007; van Dijk et al. 2007), as well as to favor imprisoning recidivist burglars at one of the highest rates in Europe, and to exceed all its European counterparts in terms of level of support for the longest possible custodial sentence in the same recidivist burglary scenario (Kühnrich and Kania 2005).

Other studies have shown that Greeks are the most likely nation on the continent to view the presence of ethnic and racial minorities in one's area of residence as contributing to a rise in crime (e.g., Semyonov and Glikman 2009; Semyonov, Gorodzeisky, and Glikman 2012); in addition, Greeks tend to perceive immigrants as the primary source of criminal danger and associated insecurities (e.g., Figgou et al. 2011). All this has been despite the fact that, at the time research was conducted, police-recorded crime rates in the country remained low by European comparison, and have risen only modestly; most of this rise was due to offenses of little criminological interest (e.g., traffic offenses such as speeding and illegal parking). The level and nature of non-Greeks' criminal involvement, moreover, fell well short of justifying fearful and punitive attitudes toward them (see Cheliotis and Xenakis 2011b for a review; see also Ceobanu 2011; Cheliotis 2017; Semyonov, Gorodzeisky, and Glikman 2012; van Dijk, van Kesteren, and Smit 2007; van Dijk et al. 2007).

Crime and Public Attitudes: A Deeper View

It is plausible that levels and patterns of public fear of crime, as well as of punitiveness, have remained incommensurate to the actual levels and patterns of criminal victimization. Indeed, in her nationwide survey in 2010–11, Giannakopoulou (2011) found a negative correlation between prior experience of personal victimization and fear of crime: respondents who reported having been victims of house burglary and theft, mugging and robbery, or sexual assault, in the past five years were significantly less likely than nonvictimized respondents to worry about suffering these respective offenses in the future. A positive correlation was nevertheless established between the experience of indirect victimization (i.e., through knowing a victim) and fear of crime.

In any case, a closer look at police-recorded crime statistics reveals rather variable trends, both in terms of levels and of patterns, across dif-

ferent offenses. Between 2011 and 2012, for example, the volume of burglaries and thefts fell by 9.2 percent, and that of robberies by 9.7 percent.
The occurrence of certain types of violent crime meanwhile underwent
an overall drop since the onset of the financial crisis, while the percentile
rise in the occurrence of other types of violent crime is far less impressive
when expressed in terms of absolute numbers and rates per units of population, but also when compared to the precrisis period. Thus, between
2009 and 2012 the total annual volume of police-recorded rapes decreased
by 21.9 percent, and by 26.3 percent as a rate per thousand inhabitants,
from 0.019 to 0.014. At the same time, while the total annual volume of
homicides rose by 15.3 percent, this was from a low 143 to a slightly higher
165 (and it actually fell by 10.3 percent between 2011 and 2012). As a rate
per thousand inhabitants, the volume of homicides rose by 16.6 percent
from 2009 to 2012, but again, this was from a mere 0.012 to just 0.014. One
way or another, the increased volume of homicides remained consistently
below the peak volume experienced in recent decades; that of 203, or 0,018
per thousand inhabitants, in 1997.

Equally, trends in the composition of offenders known to the police
problematize stereotypical representations and perceptions of ethnoracial
minorities as the prime actors behind the alleged crime boom in the country since the onset of the financial crisis. Between 2009 and 2012, for example, the absolute number of Greeks among offenders known to the police
for thefts and burglaries rose by 60.2 percent, from 5,957 to 9,545, whereas
the respective number of non-Greeks increased by a comparatively modest 13.7 percent, from 6,313 to 7,184 (also dropping slightly, by 1.7 percent,
between 2011 and 2012). In 2009 Greeks comprised 48.5 percent of all offenders known to the police for thefts and burglaries, but their proportion
had climbed up to 57 percent by 2012. With regard to robberies, the absolute number of Greeks among offenders known to the police rose by 65.3
percent between 2009 and 2012, from 782 to 1,293. The respective number
of non-Greeks underwent a significantly lower rise by 37.4 percent, from
796 to 1,094, and actually shrank by 19.4 percent between 2010 and 2012.
In 2009 the proportion of Greeks among all offenders known to the police
for robberies stood at 49.5 percent, but had reached the majority, at 54.1
percent, by 2012.

In terms of rapes, the number of Greeks among known offenders fell
by 4 percent between 2009 and 2012, from 124 to 119, while the number of
non-Greeks underwent a drop over eleven times as great, by 46 percent,
from 128 to 69. As a result, although non-Greeks were overrepresented in
proportion to their share in the general population, Greeks constituted the
majority of known rapists by any measure. Finally, as concerns homicides,
the number of Greeks among known offenders grew by only 2.8 percent

between 2009 and 2012, from 249 to 256, while the number of non-Greeks grew by 26.6 percent, from 124 to 157, although it fell by 12.7 percent from 2011 to 2012. In any case, while non-Greeks were overrepresented in proportion to their share in the general population, both in all annual counts and the overall total for the four-year period at issue, Greeks were once again responsible by any measure for most homicides.

Here it should be noted that the data available do not allow for determining whether ethnoracial minorities have been more likely to be victims of homicide in Greece, as has been established elsewhere in Europe (see, e.g., Liem et al. 2013). The heightened prevalence of racist violence in Greece over recent years, however, would seem to point in that direction, even though perpetration of homicide against members of ethnoracial minorities does not need to be motivated by the ethnoracial background of the victim. The EU ICS of 2005, for example, found the level of racist violence against immigrants in Greece to be the second highest in the EU after Belgium (van Dijk et al. 2007), while more recent reports by domestic and international NGOs claim that racist violence has escalated rapidly in the country; indeed, Greece has been described as the most acute example of the way in which the financial crisis has fueled racist violence in Europe (Rights, Equality & Diversity European Network [i-RED] 2012: 4; see also Human Rights Watch 2012; National Commission for Human Rights [NCHR] 2011a). But it should also be noted that the rate of homicides in Greece still pales in comparison to the rate of deaths by other causes. The total of 503 deaths by homicide that occurred between 2009 and 2011, for instance, was nearly eight times lower than the 3,835 deaths caused by motor vehicle accidents (a daily average of 3.5 deaths), and over twice as low as the 1,279 deaths by suicide (a daily average of just over one death).[4]

In any case, there are multiple reasons why police-recorded crime statistics in Greece need to be treated with particular caution when used as a proxy for actual crime rates. These range from the reported ease with which the Greek police file unwarranted charges (Amnesty International 2009), to their systematic overpolicing of immigrant communities, including so-called sweep or cleaning operations and a propensity to stop-and-search and arrest immigrant individuals to a greater degree than Greek persons, to the fact that immigrant individuals are easier to arrest due to the comparatively unsupportive social and physical environment in which they find themselves, to the tendency of Greek citizens to report crimes to police authorities even when cases are frivolous and their specifics largely uncertain, just as they are more likely to report crimes when offenders are believed—rightly or wrongly—to be immigrants (see further Cheliotis and Xenakis 2011b: 20–22; see also, more generally, Cheliotis and Xenakis 2016).

Indeed, given that the police forces were exempted from mass redun-dancies in the public sector (see, e.g., *Ethnos*, 20 February 2012) and that their sweep operations became more frequent and aggressive after the fi-nancial crisis broke out, it is reasonable to assume a degree of inflation in the proportional share of immigrants in police-recorded crime statistics. As concerns the prevalence of racist violence, by contrast, official data have been highly unreliable, not only because of practices of underrecord-ing and insufficient investigation, prosecution, and punishment of such cases by the police and judicial authorities (especially when police offi-cers are implicated as perpetrators), but also because of underreporting by victims due to lack of confidence in the Greek criminal justice system, fear of reprisals, and active dissuasion by the police. In the latter respect, for example, a €100 fee was introduced in 2010 as a prerequisite to the investigation of complaints against the police, while undocumented im-migrants have additionally been effectively threatened with punishment should they report their victimization. At the beginning of 2013, amid fanfare accompanying the launch of a police hotline for reporting racist violence against migrants, the chief of Hellenic Police made clear that vic-tims with irregular status would not be offered any form of immunity but, rather, would be arrested and deported (Cheliotis 2017; see also Amnesty International 2012; Human Rights Watch 2012; i-RED 2012; NCHR 2011a).

The Role of Signal Disorders and Other Indicators of Community Well-being

Given findings from past studies, it seems likely that levels and patterns of fear of crime, as well as of punitiveness, were bolstered in Greece after the onset of the financial crisis by the perceived increase in what Innes (2004) terms signal disorders (i.e., behaviors and situations that rightly or wrongly communicate to the public that the public is at risk of criminal victimization) and in various other common indicators of deterioration of community well-being.

Past research has demonstrated that fear of crime in Greece is linked to personal exposure to drug-related problems in one's area of residence, such as seeing people dealing or using drugs, or finding syringes left by drug addicts. Indeed, the rate of reported exposure to drug-related prob-lems in one's area of residence has been found to be far higher in Greece than anywhere else in Europe, as well as Australia, Canada, New Zea-land, and the United States. Although the extent of personal exposure to drug-related problems in one's area of residence in Greece has been shown not to bear a positive correlation to the actual levels of property crime (or, indeed, of drug consumption) in the country, the link between personal exposure to drug-related problems in one's area of residence and fear of crime has been found to be stronger in Greece than in any other European country (van Dijk, van Kesteren, and Smit 2007; van Dijk et al. 2007).

It has also been shown that fear of crime in Greece is linked, among other factors, to perceived high ethnic heterogeneity of one's area of residence (Semyonov, Gorodzeisky, and Glikman 2012); to perceived low quality of the built and physical environment (in terms, e.g., of cleanliness, the condition of roads, and levels of air pollution; Christakopoulou, Dawson, and Gari 2001; Vakiari and Kontargyri 2009); to perceived insufficiency of one's household income (Semyonov, Gorodzeisky, and Glikman 2012); and to low rates of welfare provision (Hummelsheim et al. 2011). As concerns specifically the association in the public mind in Greece between immigration and a rise in crime rates, it has been found to correlate positively with perceived ethnic heterogeneity of one's area of residence (Ceobanu 2011).

Following the outbreak of the financial crisis in Greece, and arguably because of it, public concerns intensified over the prevalence of several signal disorders and other common indicators of the deterioration of community well-being in the country, especially in urban areas. Whether taken singly or in concert, these concerns have included the increased concentration of poor immigrants in central locales, drug use in public places, and homelessness (see, e.g., European Commission 2011b), alongside a dramatic drop in income and severe cutbacks in welfare provision for the Greek majority.

While the distinct physical characteristics of immigrants, their poverty, and their differential use of urban space (e.g., congregating in public squares in search of work) had previously made them visible in Greek local contexts (Hatziprokopiou 2003; Kandylis and Kavoulakos 2011), such visibility became all the more prominent as the density of urban immigrant populations increased. The case of drug use in public places is similar. In itself, the rate of recorded drug use in Greece has long been one of the lowest in Europe, while the estimate of problem drug users in the country showed a decline from 2009 to 2010, as did the police-recorded rate of deaths caused by drug use. Moreover, the annual volume of police-recorded drug-related offenses and the corresponding number of accused persons dropped in the country after 2009, alongside a slight decrease in the number of individuals held in prison in connection to a drug-related offense. Yet the financial crisis brought a mix of rampant unemployment, worsening personal and household finances, the growing inability of social networks (e.g., family and friends) to provide support in the process of seeking or following drug addiction treatment, and the imposition of drastic reductions to state funding for core drug rehabilitation agencies, which pushed an increasing number of drug addicts, Greeks as well as non-Greeks, out onto urban streets. Because police sweeps of central urban areas also displaced drug addicts into new districts and neighborhoods, the categorical visibility of problem drug users inevitably heightened in the eyes of the broader public (see further Greek Monitoring Centre for Drugs [EKTEPN] 2011; European Monitoring Centre for Drugs and Drug Addiction [EMCDDA] 2011; Poulopoulos 2012).

Homelessness, unlike the concentration of poor immigrants in central locales and drug use in public places, rose following the onset of the financial crisis both as a phenomenon in itself and in terms of its manifestation, specifically in urban areas. According to aid organizations, the combination of spreading unemployment and poverty, heavy funding cuts to social services, and the suspension of housing benefits caused Greece's homeless population to swell by an estimated 25 percent between 2009 and 2011, reaching around twenty thousand people (European Commission 2012b)—too great a size to be denied convincingly by typical Greek state rhetoric (on which see Arapoglou 2004). Although half of the homeless are thought to have been concentrated in Athens and Piraeus, numbers also rose in smaller cities such as Trikala, Heraklio, and Chania. Importantly, the composition of homelessness grew to extend well beyond poor immigrants and drug addicts, and has increasingly included middle-class Greeks who have fallen into bankruptcy (European Commission 2012b), although it is the former two groups that have primarily been targeted by the police during sweep operations.

The Political Benefits of Failure

To conclude this section, Greek state elites and their chosen socioeconomic policies before and after the financial crisis not only fueled an increase in at least some forms of common property and violent crime since 2009, but also generated conditions that helped exaggerate the prevalence of such crime in the public mind, propelling to the spotlight the very "problem populations" the state and its police authorities have claimed to be sweeping. These effects, however, were not wholly counterproductive in a political sense because they furnished ample supplies of scapegoats onto which mass frustration and anger against political elites could instead be transferred and discharged. Indeed, the fact that sweep operations and other cognate control measures were implemented and gradually intensified in terms of both frequency and force lent retrospective validation to the exaggerated urgency accorded to common violent and property crime and to associated signal disorders in dominant political, media, and public discourse, just as the act of targeting particular populations invested their stereotypical perception as dangerous with the symbolic force of a fait accompli.

In a similar vein, it was not entirely counterproductive that Greek state elites publicly confessed their own failure to sufficiently come to grips with crime and related phenomena. This is a view widely shared by Greek citizens, who have long expressed low and falling levels of confidence in the police and the broader justice system of the country on the one hand, and have shown high and rising levels of support for a get-tough approach to crime control on the other (see Cheliotis and Xenakis 2011b: 9–16). Whether real or phantom, self-confessed ineffectiveness here served to signify the persistence or incessant emergence of problems that helped to justify the continued displacement of mass anger onto weak out-group minorities and the prolongation and intensification of cathartic aggression against them, thereby preempting or alleviating the political challenge to state elites and even inducing attachment to them. In the last analysis, if common property and violent crime have been politically expedient problems, it is not because they lend themselves to successful state intervention, but because they are fields where the state is able to openly acknowledge failure by way of reproducing its hegemonic power (see further Cheliotis 2013). We shall return to these points in the conclusion.

Political Violence

Albeit spasmodically, perhaps the most dramatic concern expressed in the wake of the crisis by domestic and international commentators relating to the connection between economic downturn and violent crime was about political violence (i.e., the use of physical force for political ends) and the potential breakdown of law and order, whether manifested as attacks carried out by substate groups as part of their political campaigning, or as unruly mass mobilizations. Socioeconomic pressures unleashed by the financial crisis were widely expected to continue to fuel violent campaigns waged by covert groups identified as anarchist or left wing, which were increasingly active over the 2000s (see, e.g., *Huffington Post*, 26 April 2010; Papadopoulos 2012). Such pressures were also thought to have propelled public unrest throughout the country. It was argued, for instance, that the imposition of austerity measures had produced a cycle of increasingly radicalized mass mobilizations (see, e.g., Kouvelakis 2011; Papatheodorou, Sakellaropoulos, and Yeros 2012). According to the president of Greece's NCHR, moreover, the "generalization of a sense of lawlessness in which violence becomes tolerated [was a] critical aspect" of the impact of the financial crisis on the country (NCHR 2011b: 9). Although concern about political violence was not baseless, however, the evolution of such violence since 2009 proved more complex than anticipated.

Antiestablishment Violence and Its Limits

Expectations of growing instability initially seemed to be validated by an escalation in police-recorded attacks by covert political organizations identified as left wing or anarchist, with the number of such attacks rising from thirteen in 2008 to fifteen in 2009, and twenty in 2010 (Europol 2010, 2012). In July 2010 the Sehta Epanastaton (sect of revolutionaries)—the most lethal of such organizations—promised to turn the country into a "war zone of revolutionary activity" (see *The Guardian*, 1 August 2010; Xenakis 2012). However, during the very time frame in which the impact of the austerity measures was increasingly being felt by Greek society and by Greek youths in particular, political violence from substate covert groups to the far left of the political spectrum dropped significantly. Following a series of arrests and seizures of weapons over the course of 2010 and 2011 (although there were no arrests of members of Sehta Epanastaton), only six attacks were recorded in 2011 (Europol 2012).

Similarly, assumptions that the country was on the verge of a lawless abyss also appeared to be supported by repeated outbursts of public disorder, the growing politicization of many Greeks and immigrants, and their accruing experience of mobilization. Less than a year before the financial crisis broke, Greece had experienced its worst unrest for decades. Sparked by the lethal shooting of a teenager by a police officer in Athens, December 2008 saw weeks of sit-ins, demonstrations, and clashes between protesters and police, nationwide (see further Xenakis and Cheliotis 2016). Then in May 2010, shortly after the financial crisis had been unveiled and the first package of austerity measures was being communicated to the Greek public, the ensuing trade union and political protests saw demonstrators in Athens attempt to storm the parliament building. Riots broke out in cities across the country, and the firebombing of a bank led to the death of three bank workers (Xenakis 2012).

Athens was reported by the media to have become a war zone, if at the hands of the public, in the summer of 2011 (*The Telegraph*, 29 June 2011), in October 2011 (*New York Times*, 20 October 2011), and in February 2012 (*The Guardian*, 13 February 2012; *Reuters*, 12 February 2012), each time that the Greek parliament voted to approve austerity measures in order to secure international bailout funds. The disorder that broke out in February 2012 was decried by the prime minister as the worst since 2008, and the burning of historic buildings in the center of Athens offered dramatic illustration of an apocalyptic future that—according to parliamentary debate—threatened the country (*The Guardian*, 13 February 2012). Yet, at the time of this writing in 2017, there has been no replay of the month-long unrest of December 2008. By comparison, public mobilization in the years following the onset of the financial crisis have been of a far lesser scale than precrisis mobilization. Although socioeconomic hardships helped to ignite disorder in December 2008, subsequent patterns of mobilization that accompanied harshening of socioeconomic conditions have illustrated that deterministic expectations of the relationship between the two were fallacious (Kaplanis 2011: 25). A variety of factors led to the de-escalation of social unrest over this period, including the deaths associated with the mobilization in 2010 (Renn et al. 2011). Despite the sensationalist pronouncements of politicians and journalists in February 2012, most expert observers by this point claimed there was only a small risk of a major social explosion in Greece within the next few years (Hughes 2012).

It does not seem coincidental that the level of public unrest declined as the number of incidents in which police violence is alleged to have taken place rose. According to Amnesty International, the number of reported cases alleging excessive use of force and other ill-treatment by the Greek police against peaceful protesters showed a particular increase between 2010 and 2012, the period in which the austerity measures began to be implemented (Amnesty International 2012). Any prospect of halting this apparent exacerbation of police violence toward protesters looked especially remote after the passing of Law 4058 in 2012, Article 19 of which provides for the immediate arrest and speedy referral to trial for crimes where the perpetrator is caught committing the act or shortly thereafter, unless the alleged perpetrator is a law enforcement officer carrying out the act during and because of the exercise of his duties (Amnesty International 2012: 39).

Far-Right Violence and Political Might

Strikingly, the police have not been interventionist, and have even been accused of collusion, when it comes to another form of political violence that escalated after the financial crisis began. Rising numbers of attacks carried out against immigrants by far-right political organizations (and xenophobic vigilante groups ostensibly comprising local citizens, but in which Golden Dawn was also an alleged participant), alarmed a number of independent and nongovernmental organizations (NGOs) domestically and internationally (see, e.g., Hellenic League for Human Rights [HLHR], Minority Groups Research Centre [KEMO], and Institute for Rights, Equality and Diversity [i-RED] 2010; Human Rights Watch 2012; i-RED 2012).

Although far-right violence was catapulted into the public spotlight by the electoral successes of Golden Dawn in the general elections of 2012, such violence had already been on the ascent during the first decade of the millennium, when reports began to appear with gathering frequency of fire-bombings of migrant accommodation and places of worship, as well as of attacks on Jewish, Roma, leftist, anarchist, and lesbian, gay, bisexual, and transgender (LGBT) targets (see, e.g., HLHR, KEMO, and i-RED 2010). By the end of the decade, platoons of black-clad men armed with sticks were regularly patrolling immigrant-dense districts of Athens, intimidating local shopkeepers and residents, sometimes engaging in violent assaults against immigrants and their property, and in certain cases even doing so in front of police contingents (Xenakis 2012). These vigilante groups were widely alleged to be peopled by members of Golden Dawn; the party has denied all such allegations, although members of the party have repeatedly been associated with violent attacks against immigrants (see, e.g., *E Kathimerini*, 2 June 2012). Following the onset of the financial crisis, these platoons were supplemented in Athens by less-well-marshalled formations of citizens' militias, whose actions have allegedly included dragging immigrants off public transport, as well as beating and chasing them (Human Rights Watch 2012).

Not only was far-right violence downplayed by politicians and state authorities, however, but it was also treated by them as a contributor to, rather than a detractor of, law and order. In a meeting with a delegation from Human Rights Watch in December 2010, for example, officials and prosecutors from the Ministry for Citizen Protection denied that racist and xenophobic violence was a serious or growing problem. The Greek state has long been reluctant to devise and enforce laws providing for the effective recording and prosecution of racist violence or racially motivated crimes as such (Human Rights Watch 2012: 74, 92; Xenakis 2012), and it appeared reluctant to develop a strategy for monitoring or controlling the activities of the vigilante groups that had emerged across Athens and other cities, even though the media, NGOs, and some government officials explicitly connected these groups to attacks against immigrants. On occasion, right-wing vigilantism was disavowed by politicians of the center right and center left as an inappropriate substitute for police action, yet vigilante action was tolerated as long as police work was publicly deemed to be inadequate (Human Rights Watch 2012).

Buttressing political ambivalence toward far-right violence was public support for far-right sentiments, whose appeal has broadened over recent years. According to the Demand for Right-Wing Extremism (DEREX) Index, the percentage of Greeks predisposed to right-wing extremism rose gradually from 2005 to 2009, and then saw a sharp upturn from 2009 onward. Accompanying this trend were electoral gains made by far-right parties (Popular Orthodox Rally [LAOS] and Golden Dawn) over the same period. Centrist parties PASOK and ND took a vital step in providing legitimacy to this development when, in 2011, they included the far-right party LAOS in a coalition government designed to ensure the safe passage of austerity measures through the Greek parliament (Political Capital 2012). Although the use of anti-immigrant and law-and-order rhetoric by PASOK and ND intensified over this period, their efforts to appeal to xenophobic and authoritarian sentiments were not simply prompted by the electoral gains of the far right. Not only were such efforts on the part of centrist parties evident before the financial crisis erupted, but also the greater electoral challenge to centrist parties came from the far-left SYRIZA party: while the combined far-right vote rose from 5.9 percent in 2009 to 8.5 percent in 2012, SYRIZA's share of the vote rose from 4.6 percent in 2009 to 26.9 percent in 2012.[5] The strategy of PASOK and ND was a reflection of their commitment to a socioeconomic agenda whose successful management required the deflection of public discontent about the agenda as such, the inequitable distribution of its negative ramifications on the citizenry, and the impropriety of those advancing it.

Conclusion

Just as there is no direct or even necessary correlation between economic downturn and social outcomes such as higher inequality, so too there is no inevitability in the relationship between economic downturn and lawbreaking. The design and implementation of economic, social, and criminal justice policies introduced amid a recession have a direct bearing on the impact of the recession on trends in crime and signal disorders associated with certain types of crime. Equally, the perceived fairness of such measures influences their public acceptability, affecting societal attitudes toward lawbreaking and, in turn, indirectly shaping crime trends.

In the case of Greece, the effect of the crisis on crime has been irregular and complex. Not all criminal or otherwise deviant behaviors underwent growth, and not all those linked to the crisis (whether in terms of resulting from it or being a factor in its emergence) were typically treated by political, media, and public discourse as part of the crime problem. Helping to maintain a disproportionality between fear of crime and actual victimization rates was the heightened visibility of poverty that, through a variety of signal disorders, propelled public convictions that crime risks significantly increased. Politicians contributed decisively to such perspectives by pursuing a range of policies that influenced levels and patterns of both crime and certain signal disorders, and by seeking to focus public attention on both real and phantom growth in given forms of criminal activity.

Indeed, the Greek experience attests to the role that common property and violent offenses can play in party political discourses as means of sustaining or reclaiming electoral ground and diverting public attention from socioeconomic predicaments. PASOK and ND faced a large drop in electoral support as well as increasing competition from parties of the far left and, to a lesser extent, the far right. The antipathy of the Greek public toward traditional mainstream parties increased as the state introduced disproportionately harsh austerity measures while elite corruption scandals continued to mount. Inflaming public resentment further still were worsening socioeconomic realities that intensified the economic and corporeal insecurities of the citizenry, and that, to a certain degree, were blamed on the mismanagement of the economy by PASOK and ND. These sentiments were exacerbated by the crisis-enforced contraction of the political use of clientelism, which would otherwise have provided a means of softening the impact of austerity among the masses.

Although politicians invoked a nexus between common crime and immigration as a means of deflecting public anger, however, this was just one of several strategies employed to this end. Because PASOK and ND remained committed to the reforms set out within the austerity packages, they expended a range of efforts to displace and alleviate the pressure of public discontent that was directed against them. Strategies included stressing the public's culpability for high levels of corruption that contributed to the financial crisis, and insisting that only traditional mainstream parties can secure the financial interests of the people by maintaining the country's membership of the eurozone. PASOK and ND also employed xenophobic discourses to demonstrate their solidarity with the domestic public, by drawing critical attention to the role of powerful foreign actors—such as Germany and the IMF—in shaping unpopular domestic socioeconomic policies, as well as by tying immigration to the problem of crime and the need for punitive responses.

The fact that the conjoined themes of common crime and immigration function as one of several divertive political strategies is often acknowledged in media, scholarly, and even political discourse. What has received relatively little consideration, though, is the reason why common crime and immigration are more attractive as such than other themes. In the case of Greece, while different political strategies were deployed concurrently, it is discourse about crime and immigration that was the most potent. Strategies emphasizing societal responsibility for corruption and asserting exclusive competency over the financial security of the nation targeted the assertiveness of public opposition. But in suggesting the moral backwardness and necessary subservience of the Greek public, they presented an unpalatable challenge to the dignity of the average citizen. Discursive xenophobia toward stronger interventionist powers, meanwhile, was of limited utility to mainstream political parties of the time, precisely because the decision to pursue emergency loans from abroad inevitably increased the dependence of Greek political elites on the very same foreign actors against which such discourse railed. By contrast, xenophobic law-and-order rhetoric was the sole strategy that functioned by expressing solidarity with, and promising policy priority to, the public's concerns, at the same time as being systematically applicable by dint of the weakness of its designated scapegoats and the built-in fallibility of the measures taken against them.

All this is not to imply that the use of common crime and immigration as a deflective political maneuver is bound to be wholly or durably successful. To the contrary, as suggested by the Greek case, the depth and breadth of public discontent can place limits on the effectiveness of political efforts to displace it—limits that are illustrated, for example, by the precariousness of the political status quo. At the same time, however, the extent to which ND and PASOK managed to prolong their stay in power up to 2015—even if by coalition government—in the face of very high levels of public resentment, is testimony to the efficacy of deflective political strategies, and more especially of the heated issue of crime and immigration.

Sappho Xenakis is Senior Lecturer in Criminology at the Law School, Birkbeck College, University of London. She is also codirector of Birkbeck's interdisciplinary Centre for Political Economy and Institutional Studies. Her research primarily focuses on the relationship between state power and the international transfer of law enforcement values and practices, especially with regard to organized crime and political violence. Drawing on fieldwork carried out in France, Greece, Turkey, the United Kingdom, and the United States, her work explores the mechanisms and effectiveness of foreign influence in domestic security policy. She also pursues research on the relationship between perceptions and practices of corruption, and on trends in state and public punitiveness from a political economy perspective. With Leonidas K. Cheliotis, she is also the cofounder and codirector of the Ikarian Centre for Social and Political Research.

Leonidas K. Cheliotis is Associate Professor of Criminology at the Department of Social Policy, London School of Economics and Political Science, having previously held posts at the University of Edinburgh and Queen Mary, University of London. His research is mainly focused on the political economy and social psychology of punishment in Greece and elsewhere from both national and international comparative angles, and has been published widely in top international peer-reviewed outlets. With Sappho Xenakis, he is the cofounder and codirector of the Ikarian Centre for Social and Political Research.

Notes

1. PASOK and ND saw their level of public support plummet between the general elections held in 2009 and in 2012. At the previous elections, held in October 2009 (just one month before the country's financial crisis broke), PASOK won 43.9 percent of the vote, and ND 33.5 percent. In May 2012 inconclusive elections were held in which PASOK received just 13.2 percent, while ND took 18.9 percent of the vote. The next round of elections, which took place in June 2012, allowed ND to achieve 29.7 percent of the vote, whilst PASOK support slid further to 12.3 percent. See Mylonas in this volume for further discussion of these political shifts.
2. The statistical information provided in this section on levels and patterns of crime in Greece is based on the authors' analysis of primary data that have been made available online by the Hellenic Police and the Ministry of Public Order and Citizen Protection. Calculations of rates per units of population were conducted on the basis of estimates by the Hellenic Statistical Authority (ELSTAT) of the country's total population on 1 January each year.
3. Golden Dawn also managed to attract similar levels of support in all three subsequent national elections, including those of September 2015, thereby consolidating its position as the third largest parliamentary party. This was despite the arrest and pre-trial detention in late 2013 of several of its MPs, including party leader Nikolaos Michaloliakos, on charges of involvement in a criminal organization responsible for multiple cases of homicide and a series of other serious offences, a development triggered by the murder of a Greek left-wing anti-fascist musician in the Keratsini district of Piraeus.
4. The sum of deaths caused by motor-vehicle accidents is based on primary data provided by the Hellenic Police and the Ministry of Public Order and Citizen Protection. The sum of deaths by suicide is based on primary data provided by ELSTAT.
5. Far-right votes were divided between LAOS (Popular Orthodox Rally) and the neo-fascistic party Golden Dawn. In 2009, LAOS won 5.6 percent of the vote, whereas Golden Dawn received just 0.3 percent. In June 2012, LAOS dropped to 1.6 percent, whilst Golden Dawn took 6.9 percent of the vote.

References

Amnesty International. 2009. *Greece: Alleged Abuses in the Policing of Demonstrations.* London: Amnesty International. Retrieved from https://www.amnesty.org/download/Docum ents/48000/eur250012009en.pdf.
———. 2012. *Police Violence in Greece: Not Just Isolated Incidents.* London: Amnesty International. Retrieved 23 July 2012 from https://www.amnesty.org/download/Docume nts/28000/eur250112011en.pdf.

Arapoglou, Vassilis P. 2004. "The Governance of Homelessness in the European South: Spatial and Institutional Contexts of Philanthropy in Athens." *Urban Studies* 41(3): 621–39.

Artavanis, Nikolaos, Adair Morse, and Margarita Tsoutsoura. 2012. "Tax Evasion Across Industries: Soft Credit Evidence from Greece." Working Paper, University of Chicago Booth School of Business. Retrieved 13 July 2012 from http://faculty.chicagobooth.edu/adair.morse/research/TaxEvasionWeb.pdf.

Bratsis, Peter. 2011. "Greek Corruption in Context." In Cheliotis and Xenakis, *Crime and Punishment in Contemporary Greece*, 197–206.

Box, Steven. 1987. *Recession, Crime and Punishment*. Basingstoke, UK: Macmillan.

Buehn, Andreas, and Friedrich Schneider. 2012a. "Corruption and the Shadow Economy: Like Oil and Vinegar, Like Water and Fire?" *International Tax and Public Finance* 19(1): 172–94.

———. 2012b. "Shadow Economies Around the World: Novel Insights, Accepted Knowledge, and New Estimates." *International Tax and Public Finance* 19(1): 139–71.

Callan, Tim, Chrysa Leventi, Horacio Levy, Manos Matsaganis, Alari Paulus, and Holly Sutherland. 2011. *The Distributional Effects of Austerity Measures: A Comparison of Six EU Countries*. EUROMOD Working Paper EM6. Institute for Social and Economic Research, University of Essex. Retrieved 5 August 2012 from https://www.iser.essex.ac.uk/publications/working-papers/euromod/em6-11.pdf.

Campos, Cecilia, Alistair Dent, Robert Fry, and Alice Reid. 2011. *Impact of the Recession*. Regional Trends 43. London: Office for National Statistics.

Capó Servera, Mateo, and Georgios Moschovis. 2008. "Tax Shortfalls in Greece." *ECFIN Country Focus* 4(5): 1–6. Brussels: European Commission.

Ceobanu, Alin M. 2011. "Usual Suspects? Public Views about Immigrants' Impact on Crime in European Countries." *International Journal of Comparative Sociology* 52(1): 114–31.

Cheliotis, Leonidas K. 2011. "Prisons and Parole." In Cheliotis and Xenakis, *Crime and Punishment in Contemporary Greece*, 557–91.

———. 2013. "Neoliberal Capitalism and Middle-Class Punitiveness: Bringing Erich Fromm's "Materialistic Psychoanalysis" to Penology." *Punishment & Society* 15(3): 247–73.

———. 2017. "Punitive Inclusion: The Political Economy of Irregular Migration in the Margins of Europe." *European Journal of Criminology* 14(1): 78–99.

Cheliotis, Leonidas K., and Sappho Xenakis. 2010. "What's Neoliberalism Got to Do with It? Towards a Political Economy of Punishment in Greece." *Criminology & Criminal Justice* 10(4): 353–73.

———, eds. 2011a. *Crime and Punishment in Contemporary Greece: International Comparative Perspectives*. Bern, Switzerland: Peter Lang AG.

———. 2011b. "Crime, Fear of Crime and Punitiveness." In Cheliotis and Xenakis, *Crime and Punishment in Contemporary Greece*, 1–43.

———. 2016. "Punishment and Political Systems: State Punitiveness in Post-Dictatorial Greece." *Punishment & Society* 18(3): 268–300.

Christakopoulou, Sophia, Jon Dawson, and Aikaterini Gari. 2001. "The Community Well-Being Questionnaire: Theoretical Context and Initial Assessment of its Reliability and Validity." *Social Indicators Research* 56(3): 321–51.

"Compulsory Health Checks for Migrants." 2012. *Kathimerini*, 4 January. Retrieved from http://www.ekathimerini.com/140488/article/ekathimerini/news/compulsory-health-checks-for-migrants.

Cook, Phillip J. 2010. "Property Crime—Yes; Violence—No: Comment on Lauritsen and Heimer." *Criminology & Public Policy* 9(4): 693–97.

Dobratz, Betty. A., and Stephanie Whitfield. 1992. "Does Scandal Influence Voters' Party Preference? The Case of Greece During the Papandreou Era." *European Sociological Review* 8(2): 167–80.

Douzinas, Costas. 2010. "The Greek Tragedy." *Journal of Modern Greek Studies* 28(2): 285–91.

European Commission. 2008. *Standard Eurobarometer 69: Public Opinion in the European Union: National Report Greece.* Retrieved 18 July 2012 from http://ec.europa.eu/public_opinion/archives/eb/eb69/eb69_el_nat.pdf.
———. 2009. *Eurobarometer 71: Public Opinion in the European Union.* Retrieved 18 July 2012 from http://ec.europa.eu/public_opinion/archives/eb/eb71/eb71_std_part1.pdf.
———. 2011a. *Standard Eurobarometer 74: Factsheet on Greece.* Retrieved 18 July 2012 from http://ec.europa.eu/public_opinion/archives/eb/eb74/eb74_fact_el_en.pdf.
———. 2011b. *Special Eurobarometer 355: Poverty and Social Exclusion Report.* Retrieved 18 July 2012 from http://ec.europa.eu/public_opinion/archives/ebs/ebs_355_en.pdf.
———. 2011c. *Eurobarometer 76.1: Attitudes of Europeans Towards Corruption: Results for Greece.* Retrieved 19 July 2012 from http://ec.europa.eu/public_opinion/archives/ebs/ebs_374_fact_el_en.pdf.
———. 2012a. *Standard Eurobarometer 76: Factsheet on Greece.* Retrieved 18 July 2012 from http://ec.europa.eu/public_opinion/archives/eb/eb76/eb76_fact_el_en.pdf
———. 2012b. *EU Employment and Social Situation, Quarterly Review June 2012.* Retrieved 18 July 2012 from http://ec.europa.eu/social/BlobServlet?docId=7830&langId=en.
———. 2012c. *EU Unemployment and Social Situation: Quarterly Review, March 2012.* Retrieved 14 June 2012 from http://ec.europa.eu/social/BlobServlet?docId=7548&langId=en.
European Monitoring Centre for Drugs and Drug Addiction (EMCDDA). 2011. *2011 Annual Report on the State of the Drugs Problem in Europe.* Lisbon: EMCDDA.
Europol. 2010. *EU Terrorism Situation and Trend Report.* Retrieved 7 August 2012 from http://www.consilium.europa.eu/uedocs/cmsUpload/TE-SAT percent202010.pdf.
———. 2012. *EU Terrorism Situation and Trend Report.* Retrieved 7 August 2012 from https://www.europol.europa.eu/sites/default/files/publications/europoltsat.pdf.
Figgou, Lia, and Susan Condor. 2007. "Categorising Category Labels in Interview Accounts about the "Muslim Minority" in Greece." *Journal of Ethnic and Migration Studies* 33(3): 439–59.
Figgou, Lia, Antonis Sapountzis, Nikos Bozatzis, Antonis Gardikiotis, and Pavlos Pantazis. 2011. "Constructing the Stereotype of Immigrants' Criminality: Accounts of Fear and Risk in Talk about Immigration to Greece." *Journal of Community & Applied Social Psychology* 21(2): 164–77.
Finklea, Kristin M. 2011. *Economic Downturns and Crime.* Congressional Research Service Report for Congress. Retrieved 7 August 2012 from http://www.fas.org/sgp/crs/misc/R40726.pdf.
Garland, David. 2001. *The Culture of Control: Crime and Social Order in Contemporary Society.* Oxford: Oxford University Press.
Giannakopoulou, Peggy. 2011. "Fear of Crime in Greece: A Contradiction." Unpublished MSc dissertation. Institute of Criminal Justice Studies, Portsmouth, UK: University of Portsmouth.
Gilmore, Ruth Wilson. 2007. *Golden Gulag: Prisons, Surplus, and Opposition in Globalizing California.* Berkeley: University of California Press.
Greek Monitoring Centre for Drugs (EKTEPN). 2011. *Etesia Ekthese 2011: E Katastase tou Provlematos ton Narkotikon kai ton Oinopmevmatodon sten Ellada.* Athens: EKTERN
Hagan, John H. 2010. *Who Are the Criminals? The Politics of Crime Policy from the Age of Roosevelt to the Age of Reagan.* Princeton, NJ: Princeton University Press.
Hall, Stuart, Chas Critcher, Tony Jefferson, John Clarke, and Brian Roberts. 1978. *Policing the Crisis: Mugging, the State, and Law and Order.* London: Macmillan.
Hatziprokopiou, Panos. 2003. "Albanian Immigrants in Thessaloniki, Greece: Processes of Economic and Social Incorporation." *Journal of Ethnic and Migration Studies* 29(6): 1033–57.
Hay, Douglas, Peter Linebaugh, John G. Rule, E. P. Thompson, and Cal Winslow. 1975. *Albion's Fatal Tree: Crime and Society in Eighteenth-Century England.* New York: Pantheon.

Hellenic Centre for Disease Control and Prevention (KEEPLNO). 2011. *Epidemiologike Epiterese tes HIV/AIDS Loimoxes sten Ellada: Delothenta Stoicheia eos 31.12.2011*. Athens: Ministry of Health and Social Solidarity, 2011. Retrieved 14 June 2012 from http://www .keelpno.gr/Portals/0/ percentCE percent91 percentCF percent81 percentCF percent87 per centCE percentB5 percentCE percentAF percentCE percentB1/HIV/EPIDIMIOLOGIKO percent20HIV_2011.pdf.

———. 2012. *Global AIDS Response Progress Report 2012: Greece*. Athens: Ministry of Health and Social Solidarity.

Hellenic League for Human Rights (HLHR), Minority Groups Research Centre (KEMO), and Institute for Rights, Equality and Diversity (i-RED). 2010. *Racist and Related Hate Crimes in the EU: Greece Country Report*. Thematic Study by the National Focal Point on Racism and Xenophobia (RAXEN). Retrieved 29 July 2012 from http://www.i-redited byeu/ resources/publications-files/raxen-ts-2010_racist-hate-crimes-in-greece.pdf.

Hellenic Statistical Authority (ELSTAT). 2008. "Labour Force Survey: May 2008." *Press Release*, August 12.

———. 2012. "Labour Force Survey: 1st Quarter 2012." *Press Release*, June 14.

Henry, Andrew F., and James F. Short. 1954. *Homicide and Suicide*. Glencoe, IL: Free Press.

Hollway, Wendy, and Tony Jefferson. 1997. "The Risk Society in an Age of Anxiety: Situating Fear of Crime." *British Journal of Sociology* 48(2): 255–66.

Hughes, Kirsty. 2012. "What Future for a Greece in Crisis?." *OpenDemocracy*, 24 March. Retrieved 9 August 2012 from http://www.opendemocracy.net/kirsty-hughes/what-future-for-greece-in-crisis.

Human Rights Watch. 2012. *Hate on the Streets: Xenophobic Violence in Greece*. Retrieved 13 July 2012 from http://www.hrw.org/sites/default/files/reports/greece0712ForUpload .pdf.

Hummelsheim, Dina, Helmut Hirtenlehner, Jonathan Jackson, and Dietrich Oberwittler. 2011. "Social Insecurities and Fear of Crime: A Cross-National Study on the Impact of Welfare State Policies on Crime-Related Anxieties." *European Sociological Review* 27(3): 327–45.

Innes, Martin. 2004. "Signal Crimes and Signal Disorders: Notes on Deviance as Communicative Action." *British Journal of Sociology* 55(3): 335–55.

Kandylis, George, and Karolos Iosif Kavoulakos. 2011. "Framing Urban Inequalities: Racist Mobilisation against Immigrants in Athens." *Greek Review of Social Research* 136(C): 157–76.

Kaplanis, Yiannis. 2011. "An Economy that Excludes the Many and an 'Accidental' Revolt." In *Revolt and Crisis in Greece*, edited by Dimitris Dalakoglou and Adonis Vradis, 215–28. New York: AK Press.

Karydis, Vassilis. 2011. "Immigration and Crime." In Cheliotis and Xenakis, *Crime and Punishment in Contemporary Greece*, 87–109.

Kentikelenis, Alexander, Marina Karanikolos, Irene Papanicolas, Sanjay Basu, Martin McKee and David Stuckler. 2011. "Health Effects of Financial Crisis: Omens of a Greek Tragedy." *The Lancet* 378(9801): 1457–58.

———. 2012. "Health and the Financial Crisis in Greece: Authors' Reply." *The Lancet* 379(9820): 1002.

Kosmatopoulos, Nikolas. 2012. "If Elections Could Change Things, They'd Be Illegal." *Al Jazeera*, 10 May. Retrieved 20 July 2012 from http://www.aljazeera.com/indepth/opin ion/2012/05/20125493228914268.html.

Kouvelakis, Stathis. 2011. "The Greek Cauldron." *New Left Review* 72: 17–32.

Krugman, Paul. 2012. "Greece as Victim." *New York Times*, June 17.

Kühnrich, Bernd, and Harald Kania. 2005. *"Attitudes towards Punishment in the European Union: Results from the 2005 European Crime Survey (ECSS) with Focus on Germany."* EU ICS Working Paper Series. Brussels: Gallup Europe.

Levi, Michael. 2009. "Suite Revenge? The Shaping of Folk Devils and Moral Panics about White-Collar Crimes." *British Journal of Criminology* 49(1): 48–67.

Lewis, Michael. 2011. *Boomerang: The Meltdown Tour.* London: Allen Lane.

Liem, Marieke, Soenita Ganpat, Sven Granath, Johanna Hagstedt, Janne Kivivuori, Martti Lehti, and Paul Nieuwbeerta. 2013. "Homicide in Finland, the Netherlands and Sweden: First Findings from the European Homicide Monitor." *Homicide Studies* 17: 75–95.

Lynch, Michael J. 1988. "The Extraction of Surplus Value, Crime and Punishment: A Preliminary Examination." *Contemporary Crises* 12: 329–44.

Lynn, Matthew. 2011. *Greece, the Euro, and the Sovereign Debt Crisis.* Hoboken, NJ: Bloomberg Press.

Matsaganis, Manos. 2012. "Social Policy in Hard Times: The Case of Greece." *Critical Social Policy* 32(3): 406–21.

Matsaganis, Manos, and Maria Flevotomou. 2010. "Distributional Implications of Tax Evasion in Greece." GreeSE Paper No. 31. London: Hellenic Observatory/LSE.

Matsaganis, Manos, and Chrysa Leventi. 2011. "The Distributional Impact of the Crisis in Greece." In *The Greek Crisis in Focus: Austerity, Recession and Paths to Recovery,* edited by Vassilis Monastiriotis, 5–43. London: Hellenic Observatory/LSE.

Manolopoulos, Jason. 2011. *Greece's 'Odious' Debt: The Looting of the Hellenic Republic by the Euro, the Political Elite and the Investment Community.* London: Anthem Press.

Matussek, Karin. 2011. "Ferrostaal Fined $138 Million by Court at Ex-Managers' Trial." 20 December. *Bloomberg.* https://www.bloomberg.com/news/articles/2011-12-20/ferrostaal-fined-183-million-by-court-at-ex-managers-trial

Mentinis, Mihalis. 2010. "Remember Remember the 6th of December . . . A Rebellion or the Constituting Moment of a Radical Morphoma?" *International Journal of Urban and Regional Research* 34(1): 197–202.

Mitsopoulos, Michael, and Theodore Pelagidis. 2011. *Understanding the Crisis in Greece: From Boom to Bust.* Basingstoke, UK: Palgrave Macmillan.

National Commission for Human Rights (NCHR). 2011a. *E Antimetopise tes Ratsistikes Vias apo ten Astynomia kai te Dikaiosyne.* Retrieved 13 July 2012 from http://www.demopaideia.gr/wp-content/uploads/2016/08/ethniki-epitropi-gia-ta-dikaiomata-tou-anthropou-II.pdf.

————. 2011b. *Report 2010.* Athens: National Printing Office.

Organisation for Economic Co-operation and Development (OECD). 2009. *Economic Survey of Greece, 2009,* Policy Brief. Paris: OECD.

Papadopoulos, George. 2012. "Crisis in Greece: Anarchists in the Birthplace of Democracy." *Terrorism Monitor* 10(14): 4–7.

Papatheodorou, Christos, Spyros Sakellaropoulos, and Paris Yeros. 2012. "Greece at a Crossroads: Crisis and Radicalisation in the Semi-Periphery." *Monthly Review,* March 30.

Paraskevis, D., G. Nikopoulos, C. Tsiara, D. Paraskeva, A. Antoniadou, M. Lazanas, P. Gargalianos, M. Psychogiou, M. Malliori, J. Kremastinou and A. Hatzakis. 2011. "HIV-1 Outbreak among Injecting Drug Users in Greece, 2011: A Preliminary Report." *Eurosurveillance* 16(3): 1–4.

Pearson, Geoffrey. 1983. *Hooligan: A History of Respectable Fears.* Basingstoke, UK: Palgrave Macmillan.

Pew Research Center. 2012. *European Unity on the Rocks.* Report of the Global Attitudes Project. Retrieved 19 July 2012 from http://www.pewglobal.org/files/2012/05/Pew-Global-Attitudes-Project-European-Crisis-Report-FINAL-FOR-PRINT-May-29-2012.pdf.

Political Capital. 2012. "A Broken Cordon Sanitaire: The Growing Political Relevance of the Far Right in Europe." Political Capital, Budapest. Retrieved 27 July 2012 from http://deconspirator.com/wp-content/uploads/2012/05/a_broken_cordon_sanitaire.pdf.

Poulopoulos, Charalampos. 2012. *Apologistike Synenteuxe Typou KETHEA 'Krise kai Exartese: Adiexoda kai Prooptikes' (Omilia Ch. Poulopoulou, Dieuthynte KETHEA) 25.6.2012.* Retrieved 12 July 2012 from http://www.kethea.gr/Νέα/ΔελτίαΤύπου/tabid/141/article Type/ArticleView/articleId/246/language/el-GR/Default.aspx.

Public Issue. 2011. *National Survey on Corruption in Greece–2011: Summary Presentation of Survey Results*. Athens: Transparency International-Greece.

Quinney, Richard. 1977. *Class, State and Power: On the Theory and Practice of Criminal Justice*. New York: Longman.

Radzinowicz, Leon. 1941. "The Influence of Economic Conditions on Crime." *Sociological Review* 33(1–2): 1–36.

Reiner, Robert. 2007. "Political Economy, Crime, and Criminal Justice." In *The Oxford Handbook of Criminology*, 4th ed., edited by Mike Maguire, Rod Morgan, and Robert Reiner, 341–80. Oxford: Oxford University Press.

Renn, Ortwin, Aleksandar Jovanovic, and Regina Schröter. 2011. *Social Unrest*. OECD/IFP Project on Future Global Shocks. Paris: OECD. Retrieved from http://www.oecd.org/futures/globalprospects/46890018.pdf.

Rights, Equality & Diversity European Network (i-RED). 2012. *Annual Report 2011*. Retrieved 13 July 2012 from http://www.i-redited byeu/resources/publications-files/annualreport-2011.pdf.

Samatas, Minas. 2011. "Surveillance." In Cheliotis and Xenakis, *Crime and Punishment in Contemporary Greece*, 421–42.

Schneider, Friedrich. 2012. "Size and Development of the Shadow Economy of 31 European and 5 Other OECD Countries from 2003 to 2012: Some New Facts." Working Paper. Retrieved 13 July 2012 from http://www.econ.jku.at/members/Schneider/files/publications/2012/ShadEcEurope31_March percent202012.pdf.

Semyonov, Moshe, and Anya Glikman. 2009. "Ethnic Residential Segregation, Social Contacts, and Anti-Minority Attitudes in European Societies." *European Sociological Review* 6(1): 693–708.

———. 2009. "Ethnic Residential Segregation, Social Contacts, and Anti-Minority Attitudes in European Societies." *European Sociological Review* 25(6): 693–708.

Semyonov, Moshe, Anastasia Gorodzeisky, and Anya Glikman. 2012. "Neighborhood Ethnic Composition and Resident Perceptions of Safety in European Countries." *Social Problems* 59(1): 117–35.

Semyonov, Moshe, Rebeca Raijman, and Anastasia Gorodzeisky. 2006. "The Rise of Anti-Foreigner Sentiment in European Societies, 1988–2000." *American Sociological Review* 71(3): 426–49.

———. 2008. "Foreigners' Impact on European Societies: Public Views and Perceptions in a Cross-national Comparative Perspective." *International Journal of Comparative Sociology* 49(1): 5–29.

Short, James F. 1980. *An Investigation of the Relation between Crime and Business Cycles*. New York: Arno Press.

Simon, Jonathan. 2001. "Fear and Loathing in Late Modernity: Reflections on the Cultural Sources of Mass Imprisonment in the United States." *Punishment & Society* 3(1): 21–33.

Skouras, Spyros, and Nicos Christodoulakis. 2011. "Electoral Misgovernance Cycles: Evidence from Wildfires and Tax Evasion in Greece and Elsewhere." *GreeSE Paper* 47. London: Hellenic Observatory/LSE.

Simpson, Sally S. 1986. "The Decomposition of Antitrust: Testing a Multi-level, Longitudinal Model of Profit-Squeeze." *American Sociological Review* 51(6): 859–75.

Thomas, Dorothy Swaine. 1927. *Social Aspects of the Business Cycle*. New York: Alfred A. Knopf.

Transparency International–Greece. 2010. *Countdown to Impunity: Statutes of Limitation in the European Union*. Athens: Transparency International. Retrieved from http://www.transparency.gr/wp-content/uploads/2013/09/TI-G_Report_13DEC_FINAL.pdf.

————. 2012. *National Integrity Assessment-Greece.* Athens: Transparency International. Re-
    trieved 8 July 2012 from http://files.transparency.org/content/download/545/2263/file/
    Greece_NIS_EN.pdf.
United Nations Office on Drugs and Crime (UNODC). 2012. *Monitoring the Impact of Eco-
    nomic Crisis on Crime.* Vienna: UNODC.
Vakiari, G. and K. Kontargyri. 2009. *Melete tes Epidrases pou echei e Diamorphose ton Choron tes
    Poles sto Aisthema Asphaleias ton Politon,* Unpublished BA dissertation. School of Busi-
    ness Administration and Economics, Technological Educational Institute of Thessalo-
    niki, Greece.
van de Bunt, Henk. 2010. "Walls of Secrecy and Silence: The Madoff Case and Cartels in the
    Construction Industry." *Criminology & Public Policy* 9(3): 435–53.
van Dijk, Jan, John van Kesteren, and Paul Smit. 2007. *Criminal Victimisation in International
    Perspective: Key Findings from the 2004–2005 ICVS and EU ICS.* The Hague: WODC.
van Dijk, Jan, Robert Manchin, John van Kesteren, Sami Nevala, and Gergely Hideg. 2007.
    *The Burden of Crime in the EU. Research Report: A Comparative Analysis of the European
    Crime and Safety Survey (EU ICS) 2005.* Brussels: Gallup Europe.
Varoufakis, Yanis. 2011. *The Global Minotaur: America, the True Origins of the Financial Crisis
    and the Future of the World Economy.* London: Zed Books.
Vaxevanis, Kostas. 2011. "Apo ten aletheia tes Retoreias Protimo te Retoreia tes Aletheias."
    To Kouti tes Pandoras, October 19. Retrieved 7 August 2012 from http://www.koutipan
    doras.gr/?p=10256.
Xenakis, Sappho. 2011. "Organised Crime and Political Violence." In Cheliotis and Xenakis,
    Crime and Punishment in Contemporary Greece, 241–87.
————. 2012. "A New Dawn? Change and Continuity in Political Violence in Greece." *Terror-
    ism and Political Violence* 24(3): 437–64.
Xenakis, Sappho, and Leonidas K. Cheliotis. 2016. "'Glocal' Disorder: Causes, Conduct and
    Consequences of the 2008 Greek Unrest." *European Journal of Criminology* 13(5): 639–56.

Chapter 8

The Downsizing and Commodification of Health Care

The Appalling Greek Experience since 2010

Noëlle Burgi

Introduction

Health care is one of the world's largest industries. In 2011 the world spent a total of $6.9 trillion[1] on health. Health care accounted for 10 percent of global gross domestic product (GDP) in 2013,[2] of which 59.6 percent was public expenditure. The economic, political, social, and ethical stakes are high. Depending on the purpose ascribed to health care, two opposite conceptions emerge: health care as a fundamental human right, or health care as a marketable and tradable commodity. The first defines health not merely as the absence of disease but also as a state of general physical, mental, and social well-being. It views health-care systems as a public good, as core social institutions that should be universally accessible to all on the basis of clinical need, and not the ability to pay. Enshrined in the Declaration of Alma-Alta (1978) that identified primary health care (PHC) as the key to achieving health for all, this view was also the essence of the postwar Western European social security and national health systems, and served as a landmark for the belated construction in the 1980s of the post-dictatorship Greek, Portuguese, and Spanish welfare states.

The second approach, health care as an economic transaction, became increasingly prominent in the 1990s and 2000s, along with the deepening hegemony of neoliberal social and economic doctrines. That approach was transmitted by institutions of international economic governance such as the World Bank, which successfully networked at the global level to impose a conceptualization of health care based on investor-friendly principles of health economics and cost-effectiveness analysis, and the International Monetary Fund (IMF), which prescribed relatively standard policy prescriptions focusing on maximizing private provision, imposing user fees, and prioritizing markets and competition as part of its Structural Adjustment Programmes (SAPs). The ostensible design was to increase value for money in health systems and create the conditions for sustainable economic development. A growing body of critical research, however, disputes the benefits of health commodification. Indeed, market-style devices have failed to save money or to generate proven efficiencies, let alone produce more-equitable patterns of service delivery. Quite to the contrary, the devices increased bureaucratic and overhead costs while deepening health inequalities and undermining existing public health services and research (Commission on Social Determinants of Health [CSDH] 2008; Lister 2008; Sachs 2005). Even market-friendly Organisation for Economic Co-operation and Development (OECD) researchers have recognized the complications, contradictions, and increased costs incurred by the implementation of standard health-care restructuring packages (Lister 2008: 25, 77).

Western Europe has not been immune from the trend toward commodification of health care. Since the 1980s governments have to varying degrees espoused a market fundamentalist (or neoliberal) political rationality that "casts the political and social spheres both as appropriately dominated by market concerns and as themselves organized by market rationality [and promotes] policies that figure and produce citizens as individual entrepreneurs and consumers whose moral autonomy is measured by their capacity for 'self-care'—their ability to provide for their own needs and service their own ambitions, whether as welfare recipients, medical patients, consumers of pharmaceuticals, university students, or workers in ephemeral occupations" (Brown 2006: 694 (quote); Foucault 2004). Accordingly, most Western European governments introduced measures borrowed from the one-size-fits-all package advocated by the elite community of policy-shapers and rule-makers to restructure their health and social protection systems. However, the pace of transformation was variable and was spread over several decades. European governments for the most part deliberately chose an incremental implementation method in order to contain social contention and control the transformation process. Being rich enough and relatively (albeit unequally) autonomous, the core countries among the twelve first EU members (EU-12) were and are in a position to direct the process and control the pace of change. In fact, until recently, none had experienced situations comparable to highly dependent developing countries or the countries in transition in Eastern and

Central Europe that experienced the severe, indeed coercive, conditions of SAPs. Today, however, that situation has changed: Greece has been submitted to a particularly harsh austerity regime since 2010, akin to the SAPs applied in vulnerable countries of the global South. Greece thus constitutes a particularly good analytical terrain to assess the validity of the two above-mentioned approaches.

This chapter analyzes the principal measures implemented in the Greek public health sector since 2010 and their social and ethical consequences. It brings to light the difficulties and contradictions that emerged in the reform process in which World Bank/IMF one-size-fits-all recipes—for example, cost sharing, the purchaser/provider split, activity-based systems of payment, privatization of support, and private insurance schemes—have been arbitrarily and coercively imposed on the Greek health-care system with the primary aims of cutting costs, extracting resources from the public health sector in order to repay a crushing debt load,[3] and reorienting behaviors toward the consumption of private insurance and health services. As in other key sectors for the future of the country such as higher education, prescriptions dictated by the so-called Troika of lenders (the IMF, the European Commission, and the European Central Bank) have been introduced precipitously, in total disregard and even in denial of their sanitary and social effects. In the end, the problems of the Greek National Health System (ESY) have been amplified rather than solved. The first section presents a synthetic description of the ESY on the eve of the first 2010 memorandum of understanding (MoU). That section is followed by a reminder of the comprehensiveness of health, which depends not only on primary and secondary care institutions, but also on key social determinants of health such as social security, housing, education, food security, or decent work. The chapter also discusses the main restructuring devices that were introduced in the primary, secondary, and pharmaceutical health-care sectors. The argument, based on a growing body of evidence, is that the quasi-liquidation of the weak Greek welfare state has amplified the life-threatening effects of the SAPs' market-style approach: the hope of living a decent and good life (Sen 1999) has receded and people have been made vulnerable, exposed to illness and premature death.

The Greek National Health System

The Greek National Health System (ESY) has never been particularly coherent or efficient. Created in 1983, the ESY unquestionably constituted the most important effort in Greek history to institute a genuine national health service. The original project had sought to unify a plethora of occupational funds and replace the existing incoherent primary care infrastructure with entirely new ESY public community-based urban and rural health centers, endowing all citizens with an equal access free at the point of use. However, powerful entrenched interest groups (physicians engaged in private practice, autonomous insurance funds, civil servants, trade unions, bureaucrats, and even politicians from both the opposition and ruling parties) did not allow the project to be completed as initially envisioned (Mossialos and Allin 2005). Prior to 2010, Greek health care thus formed a threefold system involving a complex mix of (1) Beveridgian-type structures, which are provided and financed by the central government through tax payments (the ESY); (2) Bismarckian-inspired bodies (a network of public health insurance funds financed by social security contributions); and (3) private services.[4]

Before 2010 the ESY included 201 rural and 3 urban health centers, which were decentralized units of the ESY regional hospitals; 1,478 rural medical posts/surgeries that were attached to health centers; and the outpatient clinics of 140 public hospitals. The centers and surgeries provided preventive, curative, emergency, and rehabilitation services free at the point of use for the rural population. Outpatient clinics of ESY public hospitals provided the urban and semi-urban population specialist and diagnostic services free of charge or with minimal copayments during the day, and on a fixed fee-for-service basis during the non-working hours.

The network of public health insurance funds included thirty-six occupational sickness funds offering different packages of PHC to some 95 percent of the population. These funds were compulsory and structured by branch or socioprofessional category. In order of importance, the first of the four main funds was the Social Insurance Institute (IKA) created in 1934 and the most important private sector workers' social security fund. It had its own primary care infrastructure with its own full-time salaried medical doctors (mostly specialists) and part-time salaried doctors who were also allowed to engage in private practice. The other three large funds belonged to the agricultural workers (OGA), the self-employed and professionals (OAEE), and the public sector employees (OPAD). All health centers purchased services (partially or exclusively) from contracted private physicians and laboratories. Users of all funds had free access to a wide range of mainly curative and diagnostic services that were either delivered at the insurance funds' primary care units or provided on a copayment basis by contracted private physicians and laboratories.

Finally, the private sector consisted of approximately 25,000 private physicians, 12,000 dentists, 400 to 700 private laboratories, and 167 operating private hospitals with their outpatient departments. Corporate-owned highly profitable diagnostic centers controlled almost all the country's biomedical equipment. Private physicians and diagnostic centers would contract with public and private health insurance funds and be paid by users as well as by the funds (on a fee-for-service basis). The private primary care sector absorbed more than 65 percent of total private health expenditure (Kondilis et al. 2012).

For a number of reasons, this complex, highly fragmented, uncoordinated system was in a state of constant difficulty before 2010. The important share of the private health sector, the lack of general practitioners, the big differences in services and coverage provided by the various insurance schemes, and real deficiencies in rural care and access rendered the system very inefficient and unequal. Moreover, the very poor pay status of both ESY and social insurance PHC workers did not make the public sector attractive and caused a series of structural problems: permanent hiring difficulties in hospitals, important understaffing (especially nurses and physicians), important shortages of intensive care units (that sometimes had to close due to understaffing), long waiting lists, and a widespread habit of slipping *fakelakia* (envelopes) to doctors (assuming the doctor has not asked for it in the first place), most often a surgeon, in order to jump up the waiting list and if possible get better treatment. Many more corrupt practices were (and remain) commonplace in the health-care sector that was notoriously mismanaged prior to the crisis. So, unquestionably, change was badly needed (Economou 2010; Ioakeimoglou 2010; Mossialos, Allin, and Davaki 2005; Siskou et al. 2008).

It must be remembered, however, that despite its shortcomings the public health system contributed to a significant improvement in public health. According to World Health Organization (WHO) data, between 1980 and 2008 noteworthy gains in life expectancy were achieved in Greece through a decrease in avoidable mortality (i.e., caused by diseases treatable by medical care), especially a remarkable decline in child mortality (down from 17.94 to 2.65 deaths per 1,000 live births during that period), and neonatal (down from 13.58 to 1.79), postnatal, and maternal mortality. Another interesting indicator can be found in the *World Health Report* (WHO 2000: 152–55), in which the Geneva-based organization ranked its 191 members. As far as the overall health system performance is concerned, Greece ranked fourteenth. France ranked first, followed by Italy (second), Spain (seventh), Norway (eleventh), and Portugal (twelfth), all of which were ahead of the United Kingdom (eighteenth), Sweden (twenty-third), Germany (twenty-fifth), Canada (thirtieth), and the United States (thirty-seventh). Even though the WHO ranking has been criticized, the report highlighted undeniable and remarkable gains in health care in Southern European states in a comparatively very short period. That progress has been largely eluded in contemporary discourse.

Reform Responsiveness and the Social Determinants of Health

During the past few years, Greece has done much better than any other OECD country in implementing the internal devaluation austerity regimes prescribed by the Troika, as indicated by figure 8.1. According to the OECD, Greece has "performed" as the "leader" of OECD's "Going for Growth reform responsiveness" (OECD 2015: 126). However, Greece has led in quite another and far more tragic way by being plunged since 2010 in a deep, prolonged, and still worsening depression, unmatched in European peacetime history. The impact of the depression on key social sectors is directly correlated to the degree of the country's reform responsiveness. As far as health is concerned, the radical downsizing of the public health-care sector (a key measure of the various MoUs imposed on Greece) has dramatically harmed public health.

Overall Reform Responsiveness for the Period 2007–14

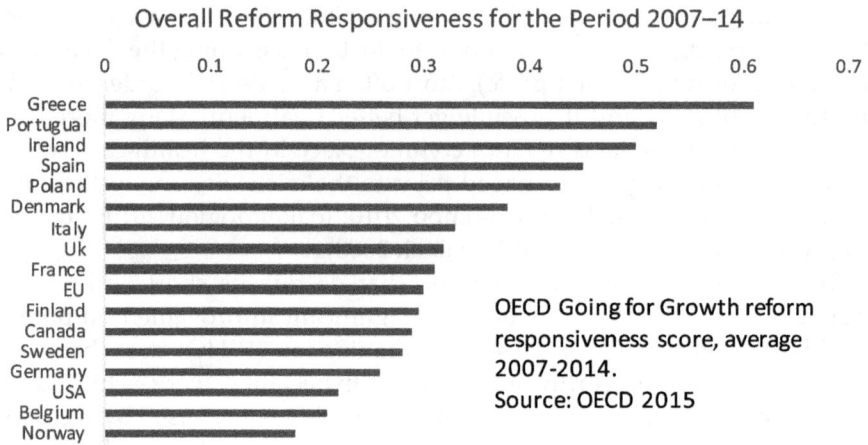

OECD Going for Growth reform
responsiveness score, average
2007-2014.
Source: OECD 2015

Figure 8.1. Eurozone: Reforms Pay Off

Public health is determined not only by the quality of health-care institutions, but also by much broader social conditions—access to schools and education, conditions of work and leisure, housing, future prospects, the state of people's communities, towns, or cities. These structural conditions of daily life constitute together "the social determinants of health and are responsible for a major part of health inequities between and within countries" (CSDH 2008: 1 (quote); Daniels 1985; Daniels, Kennedy, and Kawachi 1999). For most peripheral European countries, austerity has meant that life conditions have been abruptly transformed, leading to a deep regression with lasting health effects. The major indicators evidencing Greece's descent into the abyss are well known and need only cursory restatement here: as already indicated elsewhere in this volume, economic output has fallen more than 27 percent since 2009, resulting in the closure of thousands of small and very small businesses that are the backbone of the economy; mass unemployment affects a quarter of the population and half the youths; living standards have fallen sharply (minus 31.4 percent on average); labor rights have been severely restricted if not liquidated; public services have been largely curtailed; direct and indirect taxes have increased, representing a 337.7 percent tax burden increase for the under-privileged (Giannitsis and Zografikis 2015); economic and social inequal-ities have soared.

The downsizing of Greek public health institutions has significantly am-plified the adverse effects of austerity policies. In 2010, the first MoU im-posed drastic public health spending cuts, from 6.6 percent of GDP in 2010 to 6 percent in 2012. At the time, internationally recognized researchers and authoritative journals such as *The Lancet* estimated that the 6 percent target set by the Troika was arbitrary and abnormally low (e.g., Karaniko-los et al. 2013; Kentikelenis et al. 2014; Kondilis et al. 2013; Kondilis et al. 2012; Stuckler and Basu 2013). Greece, however, went much further than demanded by her creditors. As shown in table 8.1, public health expen-diture had shrunk to 5.7 percent of GDP in 2012; since then, it contracted further, reaching 4.6 percent in 2014 and 4.8 percent in 2016 (compared to an EU average of 6.5% and much higher ratios in the more developed countries). It must be underscored that the cutback is even more significant than it seems at first glance given that GDP itself has lost 27 percentage points since 2010. In real terms, health expenditure has therefore fallen by almost half in a few years. Further cuts are expected.

As a result there has been a recon-figuration of health-care spending. Ac-cording to Giannis Kyriopoulos (2015), former dean of the National School of Public Health in Athens, while the fund-ing of public hospitals fell by more than half between 2009 and 2014 and total health expenditure (public and private) is in sharp decline, the share of public hospital expenses in total expenditure increased 41 percent between 2008 and 2013 becoming (without means) the last resort for patients. This reflects poorer access not only to private hospital care

Table 8.1. Total Public Health Expenditure, 2004–16

Years	Percent GDP
2004	4.8
2005	5.5
2006	5.7
2007	5.6
2008	5.4
2009	6.4
2010	6.6
2011	6
2012	5.7
2013	5.1
2014	4.6
2015	4.9
2016	4.8

Source: OECD 2018.

(the share of which declined by 28 percent during the same period), but also to primary care (basic medical services, dental care, diagnoses, physiotherapy, and others) for which expenditures have fallen by 55.59 percent between 2008 and 2014. The share of pharmaceutical expenses in total expenditure nearly tripled (from 10.5 percent to 27.4 percent between 2009 and 2014) due to expanded copayments introduced by successive governments. At the same time, the disorganization of health-care facilities encouraged the quest for favoritism and some corruption with formal and informal payments to private sector doctors, up 52 percent (Kyriopoulos 2015; see also Georgakopoulos 2016).

Perverse Drug Policies

Changing doctors' and patients' behaviors regarding drug consumption and overprescription was an issue that needed to be addressed well before the 2008 global financial crisis. Pharmaceutical expenditure increased sharply in the period 2000–2009, reaching an annual rate of 12.3 percent per annum compared to an average annual growth rate among the EU-23 countries of 1.4 percent (Yfantopoulos et al 2016).[5] In 2009 Greece had the highest expenditure on pharmaceuticals among OECD countries (2.4 percent of GDP compared to an OECD average of 1.6 percent). Deep policy changes since the first bailout program led to a sharp decline. Prescribed by the Troika with the stated aim to decrease public expenditure on medicines to 1.33 percent of GDP in 2012 and 1 percent in 2014 (an objective well below the current OECD average that was achieved at the end of 2015) (Yfantopoulos et al. 2016; see also Kentikelenis et al. 2014), a wide range of policies was directed at pricing, prescriptions, monitoring assessment, and markups for wholesales and pharmacies (Carone, Schwierz, and Xavier 2012: 50–52). Increasing the use of generics and the development of an e-prescription system were among the top priorities. Today, the e-prescription system covers 99 percent of the Greek population, a network of 11,900 pharmacies and 43,000 doctors. It "supports the management and monitoring of drug prescriptions, visits to doctors, referrals to laboratory tests, and electronic medical acts" (Yfantopoulos et al 2016: 14). Other measures include the reintroduction of a positive list for pharmaceutical coverage with routine reviews investigating the price paid for medicines. Fixed rebates as well as volume rebates on all medicines sold to social security funds have been introduced. Furthermore, if spending in the public pharmaceutical budget exceeds a routinely revised ceiling, a clawback system has come into play. On the surface, this would seem to be a positive development but the reform has generated perverse effects.

Drug prices are now usually based on an average of the three lowest EU-23 prices. Substantial cost savings were thus achieved[6] without necessarily ensuring better public access to drugs because of permanent shortages, increased copayments, and the sharp fall in living standards. The factors accounting for permanent shortages are complex. Run-down hospitals very often cannot buy the medicine needed by patients and so let patients try to solve the problem by themselves. Pharmacies are in trouble. On the one hand, they have accumulated large debts because of public insurers' delays in paying them (four to five months on the average, but delays reach ten or eleven months). They were owed €0.5 billion in 2015 according to official statistics (Karamanoli 2015; Mantas 2016).[7] On the other hand, suppliers give pharmacies between one and three months payment deadlines, but they often require immediate payment. Pharmacies are then left with the option to pay their orders up front pending a reimbursement by public insurers; if they cannot afford to do so, though, they might organize informally with other pharmacies (some of them the very well-organized nonprofit social solidarity pharmacies mentioned below) to find, exchange, or borrow drugs from them, or else request patients to pay for their medicine in advance, or send patients off to try their luck elsewhere. These solutions are fragile. Very many pharmacies have closed and many others have been bought by Greek and multinational wholesalers. Wholesalers turn to other markets in search for higher profits because of Greece's relatively low prices and long delays in clearing her debts toward them. Drug makers have sometimes imposed quotas on the quantity of medicines the Greek market is supposed to need, meaning that orders are not necessarily delivered in full. They officially claim that they do not have enough stock. Some of them have stopped selling higher-priced medicines in Greece (Kresge 2012). At the same time however, pharmaceutical companies have sought to take advantage of Greece's position as one of the international reference countries for the establishment and negotiation of new drug prices.[8] Novartis, for example, allied with Greek public officials and doctors to sell some of its new products at exorbitant prices in Greece with the intention of making high profits in countries that are more populous (such as Turkey or, on a much broader scale, Brazil). The Novartis scandal is currently being investigated in Greece and the United States to establish facts and determine responsibilities. Meanwhile, international initiatives are being taken to try to moderate manufacturers' appetites due to the general crisis of public finances. In Greece the pressure on pharmaceutical companies is greater because the state requires a 25 percent discount for each new drug priced in Greece in addition to clawback and rebate reimbursements. Finally, it should be added that the Greek pharmaceutical industry is structurally vulnerable both to multinational strategies and to government policies. The industry produces high-quality generics and is an actual and potential important provider of jobs, but it can hardly ward off threats (such as price dumping) from multinational pharmaceutical industries. It is also weakened by reduced profits due to paybacks, the overall amount of which for 2014 is estimated at 30 percent of the national pharmaceutical spending budget (Anastasaki, Bradshaw, and Shah 2015).[9] While endogenous opportunities of growth are lost, the society is also deprived of a useful supplier.

To make things worse for people, a number of policies shifted part of the health-care costs to patients, causing more out-of-pocket contributions and reductions in access. Regarding medication, the benefits basket has been changed to exclude certain products and services from public coverage and introduce copayments, affecting mainly clinical tests and pharmaceuticals (private insurers have also restricted their drug coverage). Research by Gouvalas and colleagues indicates that "during the 2011–2014 period, mean percentage rate of patient contribution increased by 157.75 percent, while average patient charge per prescription in current prices increased by 65.22 percent" (Gouvalas et al. 2016 [quote]; see also Yfantopoulos et al. 2016 and Metropolitan Community Clinic of Helliniko [MCCH] Archive 2015). The share contributed by patients can in extreme cases reach 75 percent.[10] However, because of the combined effect of drug shortages, wholesalers' and drug makers' strategies, and the strict rule according to which reimbursements of medication is brought in line with the average three EU-23 lowest prices, it happens regularly that prescribed drugs either are unavailable on the market or no longer exist. Hundreds of essential drugs like insulin, anticoagulants, antidiabetic agents, or immunosuppressants either do not circulate or are difficult to find. Currently children's vaccines are unavailable. Cancer treatment medications are sometimes extremely difficult to find. This means that even when people with illnesses such as cancer are fully covered by public health insurance, they might be forced to finance most of their medication. Dysfunctions are particularly deadly for patients with chronic diseases such as diabetes or cancer. According to Dr. Charis Matsouka who at the time of the interview (2014) directed the Department of Hematology at the university General Hospital Alexandra in Athens, 40 percent of patients on chronic therapies have stopped their treatments.

Hospitals' Three-Month Horizons

Drastic measures have been introduced to restructure public hospitals and the rest of the ESY. In the past few years the country endured large hospital closures (in Athens, Thessaloniki, and elsewhere), closures and/ or mergers of a great number of clinics and specialized units, the regrouping of hundreds of labs, and the removal of some two thousand public hospital beds, if not more. In addition, public hospitals were submitted to new public management control mechanisms: hospital budgets are now managed by a private firm, the Hospital Remuneration System Company Ltd. (or ESAN AE [Etaireia Systematos Amoibwn Nosokomeiwn AE]) and various techniques aiming at controlling hospital activity and limiting doctors' autonomy have been implemented, namely a monthly data collection system for the monitoring of public hospital activity and expenditure through compulsory electronic procedures.

The Corporatization of Public Hospitals

One of the most far-reaching changes concerns the funding of public hospitals. Diagnosis-related groups (DRGs), an activity-based payments (or prospective-price-control) system based on costs associated with patient diagnosis, have replaced the previous global per day payment. The DRG method was imported to Europe from the United States despite long-standing criticism from scientific research and independent evaluations (e.g., Angell 2016; Chelimsky 1987; Davidson 2010; Dolenc and Dougherty 1985; Dougherty 1988, 1989; Fetter and Freeman 1986; Halloran and Kiley 1987). Indeed, activity-based payments are expensive. Commercialized care supporters see it as a tool to boost internal productivity because hospital revenue is directly related to their business volume (the number of acts and consultations reported). As the renowned and highly respected French medical professor André Grimaldi writes, the criterion is purely book value and does not allow distinguishing between a technical activity, which is easily quantifiable and measured, and other more-complex interventions that require time and multidisciplinary skills. In France, for instance, where an activity-based payments system was introduced in 2007, any medical consultation is now supposed to not exceed twelve minutes. The overall aim of medical practice and the shared obsession of managers and productivity-oriented doctors thus ends up being to achieve a growing number of acts rather than the delivery of general care. In other words, activity-based systems of funding are powerful managerial tools that transform the purpose of care facilities: they create business hospitals (Grimaldi 2009; on Greece, see Ioakeimoglou 2010; Polyzos et al. 2013; Economou et al. 2014). These tools have already substantially increased social insurance funds' reimbursement prices for private hospital services in Greece (Kondilis et al. 2013). According to neurologist Dr. Makis Mantas, former coordinator (until July 2015) of the Coalition of the Radical Left's (SYRIZA's) PHC program, "Activity-based payment systems increase public deficits. They have already multiplied sevenfold hospital costs. They favor private hospitals. Take the case of strabismus. That's a very simple act. The operation used to cost €70–90 in Greece. No private hospital wanted to bother. Today, the same operation costs something between €700–900. Suddenly public hospitals that used to be responsible for all of them no longer are, while private hospitals take over more and more."[11]

The advantage for private hospitals is that they can easily specialize in the simplest and lowest-risk treatments for which profits are high and caseloads predictable. By contrast, activity-based schemes lead to especially hard times for public and teaching hospitals because they remain responsible for the more complex, costly, and risky treatments even while their resources are diminished and public medical research is negatively impacted.

Modern Working Conditions

Downsizing the workforce, cutting wages, and liquidating workers' rights in the entire public sector might retrospectively be considered as one of the top priorities of Greece's creditors right from the start. In 2011 there was evidence that the cutback of public hospitals' expenditures resulted from 75 percent payroll cuts (rather than from enhanced efficiency, as successive governments claimed until 2015) (Kondilis et al. 2013; Stuckler and Basu 2013). Although public health professionals were among the lowest paid in the EU before the financial crisis, their wages have been reduced by at least 40 percent since 2010. Interviewed in 2014, Dr. Charis Matsouka said that, while she had reached the top of the hierarchy in the health system, she earned altogether €2,000 a month. Today, a newly appointed consultant's or university lecturer's average salary is about €1,100 (Ifanti et al. 2015).

The contraction of the workforce in the public health-care sector has been dramatic. Overall, from 2010 to 2016 it lost 30 percent of its workforce due to the freeze on hiring, the de facto nonreplacement of retired personnel and nonrenewed contracts for temporary staff. In 2011 alone, officials at the Athens Medical Association estimated that twenty-six thousand public health workers (up to 9,100 doctors) were about to lose their jobs (Triantafyllou and Angeletopoulou 2011). The decline of the number of doctors has been much larger than predicted by the Troika (Corriea, Dussault, and Pontes 2015) due to rapidly deteriorating working environments and conditions. Many doctors and nurses have taken early retirement. There has also been since 2010 a constant mass exodus of young and well-qualified Greek graduates, specialized physicians, and other staff seeking better working conditions outside Greece, mainly in the EU and especially in Germany. It is estimated that more than 7,500 Greek doctors emigrated in 2014, mainly to Germany where they are employed in positions below their qualifications and receive wages (€3,000 monthly) that are low compared to their European colleagues (Burgi 2014; Smith 2015).

Understaffing, patient overload, and shortages have brought public hospitals to the point of breakdown. The staff is faced with extreme work intensification, exhaustion, and burnout, leading to precarious and dangerous working conditions. Working hours have been considerably lengthened. Doctors' working time including standby periods and ordinary consultations can reach thirty-two uninterrupted hours; when doctors are on call they might work up to ninety-three hours during one week. The matter of long hours was referred to the European Commission, which in turn put the case before the European Court of Justice. The latter judged that it was illegal for employers to require such long uninterrupted periods of work.[12] The 2003/88/CE directive states that a twenty-four-hour period of work must be interspersed by at least eleven consecutive hours of rest and must not exceed maximum forty-eight hours per week. Greece has been condemned. However, as she does not have the means to hire statutory medical staff or increase health expenditure due to the MoU constraints, working conditions have not improved. Hospitals try to compensate for understaffing by recruiting self-employed nonstatutory staff on short-term contracts (and increasing numbers of undocumented immigrant health workers) (Fouca et al. 2013). This is not enough to meet the needs. In October 2015, the Panhellenic Federation of Workers in Public Hospitals (PODEIN) estimated that there were nearly 27,000 vacant posts in hospitals and 3.6 nurses (compared to 8 on average in the EU) per 1,000 inhabitants. In the meantime, there are thousands of scheduled hires that never take place and high unemployment among doctors and nurses.[13] By mid-2017 a law to conform to European working time standards in hospitals was in preparation. However, because it is still impossible to recruit statutory staff, the bill provides for an option whereby physicians who wish to do so will be able to work sixty hours a week, provided they take responsibility for their choice by signing a document (previously, excess hours were binding). As resident physicians end up leaving the ESY all over the country, intensive care units if not whole hospital departments are threatened. Hospitals have run out of the most elementary supplies. They lack everything—sheets, scissors, painkillers, blood pressure meters, sterilized equipment, vital medication, cancer screening, and appropriate equipment for surgical interventions. Some of the public cancer clinics cannot even feed their patients (MCCH Archive 2015). Since 2009 cancer clinics have been abruptly closing at various times of the day because of lack of resources, cancelling consultations without providing alternatives. In January 2016 Laiko, University General Hospital of Athens, turned away dozens of cancer patients because it could not provide vital chemotherapy that had been scheduled (MCCH Archive 2015). Services constantly struggle for additional funding in order to survive. Dr. Charis Matsouka testifies, "In the middle of the year [2014], we were on the verge of closing the lab. We asked for additional funds and they [the government] finally gave us some. But it happens every three months. So we constantly have a three months horizon. It's exhausting. And it's depressing for us."

In some extreme circumstances, newborns have been kept from their mothers until she could pay the hospital bill. Cases where cancer patients have been ejected from surgery because they could not pay €1,800 for their treatment have been reported by cardiologist Giorgos Vichas, who heads the MCCH. Such occurrences are linked to the high proportion of uninsured and have remained exceptional thanks to the ingenuity of Greek doctors who find creative ways of getting around the regulations.

Dismantling Primary Health Care

As mentioned above, the fragmented and unequal PHC network already faced important difficulties before 2010. In 2011–12 the four main social insurance funds (IKA, OGA, OAEE, and OPAD) were transferred with their staff and infrastructure to a new unique National Organization for Provision of Health Care Services (EOPYY). Considered as the way forward to ensure universality and equity of health care, the integration of social insurance funds had been hoped for since at least the foundation of the ESY in 1983. However, the changed context in the 2012 reorganization overshadowed equity. The social insurance funds absorbed by the EOPYY lost 53.5 percent of their assets in the March 2012 haircut that restructured the Greek debt. This happened because those funds had been legally obliged to have 77 percent of their disposable assets on deposit at the Bank of Greece and because they were not, contrary to banks, compensated for their losses (which amounted to about €10 billion in three months). And, of course, PHC would not be spared from cuts in social insurance health benefits, increased copayments for diagnostic tests, cuts in staff, and wage cuts (Kaitelidou and Kouli 2012; Kondilis et al. 2013).

In 2014 the minister of Health, Adonis Georgiadis, split the purchaser/ provider functions. The purchasing function remained within the jurisdiction of EOPYY while health-care provision would be assigned to a newly formed National Primary Healthcare Network (PEDY). The minister maneuvered skillfully to provoke the "voluntary" departure of half the doctors working in the health centers that had been integrated to EOPYY two years earlier. In February 2014 he closed overnight all the PHC network units and promised that they would reopen (as PEDY) within a month. PEDY structures took much longer to start (mal)functioning (an embryonic network appeared in Attica at the end of March 2014). In the meantime, approximately 6,500 to 8,000 doctors were laid off. Georgiadis announced that they would be allowed to integrate the PHC structures with the status of ESY employees on condition that they sign full-time contracts and close their private afternoon offices. Although the idea of creating a new exclusively public employment status was appreciated, it did not come with the promise to upgrade the salaries offered to the workforce: doctors would have to settle for low wages (€1,100 per month), renounce additional sources of revenue, and renounce prospects for future career progression. Many of them decided to "fire" themselves; in addition, the contract staff lost their jobs, others retired, and a minority went to courts. The latter won their cases. They were allowed to return to their jobs and keep their private practices open for a renewable period of time. Today, a mere 2,700 doctors work in the PEDY network with different employment statuses: those who returned immediately got a wage increase according to their seniority (up to €1,800), some young doctors recruited on short fixed-term contracts are paid a full time €1,100, and finally those who decided to return after winning their case in courts kept their previous rights and wage levels. The two first categories of doctors are not allowed to have other sources of revenue.

Apart from pleasing the Troika by sharply reducing the number of public sector employees, Mr. Georgiadis's initiative proved problematic. First, due to the importance of understaffing, primary care facilities (mainly those of the former IKA) have virtually ceased to function. I saw a general practitioner take care of twenty-four people in an hour and a quarter, which amounts to an average of three minutes per consultation. This is not exceptional. The work of the physician is as painful as is the situation for the patient. Patients for the most part know what they have and come only to renew their prescriptions. But there is always at least a minority who do not know what is happening to them and who will not receive the attention they need. Doctors do not have time to do much more than control health books or old prescriptions and establish new ones. In addition, they are closely monitored by the electronic platform: they cannot prescribe drugs or medical checks beyond what their individual budget allows. If they venture beyond, the system starts by issuing an Orwellian warning that appears in red letters on the computer before it locks up, and the physician, who is then fined, cannot prescribe anything else. In PHC services (as well as in hospitals), precarious physician assistants recruited on short term contracts do not want to risk their jobs or be fined. The others are also trapped by the system, so most doctors do not treat people. If necessary, they send them to the hospital where it is still possible to prescribe medications or exams freely. But it is a vicious circle, because hospital doctors are overwhelmed and do not want to spend their time issuing prescriptions.

Patients turned massively to hospital emergencies. This is the second major pitfall of Mr. Georgiadis's reorganization. To ease emergencies and address the consequences of understaffing in primary care, the minister of Health believed he could find a solution by encouraging private sector physicians to enter into agreements with the EOPYY: contracted doctors would commit to treat two hundred patients a month and be paid €2,000 monthly. This extremely costly measure for the public health system has proven very inefficient because most doctors tend at the beginning of the month to free themselves in just one week (if not faster) from their commitment to examine two hundred patients, which means that the latter are left with virtually no free PHC the rest of the time: they then have to pay for a private consultation, or go the hospital emergencies.

Such was the situation in the spring of 2017 when the current Health minister, Andreas Xanthos, launched a four-year PHC bill (Terzis 2017). Its primary objective still is to ease hospital emergencies, although the government also intends to put the whole system back on its feet. From now on, there should be only two levels of access to primary care. At the first, basic level, local health units (ToMYs) established throughout the country and located in existing centers (IKA) or in new structures, will be staffed by at least two, if possible three, doctors—a general practitioner, a pathologist, and a pediatrician. A total of 239 local units should be created within three years, fifty to sixty of which are expected to operate by the end of 2017. Where such units do not exist, private contracted doctors hired by the EOPYY should meet the needs. The minister believes that the ToMYs will cover 30 percent of basic needs and private doctors will cover the remaining 70 percent, his aim being to reverse these proportions in four years. According to Xanthos, these units could reduce the number of consultations in hospital services by about 5.5 million. At a second level, better-equipped and better-staffed health centers will replace existing services in provinces and rural areas, as well as all the structures incorporated in the national PHC network (i.e., the former PEDY). They will be open twenty-four hours a day. The government hopes to establish 240 health centers throughout the country, including Athens, by the end of 2017.

The total cost of the operation is estimated at €300 billion. It should benefit from credits guaranteed by the EU and from a gradually increasing contribution of the state budget. The operation encompasses the recruitment of 3,000 people, including 1,300 doctors. Advertised positions target general practitioners, physicians and pediatricians. They will be paid on the basis of the ESY "A" pay grid (corresponding to hospital assistant)—in other words, €1,500 to €1,600 net per month.

The initiative is welcome: it simplifies the organization of primary care, aims to create a single integrated national health system, and could correct some malfunctions. But the strict budget constraints indicate that the public system is moving toward health-care rationing. There is no way only 1,300 newly recruited doctors could meet the needs of the whole country, although the privileged profiles (general practitioners and pediatricians) correspond to a proven deficiency, since primary care services are overstaffed with specialists and understaffed with general practitioners. With only three doctors, the role of the new ToMYs is likely to be limited mainly to providing prescriptions and acting as gatekeepers that prevent the public from going to hospital emergencies. The government intends to restructure hospital emergency departments and to transform them into autonomous units with their own staff, separate from the hospital care teams; it is not yet known what that restructuring implies. On the whole, the precariousness of health-care workers will increase and the critical mass required for quality public services will be missed. Dependence on the private sector will only increase.

Encouraging Private Insurance

PHC is slowly getting reorganized to fit the principle of maximum involvement of private sector that is dear to cost-effectiveness analysts. The incremental introduction of market mechanisms in primary care merits discussion. Out-of-pocket payments are multiplying, the amounts of which might appear unimportant but seriously affect a great many people whose living conditions have deteriorated sharply. User fees for outpatient visits were raised from €3 to €5 in 2011 (the SYRIZA government removed this fee but the 2015 MoU specifies that it must be reintroduced). Medical prescriptions are limited to three drugs. If more than three are needed, doctors must add a new prescription, each of them costing the patient €1. There are also some hidden costs such as payments to schedule an appointment by phone with a doctor (Kentikelenis et al. 2014). In the near future it should be possible to schedule an appointment on the internet, which is of course a difficult option for the most disadvantaged and the elderly. Private insurance is slowly growing in the PHC market and is still relatively cheap. For instance, newspapers such as *Proto Thema* or *Anexartisia* offer their Sunday readers the possibility to collect coupons and get a "free" health card that basically will give them low-charge access to private diagnostic centers and doctors up to a very limited yearly amount. Banks also offer their clients various types of low-cost health insurance packages (e.g., a price range that might start at €85 and reach €800 yearly).[14]

These amounts are not negligible for the very poor (entire households live on a small pension that might be no more than €300–€400 a month and that is programmed to be further reduced). Alternatively, if the additional cost is affordable, it is supposed to serve an educational purpose. As Aimee Placas writes in her conclusion (this volume), austerity has a pedagogical effect. In a similar vein, a doctor told me quite abruptly in an interview, "The project is to get people used to pay until the system is finally removed." In the words of John Lister (2008: 57) from the Globalization and Health Knowledge Research Network, " One of the reasons the World Bank and other agencies have promoted user fees has been to nurture the emergence of insurance schemes even in the poorest countries." Amid other examples illustrating this point, Lister quotes Mark McEuen and Jhana McGaugh on Zimbabwe: "Among the key conclusions from a major USAID funded workshop in Zimbabwe analyzing the 'lessons learned' in health care funding was that 'user fees are vital to the introduction of any type of insurance system'" (Lister 2008: 34).

There have also been more decisive steps. Deregulation of private health services started early on at the beginning of the first bailout. For instance, Kondilis et al. (2013) mention the removal of all limitations relative to the establishment by entrepreneurs of laboratories, medical centers, and dialysis units as well as restrictions concerning the expansion of private hospitals. Similarly, contracting with private insurance companies for services delivered by public hospitals has been introduced as well as the allocation to private insurance companies of 556 luxury hospital beds in public hospitals in 2011. Just before the introduction of the new law on primary care, two big multispecialist private clinics (replacing PEDY structures) operating with leading private insurance providers and providing primary care were created in Thessaloniki and Athens.

Means-Tested Survival

Austerity does not affect everybody in the same way at the same moment everywhere. Our fieldwork and other research reveals that large groups of Greeks are unable to afford care and/or the cost of transportation to reach services. Before the advent of the global financial crisis, Greeks would go and see a doctor despite the low level of primary care. Now they tend to neglect preventive checkups; they reduce, discontinue, and even stop their treatments; and they replace their prescribed medication with cheaper alternatives. As a generalist recently (2017) told me, people have become their own doctors. Psychiatrist Spyros Sourlas reports that his patients avoid therapies and ask him instead to prescribe antidepressants.[15] Eva Karamanoli (2015: 2240) also observes that patients "ask for the cheapest treatment instead of the best." One indication of patient cutbacks is the sharp surge in dental diseases that affect an important part of the Greek population, mostly the poor and vulnerable.[16] According to a recent survey by the Hellenic Dental Association, worsening widespread dental decay is not primarily caused by changes in daily hygiene but rather by the acute fall in living standards, poverty-induced behaviors such as increased consumption of cheap high-sugar foods, and the fact that the vast majority of dental problems are left untreated for at least a year because of the inability of families to cover the out-of-pocket expenses.[17]

The 2015 MoU has a couple of pages devoted to a genuine social safety net, including a guaranteed minimum income (GMI), and access to health for all. Such concepts suggest a real improvement compared to the present Greek situation. However, progress in this area does not go farther than the World Bank's notion of an essential package of care for the poor, which abdicates equity and universalism (Missoni 2013). The general principle adopted to varying extents by most European countries in reconfiguring their welfare states has been to undermine if not abolish unconditional rights and replace previous social systems with minimum means-tested allowances for the poor, thus equalizing conditions downward (Burgi 2009, 2011). In the Mediterranean South, the new European social model nearing completion offers a safety network that barely provides means-tested survival. "Indeed what began as a 'minimum' provision became increasingly perceived as a target, effectively a 'maximum' for organizations such as the WHO" (Lister 2008: 30).

This is well illustrated by the reforms concerning unemployment benefits and health insurance. The general trend (Moreira et al. 2015) is to reduce the amounts and duration of unemployment benefits but to extend the coverage (that provides health insurance) to previously excluded unemployed groups. In Greece, before July 2011, the government provided unemployment benefits and health care to the unemployed for a maximum of one year, but patients short of financial resources could still be treated in hospitals following the termination of their benefits. After July 2011, however, new regulations stemming from the MoUs required that Greeks pay all costs out of pocket once their benefits had expired;

moreover, in March 2012, the amounts and duration of unemployment benefits were drastically reduced (from €561 to €360). In the meantime, unemployment rates (around 25 percent, 73.5 percent of which were long-term unemployed according to 2014 OECD and Eurostat figures) as well as the numbers of uninsured skyrocketed and remains huge. In 2016 Médicins du Monde estimated that there were roughly 3 million uninsured, including the self-employed that are not recorded in official unemployment numbers; Makis Mantas estimated the share of all categories of uninsured as high as 35 percent of the population, 60 percent of the total being self-employed; the figure of 2.5 million uninsured was usually put forward in official European and OECD reports.

Although these estimates cannot be verified, the unquestionable massive proportion of uninsured and pauperized people having no access to health care prompted the creation of solidarity clinics and pharmacies that are staffed by hundreds of volunteers and that have spread all over the country since the beginning of the crisis. They provide as much as possible (with very limited resources) care and medicines for free to people in need (the uninsured as well as more and more people, albeit insured, who are unable to access health services or pay for their treatment). Together with the wider social movement, solidarity clinics and pharmacies put great pressure on the government of the day to devise measures to protect the uninsured. Thus, in 2013, Minister of Health Georgiadis introduced a PHC voucher system for only one hundred thousand uninsured. His ministerial decree did not mention pharmaceutical treatment nor allow for secondary (hospitalization) care. Angry doctors from the social solidarity clinics denounced a drop in the ocean, and said that "the Ministry of Health is hoping to impress us with an aspirin, when a much more radical cure is needed" (MCCH Archive). In the summer of 2014 the minister issued another decree granting secondary health care to all uninsured under conditions to be scrutinized by special three-member committees. However, these bodies never really functioned. Instead, the uninsured admitted to hospitals were asked to sign a document in which they would recognize that they owed the hospital the cost of their treatment. Likewise, although they were allowed to go to a hospital to be examined by a doctor, if doctors prescribed medicines or further diagnostic tests, the patients had to pay out of pocket for them.

In 2016, law 4368/2016[18] and a corresponding ministerial decision (March 2, 2016) intended to correct the aforementioned deficiencies in order to guarantee "equal and universal healthcare." All citizens legally settled in Greece now have access to public health care by simply presenting their social security number. Refugees recently entered and registered in Greece (but not undocumented immigrants) are also covered. However, except for the very poor, free care does not include medicines, half the cost of which on average is borne by the patients. The exemption from user fees is subject to conditions such that only a small number, estimated at some 170,000 people, is involved (out of at least 2.5 million potential beneficiaries). Free medicines are subject to the following criteria: (1) Those with an annual income that does not exceed €2,400 for a single person (and double that amount for a couple with two children and an additional €600 per dependent person) is eligible for free medicine; (2) A person who has no income but who owns property worth up to €150,000 or more or if a person has a bank account with assets equivalent to three times the annual criterion of €200 monthly (i.e., a credit balance of €7,200) must pay; (c) Disabled people with a disability rate of less than 67 percent are not covered 100 percent; (4) Access to specialist consultation is restricted: the provision of free public health services is strictly limited to whatever public resources are available and does not extend to services that local hospitals or health centers contract to private providers. For example, an uninsured patient living in an area where the local health center that has no cardiologist and that sends insured patients to a contracted private physician, cannot access that cardiologist; she must travel, most probably to a big city, or forgo specialist care. As a result, universal access to health services and drugs is far from being achieved.

The GMI referred to in the third MoU is another component of the new European minimalist social model. The GMI has been pilot tested (November 2014 to April 2015) in thirteen local governments (one per region). EU official discourse refers to the pilot program in terms of social investment and indicates that minimum income supports (only) extreme poverty. (In the technocratic vocabulary, the term "social investment" means the opposite of hard-won unconditional rights to transfer incomes; the latter are given the derogatory qualification "social consumption.") "The policy to support minimum income (extreme poverty), under the harsh conditions of economic crisis, is considered to be a typical example of social investment" (parentheses in original) (Ziomas et al. 2015: 7).

The GMI is now called Social Solidarity Grant (KEA). It came into force in 2017 (Ministerial Decree of 24 January 2017 based on Law No. 4320/15). The scheme includes a regressive allowance slightly lower than the extreme poverty threshold[19] not exceeding €200 monthly for a single person, somewhat more depending on the size of the household—for example, €400 for a family of four or €500 for a couple and four minor children. It also includes in-kind social benefits and job-seeking assistance. Access conditions are similar to those applied to the universal healthcare legislation mentioned above. The household's income during the six months preceding the application must not exceed six times the amount of the allowance,[20] or a ceiling of €5,400 regardless of the number of persons in the household. There are also criteria for ownership, which also vary according to the size of the household. They include the taxable value of real estate in Greece or abroad (€90,000 for a single person, with a ceiling fixed at €150,000), the objective cost of all types of private vehicles (including bicycles: the total amount must not exceed €6,000), and the total amount of bank deposits or any other credit institution (€4,800 for a single person, €9,600 for two adults and two minor children, €14,400 for two adults and six minor children, with intermediate ceilings referring to the composition of households). Implementation of the scheme is entrusted to the municipalities. However, their budget constraints, the diversity of practices from one municipality to another as well as inconsistencies in the program do not allow the social services to grant the benefit of KEA to a significant proportion of applicants who are in great need.[21]

Severe Depression and Violence

Fifteen percent of the Greek population was living in extreme poverty in 2015 (compared with 10.8% in 2013 and 2.2 percent in 2009) (Hellenic Parliament 2014; Matsaganis and Leventi 2013; Matsaganis et al. 2016). Even taking into account the fact that the financial component of KEA is complemented by social benefits—that are basically limited to (always means-tested) food distribution—the new "genuine" safety net is not likely to enhance living standards and consolidate the social determinants of health. The revised European social model is heading toward limited means-tested provisions that allow survival of the poorest, but not a decent life for them.

The most immediate adverse repercussions of procyclical austerity policies (involving the downsizing of health care and other social protection institutions in response to economic downturns) are on mental well-being, risks of suicidal behavior, and interpersonal violence (homicides and domestic violence). This has been observed historically across countries and continents (Stuckler and Basu 2013). Epidemiological nationwide surveys conducted in Greece by Marina Economou and colleagues point to major depressions linked to economic hardship. The rate of severe depressions rose from 3.5 percent of the population in 2009 to 12.5 percent in 2014, a figure that persists as of this writing in 2017. Their inquiries corroborate other studies demonstrating significant increases in the rate of suicides during the three first years of austerity (plus 35 percent between 2010 and 2013) (Economou et al. 2013a, 2013b, 2016; Madianos et al. 2014). Suicides, however, represent only the tip of the iceberg. A much broader, worrying, and tenacious mental health crisis linked to surging rates of stress, anxiety, and depression is the number of children that are victims of increased (plus 30 percent) domestic violence and other forms of psychological stress associated with poverty. Spyros Sourlas[22] has observed a 30 percent increase of psychosomatic disorders (headaches, stomach aches) among children, one-third of whom are hospitalized. Gerasimos Kolaitis and George Giannakopoulos from the Department of Child Psychiatry of Athens University Medical School and Agia Sofia Children's Hospital in Athens report that they encounter "an ever-increasing number of families with complicated psychosocial adversities" (Kolaitis and Giannakopoulos 2015: 335) and that the recorded number of abused or neglected children admitted for child protection to the largest Greek pediatric hospital has risen from 81 cases in 2011 to 170 cases in 2014. The closure of local public and nonprofit mental health service units and termination of local psychosocial programs following the 2010 Greek decentralization laws, and the simultaneous introduction of SAPs leave these children, their parents, and the rest of the vulnerable defenseless. Locally more and more cases of abandoned children are occurring and dealt with through judicial and/or repressive actions instead of preventive treatment programs.

Human rights violations are greatest in the most vulnerable countries and social milieus. In Greece, one of the weakest members of the European Monetary Union (EMU), studies have reported a vertiginous list of Greek, European, and international norms, rules, and laws that have been trampled by the MoUs and successive Greek governments, including the current SYRIZA government (Debt Truth Committee 2015: 37-44; Baeten and Ghailani 2015; De Schutter and Salomon 2015). Children, women, and migrants are, as one would expect, the first victims of human rights violations. In 2012 and 2013 the Greek government orchestrated clean-up campaigns against drug users and migrants. They hunted down and insulted migrant women, warning the country against the spread of AIDS—that "can be transmitted from an illegal female migrant to the Greek customer, to the Greek family"[23]—and against so-called health time-bombs threatening Greek men and households. The latter slur was publicly articulated by Minister of Citizen Protection Michalis Chrysochoidis and Minister of Health Andreas Loverdos on 1 April 2012 during a press conference[24] in which the two men presented a new health plan (the decree GY/39A) that targeted migrants, homeless people, drug users, and sex workers as potential sources of epidemics. Decree 39A allowed the police to detain anyone for the purpose of compulsory infectious diseases testing and to publish personal data of HIV-positive subjects; it led to multiple round-up operations and the arrest, criminal prosecution, imprisonment, scapegoating, and humiliation of thousands of people. Following intense international and domestic protests the decree was overturned in May 2013 by Deputy Health Minister Fotini Skopouli, but was then restored a month later (June 2013) by incoming Minister of Health Adonis Georgiadis, and finally repealed in April 2015 by Minister of Health Panagiotis Kouroumblis (from SYRIZA) (Gamba 2013; Gkresta and Mireanu 2013; Kandylis, Daliou, and Sagia 2015; *The Lancet* 2013; Matsa 2014; Mavroudi 2013; Papastergiou and Takou 2014).

"It is important to emphasise that no systematic association exists between migration and importation of communicable diseases" (Langlois et al. 2016: 320 [quote]); Grove and Zwi 2006; Rechel et al. 2011). As Human Rights Watch researcher Judith Sunderland said at the time, "addressing infectious diseases such as HIV, hepatitis, and tuberculosis requires investing in health services, not calling the police" (Sunderland quoted in Human Rights Watch 2013). Much the same can be said of the European Union's (EU's) approach to the current flow of refugees (Skleparis 2016). Constantly exposed to institutionalized mechanisms of marginalization and discrimination that generate cumulative vulnerabilities (Smith and Daynes 2016), refugees need special care and attention. Chiara Montaldo, medical coordinator of the refugee task force, Doctors Without Borders, who was in Greece in November 2015, testified:

> We see trauma. We see growing incidences of respiratory tract infections and hypothermia. . . . We also treat skin infections, mainly scabies, prevalent in those who have been detained in unhygienic conditions, but so far we haven't observed an epidemic. . . . Signs of trauma are difficult to diagnose and manage, particularly as people are on the move. Psychologists are only treating those showing acute need and can only scratch the surface of trauma-related symptoms. Language barriers and cultural sensitivities also need to be considered. . . . [Refugees] often have acute mental health problems and trauma symptoms, notably depression and post-traumatic stress disorder (PTSD), related to organised violence, torture, human rights violation, resettlement, and traumatic migration experience. (Morgan 2015).

The refugees, however, face the greatest problems in accessing adequate health care (or any care at all), and the current policy of automatic detention in closed camps implemented in Greece in order to hold and process all refugees crossing the Aegean Sea further aggravates their health problems (World Without Torture 2012).[25] Overall, rather than estimate and respond to the refugees' health needs, increasingly complex and violent measures are taken by EU member-states to build firewalls, police their borders, detain and exclude refugees once they have crossed those borders, and finally shift the blame and the burden to Greece[26] (Cabot 2014; see also Cabot this volume). By portraying refugees "as a threat to a robust and healthy society, a threat of disease itself," by having them "screened and quarantined to avoid the spread of disease," health concerns are inverted in such a way "that the receiving population is seen to be under threat rather than attending to the health needs of the displaced" (Growe and Zwi 2006). If Europe's skewed priorities, that place an "emphasis on protection from the refugee above protection of the refugee" result in not letting refugees and asylum seekers "receive appropriate and timely health care, then this may indeed place the wider community at risk over time" and lead to the catastrophic results that this policy was purported to avoid (Grove and Zwi 2006: 1938 [quote]; Smith and Daynes 2016).

The Calculus of Power

Briefly addressing the question of the differential distribution of the livability of life, of access to a decent life, Judith Butler recently noted the need to look at those "whose lives are becoming more and more unlivable under conditions of austerity and precarity . . . we need to understand that calculus of power in order to understand that particular form of inequality" (Butler 2015 [at an ENS Seminar in Paris]). As far as the process of restructuring health care is concerned, some conclusions could be drawn that help to shed light on that calculus. In 2010, when the then prime minister of Greece, George Papandreou, asked German chancellor Angela Merkel for gentler SAP conditions, she replied that the aid program had to hurt: "We want to make sure nobody else will want this," Ms. Merkel is said to have told him (Walker 2012). The program hurt terribly and its long-term consequences will further hurt for decades. Blind and deaf to the needs of their people in this and other areas, successive Greek governments implemented the most destructive austerity regime—using "butcher's knives," as Minister of Health Andreas Loverdos acknowledged[27]—and pretended until January 2015 that their "responsible" action had increased efficiency and effectiveness in the health-care sector without impacting essential medical services (Burgi 2014; Kentikelenis et al. 2014; Stuckler and Basu 2013). Since 2010 the European Commission has seized the opportunity of the "crisis" (as well as reinforced supranational powers) to target health systems for reform in a growing number of countries (Azzopardi-Muscat et al. 2015). The European Commission is not supposed to interfere in social policies, which fall within the national competence of member-states, but it has a treaty obligation to assess the health effect of all policies, including the effect of the Troika's policies. In August 2015 it finally published a social impact assessment for the third Greek adjustment program that was, in the words of UN independent expert on foreign debt and human rights, Juan Pablo Bohoslavsky (2015: 3), "disappointing in many respects." The study, writes Bohoslavsky (2015: 3) in his End of Mission Statement, "fails to draw any lessons from what went wrong." Surprisingly, "the social impact assessment . . . does not mention the term 'human rights' even once" (Bohoslavsky 2015: 4). In the meantime, at a global level, between 2013 and 2014 "the collective wealth of billionaires with interests in [the pharmaceutical and health-care sectors] increased from $170bn to $250bn, a 47 percent increase and the largest percentage increase in wealth of the different sectors on the Forbes list. . . . Companies from these sectors spend millions of dollars every year on lobbying to create a policy environment that protects and enhances their interests further" (Oxfam 2015: 6). As the CSDH stated in its 2008 final report, "social injustice is killing people on a grand scale." (CSDH 2008: 26)

Until recently, there was some light in this dreary and indeed lethal picture. Men and women, all of them voluntary workers, have been fighting since 2009 to defeat illness and death, to restitute life and reempower the humanness of their fellow citizens. About fifty solidarity clinics and pharmacies have been created since the first one opened in Rethymnon, Crete, in 2009. Their activity and organizational skills have developed remarkably. The MCCH in Attica, for example, was established in 2010. At the beginning twenty-five people worked there; there are three hundred employees today. The first year they secured 1,200 medical consultations, and in 2015 that number was 47,000. Regardless of nationality, social status, or origin, any person in need is welcomed and given the free care and attention needed, and treated when possible, if the resources are available and if it is not too late. Many Greeks do not even know that there might be a haven where their words will be heard, their diagnoses studied, their medicine provided for. Solidarity clinics do not advertise their existence nor the name of their donors and people often end up finding them when their health situation is poor. Despite their very limited resources (that come exclusively from donations), these autonomous, independent, and self-managed groupings, that see themselves not as an alternative to public health care but as resistance bodies and that strive to enable access to health for all, have saved thousands of lives and reinstalled hope (MCCH Archive). Solidarity clinics and pharmacies, and beyond the health sector many other solidarity initiatives (Pop 2016; see also, e.g., Hart 2015), embody the social and democratic ethics that are being discarded by dominant elites, and that need to be restored to give people the means and the right to have lives worth living. For the time being, however, hope is waning because austerity became endless after Alexis Tsipras's surrender to Germany and the Eurogroup in July 2015, and because, thereafter, the Greek prime minister chose to cling to power and apply an MoU even more violent and punitive than the previous two. Apathy and despair are gaining ground. Activists and volunteers, exhausted, are quitting their organizations. Today, no one knows how the Greek society will seek to defend itself from the attacks on its very substance.

Noëlle Burgi is Senior Researcher at the National Centre for Scientific Research (CNRS; France), European Center of Sociology and Political Science (CESSP), University Paris I-Panthéon Sorbonne. Her research centers on state transformation in Europe, neoliberal governmentality, the new managerialism and its effects on individual life trajectories and identity and, most recently, the sources and effects of the deconstruction of the social state in Southern Europe, notably Greece. She received her PhD her Doctorat d'Etat (Summa cum laude) in Political Science from the Sorbonne. She recently edited *La Grande Régression. La Grèce et l'avenir de l'Europe* (2014).

Notes

1. International dollars, taking into account the purchasing power of different national currencies; World Health Organization (WHO) data.
2. Per the latest available data available from the WHO Global Health Expenditure Database.
3. The EU and the IMF have been aware since 2010 that the debt was unsustainable.
4. I am mainly basing this description on the very clear and synthetic paper by Kondilis et al. (2012). For detailed accounts, see Ioakeimoglou 2010; Siskou et al. 2008; Toundas et al. 2012; Economou et al. 2014.
5. The EU-23 member states are the coastal member states of the EU with a sea border (excluding the Czech Republic, Luxembourg, Hungary, Austria, and Slovakia, but including the United Kingdom).
6. According to Petrou and Talias (2016), €1 billion savings in 2012 (from €5.4 billion in 2010 to an estimated €3.5 billion in 2012).
7. Interview with Makis Mantas, Athens, 2016.
8. On reference pricing and price negotiations for new drugs, see, for instance, Gandjour 2013; Deloitte UK 2013.
9. And at €644 million in 2015 (see *Iatronet* 2015). The third August 2015 MoU extends the clawback ceilings for diagnostics, private clinics, and pharmaceuticals to the next three years, and prescribes further reductions in generic prices "including by making greater use of price-volume agreements where necessary." See "Greece's third MoU annotated by Yanis Varoufakis" (Varoufakis 2015: 24). The Panhellenic Association of Pharmaceutical Industries, which represents most Greek producers, and by other actors of price dumping practices, suspects multinationals in tenders for hospital drugs (Melck 2015; MCCH 2015) and reimbursement fraud has been reported (Kresge 2012).
10. Interview with Charis Matsouka, Athens, 2014. From interviewer's (author) notes.

11. Interviews with Makis Mantas in Athens, 2014 and 2016. From intervewer's (the author) notes.
12. Judgment of the Court (Ninth Chamber) of 23 December 2015. European Commission v Hellenic Republic. Case C-180/14.
13. On the recruitment of unauthorized undocumented nurses in Greek hospitals, see Fouka et al. (2013).
14. See the advertisement for Piraeus Bank: http://www.piraeusbank.gr/el/idiwtes/asfaleia/asfaleia-ygeias.
15. It costs the patient €50 to €60 to consult a psychiatrist. Whatever the cost, the patient is reimbursed €15.
16. Dental diseases can have long-lasting effects. Scientific studies find a strong correlation between bad oral health and chronic diseases such as cardiovascular diseases, diabetes, and coronary artery diseases.
17. In 2003–15, volunteer dentists of Doctors of the World examined 9,382 children in sixty-six schools in Athens and found that 81 percent needed follow-up care and 34 percent needed urgent dental care (MCCH 2015; Tagaris 2015).
18. See art. 33 of that law (in Greek): https://www.e-nomothesia.gr/kat-ygeia/nomos-4368-2016.html.
19. The term "extreme poverty" in Greece refers to a poverty threshold estimated from the cost of a consumer basket with a minimum of basic products at constant prices. That amount varies according to the localities considered. In their most recent research, Matsaganis et al. (2016) studied "Athens," "Other urban areas," and "Rural and peri-urban areas." For a single person, it amounted in 2015 respectively to €222, €216, and €182; for a couple with two children it was €640, €614, and €524 (Hellenic Parliament 2014; Matsaganis and Leventi 2013; Matsaganis et al. 2016).
20. The income would be €1,200 for a single person, a little more depending on the composition of the household, for example €3,000 for a couple and four children.
21. Interview at the municipality of Keratsini-Drapetsona, 2017.
22. Interview in Athens, 2015.
23. Comment by the then minister of Health Andreas Loverdos, 16 January 2011, quoted in Kandylis, Daliou, and Sagia, *Athens Social Atlas,* December 2015.
24. See the press release of the interview: goo.gl/yZ4WfV. See also the article published later in May by the daily newspaper *Ethnos* (in Greek): http://www.ethnos.gr/koinonia/arthro/loberdos_apasfalismeni_ygeionomiki_bomba_oi_molysmenes_me_hiv_ierodoules-63651291/.
25. A recent systematic review showed an "independent adverse effect on the mental health of asylum seekers, including PTSD, depression, and anxiety" (Filges et al. 2015, quoted in Langlois et al. 2016: 320).
26. Some self-serving and cynical EU officials and states seem to think, as one official quoted by the *Washington Post* said, "Greece wouldn't be the worst place to have a humanitarian crisis for a few months" since the population there was much more refugee friendly than those in the Balkans or Eastern Europe (Pop 2016). See also Skleparis 2016.
27. Quoted in Kentikelenis et al. 2014: 748.

References

Anastasaki, Eirini, Steven Bradshaw, and Sandip Shah. 2015. "The Greek Healthcare Reform After Troika: the Potential Impact on Global Pricing and Access Strategy." *Value in Health* 17(7): A 429.

Angell, Marcia. 2016. "Are We in a Health Care Crisis?" *PBS Public Broadcasting Service,* Healthcare Crisis: Who's at Risk? Retrieved 22 May 2016 from http://www.pbs.org/healthcarecrisis/Exprts_intrvw/m_angell.htm.

Azzopardi-Muscat, Natasha, Timo Clemens, Deborah Stoner, and Helmut Brand. 2015. "EU Country Specific Recommendations for Health Systems in the European Semester Process: Trends, Discourse and Predictors." *Health Policy* 119: 375–83.

Baeten, Rita, and Dalila Ghailani. 2015. "Politique et droit de l'Union Européenne: développements ayant un impact sur la politique nationale des soins de santé." *OSE Paper Series, Briefing Paper n°10,* April.

Blastarakos, Michalis. 2014. "E Ygeia sto Apospasma to 2015." *Health Report,* December 16. Retrieved 17 February 2016 from http://www.healthreport.gr/η-υγεία-στο-απόσπασμα-το-2015/.

Bohoslavsky, Juan Pablo. 2015. "End of Mission Statement." Athens, December 8. Retrieved 12 February 2016 from http://www.ohchr.org/Documents/Issues/IEDebt/EOM_Statement_Greece_IEForeignDebt_EN.pdf.

Brown, Wendy. 2006. "American Nightmare: Neoliberalism, Neoconservatism, and De-Democratization." *Political Theory* 34(6): 690–714.

Burgi, Noëlle. 2009. "La construction de l'État social minimal en Europe." *Politique européenne* 27(1): 201–32.

———. 2011. "Disciplining the Labour Market in Europe: The Emerging Normative Neoliberal Order." In *Europe in the Emerging World Order: Searching for a New Paradigm,* edited by Petar Bojanic, Jovan Babic and Gazela Puda, 79–92. Belgrade: Institute for Philosophy and Social Theory, University of Belgrade.

———, ed. 2014. *La Grande Régression. La Grèce et l'avenir de l'Europe.* Lormont, France: Le Bord de l'eau.

Butler, Judith. 2015. Seminar at the Ecole Normale Supérieure (ENS, Paris), November 4.

Cabot, Heath. 2014. *On the Doorstep of Europe: Asylum and Citizenship in Greece.* Philadelphia: University of Pennsylvania.

Carone, Giuseppe, Christoph Schwierz, and Ana Xavier. 2012. "Cost-containment Policies in Public Pharmaceutical Spending in the EU." European Economy *Economic Papers 461.* Brussels: European Commission Directorate-General for Economic and Financial Affairs. Retrieved 10 April 2015 from http://ec.europa.eu/economy_finance/publications/economic_paper/2012/pdf/ecp_461_en.pdf

Chelimsky, Eleanor. 1987. "Access to Posthospital Care for Medicare Beneficiaries." Statement Before the Subcommittee in Health and Long-Term Care, Special Committee on Ageing. House of Representatives, Washington, DC. 28 January. Retrieved 20 March 2016 from http://webcache.googleusercontent.com/search?q=cache: http://161.203.16.70/assets/110/101547.pdf&gws_rd=cr&ei=XRWDWemLK4f4UIfhmJAI.

Corriea, Tiago, Gilles Dussault, and Carla Pontes. 2015. "The Impact of the Financial Crisis on Human Resources for Health Policies in Three Southern-Europe Countries." *Health Policy* 119(12): 1600–5.

Commission on Social Determinants of Health (CSDH). 2008. *Closing The Gap in a Generation: Health Equity Through Action on Social Determinants of Health. Final Report of the Commission on Social Determinants of Health.* Geneva: World Health Organization. Retrieved 2 April 2015 from http://apps.who.int/iris/bitstream/10665/43943/1/9789241563703_eng.pdf.

Daniels, Norman. 1985. *Just Health Care.* New York: Oxford University Press.

Daniels, Norman, and Bruce P. Kennedy, and Ichiro Kawachi. 1999. "Why Justice Is Good for Our Health: The Social Determinants of Health Inequalities." *Daedalus* 128(4): 215–51.

Davidson, Stephen M. 2010. *Still Broken: Understanding the U.S. Health Care System.* Stanford, CA: Stanford Business Books.

Debt Truth Committee. 2015. "The Impact of the 'Bailout Programme' on Human Rights." *Preliminary Report of the Truth Committee on Public Debt.* Retrieved 1 March 2016 from http://www.cadtm.org/Preliminary-Report-of-the-Truth.

Deloitte UK. 2013. *Impact of Austerity on European Pharmaceutical Policy and Pricing: Staying Competitive in a Challenging Environment.* London: Deloitte UK Centre for Health Solutions.

De Schutter, Olivier, and Margot E. Salomon. 2015. "Economic Policy Conditionality, Socio-Economic Rights, and International Legal Responsibility: The Case of Greece 2010–2015." Legal brief preapred for the special committee of the Hellenic Parliament on the Audit of the Greek debt (Debt Truth Committee), 15 June.

Dolenc, Danielle A., and Charles J. Dougherty. 1985. "DRGs: The Counterrevolution in Financing Health Care." *Hastings Center Report* 15(3): 19–29.

Dougherty, Charles J. 1988. *American Health Care: Realities, Rights, and Reforms.* Oxford: Oxford University Press.

———. 1989. "Ethical Perspectives on Prospective Payment." *Hastings Center Report* 19(1): 5–11.

Economou, Charalambos. 2010. "Greece: Health System Review." *Health Systems in Transition* 12(7). London: European Observatory on Health Systems and Policies. Retrieved 10 Aril 2012 from http://www.euro.who.int/__data/assets/pdf_file/0004/130729/e94660.pdf.

Economou, Charalampos, Daphne Kaitelidou, Alexander Kentikelenis, Aris Sissouras, and Anna Maresso. 2014. *The Impact of the Financial Crisis on the Health System and Health in Greece.* European Observatory on Health Systems and Policies and World Health Organization Europe. Retrieved 23 March 2018 fom https://pdfs.semanticscholar.org/9a71/8dc1e383b05d96afd2dd36bba83313633e24.pdf.

Economou, Marina, Elias Angelopoulos, Lily E. Peppou, Kyriakos Souliotis, and Costas Stefanis. 2016. "Suicidal Ideation and Suicidal Attempts in Greece During the Economic Crisis: An Update." *World Psychiatry* 15(1): 83–84.

Economou, Marina, Michael Madianos, Lily Evangelia Pepou, Christos Theleritis, Athanasios Patelakis, and Costas Stefanis. 2013b. "Suicidal Ideation and Reported Suicide Attempts in Greece During the Economic Crisis." *World Psychiatry* 12(1): 53–59.

Economou, Marina, Lili Evangelia Peppou, Sofia Fousketatki, Christos Theleritis, Athanasios Patelakis, Tatiana Alexiou, Michael G. Madianos, and Costas Stefanis. 2013a. "Oikonomike Crise kai Psyhike Ygeia: Epiptoseis sten Epikratese Koinon Psyhikon Diatarahon." *Psyhiatrike* 24(4): 247–61.

Fetter, Robert B., and Jean L. Freeman. 1986. "Diagnosis Related Groups: Product Line Management within Hospitals." *Academy of Management Review* 11(1): 41–54.

Filges, Trine, Edith Montgomery, Marianne Kastrup, and Anne Marie Klint Jørgensen. 2015. *The Impact of Detention on the Health of Asylum Seekers: A Systematic Review.* Copenhagen: The Campbell Library.

Fouca, Georgia, Sotirios Plakas, Dimitrios Papageorgiou, Marianna Manzorou, Ioannis Kalemikerakis, and Zambia Vardaki. 2013. "The Increase in Illegal Private Duty Nurses in Greek Public Hospitals." *Journal of Nursing Management* 21(4): 633–37.

Foucault, Michel. 2004. *Naissance de la Biopolitique: Cours au Collège de France (1978–1979).* Paris: Gallimard-Seuil.

Gamba, Dimitra. 2013. "The Construction of Gender Identity and the Reproduction of Gender Roles by the Greek Mass Media—The Case of HIV-infected Prostitutes in Athens." School of Law, Aristotle University, Thessaloniki, Greece. Retrieved 25 June 2015 from https://www.constitutionalism.gr/the-construction-of-gender-identity-and-the-reproduction-of-gender-roles-by-the-greek-mass-media-the-case-of-hiv-infected-prostitutes-in-athens/

Gandjour, Afschin. 2013. "Reference Pricing and Price Negotiations for Innovative New Drugs." *PharmacoEconomics* 31(1): 11–14.

Georgakopoulos, Thodoris. 2016. "E Ygeia Ton Ellenon Kai E Krise—Mia Ereuna." *Dianeosis,* March. Retrieved 20 September 2016 from http://www.dianeosis.org/2016/03/greek_health_intro/.

Giannitsis, Tassos, and Stavros Zografakis. 2015. "Greece: Solidarity and Adjustment in Times of Crisis." *IMK Study,* no. 38. IMK-Hans-Böckler Foundation, March. Retrieved 25 November 2015 from http://www.boeckler.de/pdf/p_imk_study_38_2015.pdf.

Gkresta Maria, and Manuel Mireanu. 2013. "Social Control and Security in Times of Crisis: The Criminalisation of the Seropositive Women in Greece." Retrieved 5 March 2014 from https://www.academia.edu/24186347/Social_Control_and_Security_in_Times_of_Crisis_The_Criminalisation_of_the_Seropositive_Women_in_Greece_with_Maria_Gkresta_.

Gouvalas, Athanasios, Michael Igoumenidis, Mamas Theodorou, and Kostas Athanakis. 2016. "Cost-Sharing Rates Increase During Deep Recession: Preliminary Data From Greece." *International Journal of Health Policy Management* 5(12): 687–692.

Grimaldi, André. 2009. *L'Hôpital Malade de la Rentabilité.* Paris: Fayard.

Grove, Nathalie J., and Anthony B. Zwi. 2006. "Our Health and Theirs: Forced Migration, Othering, and Public Health." *Social Science & Medicine* 62(8): 1931–42.

Halloran, Edward J., and Marilou Kiley. 1987. "Nursing Dependency, Diagnosis-Related Groups, and Length of Hospital Stay." *Health Care Financing Review* 8(3): 27–36.

Hart, Keith, ed. 2015. *Economy For and Against Democracy.* New York: Berghahn.

Hellenic Parliament. 2014. *Politikes Elachistou Eisodematos sten Europaike Enose kai sten Ellada: Mia Sygkritike Analyse.* State Budget Office. September. Retrieved 22 November 2015 from http://www.taxheaven.gr/news/news/view/id/20513.

Human Rights Watch. 2013. "Greece: Repeal Abusive Health Regulation: Stop Forced HIV Testing." 3 July. Retrieved from https://www.hrw.org/news/2013/07/03/greece-repeal-abusive-health-regulation

Iatronet. 2015. Press release. http://www.iatronet.gr/eidiseis-nea/perithalpsi-asfalisi/news/32734/sta-644-ekatommyria-evrw-ypologizei-o-eopyy-claw-back-kai-rebate-gia-to-2015.html.

Ifanti, Amalia A., Andreas A. Argyriou, Foteini H. Kalofonou, and Haralabos P. Kalofonos. 2015. "Physicians' Brain Drain in Greece: A Perspective on the Reasons Why and How to Address It." *Health Policy* 117(2): 210–15.

Iglehart, John K. 1986. "Early Experience with Prospective Payment of Hospitals." *New England Journal of Medicine* 314: 1460–64.

Ioakeimoglou, Elias. 2010. "Yperesies Ygeias: Apo to Demosio Agatho sto Emporeuma." *Meletes 32.* Athens: Labour Institute INE/GSEE-ADEDY.

Kaitelidou, Daphne, and Eugenia Kouli. 2012. "Greece: The Health System in a Time of Crisis." *Eurohealth* incorporating Euro Observer, 18(1): 12–14. Retrieved 21 March 2013 from http://www.euro.who.int/__data/assets/pdf_file/0005/162959/Eurohealth_Vol-18_No-1_web.pdf.

Kandylis, George, Sofia Daliou, and Alexandra Sagia. 2015. "A City Under Siege: Military Urbanism in Modern Athens." Athens Social Atlas, December. Retrieved 20 November 2016 from http://www.athenssocialatlas.gr/en/article/under-siege/.

Karamanoli, Eva. 2015. "5 Years of Austerity Takes Its Toll on Greek Health Care." *The Lancet* 386(10010), December 5: 2239–40.

Karanikolos, Marina, Philipa Mladovsky, Jonathan Cylus, Sarah Thomson, Sanjay Basu, David Stuckler, Johan P. Mackenbach, et al. 2013. "Financial Crisis, Austerity, and Health in Europe." *The Lancet* 381(9874), April 13: 1323–31.

Kentikelenis, Alexander, Marina Karanikolos, Aaron Reeves, Martin McKee, and David Stuckler. 2014. "Greece's Health Crisis: From Austerity to Denialism." *The Lancet* 383(9918), 22 February: 748–53.

Kolaitis, Gerasimos, and George Giannakopoulos. 2015. "Greek Financial Crisis and Child Mental Health." *The Lancet* 386, July 25: 335.

Kondilis, Elias, Stathis Giannakopoulos, Magda Gavanna, Ioanna Ierokakonou, Howard Waitzkin, and Alexis Benos. 2013. "Economic Crisis, Restrictive Policies, and the Population's Health and Health Care: The Greek Case." *American Journal of Public Health* 103(6): 973–79.

Kondilis, Elias, Emmanouil Smyrnakis, Magda Gavana, Stathis Giannakopoulos, Theodoros Zdoukos, Steve Lliffe, and Alexis Benos. 2012. "Economic Crisis and Primary Care Reform in Greece: Driving the Wrong Way?" *British Journal of General Practice* 62(598): 264–65.

Kresge, Naomi. 2012. "Greek Crisis Dries Up Drug Supply As Even Aspirin Can't Be Found." *Bloomberg Business*. Retrieved 20 June 2013 from http://www.bloomberg.com/news/articles/2012-01-10/greek-crisis-has-pharmacists-pleading-for-aspirin-as-drug-supply-dries-up.

Kyriopoulos, Giannis. 2015. "Ygeia: 'Niketes' kai 'Ettemenoi' tes Krises." *The Huffington Post*, June 19. Retrieved 20 November 2015 from http://www.huffingtonpost.gr/giannis-kyriopoulos/-_583_b_7619170.html.

The Lancet. 2013. "HIV Testing in Greece: Repeating Past Mistakes." Editorial. *The Lancet* 382(9887): 102.

Langlois, Etienne V., Andy Haines, Göran Tomson, and Abdul Ghaffar. 2016. "Refugees: Toward Better Access to Health-care Services." *The Lancet* 387(10016), January 2: 319–21.

Lister, John. 2008. *Globalization and Health Systems Change*. Ottawa: Globalization and Health Knowledge Network Research Papers. Retrieved 20 April 2015 from http://www.globalhealthequity.ca/electronic percent20library/Globalization percent20and percent20Health percent20Systems percent20Change percent20Lister.pdf.

Madianos, Michael G., Tatiana Alexiou, Athanasios Patelakis, and Marina Economou. 2014. "Suicide, Unemployment and Other Socioeconomic Factors: Evidence from the Economic Crisis in Greece." *European Journal of Psychiatry* 28(1): 39–49.

Mantas interview 2016

Matsa, Katerina. 2014. "Les Addictions en Temps de Crise." in *La Grande Régression. La Grèce et l'avenir de l'Europe*, edited by Noëlle Burgi, 213–30. Lormont, France: Le Bord de l'eau.

Matsaganis, Manos, and Chrysa Leventi. 2013. "E Anatomia tes Phtocheias sten Ellada tou 2013." *Newsletter 5*. Athens: Athens University of Economics, Public Policy Research Unit. Retrieved 30 May 2014 from http://www.paru.gr/files/newsletters/NewsLetter_05.pdf.

Matsaganis, Manos, Chrysa Leventi, and Eleni Kanavitsa, and Maria Flevotomou. 2016. "Mia Apodotikotere Politike gia ten Katapolemese tes Akraias Phtocheias." *Dianeosis*. Athens: Athens University of Economics, Public Policy Research Unit. Retrieved 20 September 2016 from http://www.dianeosis.org/wp-content/uploads/2016/06/ftwxeia_version_070616_3.pdf.

Mavroudi, Zoe. 2013. *Ruins: Chronicle of an HIV Witch-hunt*. http://ruins-documentary.com/en/.

Melck, Brendan. 2015. "Greek Pharma Industry Continues to Be Caught in Austerity Crosswind." *HIS Life Sciences Blog*, 12 January. Retrieved 15 Janueary 2016 from http://blog.ihs.com/greek-pharma-industry-continues-to-be-caught-in-austerity-crosswind.

Metropolitan Community Clinic of Helliniko (MCCH) Archive. 2015. Retrieved from http://www.mkiellinikou.com/en/category/mcch/page/2/.

Missoni, Eduardo. 2013. "Understanding the Impact of Global Trade Liberalization on Health Systems Pursuing Universal Health Coverage." *Value in Health* 16(S1): S14–S18.

Moreira, Amilcar, Angel Alonso Dominguez, Catia Antunes, Maria Karamessini, Michele Raitano, and Miguel Glatzer. 2015. "Austerity-driven Labour Market Reforms in Southern Europe: Eroding the Security of Labour Market Insiders." *European Journal of Social Security* 17(2): 202–25.

Morgan, Jules. 2015. "Agencies Struggle With Europe's Complex Refugee Crisis." *The Lancet* 386(10008), November 21: 2042–43.

Mossialos, Elias, and Sara Allin. 2005. "Interest Groups and Health System Reform in Greece." *West European Politics* 28(2): 420–44.

Mossialos, Elias, Sara Allin, and Konstantina Davaki. 2005. "Analysing the Greek Health System: A Tale of Fragmentation and Inertia." *Health Economics* 14(S1): S151–S168.

Organisation for Economic Co-operation and Development (OECD). 2015. *Economic Policy Reforms: Going for Growth 2015.* Paris: OECD. Retrieved 29 January 2016 from http://www.oecd.org/economy/goingforgrowth.htm.

———. 2018. "Health Spending." https://data.oecd.org/healthres/health-spending.htm#indicator-chart.

Oxfam. 2015. *Wealth: Having it All and Wanting More.* Oxfam Issue Briefing, January. Retrieved 15 February 2016 from https://www.oxfam.org/sites/www.oxfam.org/files/file_attachments/ib-wealth-having-all-wanting-more-190115-en.pdf.

Papastergiou, Vassilis, and Eleni Takou. 2014. *Migration in Greece: Eleven Myths and Even More Truths.* Athens: Rosa Luxemburg Stiftung Office in Greece. Retrieved 20 November 2015 from http://rosalux.gr/sites/default/files/publications/migration.pdf.

Petrou, Panagiotis, and Michael A. Talias. 2016. "Navigating Through the Maze of Pricing and Affordability of Branded Pharmaceuticals in the Midst of the Financial Crisis: A Comparative Study Among Five European Recession Countries, from a Cyprus Perspective." *Journal of Pharmaceutical Policy and Practice* 9.

Polyzos, Nikolaos, Haralampos Karanikas, Eleftherios Thireos, Catherine Kastanioti, and Nick Kontodimopoulos. 2013. "Reforming Reimbursement of Public Hospitals in Greece During the Economic Crisis: Implementation of a DRG System." *Health Policy* 109: 14–22. Retrieved from dx.doi.org/10.1016/j.healthpol.2012.09.011.

Pop, Valentina. 2016. "EU Shifts Closer Toward Blocking Migrant Trail in Greece." *The Washington Post,* 25 February.

Rechel, Bernd, Philipa Mladovsky, Walter Devillé, Barbara Rijks, Roumyana Petrova-Benedict, and Martin McKee. 2011. "Migration and Health in the European Union: An Introduction." In *Migration and Health in the European Union,* edited by Bernd Rechel, Philipa Mladovsky, Walter Deville, Barbara Rijks, Roumyana Petrova-Benedict, and Martin McKee, 3–13. Maidenhead, UK: McGraw-Hill, Open University Press.

Sachs, Jeffrey D. 2005. *Investing in Development. A Practical Plan to Achieve the Millenium Development Goals.* London: Earthscan United Nations Development Project.

Sen, Amartya. 1999. *Development as Freedom.* New York: Anchor Books.

Simou, Effie, and Eleni Koutsogeorgou. 2014. "Effects of the Economic Crisis on Health and Healthcare in Greece in the Literature from 2009 to 2013: A Systematic Review." *Health Policy* 115(2–3): 111–19.

Siskou, Olga, Daphne Kaitelidou, Mamas Theodorou, and Lycourgos Liaropoulos. 2008. "E Dapane Ygeias sten Ellada: To Elleniko Paradoxo." *Archives of Hellenic Medicine I* 25(5): 663–72.

Skleparis, Dimitris. 2016. "(In)securitization and Illiberal Practices on the Fringe of the EU." *European Security* 25(1): 92–111. Retrieved from dx.doi.org/10.1080/09662839.2015.1080160.

Smith, Helena. 2015. "Young, Gifted and Greek: Generation G—the World's Biggest Brain Drain." *The Guardian,* 19 January.

Smith, James, and Leigh Daynes. 2016. "Borders and Migration: An Issue of Global Health Importance." *The Lancet* 4(2), 14 February: 85–86.

Stuckler, David, and Sanjay Basu. 2013. *The Body Politic: Why Austerity Kills.* New York: Basic Books.

Tagaris, Karolina. 2015. "The Latest Sign of Greece's Decay: Children's Teeth." *Reuters Investigates,* November 5.

Terzis, Demetris. 2017. "Etoimazoun . . . ToMY sten Protovathmia Ygeia." *EfSYN (Efemerida ton Syntakton),* 12 April.

Toundas, Giannis, with Christina Dimitrakaki, Nikolaos Oikonomou, Georgia Palkarona, and Kyriakos Souliotis. 2012. *Oi Yperesies Ygeias sten Ellada 1996–2006.* Health Services Research Centre from the Laboratory of Hygiene and Epidemiology. Athens: Athens University Medical School. Retrieved 1 March 2014 from http://www.neaygeia.gr/pdf/OiYpiresiesYgeiasstinEllada.pdf.

Triantafyllou, Konstantinos, and Chryssi Angeletopoulou. 2011. "IMF and European Co-workers Attack Public Health in Greece." *The Lancet* 378(9801): 1459–60.

Varoufakis, Yanis. 2015. "Greece's Third MoU (Memorandum of Understanding) annotated by Yanis Varoufakis." Yanis Varoufakis's online blog *Thoughts for the Post-2008 World.* Retrieved 29 August 2015 from https://www.yanisvaroufakis.eu/2015/08/17/greeces-third-mou-memorandum-of-understading-annotated-by-yanis-varoufakis/.

Walker, Marcus. 2012. "How a Radical Greek Rescue Plan Fell Short." *Wall Street Journal,* May 10.

World Health Organization (WHO). 2000. *World Health Report 2000—Health Systems: Improving Performance.* Geneva: WHO. Retrieved 20 January 2013 from http://www.who.int/whr/2000/en/.

World Without Torture. 2012. "'It's Going as Bad as It Could Go': Migrants in Greece Face Dire Detention Conditions." Retrieved 27 January 2016 from https://worldwithouttorture.org/2013/01/08/its-going-as-bad-as-it-could-go-in-greece-face-dire-detention-conditions/.

Xanthos, Andreas. 2015. Interview in *regards.fr.* Retrieved 20 November from http://www.regards.fr/web/Andreas-Xanthos-Pas-de-veritable.

Yfantopoulos, John, Nick Yfantopoulos, and Platon Yfantopoulos. 2016. "Pharmaceutical Policies under Economic Crisis: The Greek Case." *Journal of Health Policy & Outcomes Research,* February 1. DOI: 10.7365 / JHPOR.2016.2.1.

Ziomas, D., I. Sakellis, N. Bouzas, and N. Spyropoulou. 2015. *ESPN Thematic Report on Social Investment. Greece.* European Commission: Directorate-General for Employment, Social Affairs and Inclusion.

Part III

Changes in Greek Society and Culture

Chapter 9

Gendering the Crisis
Claiming New Values and Agencies beyond Destitution

Alexandra Zavos

Introduction

As chance would have it, writing this chapter coincided with my preparing a course on feminist research, to be taught at a new master's program in gender studies at one of the leading social and political science universities in Athens. I agonized over putting together the syllabus, particularly anxious about how to approach issues of performing (and problematizing) mastery and epistemic authority through notions of reflexivity and situated knowledge production, not only as topics relevant to the course, but also in the context of how I myself am positioned and interpellated, teaching as a woman and a feminist researcher in what I consider to be a masculinist institutional setting. It struck me, given the above preoccupations, that I was about to write on a topic, gender and crisis, that was far from neutral to me, far from safely removed from my own experience.

The crisis has left its marks on my life. Central to its effects is the experience of dislocation, a condition I wish to associate with the, by now, generalized regime of precarity (Biglia and Marti 2014). This dislocation— personal, professional, and sociospatial—has affective, institutional and material manifestations: a sense of insecurity and fragmentation, the diffusion of informality in work relations, the prescript of continuous professional reinvention, and an imposed nomadicity in living circumstances. As a precarious subject grappling with the task to write about the very conditions that have rendered me as such, a certain irony is not lost on me: this piece of research could have been about me. Much as I would like to, though, I cannot escape into an objectifying and detached mode of inquiry. And yet it is precisely by strategically assuming a feminist stand-point of strong objectivity, whereby I write myself into the narrative in multiple registers, that I can attain a vantage point necessary for reclaiming a sense of power.

Feminist debates on methodological reflexivity assert the need not only to address personal commitment and social positionality in the research process, but also, importantly, to account for epistemic claims in terms of social values and institutional location as well (Burman 1994), through a rigorous engagement with systemic constraints on the politics of knowledge production, with the purpose of challenging power asymmetries and silencing mechanisms inherent in academic and social science practice.[1] Keeping this in mind, it is necessary to reflect on the truth-function of the different accounts presented below,[2] and how gendering knowledge on the crisis will serve the objectives of a feminist critique that aims to interrogate both hegemonic and counterhegemonic political and institutional discourses, especially those that also claim to support radical emancipatory projects/struggles.

As a lecturer and researcher depending on temporary work contracts, I exemplify the conditions of academic precarity denounced recently by a number of Greek academics (e.g., Gavroglou 2015, who is also currently the minister of Education, Research and Religious Affairs). My current institutional location, then, can be described only as complex and contradictory: I am a member of a feminist scientific and academic community, which has to contend with unabated institutional and everyday sexism and appears to be in retreat as far as defining and defending a progressive agenda for women in public discourse and policy goes. I am a precarious subject of the neoliberal academic regime that reduces me to the position of flexible reserve labor while at the same time requiring full professionalization of academic capacities. I am an informalized adjunct of the Greek public university that struggles to secure the necessary personnel and infrastructure for carrying on research and teaching while at same time aspiring to stand as a bulwark of freedom and social justice.[3] It is at the intersection of these material and ideological constraints that I construct my account of gender and crisis.[4]

In doing so, I ask myself how much of my interest in treating the topic as an inquiry into women's practices of improvisation, innovation, and resilience[5] is colored and orientated by my own need to envision once again the possibility of a more aspirational social engagement, projected here onto my explorations of other women's alternative ways of living—including the production of counterhegemonic subjectivities, horizontal relationalities of solidarity, and different economies of value. I wonder whether my intellectual and political commitment to a feminist viewpoint is not also vital for reclaiming my own sense of power. In other words, how much does my wish to shift the dominant accounts of women in crisis from victimhood to agency reflect my own need to gain a different perspective on my own life.

In the following sections, I present a brief overview of current social research into the gendered impact of crisis and austerity, and, taking the cue from other feminist scholars, proceed to interrogate prevalent notions and accounts of crisis from a gendered perspective. Next, I discuss three recent women-initiated social enterprises as examples of cooperative entrepreneurial responses to the crisis, which draw on different understandings of gender and solidarity. Finally, taking the above into account, I return to my own experience to consider how it can inform a feminist analytics of crisis.

Overview

The gendered effects of the Greek socioeconomic crisis have been documented mostly in terms of women's changing participation in the labor market. Austerity-induced deterioration of labor conditions and social services, rising unemployment, labor deregulation, and pauperization brought on by the spiraling economic recession, affect not only women's work and gender equality, but also their family relations and daily lives (Balourdos and Spyropoulou 2012; Greek Ombudsman 2012–14; Karamessini 2014a, 2014b; Karamessini and Koutendakis 2014; Lyberaki 2014; Tsiganou 2014; Vaiou 2014, 2016).

Overall, as Maria Karamessini (2014a, 2014b) argues, while the crisis initially affected mostly men's labor participation through the collapse of the construction and production sectors, the deepening of the crisis through repeated austerity programs brought about far-reaching changes in the service economy, where most women are employed, as well: enforced part-time work, early pensioning, flexibilization, wage cuts in the public and private sector, and layoffs. While young women's unemployment is soaring and is among the highest in Europe,[6] making their entry into the labor market a very serious challenge, women in their forties and fifties have been hit very hard as well and in structurally complex ways, highlighting the interconnections between economic, social, and cultural dynamics that reflect legal, ethnic, class, educational, and age differences among women. Such consequences have been discussed at some length in recent research carried out by feminist economists and sociologists in

Greece and other Southern European countries (Karamessini and Rubbery 2014).[7]

As Dina Vaiou (2016) explains, recurrent memorandums that imposed cuts to the service and welfare sector have gradually hit women in multiple, and often invisible, ways. One of the insidious effects of these changes, which also marks the unequal class distribution of the effects of the crisis, has been the retreat (often forced by female and male unemployment) of many women in lower- and middle-income households to the private sphere of the family, in charge of care provision, a turn that seems to reinforce or reintroduce conservative assumptions about gender relations and roles in general. The precaritization of women's labor, a condition that characterized mostly migrant women's lives before the crisis began, has spread to define Greek women's labor participation and professional chances as well.[8] Most importantly, just as with migrant women before, this precaritization either remains invisible or is normalized by the (not so) latent ideologies of gender that naturalize the reinscription of women as default caretakers, expected to sacrifice themselves in the service of the family's survival. It is not surprising, therefore, that a widespread sense of disillusionment and hopelessness has set in, especially among middle-aged women who are already tied to many family commitments that circumscribe their choices and opportunities (Vaiou 2014).

An added class dimension emerges, since, as Karamessini (2014b) points out, the abolition of mainly female specializations, such as nursing, hair dressing, hair styling, and infant care from vocational training schools, and their transfer to private training colleges that charge tuition fees, renders young working-class women's access to education and professional training prohibitive, barring their entry into the labor market, a precondition for their financial emancipation. In this sense, research on the gendered impact of the crisis on different categories of women can indeed reveal important class dimensions of the crisis that would otherwise remain hidden under the general term "unemployment." Another hidden effect of the crisis, one that is nevertheless crucial for women's well-being, has been the rise in domestic violence. As Kaldi-Koulikidou and Plevraki (2014) report, domestic violence goes mainly undetected in Greece because it is intimately connected to protection of the family from public and legal scrutiny, and because there is a lack of appropriate legislation. Such violence appears, incorrectly therefore, to be lower than in other European countries. Nonetheless, police reports do indicate a significant rise in the cases reported, as well as in the use of shelters, whose services however have been disrupted by ongoing welfare cuts.[9]

What is particularly troubling, and in need of interrogation, is the fact that these changes are not part of the anti-austerity political agenda, or even publicly debated, except in tokenistic ways.[10] As Efi Avdela (2011) poignantly points out, one of the marked differences between the current crisis and the comparable crisis of the 1930s in Greece is the absence of a strong, vocal, and agonistic feminist movement to advocate for women's rights, in the context of regressive and oppressive economic and social policies. A gendered analysis cannot but situate the worsening conditions of women's lives, as well as the wide range of reactions, ranging from solidarity initiatives to the movement of the so-called squares all the way to far-right extremisms, in relation to socioeconomic but also cultural–ideological stakes, and their particular (always gendered) violence.

Feminist scholars in Greece have engaged with the crisis from different disciplinary perspectives, notably political theory, human rights, urban studies, economics, policy studies, and social anthropology, highlighting the political, economic, social, cultural and psychological impact of the crisis, as well as the effects of its management through violent austerity policies, on both women's livelihoods (e.g., unemployment, precarity, poverty, cuts on social services, rise in domestic and gender based violence) as well as on institutions and the public good (e.g., attack on labor rights, social security and welfare restructuring, rise and legitimation of the far right, pauperization, homelessness, privatization of public resources, securitization, social exclusion, and displacement). Important, if underacknowledged, aspects of the crisis, such as retrenchment of gender equality, are brought to bear on mainstream narratives of austerity (whether in favor of, or critical of, enforced restructuring) in the hopes not only of generating a more insightful and comprehensive reflection on developing trends, but also of articulating discursive and practical alternatives that challenge social destitution and disenfranchisement as well as growing racist, xenophobic, homophobic, and sexist reactions that have resurfaced in the context of diminishing rights and incomes.

A number of publications have appeared since 2010, including a special issue of the *Review of Political Science* (Pantelidou-Malouta 2013), edited collections (Brekke et al. 2014; Karamesini and Rubery 2014; Lada 2013), monographs (Athanasiou 2012; Fragoudaki 2013), as well as articles in Greek and foreign journals (Avdela 2011; Avdela and Psarra 2012; Carastathis 2015; Gaitanou 2012; Vaiou 2014, 2016), and interventions in the press (e.g., Kosyfologou 2015; Stratigaki 2013; Vougioukas 2013). The *Annual Reports* of the Greek Ombudsman (from 2012 to 2014), as well as the 2012 periodic publication of the National Centre for Social Research, *The Social Portrait of Greece,* include sections on the impact of the crisis on women, especially with regard to discrimination in the labor market, pauperization, and the consequences of welfare cuts on care services and family relations. While given focus on the effects of crisis and austerity on women's livelihoods and rights is in itself a contribution toward engendering social science research, one cannot overlook that such research more often than not reproduces a narrow conception of gender as a sociodemographic variable. Such a conception naturalizes gender binaries and their associated social roles and hierarchies, rather than confront its ideological and normative function (Pantelidou-Malouta 2010). Engendering the crisis has been a central question in the conferences "Women, Gender Equality and Economic Crisis" (Panteion University 2011), "Gender in the Crisis: the Impact and the Way Forward in Greece" (Friedrich Ebert Foundation Athens 2013), but has also appeared as a topic in other crisis-themed conferences such as "Transformations of Space in the Greek Crisis" (University of Thessaly 2013), "Crisis-Scapes: Athens and Beyond" (Athens Polytechnic 2014), "Social Inequalities in Europe" (General Secretariat for Research and Technology 2014).

Nonetheless, as Alexandra Bakalaki (2015) points out, debates deploying a feminist and gendered analysis of the crisis are still quite limited, and certainly not hegemonic in academic, or public, discourse. This point has also been raised early on by Avdela, who contends, "The crisis tends to naturalize gender and render it invisible" (Avdela 2011: 20). In the next section I will consider some of the implications of this omission of gender and what its application can bring to light.

Interrogations

Following Avdela's challenging and inspiring injunction to use the critical potential of gender as an analytical category, I will briefly outline some dimensions for interrogating what we might call the gendered architecture of crisis, and will proceed to discuss some of them as they manifest in the Greek case. In doing so I take gender not only as an index of social difference/inequality and a signifier of power relations, but also as a technology of the self and a discursive modality.

Gender and Economy

Feminists have asserted that any anti-austerity discourse that does not address women's subordination and oppression as an integral and systemic aspect of the crisis is, effectively, complicit with the very same structures of oppression, domination, and exploitation it seeks to change, and therefore can never become truly subversive and emancipatory. As Sylvia Walby maintained in her 2009 report to the UN Charter on Women's Rights,[11] the global financial and economic crisis is gendered in its causes, its effects, and, importantly, in the proposed reforms as well. In the Greek case we have seen that women are rendered—economically but also symbolically—expendable reserves in the labor market and principal care-providers, and are reconfined to the home and the private sphere, a situation that confirms Walby's earlier conclusions.

However, as Lisa Adkins (2015) contends, such feminist common sense rests on a number of assumptions: that the current (global) socioeconomic crisis intensifies and extends already existing inequalities, therefore it is "continuous with longer-term processes" (34); that socioeconomic inequalities are tied to resources and their distribution, and therefore that access to resources is a measure of inequality; that a redistributive model of justice can address this situation and serve as an alternative to austerity. The resources most commonly identified are money, income, wages, and public goods and services, but the capacities of these resources in the present crisis are left unexamined. Thus, it is assumed that if women can have access to more of these resources, other social goods such as autonomy, independence, control, and choice will be once again secured. For many European feminists, the way to claim such resources is by remembering the struggles and demands made by the feminist movement of an earlier era, a position evident in Greek feminists' responses also (e.g., Karamessini 2012; Vougioukas 2013). For Adkins, however, it is necessary to take into account changes in global financial restructuring, which have made debt, rather than needs, the defining factor in securing both wages and rights.

For Dina Vaiou, there are clear links between crisis, austerity, and neoliberalism; Greece being one of the laboratories of new and intensified attacks on labor, social rights and the equitable distribution of resources.

> One of the targets of austerity programmes to overcome the crisis, in line with the neoliberal repertoire of deregulation and downsizing of the state, seems to be the social model that has developed in different and unequal ways in Southern Europe over the postwar decades. Although this model was never fully developed in Greece, the Greek economy is rather small and peripheral in the European Union (EU) and in this sense an easier site for neoliberal experimentation on a number of frontal attacks: to demolish whatever there is of a welfare state, to attack the public sector, to abolish workers' rights, pension systems, wages and salaries, to marginalise democratic institutions and even to challenge national sovereignty. (Vaiou 2014a: 2)

Gender and Democracy

Maro Pantelidou-Malouta (2013) elaborates that the current crisis, rendered as a primarily economic crisis, a failure of fiscal and monetary policy, is in essence and in effect a crisis of democracy, hence a crisis of rights and equality. The erosion of democracy is endemic to neoliberalism and preexists the crisis, as well as precipitates it, even as it remains largely unquestioned especially in the enforcement of austerity policies and the demolition of the welfare state in favor of across-the-board privatization of the public good and public resources.[12] As Athina Athanasiou (2012) argues, the discursive-ideological construction of the crisis as an exceptional condition, rather than a continuation and intensification of conditions of violent inequality and dispossession brought on by neoliberal capitalism, not only normalizes the very same system that produces the crisis, but also legitimizes regimes of neoliberal governing through crisis management. She urges us to approach the crisis through the Foucauldian notion of a history of the present—in other words to historicize it, attending to the role gender plays in legitimizing or undoing this history.

The crisis, therefore, according to Pantelidou-Malouta (2013), must be understood as a political, ethical, and normative crisis as well as a crisis of socioeconomic reproduction; in this sense, women's rights and gender equality cannot but represent fundamental and constitutive claims for a democratic politics and a new and different vision of society that is forged out of the crisis. In this sense, also, gender represents a critical analytical lens as well as a fundamental political stake—not subservient to the economy or to class modalities of inequality, but central to any conception of justice and collective as well as individual well-being. Failure to interrogate the preexisting and pervasive relations of domination and exploitation that condition the crisis, as well as failure to integrate a gendered critique of naturalized and hierarchically ordered relations of power, results in the sense of "lack of alternatives [and] hopelessness" so pervasive in the current sociopolitical climate (Pantelidou-Malouta 2013: 14).

Gender and Nation

A discursive and gendered analysis of the crisis looks at normalized and abject subject positions, and the performativity of gender in the context of the perceived threat of national extinction. The signifying connections between aggressive manhood, injured pride, foreign-imposed socioeconomic sanctions, and national subordination, different versions of which dominate narratives of the crisis in public discourse. Their political and everyday expressions (such as the electoral rise and entry into parliament of the far-right Golden Dawn party, and the parallel rise in assaults against immigrants and homosexuals) have been discussed in a number of articles (Athanasiou 2014; Avdela 2011; Halkias 2012). Such accounts have come to discursively legitimize racist and xenophobic violence, which escalated in the aftermath of the successive austerity programs and ensuing socioeconomic deprivation, variously attributed to German and eurozone neoliberal authoritarianism as well as illegal migration and depletion of state resources (Carastathis 2015). At the same time, however, accounts of national emasculation have also come to reinforce a less extreme but nonetheless pervasive and preexisting masculinist, heterosexist nationalism that has been a staple feature of contemporary political culture in Greece, in both its right- and left-wing expressions (Athanasatou 2013; Pantelidou-Malouta 2013).[13] It is in the context of such reasserted, hegemonic masculinism that the observed regression of gender relations in public and private life needs to be analyzed and feminist critiques and resistances need to be put forth.

The ideological interrelation between gender and nation, already theorized at length by feminist scholars (Halkias 2004; Yuval-Davis 1996), needs to be rethought in the context of neoliberal crisis and austerity regimes and the resistances they engender (Brah, Szeman, and Gedalof 2015).[14] Alexandra Halkias (2012), reflecting on the December 2008 revolt and subsequent mass mobilizations, argues, "Both the patriarchal nation-state and capital are under attack, and the constitutive weakness that binds them becomes ever more visible. The nation's 'inability to pay,' in tandem with the employer's, or the family man's, marks a kind of feminization of the heretofore almighty 'father'" (Halkias 2012: 235). In other words, as Dimitrios Theodossopoulos (2014) also points out in his discussion of local indignation, loss of sovereignty in economic policy leads to a "defensive nationalism" (Theodossopoulos 2014: 489). Thus, one of the questions that needs to be asked is how structural changes in the makeup and function of the neoliberal nation-state brought about by capitalist globalization and deregulation (Brown 2015b; Sassen 2014) are ideologically represented, how subjects are interpellated (as victims, guilty perpetrators, deserving bailout recipients, unruly subjects, lazy and incompetent loafers) and whether the gender/nation nexus is reiterated, and possibly resisted. For example, debates on the changing forms and content of citizenship still stress the unabated importance of nation-state membership in the recognition of rights and entitlements, even if the nation-state is not the only significant unit and scale of belonging any longer. In this sense, national identity (with its gendered and sexualized normativities and exclusions) not only remains a salient rallying point, but it also even seems to be gaining force and solidifying around ever more exclusionary and violent narratives, as recent European racist and anti-immigrant reactions illustrate (Feischmidt and Hervik 2015).

Indeed, Anna Carastathis (2015) examines eruptions of gendered and racialized violence against migrants—the acid attack on Bulgarian laborer and union organizer Konstantina Kouneva, the murder of Pakistani laborer Shehzad Luqman, and the drowning of eleven Afghan and Syrian refugees during a coast guard pushback operation at Farmakonisi Island — in order to argue that such acts of hostility seek to reaffirm the supremacy of masculinist, heteropatriarchal nationalist identity, and are legitimized precisely through reference to the wounds suffered by foreign-imposed austerity politics.[15] Closely linked to the affective economy of hostility are the imputed moral dimensions of the crisis, the association of economic collapse with state and moral corruption, a discourse that bears clear gender significations. As Carastathis claims, "'Austerity' is constructed as a measured response of prudent economic policy, or as the duty of a responsible citizenry during national financial crisis, in which the 'sole alternative' is 'severe self-discipline or self-restraint; moral strictness, rigorous abstinence, asceticism.' . . . It is constructed as a responsible moral choice — whether for undisciplined individuals; excessive, indulgent social bodies; or fiscally irresponsible 'piggish' states" (Carastathis 2015: 74).

Gender and Social Change

Against the dominant ideological canon that renders gender invisible in the context of the crisis, gender needs to become a foundational perspective for critical analysis and social mobilization. Looking at the social spaces, practices, and discourses of resistance that emerged in reaction to the crisis, the question that comes to mind is whether particular kinds of resistances and responses carry different gendered dynamics and resonances. In other words, it is relevant here to consider whether mass mobilizations in the public sphere engender a different gender discourse and gender politics, or if they, once again, marginalize women and other non-normative social positionalities (Kaika and Karaliotas 2016), and whether, in contrast, smaller-scale and more locally focused solidarity initiatives allow for different relationalities to come forth (Arampatzi 2017; Rakopoulos 2015). And, if this is the case, what does it mean once again for a feminist critique of the public/private divide? As such, mass mobilizations, revolts, and practices of contestation appear to carry the (indelible) imprint of hegemonic leftist masculinity (Soula 2011). Indeed, as Alexandra Halkias (2016) more recently observes, in relation to the rise to power of SYRIZA and the change of guard in government, masculinities might be shifting from the fatherly and stately postures of older political leaders, to a more youthful, trendy, and irreverent style; even so, however, they are still imbued with a certain machismo.

Therefore, the main question that will frame the next part of the paper is whether, in the context of the crisis, renegotiations of gendered subjectivities are taking place, and, if so, what form they assume.

Examples

In order to explore responses to the crisis as practices of gendered subjectification, I look at social enterprises initiated and run by women in the past couple of years, in quite different social locations. I describe the initiatives in brief, drawing on their own (published and oral) accounts, and subsequently consider what issues such endeavors raise in terms of dealing with the crisis, as well as engendering a different politics of self and solidarity. In doing so, I take into account the danger of creating a narrative of success stories, rendering women's hardship invisible. It is therefore necessary to walk a fine line between acknowledging the detrimental effects and probing the possibilities that a feminist or women-centered approach might introduce.

Such social enterprises have been discussed in terms of the growth of a solidarity and social economy, including both new collective and cooperativist forms of economic activity (Social Cooperative Enterprise, or KOINSEP)[16] as well as of the rise of nongovernmental organizations (NGOs) and their role in substituting the welfare state, but also as a form of increased engagement and reactivation of civil society actors concerned with the commons (Agelopoulos 2013; Rakopoulos 2014; Vaiou and Kalandides 2017).

The three examples discussed next should not be considered as representative but only as indicative cases of social enterprises; they were chosen in terms of their diversity in order to illustrate different trends, especially with regard to the foregrounding, as well as intersection, of gendered, sexual, cultural, and ethnicized identities in the construction of economic and/or sociopolitical alternatives.

Beaver: A Queer Collective-Bar by Women Activists

"In January 2012 we had a spontaneous idea about the creation of a space run by women, that would be open to people and groups who find it otherwise difficult to "belong" somewhere, and that would be also a fun hangout for us to meet. It was that concept that brought all of us together and finally came to fruition in September 2013."[17]

As the collective explains on its Facebook page, setting up a queer space was the result of a long process of activism, critique, and dreaming, mixing together gender and sexual politics, friendship, and work, transformed in the context of the crisis:

> Some of us were old friends, some of us knew each other from participating in
> the same feminist political movements and had met through these initiatives,

and some of us played basketball together! Whether acquainted or not, we all shared a common point of view about the ways in which we (don't) want to see labor, class and gender relations be formed and acted out. Our primary aim was to build a non-oppressive work and meeting environment, free from hierarchies, and with a clear focus on the quality of working time and social efficiency of our services. Particularly, a space designed for women, who in this time of economic crisis are becoming increasingly vulnerable to labor and other kinds of exploitation.

As one of the few queer spaces in Athens, Beaver certainly captures a niche market and has a steady and dedicated clientele that uses the space for entertainment as well as for a social hub. The collective's explicitly endorses a nondiscriminatory policy in its open-access Facebook statement: "Our cooperative's, and especially beaver's principle and priority is to ensure practical and essential access to all population groups regardless of their social or physical characteristics," provides a (novel for Greece) social and ideological reference that attracts a younger generation concerned with issues of social justice not only in the abstract but in everyday life as well.

Initiatives such as this one come under the category of employment collectives and, as Vaiou and Kalandides (2017) argue, can be located somewhere between resilience and social innovation practices, combining livelihood activities with prefigurations of an alternative future. As the collective itself states on its Facebook page, "After all, creating and running such projects all around the world means advocating precisely this: the de-education from the capitalist mode of labor relations and the cultivation of solidarity, comradeship and mutual understanding, as opposed to individualism, the rationalism of achieving maximum individual benefit, and individual solutions. And finally, the need of creating horizontal networks of cooperation, of abolishing the misconceived notion of competitiveness, steering clear from the concept of masters/bosses and other similar calamities."

The cafe was set up as a KOINSEP, a new, tax-light, legal form for small business ventures that attempts to introduce business models that are more horizontal, and to help reignite small-scale commerce and services. However, the collective stresses the collective rather than the business side of things, and the importance of fairness vis-à-vis both producers and consumers, who are renamed participants in a network of exchange relations characterized by greater social, economic and ecological justice. As mentioned on their Facebook page, "In regards to supplying beaver with the necessary products, our aim is to create a network of suppliers on the basis of product quality, an equitable and sustainable relation between quality and cost, and a cooperative model of economic exchange, which will enable the offer of products and services on the lowest possible price. Our basic principle is to treat the recipients of our services as collaborators in the production process and not just mere consumers/customers." The idea of customers-as-collaborators, which displaces the common consumer identity one assumes in the public sphere, speaks to an anticapitalist and anti-neoliberal politics, as well as to a feminist ethic of participation, cooperation, and active engagement in producing the commons.

The cafe consists of a high-ceilinged single-room ground-floor space—previously a grocery—and a covered sidewalk with tables in front. The space was renovated by the women themselves and combines an industrial with an unfinished, do-it-yourself look, with mismatched tables and chairs, and odd assortments of plates and glasses, some of which came from the women's own homes. The menu offers beverages, drinks, sweets, and light meals prepared on the premises. The space and the service have a certain youthful, amateurish flair. The cafe also organizes public events, discussions, film screenings, DJ nights, and other cultural and solidarity activities.

A year into the enterprise, Beaver has managed to pay off all start-up costs and, while still supporting the wages of five workers, has started making a small margin of profit. Making a modest living through such an enterprise is an important but labor-intensive effort since, in addition to daily working hours, time and energy are also taken up in collective decision making and programing, an integral part of the initiative's identity and work-politics. Having set a clear goal not to incur debt, they are particularly proud of their debt-free record, something that also distinguishes them from other such experiments that, as they comment, are heavily in debt, and cannot keep "tidy books." For them it is a matter of pride and principle to keep finances in good order. This does raise some questions as far as gendered notions of tidiness, orderliness, and the successful management of household finances goes. Along with the concern to offer good service and keep the customer pleased, which again links to gendered notions of service and pleasing others, questions arise as to whether such notions can be reiterated in ways that displace them from their original ideological function.

Another important aspect of the enterprise relates to the issue of visibility and spatialization of gender and sexuality. Gazi, the neighborhood where the cafe is set up, has been associated with a new, more youthful, entertainment scene in Athens, and, notably, a gay-friendly city area, much like so-called gay villages in other European cities. In this sense, Beaver is continuing the growing trend of developing services catering to a gay clientele but at the same is also changing it by introducing new work-practices that depart from usual profit-making market rationalities.

It can therefore be considered both a social and a business experiment, in terms of its labor and identity politics.

Exi Okades Ki Ena Drami: A Collective Delicatessen-bakaliko by a Group of Mothers[18]

"The collective effort of a group of women for a grocery store that believes in produce from the Greek land and in fair trade."[19]

As their founding story goes, a group of five mothers, who met at the parents' association of their children's school in the Athenian neighborhood of Holargos, and who, as they like to joke, graduated from primary school together, decided to cooperate and open a store that would "sell good food products [because] as mothers, quality food and cooking are among our keen interests."

The opening statement on their Facebook page reads, "'*Six okades and one drami*' was created in order to find and showcase good produce from the Greek earth, and elsewhere, that come from good producers and good people. To introduce them to the younger generations and remind them to the olders. On this journey we look for fellow travelers. 'Six okades and one drami' are open and waiting for you."

In search for ways to enhance their families' incomes, their idea to open a grocery in their own neighborhood where they were well known and people would trust them, offering selected food items (eggs, dairy products, wine, hams, pasta, and legumes) from small producers all over Greece, tapped into a more general trend toward supporting Greek products to help the failing economy. Such local products have long been considered of higher quality than mass-produced goods offered in supermarkets, and capture also a taste for local specialties that many Greeks share. The idea of celebrating a Greek cuisine, also promoted on numerous food shows on Greek TV, combines notions of authenticity, tradition, and purity, which locally produced food is supposed to incorporate, with fashionable cultural culinary practices presenting a new kind of stylish domesticity that Greek women can aspire to and take pride in, with nothing to envy from their counterparts in the rest of Europe.[20]

The grocery was set up in a spacious ground-floor store with a large garden in front, where people can hang out. It is furnished with large shelves and old and modern furniture mixed together. As the women explain, it took them five months to get it up and running, since they had to rely on their own work and limited resources; they did not want to get a bank loan or go into debt. They stress that it is founded on friendship, trust, and relying on each other. The sense of intimacy that they share is projected outward, since the store invites its customers and friends to drop by for coffee and treats, as well as for heart-to-heart talks, becoming a kind of neighborhood hub. The store also maintains a Facebook page where the women publish daily recipes, food and nutrition tips, and seasonal stories of an informative and entertaining character, as well articles on environmental issues and ethical consumption.

Thus, it is not uncommon to come across references to traditional Greek values together with discussions of more Western movements such as fairtrade and global food justice. Indeed, the grocery seeks to function not only as a food market but also as a social center, engaging in various solidarity and awareness raising actions, such as gathering and distributing food to refugees, women's shelters, and pauperized neighbors. For example, the grocery participates in a crisis-inspired food-in-waiting initiative, where customers that are more well-off can buy food credits for those in need, to be cashed in at the store. It also liaises with other newly formed food cooperatives around Athens to organize discussions with invited guests, or parties for livening up the neighborhood.

As the title "From Mothers to Grocers" of a showcase article in the culinary section of the daily newspaper *Kathimerini* illustrates (Karapiperi 2015), the articulation of traditional female roles with activities that are more entrepreneurial, such as running a grocery store, is desirable and saluted. Indeed, the nexus of motherhood and good business practice seems to exalt both, constituting a kind of affective economy of food. Food is invested not only with nutritional value, but also with care, healing, and loving properties. To prepare a good meal with pure Greek raw materials, from equally pure and ethical small Greek producers, is the highest value a mother can offer her family and, most importantly, her children, the future generation. At the same time, while being an exemplary mother, she can also contribute to the family's financial well-being. "Doing business with pleasure" is possible and effective, the message seems to be.

Along with love, pride is another key affect in this culinary economy. As the article (Karapiperi 2015) commends, "They discovered the produce one by one, know them well, and speak about them with 'love and pride.'" The individualized attention to each produce is reminiscent of the kind of loving and proud attention mothers give to their children, and we assume, by extension, to their customers. A chain of investments takes shape: one feels pride in Greek food and cooking, in being a good mother, in being a good neighbor and a good person, a responsible businesswoman, and an ethical consumer and humanitarian citizen. Memory as nostalgia for the good life, also invested with ethical and affective value, serves as the motivating factor. As the women explain on their Facebook page, "*Six okades and one drami* is a grocery store that a group of women friends from Holargos dreamed of and set up, in a *nostalgic mood,* with main goals in life good food, good company and faith in collective efforts" (my italics). The reinvention of tradition around (romanticized and essentialized) notions of food, care, and community, exemplified in this new entrepreneurship, comes to form the recipe for overcoming the crisis.

Of the many issues regarding the cultural politics of gender, nation, and crisis such an enterprise raises, I will consider briefly the questions of hybridity and class. The particular ideological contours of this new entrepreneurship seem to combine contrasting positions between what are considered old and new, and local and foreign practices; traditional and contemporary life styles and roles; as well as business strategy and social engagement. In this sense, it could be understood as a kind of historically and culturally situated hybridity that mixes heteropatriarchal gender subjectification with new discursive interpellations around ethical consumption and solidarity economies. In this sense, it does not break with mainstream gender roles, but supplies them with additional topical content that enhances their cultural capital. At the same time, the class dimension of this kind of gendered entrepreneurialism is to be noted as well, manifesting as an aspect of the specific, lower- and middle-class neighborhood to which the initiative addresses itself. Both the identities of traditional mother and grocer, as well as notions of good food and good company, or good people, bear popular working-class connotations and histories. In this case, it is the projection of these identities onto both local and global concerns that could account for its growing success.

Melissa: A Network of Migrant and Greek Women Activists

"Melissa is a network of migrant women in Greece, promoting empowerment, communication and active citizenship."[21]

Melissa (meaning "bee" in Greek) is a network founded in September 2014 as a civil society umbrella organization bringing together several preexisting migrant women's groups, and individual migrant women, who wished to consolidate and collectivize their action on migration and integration politics in Greece. As mentioned on their Facebook page, "This shows the great desire of migrant women to become socially active. Many of the women who came were already engaged in social activism, but there were others who had never spoken in front of an audience. It was very important to witness women take the stand and with trembling voice claim their active participation in society. This gave us a lot of strength, and thus we managed to set up this initiative."

The network is multicultural; its founding members include six women from Albania, Greece, Nigeria, the Philippines, Russia, and Zimbabwe. As Nadina Christopoulou, its acting director, remarks, "In the first meeting more than 100 women attended from over 30 countries" (quoted in Chondrogiannos 2015). It also seeks to establish an international profile, linking with international NGOs (such as Humanity in Action and the Asian Development Bank), international and European volunteer groups, as well as securing funding from abroad, and in this sense it is not by chance that it was one of the venues visited by Secretary of State John Kerry on his visit to Greece in December 2015.[22] Some of its founding members also participate as grassroots members in international institutions such as the United Nations High Commissioner for Human Rights.

Melissa was set up in an old neoclassical building in the center of Athens, near Omonoia Square, which used to be the headquarters of the Greek Forum of Migrants. Reusing a space already associated with migrant activism establishes a sense of continuity: it is an address that is well-known known to migrant and Greek activists. Volunteers have renovated the rooms, which convey an atmosphere of airy, colorful coziness, a marked departure from the types of spaces commonly encountered in social movement settings. In fact, the ambience of the space matches to some extent the activities of the organization, which, although multifarious, center on providing what might be coded as "nurture," rather than on spearheading political campaigns and mass mobilizations, as activist antiracist groups usually do.

So, for example, in September 2015, during one of the first refugee occupations in Athens, a group of women from the organization set up a volunteer kitchen to prepare daily breakfast meals for the refugee children squatting in the nearby square. As the women in the group explained, they believed they had to offer care and support to those in need, having themselves experienced suffering and displacement. "These people are experiencing great difficulty. We thought it was important to help, even if it's only a little. We decided to offer the children the breakfast they didn't have. As migrant women we know firsthand the difficulties they are facing. We are mothers and we know we cannot abandon them without help. We had to do something" (Maria Ohilebo quoted in Chondrogiannos 2015). Here, it is more about practicing antiracism as a living-and-working-together project, as an expression of sociality and care, rather than as part of a distinct political program. Therefore, while engaging in what has been termed "participatory politics" (usually associated with grassroots activism or active citizenship), this action is not politicized in the strict sense; rather, it is claimed as a "politics of care," as one of their Facebook posts quoting Audre Lord suggests.[23]

Today, the network's activities expand to further areas of solidarity and empowerment, including projects such as the backpack-for-the-road initiative (providing backpacks with essentials for refugee children to carry on their way to other European destinations), Greek language classes, yoga, psychodrama, individual psychological support, knitting and storytelling evenings, gospel choir practice, African dance classes, web-radio workshops, and leadership development seminars. The network tries to develop social interventions that incorporate artistic and cultural activities aimed at empowerment, training, and networking, in a celebratory spirit. In this sense, it moves away from more-traditional antiracist mobilizations or migrant integration advocacy, toward human rights/active citizenship approaches. An important part of Melissa's work is fundraising, as well as liaising with various Greek public agencies and private organizations, and keeping up a presence in the Greek and international press (e.g., Al Jazeera) and on social media, in order to promote social visibility and secure donations.

I am not able here to further analyze this network from an organizational perspective, but I will pose some questions on intersectionality and citizenship from a feminist perspective. "Active citizenship," a term used explicitly on Melissa's Facebook page, is invoked as a form of civic engagement that can foster social inclusion at the level of civil society. "Melissa is a network for migrant women living in Greece. It aims to strengthen the bonds among them, to promote empowerment and active citizenship, and to build a bridge of communication with the host society." As such, active citizenship does not reference antagonistic politics that mobilize struggles for institutional change, as antiracist discourse in Greece often does (Zavos 2010), but rather reinscribes migrant women's activism and activities as practices of participation. Active citizenship is, hence, a form of integration from below that can lead to a sense of pluralist belonging, in spite of strict and exclusionary migration policies. In this sense, the identity and work of the network is defined as "networking, advocacy and capacity building," a vocabulary that draws more on development than on social movement discourse and, thereby also, shifts the ideological premise of migration politics in Greece.

The group is represented as "different (migrant and Greek) women who want to work together on migrant women's and children's rights from a feminist approach," therefore empowerment integrates both migrant and feminist aims. In this respect, it is important to consider the multiple axes of discrimination that the women in the organization face, including sexism, racialization, and minoritization. These experiences are tied up with issues of citizenship and rights, which are still unresolved for most of its members. "It's just that they kill your dreams here. I don't know why it is so difficult to get to your goal. I feel like I am in this country, and I am still in a shell trying to come out. And I can't see myself coming out," says Jessica Anosike in an interview for Al Jazeera (quoted in Psaropoulos 2015).

Or as Beata Pastor, interviewed about the new nationality code, remarks, "I was born here. I live here. I go to school here. I know the language, I know how to read and write, I can communicate here. My friends are here. I lived here all my life. Whatever a Greek has gone through, I have been through. Not really part of this society in papers. But I feel I belong to this society" (quoted in Psaropoulos 2015). When speaking out about their experiences in public they are often represented as volunteers from the network Melissa, which means that participating in the organization gives them not only a community to belong to, but also a public status.

The identity of the network, while antidiscriminatory, still poses questions both with regard to the complex power relations such a heterogeneous group of women must negotiate, internally and externally, and as concerns the professionalization of solidarity and care that advocacy work entails.[24] However, the air of novelty and the aspirational global outlook that Melissa projects also contrasts with the sense of closure and staleness that Greek politics and public life otherwise exude. Melissa therefore presents an attractive alternative for migrant women who are themselves, in a sense, the living subjects of the invoked globalization.

Conclusion

Looking at all three examples together, I will draw out and discuss some shared aspects, looking for possible underlying dispositions. One of the senses that comes through is that spaces of work need to be spaces of sociality as well; business needs to integrate a sense of intimacy and coziness. Along with this, the sense that people need to feel they are contributing or doing politics through their everyday life, not as an exceptional or external engagement. Whether this is neoliberal rationality rewriting politics as lifestyle or a radical shift is a question for debate (Brown 2015a). Finally, considering the reinvention of traditional roles, such as motherhood, as entrepreneurship or activism begs the question: is this the uncanny return of the familiar or a chance for change?

In all three cases, it is women between the ages of thirty and fifty who are starting up something new, having worked either in the same field of employment or in other jobs. In this sense, the enterprises build on already existing professional experience of some kind. It is perhaps because of this, also, that all three groups refuse to incur debt, but also appreciate and prioritize the value of working collectively. Age, and the turmoil of crisis, also combine toward a sense of timing; it is the right moment to try something new. Crisis, though present, is not a dominant narrative for their endeavors; rather, it forms the background—and trigger—against

which the sense of this being the right moment ripens. Under other circumstances, perhaps the impetus for embarking on such an experiment
would not gather. Friendships are important, even a key component, to
all three cases. They form the ground on which relationships of trust and
affection can be mobilized into more-demanding undertakings, offering
at the same time a sense of intimacy and support to face the difficulties
of bringing their dreams to life and sustaining them. Identities are also
a dominant motif, whether referencing sexuality, motherhood, or migration. Identities are both connecting tissue as well as a recognizable face
that addresses itself to specific publics. Scale is another important factor.
In the case of the Exi Okades ki Ena Drami grocery and Beaver, the neighborhood is a defining circumstance, either because of the networks it en-
ables, or because of the cultural and class profile it establishes. Finally,
all three cases can be regarded as examples of hybrid cultural-economic
practices that straddle different, sometimes competing, ideological interpellations. As such, then, they raise interesting political questions, such as
whether they reproduce traditional heteropatriarchal norms or displace
them, whether they collude with lifestyle neoliberalism or undermine it,
whether they operationalize neoliberal governance or resist it, that cannot
be conclusively answered because their hybrid character itself precludes
conceptual closure. Finally, all three examples entertain some form of nur-
turing that might be gender-role related but might also be connected to
the crisis and the inflated need for care it engenders.

In closing, I return to my opening thoughts and ask myself if writing
this chapter has given me a different perspective on the crisis and my experience of it. Crisis raises issues about knowledge politics and the role of
the university in critiquing and challenging old and changing regimes of
gender and power. As feminist teachers and researchers, are we uphold-
ing a defunct system or resisting and subverting it? As with many other
public institutions, severe financial cuts and austerity politics impact the
function and reproduction of the university, which in the end survives
more through the personal commitment of its servants, rather than any
state policy, the master of arts degree (MA) in gender studies being a case
in point. At the same time, it is clear that old institutions are in crisis, and
people need more-flexible and more-companionable spaces and ways of
working together. As the students of the newly founded MA in gender
studies indicate, it is issues of sexuality and social justice—rather than
traditional politics—that engage and motivate a younger generation that
is growing into adulthood in the middle of the crisis. The choice to pursue gender studies is often discussed as a moment of choosing personal
autonomy and a space of freedom, also freedom from familial and societal expectations, especially in the context of the crisis where strong fears

about the future make every choice not only matter, but also seem irrevocable; each choice needs to be economically rationalized and justified. Politics for these students might be less external and more embodied, molecular—an affective disposition rather than a set of imperatives. Where do I/we meet with others in such initiatives? Do paths cross? What happens when they do?

Alexandra Zavos obtained her doctoral degree in 2010 from the Department of Psychology, Manchester Metropolitan University. Her work focuses on gender and migration in Greece and Southern Europe, with a special emphasis on migrant women's citizenship claims and practices in the context of social movements and integration politics. She is affiliated with the Center for Gender Studies at Panteion University and has worked as researcher on the European-funded projects GEMIC and MIG@ NET, as well as the research and training project Universities Supporting Victims of Sexual Violence (USVSV). She teaches sociology of gender at the University of Crete. Some of her research has been published in the *Annual Review of Critical Psychology* (2008, 2017); in *Qualitative Research in Psychology* (2009, with Barbara Biglia); and in *Feminist Review* (2010, with Helen Kambouri). She has contributed book chapters to the edited collections *The Gender of Migration* (in Greek) (Metaixmio, 2009), *Gender and Migration: Feminist Perspectives, Political Interventions* (Zed, 2010), *Feminism and Migration: Cross-Cultural Engagements* (Springer, 2012), *Immigrant Protest* (SUNY Press, 2014), and has coedited the book *Gender, Migration, Interculturalism* (in Greek) (Nissos, 2013). More recently, she coedited the special issue, "Changing Landscapes of Urban Citizenship: Southern Europe in Times of Crisis" of the journal *Citizenship Studies* (2017, with Penny Koutrolikou and Dimitra Siatitsa).

Notes

1. The notion of "pathologized presence/normalized absence" coined by Ann Phoenix (1990: 91), refers to racialized and gendered exclusions of nonnormative subjectivities from research. I will argue here that in the context of the crisis, but also more broadly, gender is precisely one of those nonnormative categories of analysis that easily disappears from public as well as academic discourse, especially when it is the politics and sovereignty of the nation itself that is at stake.
2. Maria Tamboukou (2012) uses the Foucauldian notion of parrhesia, speaking truth to power, to ask what it means for academics in dark times, such as these, to undertake the risky practice of truth-telling. A gendered and feminist analysis of the Greek crisis

does not only document, but also seeks to intervene in how it is represented, lived, and resisted. As Giorgos Agelopoulos (2013) notes, it is necessary to question the metaphysics of crisis or, in other words, to question how the crisis reified and naturalized and, importantly, how it affects different subjects differently.

3. See, for example, the workshop organized by the Nikos Poulantzas Institute on the Democratic University of the 21st Century (12 May 2016).

4. My understanding of neoliberalism is informed by Wendy Brown's conceptualization of neoliberal rationality, which pervades all aspects of our social, economic, political and cultural worlds, put forth in her recent book *Undoing the Demos* (2015b). As I cannot here elaborate at greater length, I quote from an interview in the Greek newspaper *Avgi*, "Neoliberalism is not just an economic policy, but a whole governing rationality through which we are ruled, both as regards the state, as well as in schools, prisons, social services and workplaces. Neoliberalism reconstructs the social sphere, social relations and the person in the model of the market; therefore, it reconstructs political life, the state, and democracy as well. As Thatcher had said: "Economics is a method, the goal is to change the soul." Therefore, "responsibilization," "incentivization" and a whole series of "good practices," which are widespread in schools, hospitals, workplaces and governments are transformed into tools of neoliberal political rationality" (Brown 2015a). In this sense, the academy is also rendered neoliberal through the flexibilization of intellectual labor and the transformation of the academic into a manager of personal resources. In her own words, "Above all, it casts people as human capital who must constantly tend to their own present and future value" (Brown 2015a).

5. The politics of social innovation and resilience are controversial since they can be inscribed both as neoliberal notions of resourceful individualism (those who float and those who drown), as well as anti-systemic solidarity alternatives (Fainstein 2015; Vaiou and Kalandides 2017).

6. Overall female unemployment in Greece reached 29.7 percent at the end of 2012 (Karamessini and Koutentakis 2014); unemployment rates for young women (aged 20–29) were significantly higher, reaching 48.2 percent for the same period (Anastasiou, Filippidis, and Stergiou 2015).

7. According to Karamessini and Rubbery (2014) and others (Tsiganou 2014), the reversal of labor status between men and women that occurred in the first years of the crisis—male unemployment rose more than female, and men's wages shrunk closer to women's already low levels—did not, in fact, signify improvement in women's labor position, but, rather, an overall attack on labor, men's labor included. Indeed, as the authors argue, an unseen effect of crisis and austerity is the widespread use of women's, including migrant women's, undocumented and/or unpaid labor; that labor falls outside state regulation and is, hence, vulnerable to high levels of exploitation and abuse.

8. In addition, loss of family income renders migrant women's domestic services unaffordable; Greek women's entry into the labor market over the past three decades depended on those services, further curtailing their capacity in seeking paid employment.

9. "The Greek Police report that when the economy began to collapse in 2009 they observed an alarming increase in cases of domestic violence. In comparison with previous years, domestic violence was up 53.9 percent in 2011 and 22.2 percent in 2012. Ten women were murdered by an intimate partner in 2011, five in 2012, and eight in 2013" (Svarna 2014).

10. As Maria Stratigaki (2013) points out, the introduction of gender mainstreaming policies in Greece has been slow, well behind other European countries, and has been further hampered by the economic crisis.

11. "The impact of the financial and consequent economic crisis is gendered. This gendering is linked to gender differentiated, segregated/segmented sectors of the economy with boundaries constructed by a mix of structural capacities and discrimination:

(formal paid/informal/family worker/domestic care-work), with different levels of gendered control over resources that are intricately related to gendered cause and gendered consequence. The financial and economic crisis has detrimental consequences for women's human rights as well as for gender equality, poverty and human and economic development" (Walby 2009: 27).

12. According to Pantelidou-Malouta, "The search for the deeper reasons for the current socio-economic and financial crisis, which quickly transformed, because of the way it was managed, into an obviously political one, as well as a crisis of democracy, is not encouraged. The invoked reasons point to blaming the victims. (...) Hence, even though the current crisis pertains to the historical core of the relationship between economy and politics and even though it only enlarges and worsens the odious components of the neoliberal worldview, it does not lead to a wholesale rejection of the existing system" (Pantelidou-Malouta 2013: 11–12, my translation). Regarding the crisis of democracy, Nancy Fraser (2016) points out that, "increasingly, even if you have states that claim or would like to be genuinely responsive to their citizens (which is not always the case, obviously), even in the best case scenario, such states increasingly lack the capacity to implement policies that their own citizens might demand of them, or might look for. That's one aspect of the crisis of democracy" (Fraser 2016: 7). And according to Wendy Brown (2015b) "From the moment the neoliberal vision organises every activity in the logic of the market, assuming each person acts solely on economic criteria, democracy cannot survive. The power of the people depends on popular sovereignty, and this in turn on the equal access to political power. Markets have no use for popular sovereignty or equality; they are organized on the basis of antagonism, winners and losers, and powers that are not subjected to any control. Consequently, when the principles of the market prevail in political life, not only do they erode democracy, they plunder its meaning and attack its very value. Neoliberalism regards the markets as the ultimate value; this is war against democracy."

13. Recent research on Golden Dawn discourse highlights the intersection of gender and nationalism, and the resurgence of antifeminist positions that regard motherhood and family as the appropriate and pivotal roles for women, who (should) wish to serve the nation/fatherland. In their Women's Front website, for example, women are interpellated as mothers of the nation. Feminism and equality are seen as unpatriotic, not only because they are Western but, mainly, because they (mis)lead women and threaten the biological and cultural reproduction of the nation (Psarra 2014). This point is also raised by Karpozilos (chapter 4 this volume), who argues, "The creation of the White Women Front underlined the effort of Golden Dawn to counter its male-dominated image and to promote a renewed nationalist gender agenda that focused on women as 'mothers of the nation [who] ought to safeguard our Race and the future of our children'" (84).

14. Phoenix et al. in their editorial to the Feminist Review Special Issue on "The Politics of Austerity" note, "We were interested in exploring the ways in which the global ascendance of neo-liberal policies and discourses is enmeshed with the crisis in global capitalism, and how divides of class, gender, race, ethnicity, sexuality and disability are being exacerbated at local, regional and global levels in the neo-liberal response to the crisis. We asked what a feminist response to the crisis and its purported solutions might look like, and what feminist alternatives to the austere, neo-liberal state and economic policy are emerging in contemporary scholarship and activism" (2015: 1).

15. "The latter, affective dimension of austerity politics is crucial in securing public assent to increasingly authoritarian forms of capitalism, and in rendering the appearance of democratic legitimacy to client states. The fomentation of hostility towards gendered and radicalized social groups that are made to embody parasitism, disease, perversion, defilement and weakness is part of a nation-building project that conceals while supporting violent processes of accumulation by dispossession" (Carastathis 2015: 91).

16. KOINSEP were introduced in 2011 as a new legal form to enable the development of social economy, identified as "the sum of economic, business, productive and social activities, which are taken up by companies or persons' associations, whose purpose is the pursuit of collective good and the service of general social interests" (Stavroulakis n.d.).
17. All quotes are from the Beaver Collective Facebook page. Retrieved from https://www .facebook.com/collectivabeaver/info/?tab=overview.
18. They explain, "Oka was the unit of measurement of the Ottoman empire that remained in use even after the empire dissolved into different states, often in parallel with the kilo. Each oka was divided into 400 drams. In Greece, okas and dramia were in use until July 1st 1959!" It is relevant to note here that the "Ottoman oka" evokes "authentic" oriental culinary traditions and dishes, such as those of the renowned Turkish and Asia Minor cuisine, which is claimed to surpass even Greek high standards.
19. All quotes are from their Facebook page. Retrieved from https://www.facebook.com/ Έξι-Οκάδες-και-ένα-Δράμι-618404761592925/info/?tab=overview fn19.
20. For example, the popular expression "*gourmedia,*" used for Greek delicacies, represents a popularized and Greekified adaptation of the French term "gourmet" that references and mocks its foreign and bourgeois connotations.
21. All quotes are from Melissa's Facebook page. Retrieved from https://www.facebook .com/Melissanetworkgreece33/info/?tab=page_info.
22. "Yesterday at Melissa, we shared with John Kerry our stories of resilience, our efforts to contribute, and our vision of society as an open beehive of communication and creative exchange" (Christopoulou quoted on Melissa's Facebook page: https://www .facebook.com/Melissanetworkgreece33/photos/pb.483189245190300.-2207520000 .1456758342./525730437602847/?type=3&theater).
23. "Caring for myself is not self-indulgence, it is self-preservation, and that is an act of political warfare" (Audre Lorde quoted on Melissa Facebook page).
24. As Heath Cabot (chapter 10 this volume), discussing the tensions between the Solidarity Movement and NGOs in the context of the refugee crisis, observes, "Many participants cite these aspects of solidarity as distinguishing the movement from other spheres of civil society, especially NGOs. In contrast, solidarians tend to frame NGOs as hierarchical, grounded on monetary compensation and the professional capacity for expertise (or the building of professionalism through formal internships and practicums)" (291).

References

Adkins, Lisa. 2015. "What Can Money Do? Feminist Theory in Austere Times." *Feminist Review* 109(1): 31–48.
Agelopoulos, Giorgos. 2013. "Krise kai Protovoulies Alleleggias Oikonomias: Mia Anthropologiki Proseggisi." Seminars on the Crisis, Thessaloniki, Greece. Retrieved May 11 2016 from http://slideplayer.gr/slide/1960055/.
Anastasiou, S., Konstantinos Filippidis, and Konstantinos Stergiou. 2015. "Economic Recession, Austerity and Gender Inequality at Work. Evidence from Greece and Other Balkan Countries." *Procedia Economics and Finance* 24: 41–49.
Arampatzi, Athina. 2017. "The Spatiality of Counter-austerity Politics in Athens, Greece: Emergent 'Urban Solidarity Spaces.'" *Urban Studies* 54(9): 2155–71.
Athanasiou, Athina. 2012. *E Krise os Katastase "Ektaktes Anagkes" Kritikes kai Antistaseis*. Athens: Philippotis.
———. 2014. "Governing For the Market: Emergencies and Emergences in Power and Sub-

jectivity." In *Crisis-Scapes: Athens and Beyond,* edited by Jaya K. Brekke, Dimitris Dalakoglou, Christos Filippidis, and Antonis Vradis. Athens: Synthesi. Retrieved 11 May 2016 from Crisis-scape.net: http://crisis-scape.net/resources/conference-publication.

Athanasatou, Ioanna. 2013. "Phylo, Ypokeimenikoteta, Zoe sto Orio: Anazetontas ton Feminismo ten Epoche tes Krises." *Ellenike Epitheorese Koinonikes Epistemes* 41: 103–12.

Avdela, Efi. 2011. "To Phylo sten (se) Krise, e ti Symvainei stis 'Gynaikes' se Chalepous Kairous." *Sygchrona Themata* 115: 17–21.

Avdela, Efi, and Angelika Psarra. 2012. "Apokryphes Ptyches tes Melanes Psephou." *Sygchrona Themata* 117: 4–5.

Bakalaki, Alexandra. 2015. "Crisis, Gender, Time." *AllegraLab.* Retrieved 11 May 2016 from http://allegralaboratory.net/crisis-gender-time/

Balourdos, Dionysis, and Natalia Spyropoulou. 2012. *To Koinoniko Portraito tes Elladas 2012. Opseis tes Krises.* Athens: Ethniko Kentro Koinonikon Ereunon.

Biglia, Barbara, and Jordi Bonet Marti. 2014. "Precarity." In *The Encyclopedia of Critical Psychology,* edited by Thomas Teo, 1488–91. New York: Springer.

Brah, Avtar, Ioana Szeman, and Irene Gedalof. 2015. "Feminism and the Politics of Austerity." *Feminist Review* 109: 1–7.

Brekke Jaya K., Dalakoglou Dimitris, Filippidis Christos, and Antonis Vradis, eds. 2014. *Crisis-Scapes: Athens and Beyond.* Athens: Synthesi. Retrieved 11 May 2016 from Crisisscape.net: http://crisis-scape.net/resources/conference-publication.

Brown, Wendy. 2015a. "O Neophileleutherismos den einai aplos mia Oikonomike Politike, alla ena Oloklero Systema Logikes." *E Avgi,* November 29.

———. 2015b. *Undoing the Demos. Neoliberalism's Stealth Revolution.* Cambridge, MA: Zone Books.

Burman, Erica. 1994. "Feminist Research." In *Qualitative Methods in Psychology,* by Peter Banister, Erica Burman, Ian Parker, Maye Taylor, Carol Tindall, 121–41. Buckingham, UK: Open University Press.

Carastathis, Anna. 2015. "The Politics of Austerity and the Affective Economy of Hostility: Radicalized Gendered Violence and Crises of Belonging in Greece." *Feminist Review* 109: 73–95.

Chondrogiannos, Thodoris. 2015. "Melissa: The Migrant Women Who Stand on the Side of Refugees." Popaganda, 8 December. Retrieved from http://popaganda.gr/melissa-metanastries-pou-apofasisan-na-stathoun-sto-plevro-ton-prosfigon/.

Fainstein, Susan. 2015. "Resilience and Justice." *International Journal of Urban and Regional Research* 39(1): 157–67.

Feischmidt, Margit, and Peter Hervik. 2015. "Mainstreaming the Extreme: Intersecting Challenges from the Far Right in Europe." *Intersections. EEJSP* 1(1): 3–17.

Fragoudaki, Anna. 2013. *O Ethnikismos Kai I Anodos Tis Akrodexias.* Athens: Alexandreia.

Fraser, Nancy. 2016. "The Battle for Neoliberal Hegemony: An Interview With Nancy Fraser." *OpenDemocracy,* 19 January.

Gaitanou, Eirini. 2012. "Feminism in Times of Crisis: Woman Struggle in Greece." Paper presented at the Historical Materialism, 9th Annual Conference, London, November 7–11. Retrieved May 11 2016fro https://www.academia.edu/5474862/Feminism_in_times_of_crisis_Woman_struggle_in_Greece.

Gavroglou, Kostas. 2015. "Mia Nea Atzenda gia ta Panepistimia." *CHRONOS* 29. Retrieved May 11 2016 from http://www.chronosmag.eu/index.php/ggl-g-pps.html.

Greek Ombudsman. 2012–14. *Eidikes Etesies Ektheseis: Fylo kai Ergasiakes Sheseis.* Department of Gender Equality, Athens. Retrieved 11 May 2016 from http://www.synigoros.gr/?i=isotita-ton-fylon.el.ifeidikesektheseis.

Halkias, Alexandra. 2004. *The Empty Cradle of Democracy: Sex, Abortion and Nationalism in Modern Greece.* Durham, NC: Duke University Press.

———. 2012. "E Koinoniologia tes Sexoualikotetas, oi Arrenopotetes kai o Emphylos Dekem-
vres." In *Soma, Phylo, Sexoualikoteta. LOATK Politikes sten Ellada*, edited by Alexandra
Halkias and Anna Apostolleli, 215–49. Athens: Plethron.

———. 2016. Roundtable Discussion at the Body and Public Space Event, ONASSIS Cultural Center, Athens, 4 March, 2016. Retrieved 11 May 2016 from http://www.sgt.gr/
eng/SPG1515/?.

Kaika, Maria, and Lazaros Karaliotas. 2016. "The Spatialization of Democratic Politics: Insights from Indignant Squares." *European Urban and Regional Studies* 23(4): 556–70.

Kaldi-Koulikidou, Theodora, and Styling Plevraki. 2014. "Domestic Violence Against Women
in Greece." In *Family Violence from a Global Perspective: A Strengths-Based Approach*, edited
by Sylvia M. Asay, John De Frain, Marcee Metzger, and Bob Moyer, 94–107. London:
Sage.

Karamessini, Maria. 2012. "E Ellenike Krise se Europaike Prooptike: Feministike Kritike." *E
Avgi*, October 11.

———. 2014a. "Structural Crisis and Adjustment in Greece: Social Regression and the Challenge to Gender Equality." In *Women and Austerity. The Economic Crisis and the Future
of Gender Equality*, edited by Maria Karamessini and Jill Rubbery, 165–84. London:
Routledge.

———. 2014b. "Tessera Chronia Mnemonia: Epiptoseis kai Antistaseis apo te Meria ton Gynaikon" *REDNotebook*, March 26.

Karamessini, Maria, and Franciscos Koutentakis. 2014. "Labor Market Flows and Unemployment Dynamics by Sex in Greece During the Crisis." *Revue de l'OFCE / Débats et
Politiques* 133: 215–39.

Karamessini, Maria, and Jill Rubbery. 2014. "The Challenge of Austerity for Equality: A Consideration of Eight European Countries in the Crisis." *Revue de l'OFCE / Débats et Politiques* 133: 15–39.

Karapiperi, Dafni. 2015. "Exi Okades Ki Ena Drami: Apo Mamades Mpakalises." *Kathimerini*,
15 December. Retrieved from http://www.kathimerini.gr/842233/article/gastronomos/
agora/e3i-okades-kai-ena-drami-apo-mamades-mpakalisses.

Kosyfologou, Aliki. 2015. "Gynaikes kai Litoteta." *REDNotebook*, September 7.

Lada, Sasa. 2013. "When Gender Did (Not) Meet the Crisis. Displaced Bodies and Absent Approaches." Round table at the Transformations and Re-inscriptions of Greece in Times
of Crisis Conference, Volos, November 1–3, 2013.

Lorde, Audre. 1988. *A Burst of Light: Essays*. London: Sheba Feminist Publishers.

Lyberaki, Antigone. 2014. "GREECE: Gender Equality, Development and Women's Rights
in the Eu Mediterranean Basin in the Years of Financial, Political and Social Crisis." In
*The Impacts of the Crisis on Gender Equality and Women's Wellbeing in the EU Mediterranean
Countries*, 71–138. UNICRI. Retrieved May 11 2016 from http://www.unicri.it/news/
files/VAW_draft_last_lowq.pdf.

Pantelidou-Malouta, Maro. 2010. "E 'Anisoteta ton Phylon' os Provlema Politikes. Arretes
Paradoches tes Sygchrones Politikes Analyses." In *Phylo kai Koinonikes Epistemes ste Syg-
chrone Ellada*, edited by Venetia Kantsa, Vassiliki Moutafi, Evthymios Papataxiarchis,
257–73. Athens: Alexandreia.

———. 2013. "Apo te Skopia tou Phylou: Opseis tes Krises." *Ellenike Epitheorese Politikes Epistemes* 21: 9–34.

Phoenix, Ann. 1990. "Social Research in the Context of Feminist Psychology." In *Feminists and
Psychological Practice*, edited by Erica Burman, 89–103. London: Sage.

Psaropoulos, John. 2015. "Greek immigration policy: A lesson for Eastern Europe?" *Al Jazeera*, 9 December. Retrieved from https://www.aljazeera.com/indepth/features/2015/12/
greek-immigration-policy-lesson-eastern-europe-151206054018282.html.

Psarra, Aggelika. 2014. "Melanas Zomos e Maska Prosopou me Avokanto? Emphyles Ptyches tou Ellenikou Neonazismou." *Archeiotaxio* 14: 129–56.

Rakopoulos, Theodoros. 2014. "The Crisis Seen from Below, Within and Against: from Solidarity Economy to Food Distribution Cooperatives in Greece." *Dialectical Anthropology* 38: 189–207.

———. 2015. "Solidarity's Tensions. Informality, Sociality, and the Greek Crisis." *Social Analysis* 59(3): 85–104.

Sassen, Saskia. 2014. *Expulsions: Brutality and Complexity in the Global Economy.* Cambridge: Harvard University Press.

Soula, M. 2011. "The Commonalities of Emotion: Fear, Faith, Rage and Revolt." In *Revolt and Crisis in Greece,* edited by Dimitrios Dalakoglou and Adonis Vradis, 199–203. New York: AK Press.

Stavroulakis, Konstantinos. n.d. "Ftiaxte Mia KoinSEp." Koinsep.org. Retrieved from http://koinsep.org/τι-είναι-οι-κοιν-σ-επ/.

Stratigaki, Maria. 2013. "E Politike Isotetas ton Phylon ste Dike tes Oikonomikes Krises." *Ellenike Epitheorese Politikes Epistemes* 41: 60–83.

Svarna, Foteini. 2014. "Financial Crisis and Domestic Violence: the Case of Greece." *The WIP,* May 29. Retrieved 20 June 2016 from http://thewip.net/2014/05/29/financial-crisis-and-domestic-violence-the-case-of-greece/.

Tamboukou, Maria. 2012. "Truth Telling in Foucault and Arendt: Parrhesia, the Pariah and Academics in Dark Times." *Journal of Education Policy* 27(6): 849–65.

Theodossopoulos, Dimitrios. 2014. "The Ambivalence of Anti-Austerity Indignation in Greece: Resistance, Hegemony and Complicity." *History and Anthropology* 25(4): 488–506.

Tsiganou, Joanna. 2014. "The Impact of Crisis on Gender Inequality the Greek Case." Presentation at the Social Inequalities in Europe Conference, Athens, June 20. Retrieved 11 May 2016 from http://www.gsrt.gr/inequalities/en/speakers/pdf/Tsiganou_presentation.pdf.

Vaiou, Dina. 2014. "Is the Crisis in Athens (also) Gendered? Facets of Access and (In)visibility in Everyday Public Spaces." *City* 18(4–5): 533–37.

———. 2016. "Tracing Aspects of the Greek Crisis in Athens: Putting Women in the Picture." *European Urban and Regional Studies* 23(3): 220–30.

Vaiou, Dina, and Ares Kalandides. 2017. "Practices of Solidarity in Athens. Reconfigurations of Public Space and Urban Citizenship." *Citizenship Studies* 21(4): 440–54.

Vougioukas, Anna. 2013. "Dikaiomata ton Gynaikon kai Sygchrona Diakyveumata." *E Avgi,* June 13.

Walby, Sylvia. 2009. "Gender and the Financial Crisis." Paper for UNESCO project on "Gender and the Financial Crisis," April 9. Retrieved 11 May 2016 from http://www.lancaster.ac.uk/fass/doc_library/sociology/Gender_and_financial_crisis_Sylvia_Walby.pdf.

Yuval-Davis, Nira. 1996. *Gender and Nation.* London: Sage.

Zavos, Alexandra. 2010. "Gender, Migration and Anti-racist Politics in the Continued Project of the Nation." In *Gender and Migration: Feminist Perspectives, Political Interventions,* edited by Ingrid Palmary, Erica Burman, Khatidja Chantler, and Peace Kiguwa, 15–30. London: Zed.

Chapter 10

From the Twilight Zone to the Limelight

Shifting Terrains of Asylum and Rights in Greece

Heath Cabot

Introduction

In 2008 I conducted an interview with a refugee advocate from the European North who had recently begun a project on Lesvos, the Greek Aegean island that, since the early 2000s, had become a key site of crossing for asylum seekers and migrants entering Europe. The advocate explained that it was "obvious" to anyone working on asylum in Europe that Greece was "the place" to do a successful advocacy project. "Everyone knew terrible things were happening in Greece," he explained, "but no one was talking about it."

We went on to discuss the detention and policing situation in Lesvos: the notorious Pagani detention center (closed in 2009), and the frequent unofficial pushbacks of asylum seekers to Turkey (of which local lawyers and advocacy groups had intimate knowledge, but which European powers had hitherto ignored). We also discussed the Evros land border in the north of Greece, with its river, marshlands, and nature preserve popular with bird watchers. He told me that Evros was a "twilight zone" for both the difficulty that advocates faced in accessing its squalid detention centers, and the nightmarish accounts of refugees and migrants who passed through the area. Indeed, some of the refugees I met during my research on asylum had themselves encountered the *narkes* (landmines) buried in

---

the marshes from earlier conflicts with Turkey. These landmines were notorious for blowing legs off border crossers, and riddling the unlucky with shrapnel, sometimes with fatal consequences.

In the intervening years since that 2008 interview, I have often ruminated on this conversation as I have watched Greece become a site that is now very much talked about. Greece has since moved out of the darkness of that twilight zone, so to speak, into the global limelight via two overlapping crises: first, Greece's role in the global "financial crisis" owing to its unsustainable debt; and second, in 2015–16, for its crucial geopolitical position in the "refugee crisis." More than 800,000 of the 1 million people seeking refuge in Europe in 2015 entered through Greece, primarily through the Aegean islands; 500,000 or more of them entered via Lesvos. This refugee crisis, rightfully, garnered extensive press coverage, sparked heated policy and political debates, and mobilized donors and volunteers both in Greece and throughout the world. The United Nations High Commissioner for Refugees (UNHCR), as well as international organizations such as the International Rescue Committee (IRC) and Doctors of the World, and Greek and European nongovernmental organizations (NGOs), strived to meet the often-urgent needs of those entering Greece. Meanwhile, volunteers from all over the world traveled to Greece to participate in the humanitarian response. Perhaps most striking was the scale of the response of Greeks and other locals on the ground, through the mobilization of informal, but highly organized networks based on the principle of *allileggii* (solidarity) with refugees.

Since 2005 I have studied asylum in Greece from an anthropological perspective, focusing on the peculiar dilemmas that Greece has faced as a threshold of Europe. My book, *On the Doorstep of Europe: Asylum and Citizenship in Greece* (Cabot 2014), examined the crucial role of the Greek NGO sector and other civil society groups in offering legal aid and social support to asylum seekers. I conducted anthropological fieldwork in Greece between 2005 and 2011, before the civil war in Syria and the rise of the Islamic State. At that time, Iraqis and Afghans, along with others from Southeast Asia and sub-Saharan Africa, were the primary groups seeking refuge in Greece from wars spearheaded by the United States and NATO, and from both economic and political forms of violence. Greek and other European organizations specialized in issues of asylum began speaking of a "humanitarian crisis" in the Aegean as early as 2007 (see PRO ASYL et al. 2007). The dangers of border crossings, the lack of access to the asylum system and social services, the grinding fear of moving and living with precarious status—these were already everyday crises for my field interlocutors in Greece, long before they made headlines in the broader Euro-American world.

Since then, there have been material changes in the global configurations of power and violence that led to unprecedented movements of people into the European Union (EU) in 2015–16. I cannot speak directly to the specific histories that caused refugee movements from Syria. In earlier work, however (Cabot 2014), I highlighted in detail the structural problems that continue to impact EU and Greek migration and asylum regimes: the dearth of resources for member-states and civil society groups to provide services to refugees, the lack of social support for refugees themselves, the ambiguous responsibilities of member-states in granting safe haven, and deeply problematic and inequitable legislation at the EU level (see Magliveras 2011; McDonough and Tsourdi 2012; Papageorgiou 2013; Rozakou 2006, 2012). For those I met in my earlier research on asylum, it was obvious that not just the Greek state but also the EU was deeply, perhaps even willfully, ill-prepared for earlier refugee movements—let alone the war in Syria. These systemic deficiencies have persisted and perhaps even increased, combined with what Karpozilos, and Xenakis and Cheliotis, in this volume, describe in terms of the increasing political violence and criminalization affecting migrants in Greece under austerity. In the meantime, however, as Burgi shows us in her analysis of the Greek health-care system (this volume), economic instability and debt in Europe's poorer countries, and the forms of neoliberal governance at work in austerity policies, have made it even more difficult for member-states like Greece to provide care and support to both citizens and noncitizens (see Athanasiou 2012; Davis 2015; Douzinas 2013; Knight 2015; Lazzarato and Jordan 2012, 2014; Rakopoulos 2014; Stuckler and Basu 2013).

In this chapter, following the provocations of the editors, I consider some of the key changes that have taken place with regard to asylum and refugee issues under austerity, in the face of what EU Migration and Home Affairs Commissioner Dimitris Avramopoulos (2015) described as "the worst refugee crisis in Europe since World War II." Yet I also emphasize the many continuities that undergird the current moment of crisis. I argue that many of those events that have become visible as new (including the "crisis" itself) are in large part products of existing structural inequities, and of often systematic policies and practices: Greece's geopolitical and economic marginality in Europe, increasing projects of securitization, legislative patterns that have persistently outsourced the problem of migration and asylum to the EU's external borders and beyond, and, finally, the ongoing neoliberal devolution of rights and services necessary for livable (let alone good) lives to venues outside the state. Ultimately, I suggest that the changing context of asylum in Greece in the age of austerity indicates a crisis in the state of rights in Europe today, for both citizens and noncitizens.

Chasing the Limelight

Conducting scholarship in sites and times of "crisis" is a challenge that more and more social scientists are confronting, because this historical moment is punctuated with multiple crisis discourses and hot spots.[1] At such moments, it is easy to forget that change is always happening, even in periods of apparent stasis; time seems to speed up, and the present simultaneously acquires an added density (Cabot 2015). *Krisi* (crisis), which in Greek means also judgment, also denotes a point of reckoning when we engage collectively, though in deeply heterogeneous ways, in rethinking the past, present, and future (Roitman 2014). The common sense of everyday structures, practices, and life-worlds is thrown into question (Gluckman 2006 [1965]; Turner 1974).

Even critical accounts of crisis, however, frequently neglect the continuities that undergird these moments of rapid change and the often-entrenched practices and sociopolitical forms that underlie them. Crisis has a bewitching quality for researchers, making certain topics and places dangerous and exciting when they were not before, and promoting an urgent need to be on the frontlines of whatever is coming next. But crisis thinking is distracting, encouraging us to approach such moments as exceptions to the social and political order (Agamben 2005; Athanasiou 2012). Crisis thinking is also dangerous for how it reifies power relationships and active decisions that lie behind political and economic realities, presenting certain injustices as given and perhaps unavoidable. The editors of this volume are careful to talk about "Greece under austerity" as opposed to "crisis Greece," highlighting how economic and financial instabilities (read as "crisis") cannot be excised from the austerity packages that Greece has been made to adopt since 2010. The concept of austerity, for instance, helps us critically analyze a political reality, a set of intentionally crafted and imposed policies and practices, whereas crisis speaks to the mystical authority of the market. Similarly, the language surrounding the "refugee crisis" strips European governments and decision makers of responsibility for a situation that has been, as I argue here, in the making for years.

Like many of the other authors in this volume, I can chart Greece's ascension into the arena of scholarly and public attention to the financial crash of 2010. When I began my graduate research on asylum in Greece in 2003, however, Greece was not deemed a particularly exciting or socially relevant place to be doing research. I had to respond to frequent questions of, "Why Greece?"—asked to justify why this site was interesting or promising.[2] At that time, Greece was enjoying the so-called good years of neoliberal development, excessive borrowing, and deregulation (see Placas this volume; Placas 2011, 2016) associated with the Olympic Games and recent accession to the euro.[3] However, Greece was still largely approached by more global publics as a friendly, disorganized, and somewhat backward country on Europe's Mediterranean margins. Within Europeanist anthropology, meanwhile, Greece was certainly the site of deeply respected work but was still often framed as a bit old-fashioned: a place to study (certainly interesting, but not always sexy) topics such as the uses of history, kinship, village life, and gender roles (largely associated with more traditional anthropology). Greece did not have the added political-economic interest of the postsocialist world, and was also lacking the (post) colonial connections that have made, for instance, England and France particularly intriguing for questions of identity, power, erasure, hybridity, and the like. Finally, as a site for the study of migration, Greece was, at that time, also of lesser interest than Spain (the Canary Islands and Melilla) and Italy (Lampedusa), which had entered the limelight earlier as problem areas with regard to issues of migration and asylum.

Having begun my work in a context in which scholars of Greece were marginalized almost as much as Greece has been, I am still somewhat amazed by Greece's ascension as a hot spot of scholarly and media interest (see also Cabot 2016). The concept of "crisis" has swept Greece up and catapulted it into the center of attention. But this limelight should elicit more questions than it does. What was going on behind the scenes, in those uninteresting, gray, twilight zones that characterized precrisis refugee and asylum politics in Greece?

Continuities and Changes

In 2015 global publics were confronted with Greece's position as Europe's doorstep and the stark role of border regimes in shaping people's capacity to live, die, move, or remain stuck not just outside the EU, but also within its territorial boundaries. Images circulated in the news and on social media: of a desperate rush to reach Europe, of people landing on Aegean shores, of deaths and drownings, and enormous numbers in limbo in makeshift camps in Greece and elsewhere in the Balkans as they sought to enter contiguous European territory. Some European leaders and citizens expressed the need to welcome refugees; others (especially after the Paris attacks in January 2016) emphasized the danger of the so-called floods, tides, and waves of migrants, who not only were non-European, but also were largely Muslim. In March 2016 a statement was signed by the European Union and Turkey allowing European authorities to return irregular migrants to Turkey. This controversial decision has furthered reinforced the marginality of Greece even as it has altered the territorial profile of Europe by extending bordering practices not just to the edges of Greece but also beyond, to Turkey itself.

The refugee crisis of 2015–16 threw into sharp relief longstanding European patterns of governance and border legislation. EU approaches to border management, combined with unique geopolitical factors, have, since at least the early 2000s, made Greece both a crucial point of arrival and the "prison of Europe," to cite the succinct description of one of my field interlocutors (an Iranian refugee speaking in 2011). Greece is a site where people have long sought to arrive but that they usually also strive (often unsuccessfully) to leave (Cabot 2012; Triandafillydou and Maroufof 2009; Papadimitriou and Papageorgiou 2005).

During the first years of my fieldwork (2005–8), Greece's geopolitical position, with land and sea borders imminently close to Turkey, made it the primary entry point for persons fleeing the wars in Iraq and Afghanistan. Moreover, the emergence of new consumer markets in Southern Europe (Rosen 2011) had also made Greece (like Italy and Spain) a key site for many different forms of labor-related migration (see also Placas this volume, Rosen this volume), primarily from China, Southeast Asia, and West Africa (Fouskas 2013). Increasingly militarized policing measures in other regions of Europe's Mediterranean also redirected to Greece boats that were originally headed to Italy and Spain from the African coast. Few migrants and asylum seekers I met during my research described Greece as their stated destination. However, Greece's peculiar position as an outpost of noncontiguous EU territory presented border crossers with further challenges as they sought to move deeper into the EU. Many paid smuggling networks for passage to the North. Others attempted to cross on their own from the port city of Patras by hiding themselves in container trucks or climbing the port-side fence and embarking ferries bound for Italy. From Greece, the road that many sought to travel often extended as far as Norway, Sweden, and the UK, but France and Germany were also highly sought-after destinations. Despite attempts to leave, however, many who were apprehended and detained applied for asylum in Greece,[4] and for others, the fear of arrest and detention made an asylum application expedient and even necessary. As a result, many of those hoping to move on to elsewhere in Europe became stuck in Greece.

The spatial politics of EU immigration and asylum law are contradictory. On the one hand, EU legislation frames the EU as a smooth, homogeneous space, "as natural, innocent, and absent of systems of domination" (Volpp 2012: 456). However, the vision of a Common European Asylum System, which is crucial to the legislative frame of immigration and asylum in Europe, does not sufficiently take into account the differential positions and capacities of member-states. Moreover, in many cases EU legislation reinforces existing power differentials and exacerbates the marginality of border states. The Dublin Regulation, first signed in 2003 and recently renewed in 2013 (producing "Dublin III"), requires that asylum seekers apply for protection and then remain in the country where they first enter EU territory. This law was initially articulated as a way to encourage responsibility or burden sharing among member-states. However, given that most people enter Europe via the borders, it has long had the effect of constraining asylum seekers to border countries. The early years of my research were rife with people in the asylum system struggling to survive while stuck in Greece, unable to leave owing to internal European policing regimes. Many others were caught in the Dublin system, shuttling back and forth between Greece and other places in the European North where they worked, had families, or otherwise made their homes. Since its inception, the Dublin system has been variously challenged, invoked, selectively applied, and suspended by member-states (Brekke and Brochmann 2015; Thielemann and Armstrong 2013). Most crucially, in 2011 a case brought by an Afghan asylum seeker to the European Court of Human Rights, *M.S.S. v. Belgium and Greece*,[5] exposed a level of brutality in Greek detention systems that the Court deemed unacceptable, alongside highly precarious access to the asylum system and social services. This decision highlighted the Greek state's ongoing incompetence in this area, as well as lack of political will to institute meaningful changes in asylum and reception systems. It also incited a moratorium on Dublin returns to Greece, which, until recently (March 2017), has been adhered to fairly consistently (Moreno-Lax 2012).

   At the national level, in the mid-2000s the (then relatively untried) Greek asylum process faced an enormous spike in applications, increasing from around five thousand applications in 2005 to approximately twenty-five thousand in 2007 (Cabot 2014; McDonough and Tsourdi 2012; Papageorgiou 2013). These larger numbers concurrently placed greater pressure on both asylum bureaucracies and civil society mechanisms of support. Meanwhile, because most applicants remained in the system for a matter of years, the number of backlogged cases grew, eventually reaching fifty-two thousand in 2010, the fourth-largest number of backlogged cases globally (after South Africa, Ecuador, and the United States) (UNHCR 2010). The Greek state provided access to health care and the right to work to those awaiting decisions on their asylum claims, but other often-urgent social needs (primarily housing and food) were left almost entirely to civil society organizations and collectivities, primarily the (at that time very few) NGOs focused on asylum-related issues. As I write in detail elsewhere (Cabot 2012), applicants, finding themselves in this state of limbo (often for many years), had to deal with the difficult challenges posed by precarious, indeterminate status and negligible social support.[6] NGOs such as my primary field site sought to provide important, though limited, forms of assistance. A further difficulty was that even those who eventually did receive asylum in Greece found themselves without meaningful assistance in finding housing and employment.

By 2010 Greece had become a crucial area of concern for advocates and government officials in Europe, initiating significant legislative changes to make Greece compliant with European directives. These legislative shifts had important impacts on the ground, even if they were relatively slow to emerge. Asylum applications used to take place through the police authorities (primarily in Thessaloniki and in Athens), generating nightmarish scenes of hundreds in line waiting for days, weeks, or months, to apply, as police monitored the crowd, often doing so violently. Those successful in making an asylum application then went to a more in-depth hearing in front of a committee in order to receive a final decision from what was then known as the Ministry of Public Order and Citizen Protection (again, often after years in limbo). In 2011, however, the Greek parliament approved Law 3907/2011, which established a new asylum system meant to institute greater transparency and compliance with relevant EU directives: a new, semi-independent asylum authority, new employees, and regional offices for applications. This new system was not enacted until 2013, and even then, both the old and new systems functioned simultaneously: new applicants would enter the new system, whereas those who had applied under the old remained in that process until they received a decision. The police authorities stopped reviewing all applications in 2015.[7]

Geopolitically, practices of border management, policing, and securitization initiated further adaptations in routes and tactics of border crossing. In 2009 forces from the EU border management service, the European Border and Coast Guard Agency (Frontex), began policing the Aegean much more aggressively, a move that redirected most migration traffic to the North, and by 2010 the Evros border had become the most crossed border in Europe. This emergent "crisis" in Evros, in turn, generated the deployment of Frontex rapid response units to the Evros region. The construction of a border fence in Evros was initiated under the Panhellenic Socialist Movement (PASOK) government of George Papandreou, who in other respects was much more open on questions of migration, particularly in comparison to the earlier, conservative government of Kostas Karamanlis (New Democracy, or ND). Antonis Samaras, from a more conservative wing of ND, completed the fence. While EU funds were not expressly used for the construction of the fence, surveillance equipment was accessed via EU programs, and Frontex continued to participate in securing the border (see Feldman 2012). With massive displacements from Syria in 2015–16 the Aegean Sea (and the Greek islands) emerged again as the primary theater of crossing.

In the contemporary context, policing practices in the Balkans and within European territory have made passage from Greece even more fraught and complex. In 2015–16, with no viable way to move between Greece and Italy, the hundreds of thousands entering Greece had to find a way North, leading to the emergence of the so-called Balkan Route, in which people exited not only the Schengen area, but also European Union territory in order to reenter again. This route was closed in spring of 2016, positioning thousands in muddy, makeshift camps in Idomeni, near the border with Macedonia (Former Yugoslav Republic of Macedonia, or FYROM). Meanwhile, the effects of the EU/Turkey agreement of Spring 2016 were swift and palpable, instituting a fast-track border procedure at the hot spots in which those asylum seekers found not to constitute vulnerable categories of people are marked to be sent back to Turkey (Rozakou and Kalir 2016).[8] While returns to Turkey have taken place, many still remain at the hot spots awaiting processing and examination, highlighting the ongoing strategic use of limbo and uncertainty as key governance tactics in Greek (and European) asylum regimes (Cabot 2012; Rozakou 2017a).[9] The walling up of the northern borders has made Patras again a site of dangerous internal European crossings, and people can be seen trying to climb the port-side fence, attempting to board ferries headed for Italy.

Now, with the heavy policing of EU internal borders, and with arrivals continuing (though in vastly diminished numbers), refugees and asylum seekers in Greece face extreme difficulty in relocating to elsewhere in Europe, both formally and informally. Those who made applications for asylum before 20 March 2016, and the institution of the EU/Turkey Statement, might have their cases examined by other European countries. Yet relocation processes are protracted, and success is anything but guaranteed.[10] Others must await the examination of their claims in Greece. Still, advocates and refugees alike speak openly of informal methods of transit, and of the steady leakage of European internal borders, through which refugees in Greece continue to relocate via smuggling routes to other European countries.[11]

Expanding one's temporal scale of analysis beyond a snapshot view of the current refugee crisis highlights some of the ongoing structural difficulties that characterize EU border regimes. The violent effects of these contradictions are felt, of course, primarily by border-crossers themselves, as well as, to lesser degrees, by advocates and others working at the borders. Governance practices at EU, national, and regional levels have persistently placed Greece in a contradictory position regarding its own territorial sovereignty, on the one hand, and its responsibility to regulate Europe's borders, on the other. Greece must guard the frontiers of Europe, always subject to critiques and interventions with regard to European-level security needs. Meanwhile, the need for a humane, functioning asylum system that complies with European standards has also made Greece the ongoing subject of critique for its own (very real) inadequacies in the treatment of asylum seekers. These systemic challenges do not excuse the actions of Greek governments that persistently have been unable or unwilling to respond meaningfully to various refugee movements over the years. Most recently, accounts have documented significant deficiencies in policy and practice instituted by the current Coalition of the Radical Left (SYRIZA) government, specifically in the use and misuse of funds (see Howden and Fotiadis 2017). With regard to asylum seekers themselves, these contradictory regimes of border management have only intensified with the current refugee crisis, placing those seeking refuge in Europe in increasingly untenable positions. Facing extraordinary dangers in the crossing to Europe, refugees entering Greece now — as before — must navigate protracted dangers and struggles within Europe: facing extreme difficulties in finding meaningful protection in Greece but often unable to move elsewhere.

From NGOs to Solidarity

I first went to Lesvos in 2006 with workers from the Athens-based refugee advocacy NGO where I conducted much of my fieldwork, which at the time was one of the few of its kind in Greece. It was late November, when crossings become particularly dangerous. A boat carrying forty-five Afghans had arrived, most of them appearing to be minors. I accompanied two pro bono lawyers who met with the boys in the courtyard of the Pagani detention center, a concrete space open to the elements, with just a roof to shelter them, and bars on the windows and doors. As the lawyers, with the help of an interpreter, informed the boys of their right to asylum, a local woman — a volunteer social worker — circled our makeshift meeting space, bringing the boys sweaters and cleaning their faces with the rough care of a Greek grandmother.

At that time, Lesvos, along with the other large islands in the Eastern Aegean, including Samos, Kos, and Leros, had already become relatively accustomed to refugee arrivals. However, with the lack of a local, state-sponsored infrastructure for reception, NGOs from the mainland often provided assistance. Since then, the Eastern Aegean has become a hub of not just refugee arrivals but also of modes of humanitarian governance that extend far beyond the formal designation of NGOs. These initiatives have been extraordinary in both their scope and their capacities to mobilize and organize voluntary labor and resources (Papataxarchis 2016; Rozakou 2016b). NGOs and international organizations have, of course, been active in the emergency response in 2015–16, and the number of professional organizations, both Greek and non-Greek, dealing with refugee issues has also exploded. But, perhaps even more strikingly, and especially in the early days of the crisis of 2015 (late summer and fall), locals from throughout Greece, in collaboration with volunteers from throughout Europe and the world, developed modes of assistance and support in spheres sharply demarcated as outside of, and perhaps even antithetical to, the NGO and nonprofit sector. Instead, these initiatives were explicitly framed as informal and nonprofessionalized, consisting of citizens acting in solidarity with the other. The very woman who I met working as a social worker ten years ago in Pagani is now locally famous as a stolid leader in what has become known as the Greek *kinima allileggiis* (solidarity movement).

The solidarity movement refers to the deeply heterogeneous network of initiatives that seek to collect and redistribute resources to people in need, including Greek citizens, long-term migrants, and newly arrived refugees. These initiatives include *pantopoleia* (groceries), anti-middlemen markets (Rakopoulos 2015), food and clothing banks (Theodossopoulos 2016), soup kitchens, pharmacies and clinics, and even language classes and other opportunities for continuing education. The solidarity movement can be framed, in part, as a response to rising poverty and unemployment accompanying austerity, though it can also be traced to the forms of protest and civic action (including direct democracy) that have emerged among an increasingly politicized and active populace (Giovanopoulos and Mitropoulos 2011; Panourgia 2011). Furthermore, the solidarity movement often positions Greeks and non-Greeks alongside each other as sharing common predicaments and political projects.[12] For instance, many active in the movement have long engaged in actions meant to provide support to migrants and refugees. A number of those active in the solidarity movement explained to me that the 2011 hunger strike by three hundred migrants demanding papers was particularly important in catalyzing the collective organizing that undergirds solidarity networks.

Recent scholarship (including my current research on social solidarity clinics and pharmacies; see Cabot 2016; Rakopoulos 2016) highlights both the novel and the creative aspects of solidarity, as well as its roots in longer Greek histories of resource pooling and redistribution, which other anthropologists have examined in both rural and urban contexts (Bakalaki 2008; Du Boulay 1974; Friedl 1962). For many participants themselves (many of whom call themselves solidarians), solidarity, as an organizing and ideological principle, marks the movement as unique, in contradistinction to other forms of service provision, including state formations, NGOs, or more traditional forms of charity or philanthropy (Theodossopoulos 2016).[13] In the talk of many participants, as well as in the discursive trends that frame the movement, solidarity is grounded on lateral, explicitly antihierarchical modes of organization and resource distribution. I have, for instance, been told repeatedly that solidarity is equally open to all, and that there are no leaders among these collectives (even if leaders often seem to emerge in practice). Conceptually, this horizontalism also includes those who receive assistance. Maria, a volunteer at a solidarity clinic in Athens, explained to me that solidarity is different from humanitarianism or philanthropy because it is not based on a *keno* (gap) between the one who offers support and the one who receives it. Indeed, I have met a number of people who participate as volunteers in solidarity initiatives and who also receive assistance. Furthermore, at a time when the misappropriation of funds (by the Greek state and banks) is seen as inextricable from the current period of austerity, many solidarity initiatives seek to subvert what Katerina Rozakou (2016b) describes as the polluting tendencies of money by eliciting donations of material resources and labor, while resisting or rejecting outright monetary donations. This rejection of capital is not just an attempt to produce alternative (noncapitalistic) modes of exchange, but also an acknowledgment of how money often generates mistrust and speculations about corruption or misuse of funds. Finally, these initiatives are notable for their valuation of informal, nonprofessionalized forms of voluntary participation (Rozakou 2016a). While the role of professionals is unavoidable in certain cases (such as volunteer doctors in the clinics), solidarity networks are framed as venues where anyone (expert and layperson alike) is allowed to take part.

Many participants cite these aspects of solidarity as distinguishing the movement from other spheres of civil society, especially NGOs. As such, solidarians tend to frame NGOs as hierarchical, grounded on monetary compensation and the professional capacity for expertise (or the building of professionalism through formal internships and practicums). Of course, the practice of solidarity might look very different from how it is imagined and described. For instance, one volunteer explained to me that no matter what people want to call these initiatives, they are a form of charity. Likewise, despite solidarity's rejection of money, rumors—true or not—abound among volunteers and beneficiaries about monetary donations that are accepted behind the scenes.[14] Such moments of internal critique, while commenting on the weaknesses or challenges of solidarity in practice, do not question the underlying ideological matrix of solidarity itself.

With the refugee crisis of 2015–16, drawing on existing know-how and networks, solidarity initiatives mobilized and coordinated to generate a wide-ranging, yet highly effective, response meant to welcome refugees.[15] These efforts were featured and celebrated in the international press, even garnering a Nobel Peace Prize nomination. Still, many solidarians themselves would remind us that this movement, a topic of such celebratory discourse, is itself largely a product of the failure of state and EU infrastructures to provide rights and livable livelihood to refugees—as well as to Greek citizens. The devolution of rights not just to formal civil society groups (NGOs) but, in the form of solidarity, to the ordinary person, highlights the ongoing precaritization of rights and services for both citizens and noncitizens attached to neoliberal policies and practices (Muehlebach 2012).[16]

Remaking the Ground of Rights

As I have just shown, bordering practices have rendered the right to asylum increasingly precarious for seekers of refuge. Through austerity, the right to livable livelihood has become increasingly precarious for citizens as well. The neoliberal quality of austerity policies has been extensively documented in the literature cited throughout this volume, and their neoliberal effects are thrown into particularly high relief by the changing terrain of both human and social rights evident on Europe's margins. When I speak of rights here, I refer, first, to international human rights: the legislative apparatuses formed at international, EU, and national levels, that, formally speaking, "should" apply irrespective of one's status within a national territory (i.e., whether or not one is a citizen). Yet I also invoke a particular vision of the relationship between person and society implied in the organization of the welfare state in Europe, the notion that by performing the obligations of citizenship (in particular, complying with taxation), one has access to those things necessary for not just a livable life, but also a good one. These consist of social rights, and workers' and citizens' rights, including health care, education, housing, safe retirement, a clean environment, and so on. These conceptions of rights are linked but differentiated. There is a robust debate among scholars and practitioners about whether social rights (such as health care, for instance) should be framed as human rights (see, e.g., Farmer 2005). Formally speaking, however, international human rights are supposed to apply to all people, irrespective of a person's legal status, whereas citizens' rights apply primarily to those who are, in fact, citizens.

Critical legal scholarship has, however, shown that one's legal status matters deeply in whether one can access or realize international human rights. Perhaps most famously, Hannah Arendt (1976 [1951]) demonstrated that citizenship within a national territory in post–World War I Europe was a determining factor in realizing even the right to life, while stateless persons and refugees, squeezed out of regimes of legal protection, were ascribed to the margins of life. As discussed earlier, even as the rights of refugees are formally recognized in both international and European law, the rights of refugees on Europe's margins have, in practice, become increasingly precarious. Concurrently, the rights of citizens in Greece have also been destabilized through a variety of factors—in particular, austerity measures. The extant Greek welfare state has been persistently dismantled by policies that explicitly attack the public sector (see Burgi this volume). In my current research I have conducted numerous interviews with Greek citizens who no longer have access to health care, retirement, and social support. A number of my interlocutors have emphasized that this shared predicament makes their positions similar to those of refugees and migrants; some have even used the term *esoteriki prosfiges* (internal refugees) to describe Greeks who themselves have been displaced from the workforce and frameworks of social assistance. In Greece today the state of rights for both citizens and noncitizens is deeply uncertain, a feature that has often been framed as the result of neoliberal governance (Allison 2013; Muehlebach 2012).

In discussions of neoliberalism, we often hear of a rolling back or stripping down of the welfare state. But Pierre Bourdieu (1998) offers a more precise metaphor for the trends toward neoliberal governance at work in Europe, the costs of which are felt so deeply at its borders. In a speech from the mid-1990s, when the eurozone was on the horizon but as yet unrealized, he discussed the dangers of this imagined polity grounded on shared currency and financial interests. He describes the state as having two hands: the right hand in charge of the management of economy and finance, the left in charge of welfare and social services. The problem under neoliberalism, he explains, is that the right hand no longer wants to know what the left hand is doing—and more importantly, does not want to pay for what it does. He critically acknowledges the possibilities that supranational government (specifically the EU) could also offer for a revitalization of the welfare state, through legal and governmental apparatuses that might reestablish nation-states as safe havens for both citizens and noncitizens. However, the age of austerity seems to have confirmed Bourdieu's fears rather than his hopes for Europe. European laws and policies continue to encourage what is good for capital (the free movement of goods, elite labor, and money), while European commitments to rights have waned. Through austerity, EU bodies have placed active strangleholds on even national governments' capacities to protect and care for citizens and noncitizens. As such, rights are now distributed differentially across and within Europe, leaving states and persons (both citizens and refugees) on the margins in positions of increasing precariousness.

Even in such sites of precariousness, however, rights frameworks are dependent on, and presuppose, particular social configurations through which persons do or do not become recognizable to others as subjects of rights. Regardless of their formal instantiation in law, rights are interpreted, negotiated, claimed, and realized locally and interpersonally, through multilevel and multivalent translations and mistranslations (Merry 2006). During my own ethnographic engagement in Greece, I have observed a distinctive shift in the grounds on which both refugees and citizens may be recognized as rights-bearing subjects. Formally speaking, both refugees and citizens are supposed to be recognized by state governmental bodies as entitled to rights. However, in Greece today the distribution of services necessary for livable livelihood, for both citizens and refugees, has been increasingly outsourced to venues outside the state. Rights are thus grounded increasingly on social, rather than on legal and political, grounds of recognition.

One must also consider whether the (deeply necessary) services provided by NGOs and solidarity networks alike are, in fact, rights-based, given that they lack the consistency and legitimacy of state bureaucratic and legal structures. Many scholars of humanitarianism, for instance, have argued that the ethic of care, whether framed in terms of compassion (Fassin 2005), hospitality (Cabot 2014; Rozakou 2012), or in this case solidarity (Theodossopoulos 2016), undermines the aspects of entitlement that are formally endemic to rights-based infrastructures.[17] As the right to refuge in Europe has been increasingly devolved not just to the borders but also to formations explicitly marked as nonstate, this right itself has been thrown into question.

Yet, scholarship has also shown that nonstate institutions and networks are always crucial for the recognition and practice of rights. Humanitarian and rights-based NGOs have attested to their ambivalent position vis-à-vis the state (Ferguson 1994; Fisher 1997). Ferguson and Gupta (2002) for instance, famously argued that neoliberal governmentality must be considered in terms of a respatialized state, which is intimately entangled in institutions and networks marked as civil society.[18] Political anthropologists themselves have been pushed to reconceptualize how they and their interlocutors frame the boundary between state and nonstate. This was a crucial tension that I explored in my earlier research on asylum, in which the limited capacity and willingness of the Greek state to receive and support asylum seekers and refugees was widely discussed by state employees, NGO workers, and refugees alike. NGO workers spoke of the ambiguities and contradictions that they negotiated in their work: having the desire and responsibility to help those seeking assistance, but without the capacity, resources, or legitimacy of an (imagined, but nonexistent) state infrastructure for assisting asylum seekers and refugees. Workers often voiced frustration at how they did "the state's work." Still, the NGO's role as a formal organization, with close ties to the state (financially, bureaucratically, and socially), and its professionalized, bureaucratically robust approach, made it distinctly state-like. Thus, well before the current refugee crisis, a small, professionalized sphere of NGOs and international organizations took on the crucial, though highly imperfect, work of seeking to ensure rights and services for asylum seekers and refugees, emerging as a kind of shadow state beneath and alongside the formal state.

The rise of solidarity networks in austerity Greece, while certainly innovative, also attests to the increasing precaritization of rights. Through solidarity, rights and services are no longer based on one's recognition as a rights-bearing-subject by the state or even by a shadow state (such as an NGO). Rather, such recognition is increasingly grounded on lateral, informal networks, shared socialities, and an explicit rejection of professionalized, hierarchically structured labor. Solidarity initiatives, like NGOs before them, have taken on the task of remaking a venue for the distribution of rights and services outside the state, at a moment when the state of rights has, in many ways, failed. However, the state and the shadow state remain constitutive frameworks against which solidarity claims a space for itself. In the summer of 2015, at a small festival of solidarity networks in the historically leftist neighborhood of Kaisariani, I read a poster meant to educate citizens on what is and is not solidarity. One of the very first distinctions mentioned was that solidarity structures are not NGOs. Yet solidarians' persistent engagement in drawing such distinctions itself underscores the continuing slippage between those who seek to provide rights and services outside the state and the specter of the state itself. Because the state under austerity has been increasingly absent (and hamstrung) in its provision of rights to both refugees and citizens, alternative venues have emerged for the realization of livable livelihood and rights. Still, behind this increasingly neoliberalized state, a failed vision of the European state as a state of rights remains, emerging as a kind of specter in the venues where rights are indeed (if only partially) remade. This specter haunts the projects of NGO workers and solidarians alike.

Conclusion

By the time this article is published, we will certainly have entered a new phase of Europe's border contest; Greece might or might not be in the limelight. Still, as I have tried to show, a focus on "crisis" does little to underscore the systemic and structural factors that make crises possible — crises that most often unfold in the twilight zones far beyond the range of public interest and attention. The refugee crisis must be understood not as a simple aberration, but in part as an effect of longstanding patterns of securitization and neoliberalization instituted, quite systematically, through European financial and migration-related policies and practices. To return to Bourdieu (1998), in a talk he gave to the trade unions of Athens in 1996 on the dangers of neoliberalism, he called on the need for the combined critical power of intellectuals, workers, and associations of all kinds to question the withering away of the state of rights. My various research interlocutors, both then and now, before and after the onset of austerity, have sought to provide venues for rights and livable livelihood against the backdrop of what has increasingly become a crisis, a moment of reckoning and judgment, regarding the state of rights in Europe today.

Heath Cabot is Assistant Professor at the University of Pittsburgh in the Department of Anthropology. She is the author of *On the Doorstep of Europe: Asylum and Citizenship in Greece* (University of Pennsylvania Press, 2014). Her research interests include political and legal anthropology, asylum and human rights, the anthropology of ethics, advocacy, and activism. Her current research concerns social insurance and community-based health care in Greece. She is currently the coeditor of the *Political and Legal Anthropology Review*.

Notes

1. I have also presented a similar argument regarding crisis and continuity in an essay for *Allegra Laboratory* (Cabot 2015).
2. In a field that has been famed for its appreciation of everyday life and small, even out-of-the-way places, this might rightfully strike some as contradictory.
3. The Olympics of 2004 are a case in point regarding the ways in which Greece remained marginal in the global public eye, even as it symbolically entered the modernity of the contemporary Olympic games. Even as Greece renovated its metro system and built quite extraordinary infrastructures for the games, international media coverage focused on aspects of disorganization and corruption, such as the "last-minute" aspects

of the building process, and the "corruption" of taxi drivers and hotel operators who overcharged tourists.

4. Indeed, in migration literature, the concept of transit countries versus destination countries has been increasingly complexified, as it has become clear that persons increasingly spend significant time in countries where they might never have intended to stay, while places that people might in fact seek to reach also become places of transit (see Coutin 2005).

5. Grand Chamber, European Court of Human Rights, January 2011. M.S.S. v. Belgium and Greece.

6. As the M.S.S. decision itself shows, while housing and social support for asylum seekers is always an issue in Europe, the dearth of social support to asylum seekers in Greece is particularly noteworthy in comparison (see, e.g., Clarke 2013; Ioakimidis, Santos, and Martinez Herrero 2014; Norredam, Mygind, and Krasnik 2006).

7. With the enormous numbers entering Greece in 2015–16, the Greek government—at the behest of the European Union (EU)—created hot spots on the Greek islands, with the formal goal of registering asylum seekers and granting them temporary permission to stay in order to apply for asylum. With the inauguration of the Turkey/EU deal in March 2016, however, these hotpots have effectively become, in the words of one interlocutor (a worker on Lesvos) "detention centers," where many people are subject to removal to Turkey. Meanwhile, the problem of housing and services for those in limbo are extremely concerning.

8. After the institution of the agreement, asylum committees in Greece initially refused to make decisions that would return asylum seekers to Turkey on the grounds that Turkey cannot be deemed a safe third country. This sparked the minister of migration, Giannis Mouzalas, to reconfigure the personnel on the asylum committees in order to make them more restrictive.

9. The fear of being returned to Turkey, along with other policing measures, seems to have served as a deterrent. It is also noteworthy how policing on the opposite side of the Aegean (from the Turkish coast) seems also to have limited arrivals in Greece. For a detailed overview of how the hot spots are supposed to function, see European Council for Refugees and Exiles (2016).

10. As in all asylum regimes, decision-making for country relocation is subject to the shifting political and social contexts of the examining country. For instance, recently I have heard numerous accounts (from advocates and asylum seekers) of palpably restrictive decisions rendered by Germany and France, in particular.

11. By the time this chapter is published, the asylum system in Greece will almost certainly have undergone significant changes. The Asylum Information Database (AIDA) provides frequent updates on asylum systems. The most recent is this summary of the key changes to the Greek asylum procedure in 2016–17 (Asylum Information Database and the Greek Council for Refugees 2017).

12. As Anna Carastathis (2015) shows, another trend has been forms of hostility to migrants that frame increasing racism as a result of austerity and the bitter pill that Greeks have had to swallow.

13. Whereas solidarity is a concept most often associated with the more radical left (Rozakou 2006), it has exploded in the public sphere since the onset of economic collapse in Greece. The current politicization of solidarity, however, tends to elide the ways in which this category has often been associated with spheres of civil society that so-called solidarians themselves would reject, including Allileggii, the NGO of the Orthodox Church, that significantly predates the crisis.

14. These rumors themselves highlight the role of money as a moralizing force in austerity Greece, as a way either to claim moral purity or to ascribe moral impurity.

15. As the reception challenges in Greece have become more chronic, formal NGOs and international organizations have now become relatively dominant, not so much super-seding as functioning alongside and sometimes overlapping with solidarity initiatives (though not always in harmony). As the relative urgency of the situation has waned, some solidarity groups have disbanded. Other collectivities with roots in the solidarity movement have taken on the status of formal NGOs or nonprofits, an example of what Katerina Rozakou (Rozakou 2017b) refers to as the "NGOification of solidarity."
16. As I argue in a recent article, solidarians themselves are rarely naïve about these over-laps between solidarity and neoliberalization, and they often engage in heated mo-ments of internal critique and debate regarding solidarity's role as an emancipatory force that is, simultaneously, entangled in neoliberal tendencies (Cabot 2016).
17. In my book *On the Doorstep of Europe* (Cabot 2014), I show how the concept of hospi-tality, based on asymmetry and obligation, is contradictory to the enactment of rights-based assistance, which are grounded on entitlement.
18. Such approaches are, of course, grounded in the Foucauldian argument that modernity is characterized by the pastoralization of governmental power and its diffusion into the arenas of ethics and care of the self (Foucault 1988).

References

Agamben, Giorgio. 2005. *State of Exception*. Chicago: University of Chicago Press.

Allison, Anne. 2013. *Precarious Japan*. Durham, NC: Duke University Press.

Arendt, Hannah. 1976 [1951]. *The Origins of Totalitarianism*. New York: Harcourt.

Asylum Information Database and the Greek Council for Refugees. 2017. *Country Report: Greece*. Brussels: The European Council for Refugees and Exiles. Retrieved from http://www.asylumineurope.org/sites/default/files/report-download/aida_gr_2017update.pdf.

Athanasiou, Athina. 2012. *E Krise Os Katastase Ektaktes Anagkes*. Athens: Savvalas.

Avramopoulos, Dimitris. 2015. "A European Response to Migration: Showing Solidarity and Sharing Responsibility." Brussels, August 14.

Bakalaki, Alexandra. 2008. "On the Ambiguities of Altruism and the Domestication of Emo-tions." *Historein* 8: 83–93.

Bourdieu, Pierre. 1998. *Acts of Resistance: Against the Tyranny of the Market*. New York: Polity.

Brekke, Jan-Paul, and Grete Brochmann. 2015. "Stuck in Transit: Secondary Migration of Asylum Seekers in Europe, National Differences, and the Dublin Regulation." *Journal of Refugee Studies* 28(2): 145–62.

Cabot, Heath. 2012. "The Governance of Things: Documenting Limbo in the Greek Asylum Procedure." *Political and Legal Anthropology Review* 35(1): 11–29.

———. 2014. *On the Doorstep of Europe: Asylum and Citizenship in Greece*. Philadelphia: Uni-versity of Pennsylvania Press.

———. 2015. "Crisis and Continuity: A Critical Look at the "European Refugee Crisis." *Al-legraLab*, November 10.

———. 2016. "Contagious Solidarity: Refiguring Care and Citizenship in Greece's Social Clinics." *Social Anthropology:* 24(2): 152–166.

Carastathis, Anna. 2015. "The Politics of Austerity and the Affective Economy of Hostility: Racialized Gendered Violence and Crises of Belonging in Greece." *Feminist Review* 109: 73–95.

Clarke, Jennifer. 2013. "Transnational Actors in National Contexts: Migrant Organizations in Greece in Comparative Perspective." *Southeast European and Black Sea Studies* 13(2): 281–301.

Coutin, Susan. 2005. "Being En Route." *American Anthropologist* 107(2): 195–206.
Davis, Elizabeth. 2015. "'We've Toiled without End': Publicity, Crisis, and the Suicide 'Epidemic' in Greece." *Comparative Studies in Society and History* 57(4): 1007–36.
Douzinas, Costas. 2013. *Philosophy and Resistance in the Crisis: Greece and the Future of Europe.* Cambridge, UK: Polity Press.
Du Boulay, Juliet. 1974. *Portrait of a Greek Mountain Village.* Oxford, UK: Clarendon Press.
European Council for Refugees and Exiles. 2016. *The Implementation of the Hotspots in Italy and Greece: A Study.* Brussels: European Council for Refugees and Exiles. Retrieved from https://www.ecre.org/wp-content/uploads/2016/12/HOTSPOTS-Report-5.12.2016.pdf.
Farmer, Paul. 2005. *Pathologies of Power: Health, Human Rights, and the New War on the Poor.* Berkeley: University of California Press.
Fassin, Didier. 2005. "Compassion and Repression: The Moral Economy of Immigration Policies in France." *Cultural Anthropology* 20(3): 362–87.
Feldman, Gregory. 2012. *The Migration Apparatus: Security, Labor, and Policymaking in the European Union.* Palo Alto, CA: Stanford University Press.
Ferguson, James. 1994. *The Anti-Politics Machine: "Development," Depoliticization, and Bureaucratic Power in Lesotho.* Minneapolis: University of Minnesota Press.
Ferguson, James, and Akhil Gupta. 2002. "Spatializing States: Toward an Ethnography of Neoliberal Governmentality." *American Ethnologist* 29(4): 981–1002.
Fisher, William. 1997. "Doing Good? The Politics and Anti-Politics of NGO Practices." *Annual Review of Anthropology* 26: 439–64.
Foucault, Michel. 1988. *The History of Sexuality.* New York: Vintage Books.
Fouskas, Theodoros. 2013. "Low-Status Work Consequences on Immigrant Workers' Organization: The Cases of Five Immigrant Groups in Athens." *International Review of Sociology* 23(3): 671–98.
Friedl, Ernestine. 1962. *Vasilika: A Village in Modern Greece.* New York: Holt.
Giovanopoulos, Christos, and Dimitris Mitropoulos, eds. 2011. *Demokratia under Construction: Apo Tous Dromous Stiw Plateies.* Athens: A/Synecheia.
Gluckman, Max. 2006 [1965]. *Politics, Law, and Ritual in Tribal Society.* London: Aldine Transaction.
Howden, Daniel, and Apostolis Fotiadis. 2017. "The Refugee Archipelago: The Inside Story of What Went Wrong in Greece." *Refugees Deeply.* Retrieved from https://www.newsdeeply.com/refugees/articles/2017/03/06/the-refugee-archipelago-the-inside-story-of-what-went-wrong-in-greece.
Ioakimidis, Vasilios, Clara Cruz Santos, and Ines Martinez Herrero. 2014. "Reconceptualizing Social Work in Times of Crisis: An Examination of the Cases of Greece, Spain and Portugal." *International Social Work* 57(4): 285–300.
Knight, Daniel M. 2015. *History, Time, and Economic Crisis in Central Greece.* New York: Palgrave Macmillan.
Lazzarato, Maurizio. 2012. *The Making of the Indebted Man: An Essay on the Neoliberal Condition,* translated by Joshua David Jordan. Cambridge, MA: Semiotext(E).
———. 2014. *Signs and Machines: Capitalism and the Production of Subjectivity.* Los Angeles: Semiotext(e).
Magliveras, Konstantinos D. 2011. *Migration Law in Greece.* Alphen aan den Rijn, The Netherlands: Kluwer Law International.
McDonough, Paul, and Evangelia Lilian Tsourdi. 2012. "The 'Other' Greek Crisis: Asylum and EU Solidarity." *Refugee Survey Quarterly* 31(4): 67–100.
Merry, Sally Engle. 2006. *Human Rights and Gender Violence: Translating International Law into Local Justice.* Chicago: University of Chicago Press.
Moreno-Lax, Violeta. 2012. "Dismantling the Dublin System: Mss V. Belgium and Greece." *European Journal of Migration and Law* 14(1): 1–31.

Muehlebach, Andrea Karin. 2012. *The Moral Neoliberal: Welfare and Citizenship in Italy.* Chicago: University of Chicago Press.

Norredam, Marie, Anna Mygind, and Allan Krasnik. 2006. "Access to Health Care for Asylum Seekers in the European Union—a Comparative Study of Country Policies." *European Journal of Public Health* 16(3): 285–89.

Panourgia, Neni. 2011. "The Squared Constitution of Dissent." Hot Spots, *Cultural Anthropology website, October 29.* Retrieved from http://www.culanth.org/fieldsights/252-the-squared-constitution-of-dissent.

Papadimitriou, Panayiotis, and Ioannis Papageorgiou. 2005. "The New Dubliners Implementation of European Council Regulation 343/2003 (Dublin-Ii) by the Greek Authorities." *Journal of Refugee Studies* 18(3): 299–318.

Papageorgiou, Ioannis. 2013. "The Europeanization of Immigration and Asylum in Greece (1990–2012)." *International Journal of Sociology* 43(3): 72–90.

Papataxarchis, Evthymios. 2016. "Being 'There': At the Frontline of the 'European Refugee Crisis'—Part 1." *Anthropology Today* 32(2): 5–9.

Placas, Aimee 2011. "Trickle-Down Debt." Hot Spots, *Cultural Anthropology Website,* October 31. Retrieved from http://www.culanth.org/fieldsights/257-trickle-down-debt.

———. 2016. "Money Talk." Hot Spots, *Cultural Anthropology Website,* April 21. Retrieved from http://www.culanth.org/fieldsights/856-money-talk.

PRO ASYL and Group of Lawyers for the Rights of Refugees and Migrants, Athens. 2007. *The Truth May Be Bitter but It Must be Told: The Situation of Refugees in the Aegean and the Practices of the Greek Coast Guard.* Franfurt: PRO ASYL. Retrieved from https://www.proasyl.de/material/the-truth-may-be-bitter-but-it-must-be-told/.

Rakopoulos, Theodoros. 2014. "The Crisis Seen from Below, Within, and Against: From Solidarity Economy to Food Distribution Cooperatives in Greece." *Dialectical Anthropology* 38: 189–207.

———. 2015. "Solidarity's Tensions: Informality, Sociality and the Greek Crisis." *Social Analysis* 59(3): 85–104.

———. 2016. "Solidarity: The Egalitarian Tensions of a Bridge Concept." *Social Anthropology* 24(2): 142–151.

Roitman, Janet L. 2014. *Anti-Crisis.* Durham, NC: Duke University Press.

Rosen, Tracey. 2011. "The 'Chinese-Ification' of Greece." Hot Spots, *Cultural Anthropology Website,* October 30. Retrieved from http://www.culanth.org/fieldsights/253-the-chinese-ification-of-greece.

Rozakou, Katerina. 2006. "Street Work: Oria Kai Antiphaseis Ton Synanteseon Ellenon Ethelonton Kai Prosphygon." In *Oi Peripeteies Tes Eterotetas: E Paragoge Tes Politismikes Diaphoras Sten Semerine Ellada,* edited by Evthymios Papataxiarchis, 325–55. Athens: Alexandria.

———. 2012. "The Biopolitics of Hospitality in Greece: Humanitarianism and the Management of Refugees." *American Ethnologist* 39(3): 562–77.

———. 2016a. "Crafting the Volunteer: Voluntary Associations and the Reformation of Sociality." *Journal of Modern Greek Studies* 34(1): 79–102.

———. 2016b. "Socialities of Solidarity: Revisiting the Gift Taboo in Times of Crises." *Social Anthropology* 24(2): 185–99.

———. 2017a. "Nonrecording the 'European Refugee Crisis' in Greece: Navigating through Irregular Bureaucracy." *Focaal: Journal of Global and Historical Anthropology* 77: 36–49.

———. 2017b. "Solidarity #Humanitarianism: The Blurred Boundaries of Humanitarianism in Greece." *AllegraLab,* September 27. Retrieved from http://allegralaboratory.net/solidarity-humanitarianism/.

Rozakou, Katerina, and Barak Kalir. 2016. "'Giving Form to Chaos': The Futility of EU Border Management at Moria Hotspot in Lesvos."*Governing Mobility through European Hotspot Centres Forum, Society and Space.* Retrieved from http://societyandspace.org/2016/11/

16/giving-form-to-chaos-the-futility-of-eu-border-management-at-moria-hotspot-in-lesvos/.

Stuckler, David, and Sanjay Basu. 2013. *The Body Economic: Why Austerity Kills—Recessions, Budget Battles, and the Politics of Life and Death.* New York: Basic Books.

Rakopoulos, Theodoros. 2016. "Solidarity: The Egalitarian Tensions of a Bridge Concept." *Social Anthropology* 24(2):142–151.

Thielemann, Eiko, and Carolyn Armstrong. 2013. "Understanding European Asylum Co-operation under the Schengen/Dublin System: A Public Goods Framework." *European Security* 22(2): 148–64.

Triandafillydou, Anna, and Michaela Maroufof. 2009. "Idea Project Report." Retrieved 18 April 2010 from http://www.eliamep.gr/.

Turner, Victor W. 1974. *Dramas, Fields, and Metaphors; Symbolic Action in Human Society, Symbol, Myth, and Ritual.* Ithaca, NY: Cornell University Press.

United Nations High Commissioner for Refugees (UNHCR). 2011. UNHCR Global Trends 2010.

Volpp, Leti. 2012. "Imaginings of Space in Immigration Law." *Law, Culture and the Humanities* 9(3): 456–74.

Chapter 11

Giname Kinezoi!
(We've Become Chinese!)
Critical Developments in
the Imaginary of Chinese Capitalism

Tracey A. Rosen

Introduction

Throughout the period of Greece's sovereign debt crisis, the specter of China has been continually invoked to express anxieties about the nation's future. In the wake of austerity measures designed to create a more flexible labor force, the neologism *kinezopoiisi* (Chineseification) has been increasingly used to reference the dismantling of state protections and the overall degradation of Greek life. The unwelcome prospect of Greeks working for "Chinese wages" under "Chinese conditions" has stoked resistance across the political spectrum, including the radical left and extreme right.

Yet the possibility of "becoming Chinese" is not uniformly taken as negative. For instance, in the summer of 2008, at the time China was hosting its first Olympics, a prominent Greek electronics and appliances chain store, Kotsovolos, ran a very telling, award-winning ad campaign: "With prices so low, you'll think we've become Chinese!" the TV and radio ads boasted as the company's stores around Greece were festooned with red paper lanterns and banners exclaiming, "We've become Chinese!" Indeed, for some, the adjective Chinese not only suggests increased access to a greater and cheaper variety of goods, but it also suggests sanguine promises of jobs, investments, and global integration. For instance, in a 2015 op-ed by the managing editor of the mainstream daily newspaper *E Kathi-*

Notes for this chapter begin on page 318.

merini, Alexis Papahelas hails the current Chinese Communist Party's authoritarian style of leadership as a model to be emulated (Papahelas 2015). Exhorting the prime minister to "Do it like the Chinese," Papahelas advises Tsipras to ignore his constituents and shed the clunky, outdated Soviet orientation which is seen as an obstacle to Chinese investments into Greek infrastructure. The window of opportunity for the Chinese windfall is small, he presses, and Chinese investors will not wait long when the UK, Serbia, and other countries are rolling out the red carpet.

Presaging alternative futures of progress and decline, salvific windfall and civil erosion, China stands in as a figure for the larger structural contradictions of Greece's engagement with global capitalism.[1] As Greece has become more vulnerable through the debt crisis and austerity, this ambivalent coupling of hope and fear has only amplified. In this chapter, I examine how this figure of China has emerged—and how it continues to evolve—in relation to Greece's turbulent integration into European and global markets. I begin by examining the heady period of the introduction of Chinese migrants, commodities, and capital into Greece that paralleled Greece's Europeanization.[2] I argue that new, ethnicized categories of productive labor and value have been transformed alongside these new patterns of capital flow, and I consider the shifts in everyday practices and ideologies that have and have not occurred through the sovereign debt crisis and ensuing regime of austerity. While the sovereign debt crisis here serves as a narrative device that marks an important moment in Greece, I am wary of contributing to temporal narratives of a "prior to" and a "post" that would obscure the way in which the Chinese–Greek interactions and markets are tied to larger processes and ongoing crises of global capitalism. The upshots of neoliberal reforms associated with Europeanization are not reducible to any simple narrative of decline or resilience, but are rather multiple and complex. Below, I attempt to clarify this complexity by providing three ways in which Chinese–Greek economic relations have developed over the course of the past two decades.

Chinese Migrants and Commodities in Europeanizing Greece

Chinese migrants and commodities began entering Greece in significant numbers at the turn of the millennium as both China and Greece had undertaken major transformations integrating into the global market a decade earlier. Expressed in Athens and Beijing's success in winning the bid to host the Olympic Games, both Greece and China were undergoing a renewal of their status as cosmopolitan, open nation-states. These parallel trajectories of the two nation-states, along with a shared connection as the birthplace of Eastern and Western civilization, respectively, become an important platform though which twenty-first-century bilateral negotiations and trade are executed.

China's historic entry into the World Trade Organization in 2000 followed a decade of reforms initiated to open up the country to international markets. The steady embrace of capitalism saw the corporatization of Chinese state-owned enterprises, the expansion of private property, and the increased courtship of foreign direct investments, among a myriad of other reforms designed to stoke business and entrepreneurship. At the popular level, individual subjects were also in the process of a kind of privatization as new values and ideologies of self-actualization and enterprise began to take root (see Chu 2010; Liu 2002; Zhang 2001; Zhang and Ong 2008). Though soap operas, advertisements, and other forms of discourse, individuals were encouraged to cultivate their entrepreneurial spirit and seek their fortunes away from home (Liu 1997). The vast majority of these individuals moved within China, but competition and new opportunities prompted many of China's floating population of internal migrants to set their sights on Europe.

Southern and Eastern Europe was seen as a peripheral but lucrative frontier and attracted Chinese merchants with untapped markets resulting from the fall of the Soviet bloc in the East (Pieke et al. 2004) and economic globalization in the South. Possibly the most significant story of Chinese migration to Europe comes from the Umbrian textile center of Prato. In the late 1980s Chinese migrants were brought to the traditional manufacturing city by subcontractors producing high-quality, brand-name fashion. Chinese migrants were initially used as cheaper, skilled labor; they slowly began to take ownership of the subcontracting firms, eventually turning them into final firms where those migrants controlled the entire process from design to sales (Dei Ottati 2009). Prato has emerged as the heart of Chinese textile manufacture in Europe and is understood to have the highest concentration of Chinese nationals of any city in the European Union (EU) (Donadio 2010). As Antonella Ceccagno (2003, 2009) notes, in 2003 there were four thousand Chinese firms in a city of fewer than two hundred thousand.

It was through Italy, and specifically Prato, that many Chinese entrepreneurs got their initial foothold into the Greek market. While Prato was becoming saturated with production houses, Greece provided a new market for Chinese merchants to sell "Made in Italy" fashion. At this time, Greece's liberalization was largely guided through its own political and economic reforms during the 1990s and 2000s within the overarching framework of its Europeanization. The 2001 adoption of the new European currency along with other large-scale Europeanization efforts, such as the removal of religion from identity cards and the signing of the Schengen Agreement in 1985, created a more flexible and globally integrated populace. Equipped with a new consumer subjectivity and choice in the marketplace, as described in the next chapter, this volume, by Aimee Placas, the nation was beginning to enjoy a new, elevated status.

The boon in consumerism and consumer choice, however, was accompanied by a corresponding decline in production. Liberalization proved particularly disastrous for the Greek textile industry. One of the traditional sectors of the Greek economy—Greek apparel, shoe, and toy manufacturers—was forced to compete with multinational companies under a new regime of lifted price controls and extended legal working hours (Bennison and Boutsouki 1995). The vast majority of the Greek enterprises were small family firms, 90 percent of which had ten employees or fewer (Lyberaki 2011). Wages were too high to compete with the influx of cheaper imports and too undercapitalized to compete with expensive European manufacture. Some firms survived by upgrading their industry; however, this was increasingly difficult because bank deregulations saw a rise in the cost of loans. Other firms resorted to what David Harvey (1989, 2011) refers to as a spatial fix by moving their factories across the border into Bulgaria or other neighboring countries.

The demise of the textile industry is set in contrast to the rosier picture of economic revitalization that usually characterizes Greece's economy between 1995 and 2007. While it is largely accepted that there has been a rise in real wages in the 1990s and 2000s, the rise was uneven, and behind the appearances lay a creeping gap between price inflation and wage stagnation. As Spyros Sakellaropoulos (2010), for instance, notes, figures from the European commission demonstrating the rise of purchasing power of average wages were manipulated and greatly overestimated.[3] Between 1996 and 2004 the proportion of household income savings fell by almost half, and in 2006, the supposed height of Greece' economic success, 21 percent of the population were living below the poverty threshold (Sakellaropoulos 2010), the highest in the EU, according to World Bank figures (2012). At the same time, there was a sharp spike in consumer credit following the new availability of loans at unprecedentedly low interest rates following Greece's adoption of the euro (see Placas 2016; Placas this volume). The sudden access to credit helped ramp up competitive displays of conspicuous consumption (Veblen 2013) among Greece's economic elite, many of whom used credit to purchase home renovations and luxury items, such as second cars and designer fashion.

Yet while new forms of material wealth were increasingly on display among the affluent minority, the larger majority of Greece's population were using new loans to make ends meet: for example, to pay for groceries, energy bills, and taxes (Doulos and Katsaitis 2014). In short, income inequality was high.[4] The initial success of Chinese merchants lay in their ability to tap into this gap between increased consumer desires and limited access for a large public. By importing cheap fashion directly from Prato, Chinese merchants provided many Greeks with a way to engage in the same shopping and sartorial patterns as their wealthier Greek and European counterparts. The speed and efficiency by which cheap and fashionable clothes were able to enter the Greek high streets were critical to this success. One common pathway by which this is accomplished was the use of digital cameras to capture the latest trends in window displays in Rome and Milan (and other European centers of fashion). "Close to fashion" and churned out at exceptionally high and fast rates, Chinese merchants offered large stocks and varieties of clothing for much cheaper prices. In short,"fast fashion"—cheaply and quickly manufactured clothing following the latest trends—had taken Greece by storm: the nation, armed with new credit and a new sense of itself as no longer marginal but rather on par with the consumption patterns and material lifestyles of Western Europe, sought to wear its new status. Chinese middlemen helped bridge Greece and the rest of Europe by providing inhabitants at the lower end of the economic spectrum the ability to consume and dress like Europeans.

A Different Kind of Migrant

Despite the dominance of popular and scholarly narratives professing ethnic homogeneity prior to the end of the twentieth century, the Greek nation-state has been a locus of migration since its inception. However, it is true that new patterns of labor-specific migration began in the 1970s, with seasonal guest workers drawn from Asia and Africa (Cavounidis 2002; Triandafyllidou 2010; Yousef 2013),[5] and was heavily intensified after the fall of the Eastern bloc—most specifically Albania—in the early 1990s (Baldwin-Edwards 2004; Lawrence 2005). As a number of scholars have noted, the projection of criminality, danger, and contamination onto the laboring migrant operated as a way to perform a newly elevated European status (Bakalaki 2003; Karydis 1992). In other words, by representing migrants as backward and criminally envious, Greece and Greek lifestyles were established as coveted, legitimate, and modern.

   Chinese migrants constitute both a continuation and a distinct departure from the general discourse surrounding migrant laborers. Like these other migrants, Chinese migrants were also associated with new patterns of globalization and Athens' refurbished role as a cosmopolitan European center. This had less to do with Chinese merchants' facilitation of the latest

European-style fashions to Greece, as explained above, and more with the new presence of Asian faces and habits that mirrored the ethnic diversity of other major European capitals. Like migrants of other nationalities, Chinese migrants were also associated with danger and criminality. Yet, the particular form that this danger, criminality, and globalized threat takes is critically different.

To understand why the Chinese migrant threat takes a different shape, it is first important to note that Chinese migrants are the first migrant group to enter Greece as petty merchants, with cash and commodities rather than labor as their form of capital. That is, it is precisely their role as entrepreneurial middlemen that has helped put them in a markedly different discursive niche. As opposed to other laboring migrants who entered Greece in the early to mid-2000s and were often characterized by poverty and victimhood, the Chinese merchants were often visibly successful. As one longtime shop owner from Fujian explained to me, "In the early days, Chinese people were making a lot of money. They would come selling shoes on the street. And the next year they would own a shop, and the next year, multiple shops with fancy cars." The tremendous confusion surrounding the quick enrichment of the Chinese could often lead to resentment and suspicion among their neighbors.

A second important distinction between Chinese and other groups of migrants is that while people of various nationalities were becoming more visible on the city streets of Greece, Chinese migrants were mostly discernable—not through their bodies, but through their transformation of the built environment. In just a few years, the emergence of Chinese wholesale and retail shops changed the face of Athens' historical center. Located in between the downgraded and gentrifying areas of the historical center (Omonoia Square and Psiri), Chinese-owned shops were established along Athens' main avenue linking the city to the port of Piraeus. This pattern also occurred in Thessaloniki, where Chinese shops were situated on the margins of the historical center's gentrifying area, with immediate access to the city's port. Smaller cities and the rural periphery also saw a dramatic rise of Chinese shops as a local fixture.

Perceived not through any immediate, corporeal presence but through signs of their shops and commodities, Chinese middlemen may be viewed as the conceptual foil of the material, bodily labor of the "Albanian." As Albanians and other manual migrant laborers[6] took up jobs in construction, agriculture, and domestic work, they were viewed as engaging in productive labor that helped the Greek economy thrive. However feared and maligned migrants were and continue to be, by taking up the labor from which Greeks had been distancing themselves, these workers physically transformed the nation: converting dirt into cleanliness, raw materials into buildings, fields into food. For instance, the contributions of Albanian manual labor to the Greek nation was powerfully symbolized in the success of eleventh-hour construction projects for Athens' Olympics. Moreover, the (mostly female) laboring migrants are invited into the intimate spaces of the Greek home when they are charged with the hands-on care of the nation's children and elderly. Predictably, one of the anxieties created by these migrants, and particularly their children, is that they were getting too integrated and threatening to dilute the fabric of Greek ethnonational identity.

Chinese migrants, on the other hand, were criticized for not integrating enough. In direct contrast to the physical, embodied presence of the migrant manual laborer, Chinese middlemen were not viewed as producing national value but extracting it. One way in which such extraction is seen to occur is through the repatriation of profit back to China and lack of investment into the neighborhood. As one local worker complains to the center-left daily newspaper *Eleftherotypia*, "The Chinese don't even spend a Euro in the neighborhood. The Chinese bought that [pointing to a building on Kolokynthous] recently. They paid 100,000 euros and they don't even have an elevator or central heating" (G. D. 2007). Another coffee-shop owner related to me his experiences of his Chinese neighbors on Koumoundourou Square: "Chinese people rarely come in, when they do it is for tea. They are closed, they don't give money to the neighborhood, they cook food for one another, and rarely will come in and ask me to break some money. The Chinese bring gypsies etc., wherever they go, they sink the area. The area has gotten rough, Chinese have brought up the rent up, as well as the *aera* [transfer fees], and products must be very cheap. They work like ants, and have no private life, there is one boss and the other workers who work like slaves."

The criticism that the Chinese merchants do not invest in the neighborhood was one that I frequently encountered during fieldwork among merchants and neighbors of the central Athens area where the Chinese wholesalers are set up. An organizer of the central Athens residents' association with a considerable public profile expressed a number of sympathies for his Chinese neighbors and contrasts the coffee shop owner's description of the Chinese "sinking" the neighborhood. Rather, he credits them with revitalizing downgraded Koumoundourou Square where he lives above his family's shop. Yet, despite his progressive leanings, he also echoes very common complaints about his new neighbors:

> They [the Chinese] are taking the whole area over like a virus. They've bought up all the shops in the area and have completely changed the character of the neighborhood. Their shops are extremely bare, no money is invested. They

don't repair or renovate anything and the outside of their shops are filled with trash from the packaging. They are introverted and don't speak with white people, and pretend not to speak Greek . . . or they will only know Greek numbers. They eat in their shops with their own food. They work all day, how can they have a good time? The Chinese are like parts of an army, the Pakistanis are more natural. The more East you go, the worse it gets.

Such lack of financial investment into the neighborhood easily extends into a sense of a general lack of investment into the environment, their stores, and themselves. These interpretations of the Chinese negligence became moral censures of greed and machine-like self-denial. As another Greek shop owner in Omonoia explained to me, "The Chinese work longer hours because they are greedy. They help each other a lot, borrowing lots of money. They aren't afraid, they have no personal life. You can see them drinking lots of water during the day, they act like machines with no feelings." Lack of investment in shops along with putative ability to live without heat or air conditioning render Chinese nationals as machine-like profiteers. This characterization of the Chinese is further aided by the experience that Chinese people are rarely seen, while their shops and commodities are everywhere. Again, in contrast to the manual laborers creating productive value, the experience of the Chinese was abstract networks of value extraction. This ghostly absent presence only worked to heighten their strangeness and untrustworthiness. As Lacan (1999) has theorized, the Other emerges as such because they enjoy differently. The Chinese merchants and workers were seen to perversely enjoy nothing, except perhaps labor and profit, and the Greek described them as machines who "only drink water" and "only know Greek numbers." This characteristically contrasts and amplifies the Greek national self-stereotypes as carefree, Zorba-like revelers of the gambit of human emotion and experience.

Moreover, the imputed lack of attention of the Chinese to their own physicality carries threats of contamination to the health of the larger Greek public. One way in which this was expressed is the moral panic and a spate of rumors that circulated with regard to the dubious quality of Chinese products as harmful to Greek consumers' health.

Indeed, they were often characterized by the underworld, with connections to Italy and Italian Mafia as sensationalized in the 2008 popular Italian film, *Gomorrah* (Garrone 2009). The Chinese were also accused of unfair competitive practices: general tax evasion, not giving receipts, smuggling imports from China, operating without proper registration, and working illegally on Sundays. The assumed duplicitousness of the Chinese commodities is reflected in an assumed duplicity of the Chinese merchant, and the shared resemblance of Chinese commodities and merchants are well represented in rumors that Chinese merchants are similarly seen to be counterfeiting the histories of their identity and their stores (e.g., there are rumors that they recycle passports and identity cards from the deceased, use unregistered ghost ships in international waters as mobile factories, and transfer store ownership to avoid taxation). Yet, in addition to the old-time Mafia connections, the Chinese were also viewed as armaments of the powerful, massively expanding Chinese state. While the response to the Chinese by the Greeks could be multivocal and often ambivalent, there was an almost unanimous consensus that the Chinese were able to mobilize cash so quickly because they were paid by the Chinese state to set up shop in Greece.

In short, the Chinese—unfairly competitive, abstractly networked, and extractive—provided many Greeks with an embodied model by which Greece's further integration into global capitalism was rendered tangible and expressed. In 2009 the newly privatized port of Piraeus, the largest port serving the Mediterranean, was leased by the Chinese state-owned enterprise, China Ocean Shipping Company (COSCO). This spurred a new form of anti-Chinese reaction to the envisaged lowering of wages and working outside of union demands. As mentioned above, the term "Chineseification" (*kinezopoiisi*) was coined to describe the contagion of Chinese forms of labor and quality of life. This discourse piggybacked on the homegrown discourse of Chinese working in their shops all day and the global reputation for China as the low-wage workhouse of the nation. This discourse also expressed the perception that the country's value was being siphoned off by Chinese merchants returning their profits from Greece to China, as the COSCO deal projected what was occurring at the small, mercantile level to the level of national industries and policies.

From Economic Problem to Crisis

I turn my discussion here to the period of "crisis" following the domino of events precipitated by the Panhellenic Socialist Movement's (PASOK's) revelation of its inherited deficit in October 2009. In this period, the familiar form of moral panic expressed over migrants entering Greece would often give way to its inversion, as media headlines clamored, "The Albanians are fleeing Greece." Finding themselves no longer in a land of opportunity but, rather, on a rapidly sinking ship, Greece's inhabitants were interpellated as victims of the crisis regardless of ethnicity or citizenship status. For its part, the numbers of Greece's Chinese community were swiftly dwindling. Anecdotes collected from the Chinese daily newspaper and local Chinese and Greek shopkeepers point to 30 percent to 50 percent of the Chinese community closing shop to return to China or to continue their sojourn to other countries in Europe or, sometimes, Africa. The crisis also appears to have hit the Chinese community asymmetrically, as it did the larger nation. For example, I encountered a few cases where unfortunate shop owners, lacking the money or papers to leave Greece, found themselves working for former competitors who benefitted by the cheaper rents and decreased competition.

In my interviews with Chinese merchants after 2009, I heard many accounts of Greece's *jingji wenti* (economic problem).[7] The "economic problem" (and, less often, *jingji weiji* or economic crisis) could be used as a shorthand to explain a number of everyday obstacles, such as garbage on the street, police crackdowns, and crime. But mostly it was used to explain why business was going poorly and/or why people had left Greece. Yet, early into my fieldwork in the summer of 2007, the Chinese merchants I interviewed were already complaining of the "economic problem" to cite their business's lack of success. Two complaints were repeatedly recounted: first, "The Greeks have no money," and second, "There are too many Chinese."

These complaints about the "economic problem" in 2007 are easily tied to a number of issues associated with Greece's Europeanization and the vicissitudes of global capitalism as discussed above. However, post 2009 the global ebb and flow of people and commodities associated with the opening of European borders to capital circulation often is subsumed under the larger narrative of Greece's financial crisis. This is true about the use of the word "crisis" by Greek merchants who similarly used the term to discuss the demise of the textile industry. What this demonstrates is that as much as the word "crisis" might be deservedly tied to a particular event, it also serves as an overdetermined mode of thinking. It is a label that is so easily and readily applied to a situation that the state of crisis takes on a chronic dimension (see Vigh 2008). One of the important points about crisis, as Janet Roitman (2013) has noted, is that it bifurcates collective historical consciousness into a before and after, and carries a moral demand that the latter should break from the former. Closely following Reinhart Koselleck, Roitman explains that this moral demand creates a blind spot that unwittingly smuggles in a (Christian) epistemology and eschatology by which past knowledge is rendered false and the future contains the promise of both revelation and redemption. The political upshot of this process, according to Roitman, is that the wrong questions are asked. For instance, taking the U.S. mortgage crisis as an example, she points out that the narrative of crisis prompts the question, "Why were homes overvalued?" instead of, "How are house prices determined?" The former question seeks to rectify an assumed natural equilibrium of the market, whereas the latter

question—untethered to the "metaphorics of the eighteenth century"—
seeks to understand the larger process through which home values are
established (Koselleck 2002: 242). With Roitman's metacritique of crisis in
mind, the next section aims to lay out three different forms of postcrisis
development of Chinese–Greek market relations that provide empirical
complexity and confound any neat teleology of crisis.

More of the Same

After three decades supplying the domestic market with Greek clothing,
the low-cost, fast-fashion Sprider Stores closed its doors in the fall of 2013.
Sprider Stores was a large chain store with brand presence on the high
streets of cities and neighborhoods and was the highest-profile Greek alternative to the Chinese low-cost, retail clothing. Both a beneficiary and
a casualty of Greek economic revitalization, Europeanization, and economic crisis, Sprider Stores' rise and fall might be viewed as emblematic
of the rise and fall of the Greek textile industry as a whole.

Starting as a wholesale manufacturer of beach clothes in 1971, Sprider
Stores branched outside the domestic market, exporting wholesale merchandise to Europe and the United States in the 1980s. In the 1990s it
opened its first retail stores in Greece, broadening its product line, and
after 2000 it expanded its retail reach in the Balkans and Eastern Europe.
From eleven stores in Greece in 1999, it grew to one hundred and ten
stores abroad and domestically ten years later. Listed on the Athens stock
exchange in 2004, by 2009 investors had begun to view the chain as dangerously overextended, and the company started to close almost half of
its stores. The beginning of its precipitous decline was marked in 2012,
following a fire in one of its largest factories, a fire that authorities claimed
was purposely set to collect insurance money. Unable to secure loans from
domestic or international banks, in 2013 Sprider Stores applied for Article 99 (the corporate bankruptcy restructuring law) but was denied. The
abrupt collapse of the company left around eight hundred employees suddenly out of work. In several stores the workers staged occupations to
protest the closings.

In a number of cities, including Sparta, Patra, and Preveza, the vacant
Sprider stores were rented out by Chinese merchants selling fast fashion.
The response to the transfer of the retail spaces to Chinese hands change
elicited familiar reactions. First, there was a widespread sentiment that the
new Chinese renters indexed the demise of the larger local market. As one
internet blogger reported from the northern Greek town of Preveza, "Chinese merchants deliver the knock out punch [*charistike vole*] to the Preveza
market. The former Sprider is becoming a Chinese superstore. If it is not

enough that the stores of Preveza are mostly empty of customers, now the Chinese merchants, who have enjoyed special tolerance from the Greek state, come to give the final blow" ("Charistike Vole " 2014).

The characterization of Chinese stores as delivering the final blow to a crisis-torn economy is one that I have encountered as early as 2004, during the height of Greece's economic revitalization. In these earlier cases, the Greek state is similarly blamed for its willful negligence. Similarly, the earlier cases also use the concept of crisis to bridge the end of Greek with the rise of Chinese mercantile activity. The blogger continues with other familiar discursive points: "Many professionals will be directly affected by the introduction of Chinese garments, shoes, curtains and relief items to be housed in large space where the SPRIDER store used to operate on Ioanninon Avenue. This store will not have any restrictions covering its operation nor its products, and most importantly it will not employ Greeks as staff. Most people are familiar with how these typical Chinese traders leave no money in the local market but only seek profit." ("Charistike Vole" 2014).

A report from *Veriotis,* an online local news site covering the small city of Veria, lodges similar complaints:

> **Raid of Chinese Shops in Veria:** Thousands of square meters are now occupied by Chinese shops in Veria. In the last month we've received . . . a raid of Chinese "cheap" ["*fteniarikon"*]shops. The closed super-market "Arvanitidi" on Alexander Street was taken by the Chinese! The Chinese took the regional "Sprider" stores that were closed. The Chinese took two to three stores that closed in Pieria. The fact that they constantly open new shops means that they are preferred by consumers, who now have little money to spare. But how can a person from Veria compete with a Chinaman, when the latter enjoys numerous exemptions, while "our" traders, . . . who don't enjoy the same exemptions, give "blood" to tax hikes, banks and bureaucracy. (Epidrome Kinezikon magazion 2013)

Second, from the perspective of such residents not only do the Chinese deliver the final blow to the Greek market taking advantage of the crisis, but they also do so in a manner that exploits the trust of Greek consumers toward Greek goods. After the transfer of ownership to *Kinezika symferonta* (Chinese interests), immediate complaints that the Chinese had done nothing to change the store, including the Sprider sign and the Sprider bags, began to circulate. As one TV news journalist from the Laconian news channel Apela.gr reports, "Our fellow citizens have been talking a lot about the reoperation of the Sparta's chain store, Sprider, because its doors are once again open. However, reality is not as it appears. At this point the store is run by Chinese interests. At this address everything has been left the same, except for, of course the merchandise. Is this an oversight or is it on purpose? ("Georganes gia Kineziko Sprider" 2013). The reporter interviews the president of the Commercial Association of Sparta who accuses the Chinese of intentionally misleading the public. Informing viewers that he cannot legally prosecute, he urges the Greek public to lodge consumer complaints.

The idea that the Chinese are understood to "not play fair" is grounded and rather overdetermined by the popular Greek expression to *kano to kinezo* (make like the "Chinaman")[8]. The expression refers to playing stupid, to donning a mask of inscrutability or stupidity to hide underlying and nefarious intentions. Again, while the looming menace of other migrant groups might be read through the threats of physical, embodied violence, the Chinese threat is essentially one of uncanny mimicry and vampiric value extraction. As the logic goes, not only do the Chinese damage local and national economic reproduction through a kind of expropriation, but they also do so in the diabolical manner of exploiting the innocent goodwill of Greek consumers looking to contribute to their economy by buying Greek. The sense of the state-backed network of Chinese interests having taken up home in the shell of Sprider replays this obsession with making like the "Chinaman" in Greece's brave new world where "reality is not as it appears."

The Changing Face of Kerameikos

I was alerted to the buying up of Sprider stores in the summer of 2016 by a second-generation Chinese store owner with a shop on Kolokynthous in the heart of Athens' wholesale district in Kerameikos. In his early twenties, Huajian took ownership of a wholesale shoe shop from his parents who had moved to Greece in 2000 from Li'Ao in the Wenzhou prefecture of Zhejiang. Huajian explains to me that as far as he knows half of the Chinese merchants have left due to the economic problem. At the time of my interview, Huajian referenced his biggest "economic problem" by showing me a ten-page government form he was filling out in order to bypass the current capital controls to send money to Prato to buy his stock.

Despite the ongoing crisis, the shop that Huajian runs looks markedly upscale compared to the Chinese shops I studied between 2007 and 2011 in Kerameikos. In fact, the entirety of the neighborhood's appearance has been transformed in a manner that seems to be strikingly inconsistent with the usual picture of economic crisis. Compared to the shops from a decade earlier, which were usually bare-bones operations with stock haphazardly piled in open cardboard boxes, many of the new Chinese shops are larger and have been renovated and designed with customer experience in mind. Walking around the neighborhood, it is immediately visible that more capital has been invested in overhead to update shop signs, sample displays, and storefront windows. Another transformation that confounds the image of economic crisis is the sudden arrival of dozens of Greek-owned wholesale clothing shops around 2013 where only a couple existed before. The Greek stores, which sell Greek- and Bulgarian-made manufactured items, are similarly upscale and design conscious.

While these transformations appear to be at odds with the crisis, Huajian explains that they are, in fact, a function of the crisis. Accordingly, competition grew increasingly fierce among Chinese shops during the crisis and many businesses did not survive. Those that did survive needed to shore up their capital and spend more money on the presentation of their shop in order to distinguish themselves and compete. A similar explanation was given to me by several Greek shop owners who explained that the mass influx of Greek stores in Kerameikos do not represent a renaissance of Greek manufacture. Rather they are an effect of larger Greek firms consolidating, contracting, and moving into the neighborhood in order to share in the market created by the Chinese wholesalers.

One of the upshots of increased competition is that there is greater market integration between Greek and Chinese enterprises that are evolving together. This market integration can be viewed in a number of ways. At the level of labor, Greeks shops are beginning to hire Chinese labor for their knowledge of the industry, language ability, and legal vulnerability. On the other hand, whereas Greek merchants began buying cheaper Chinese merchandise several years after the Chinese merchants began entering Greece, Chinese merchants are beginning to buy Greek wholesale clothing as well. In terms of the shop appearance, Chinese-owned shops look more like Greek stores and are no longer adorned with telltale red lanterns that so conspicuously marked them when the Chinese shops first arrived.

Yet, while the market appears to be getting more integrated and the "ethnicity "of the merchandise more confused, there is also a greater emphasis on nation branding. Again, while Greek stores are increasingly eager to advertise their merchandise as "Made in Greece," it is not uncommon to find a "Made in Greece" sticker affixed over one that says "Made in China." This confusion is sometimes exploited at the retail level in hipper areas (such as the leftist neighborhood of Exarchia) where stores specializing in Greek hand-made goods pepper their inventory with Chinese merchandise in an attempt to sell clothing with much higher margins.

New Patterns of Chinese Investment

As Chinese petty entrepreneurial businesses have closed, China's newly generated wealth has been directed to other sectors of the Greek economy.

These investments are run through both private and state-owned enterprises. The most prominent and earliest of these investments came in 2008 from state-owned COSCO's thirty-year lease of Piraeus's Pier II container terminal for €490 million. The following year the terms of the lease were updated, adding five years for building a third, deep-water container port, Pier III. In January 2016 COSCO was the only bidder in the Coalition of the Radical Left's (SYRIZA's) privatization of the port for which they offered €368.5 million for a 67 percent stake, wresting majority ownership from the Greek state. In an attempt to quell protests of Greek patrimony being alienated to Chinese hands, Xu Lirong, president of COSCO, pledged to maintain jobs and make Piraeus into the center for Asian distribution of imports to Europe. However, unions have been banned in all COSCO-operated activities. This comes with further prospects of modernization of the ports, including creating high-speed railway to the Balkans and central Europe, a freight center, and a logistics hub. Additional corporate interests include speculation about rare earth mining and a hydro airport in Corfu.

There is an interesting ambiguity with regard to the price paid for the port: either COSCO is viewed as having paid too much (thus mirroring the way in which local merchants are viewed to have overpaid the value of stores) or as having paid too little. The first interpretation renders Piraeus as a necessary strategic mercantile outpost to be gained by the Chinese leviathan at any and all costs. The second interpretation expresses the sentiment that the value of national patrimony cannot and should not have a price or be priced. This is the interpretation that invokes the threat of "Chineseification" and the loss of national sovereignty.

As "Chineseification" and the fear of a new, defanged regime of non-unionized labor emerge, Greece (along with Cyprus and Portugal) has extended residency opportunity to anyone able to afford €250,000 worth of real estate.[9] Chinese investors are well represented in this group of potential buyers, among those from Russia, the United Kingdom, and other Europeans. For instance, in 2015 the Chinese investment firm Pyrros invited three hundred of its shareholders to Athens, where they were given a crash course to on how to invest in real estate. Such events accentuate the fault lines between Greeks who have much to lose and those who have much to gain. Members in the latter category, such as Georgakos Properties and Parthenon Real Estate Group, implicitly contest those in the former category by emphasizing the notion that Chinese buyers are not looking for investment, but an opportunity to send their children to European schools and live a European lifestyle.

Perhaps the most visible sector of the economy that has benefited from Chinese wealth is in tourism from mainland China, from which both Greek and Chinese nationals seek to profit. While many Chinese tourists appear to visit Greece as one leg of a larger European tour, the island of Santorini has become a very popular destination for Chinese flying directly from the mainland. The island featured prominently as a romantic destination in the 2014 film *Beijing Love Story* (Chen 2014), China's highest-grossing film to date, which was based on a television series. According to one informant, whose Fujianese father runs a tourism agency in Athens, Chinese tourists are solely responsible for making the island a viable winter tourist destination: the number of hotels open during the winter months, catering almost exclusively to Chinese tourists, has skyrocketed. According to German broadcaster Deutche Welle, the Chinese tourist population increases by 20 percent each year ("Greece: Boom in Chinese Tourists" 2017), providing a commodified, exotically Western form of love by which China's burgeoning middle-class couples seek to distinguish themselves.

Conclusion

By presenting itself as a commodity that allows Chinese tourists mark their social status, Santorini inverts the typical narrative of exploitation by Chinese traders. Indeed, in addition to the introduction of Chinese small- and large-scale investments in Greece, a small but not insignificant number of Greek businesses are increasingly exporting to China. The question, however, is not whether Chinese money is invested in Greece but rather how and to whom. As one Greek truck driver pithily explained to the *Wall Street Journal* in 2013, "the [Greek] exports [to China] don't help me" (Areddy 2013).

In this chapter I have attempted to demonstrate how China articulates Greece's complex and multidimensional experience of Europeanization and its larger form of economic globalization. While the Greek sovereign debt crisis might provide a narrative marker by which the transformations of value and identity are assessed, these transformations have been occurring steadily throughout the past several decades as global trade patterns coalesce with local understanding of self and other. For instance, while narratives of Chinese merchants as abstract, state-backed forms of value extraction continue to be expressed, such as in the case of Sprider presented above, new ideological forms and trade relations continue to unfold in both predictable and unpredictable ways.

Tracey A. Rosen is college fellow and lecturer in social studies at Harvard University. She was the 2016–17 Ted and Elaine Athanassiades Postdoctoral Research Fellowship in Hellenic Studies at Princeton University, and received her PhD in anthropology from the University of Chicago. Her research has focused on Chinese migrant merchants and the impact of Chinese business in Greece with fieldwork in Greece, Italy, and China.

Notes

1. This argument is fully developed in my Ph.D. dissertation on the subject (Rosen 2015).
2. By "Europeanization" I refer to a set of material and ideological practices that bind the processes and goals of modernization and neoliberalism and are guided by a vision of a territorial integration of economy, politics, law, value, and identity (see Borneman and Fowler 1997; Featherstone 1998).
3. As Sakellaropoulos (2010) explains, what is omitted from the calculation is how the averages are hiked by large payouts to executives, the treatment of overtime as regular wages, and the difference between average rate of inflation and rate of price rises for basic necessities.
4. While income inequality in Greece has become an important issue after the crisis, however, the rate has not dramatically changed. For instance, the Gini coefficient and the share ratio between the highest and lowest 20 percent of incomes are higher in 2006 than in 2011 (Mitrakos 2014).
5. These included migrants from Bangladesh, Egypt, Pakistan, and the Philippines.
6. "Albanian" in Greek can be used as dismissive shorthand to denote a manual laborer of any nationality.
7. "Economic problem" could also be translated from Mandarin into "economy problem" as well as the plural form of both of these.
8. I have decided to translate "to kinezo" into the pejorative English term "Chinaman" as it bears the most faithful relationship to the Greek. However, much is lost in translation here as the term indexes a different history and bears different connotations. For instance, the English phrase, "its all Greek to me" to denote the inscrutability of a communicative act appears as "its all Chinese to me" in Greek and other countries in the Balkans. The phrase "kano to kinezo" draws from this tradition which historically may have pointed more to the inscrutability of the language and not the person (as in the English use of "Greek"). However, in present usage, I argue that the perceived inscrutability of the language is indeed reflected in the perceived inscrutability of Chinese people and thus the term does resemble some of the offensive connotations as the English term "Chinaman."
9. This is not new or unique compared to other countries, however the price is particularly low.

References

Areddy, James T. 2013. "Greek Exports Take Aim at Chinese Palate." *Wall Street Journal,* 10 July, sec. Business. Retrieved 12 July 2014 from http://www.wsj.com/articles/
Bakalaki, Alexandra. 2003. "Locked into Security, Keyed into Modernity: The Selection of Burglaries as Source of Risk in Greece." *Ethnos: Journal of Anthropology* 68(2): 209–29.

Baldwin-Edwards, Martin. 2004. "Immigration into Greece 1990–2003: A Southern European Paradigm?" European Population Forum 2004. Geneva: United Nations Economic Commission for Europe.

Bennison, David, and Christina Boutsouki. 1995. "Greek Retailing in Transition." *International Journal of Retail & Distribution Management* 23(1): 24.

Borneman, John, and Nick Fowler. 1997. "Europeanization." *Annual Review of Anthropology* 26(1): 487–514

Cavounidis, Jennifer. 2002. "Migration in Southern Europe and the Case of Greece." *International Migration* 40(1): 45–70.

Ceccagno, Antonella. 2003. "New Chinese Migrants in Italy." *International Migration* 41(3): 187–213.

———. 2009. "Chinese Migrants as Apparel Manufactures in an Era of Perishable Global Fashion: New Fashion Scenarios in Prato." In Smyth, French, and Johnson, *Living Outside the Walls,* 42–74.

Chen, Sichent, dir. 2014. *Beijing Love Story.* Los Angeles: China Lion Film.

Chu, Julie Y. 2010. *Cosmologies of Credit: Fuzhounese Migration and the Politics of Destination in China.* Durham, NC: Duke University Press.

Dei Ottati, Gabi. 2009. "Italian Industrial Districts and the Dual Chinese Challenge." In Smyth, French, and Johnson, *Living Outside the Walls,* 26–41.

Donadio, Rachel. 2010. "Chinese Remake the 'Made in Italy' Fashion Label." *New York Times,* 12 September. Retrieved 17 October 2017 from http://www.nytimes.com/2010/09/13/world/europe/13prato.html.

Doulos, Dimitris, and Odysseas Katsaitis. 2014. "Fiscal Austerity and Export Performance: The Case of Greece." *International Advances in Economic Research* 21(1): 121–22.

"Epidrome Kinezikon magazion ste Veroia." 2013. *Veroiotes.gr,* 12 November. Retrieved 16 October 2017 from http://www.veriotis.gr/2013/12/blog-post_3320.html.

Featherstone, Kevin. 1998. "'Europeanization' and The Centre Periphery: The Case of Greece in the 1990s." *South European Society and Politics* 3(1): 23–39.

Garrone, Matteo, dir. 2009. *Gomorrah.* New York: Criterion Collection.

G. D. 2007. "Tsainataoun sten kardia tes Athenas" *Eleftherotypia (Enet).* Retrieved 1 November 2008 from http://archive.enet.gr/online/.

"Georganes gia Kineziko Sprider." 2013. *Apela.gr,* 23 December. Retrieved 17 October 2017 from https://www.youtube.com/watch?v=CJ7-VeHrpDE.

"Greece: Boom in Chinese Tourists." 2017. *Deutsche Welle,* 27 July. Retrieved 17 October 2017 from http://www.dw.com/en/greece-boom-in-chinese-tourists/av-39852436.

Harvey, David. 1989. *The Condition of Postmodernity.* Hoboken, NJ: Wiley-Blackwell.

———. 2011. *The Enigma of Capital: And the Crises of Capitalism.* Oxford: Oxford University Press.

Karydis, Vasilis. 1992. "The Fear of Crime in Athens and the Construction of the 'Dangerous Albanian' Stereotype." *Chronica* 5.

Koselleck, Reinhart. 2002. *The Practice of Conceptual History: Timing History, Spacing Concepts.* Stanford, CA: Stanford University Press

Lacan, Jacques. 1999. *The Seminar of Jacques Lacan: On Feminine Sexuality, the Limits of Love and Knowledge.* Edited by Jacques-Alain Miller and Bruce Fink. New York: W. W. Norton & Company.

Lawrence, Christopher. 2005. Re-Bordering the Nation: Neoliberalism and Racism in Rural Greece. *Dialectical Anthropology* 29(3–4): 315–34.

Liu, Xin. 1997. "Lukang: Commerce and Community in a Chinese City." *American Anthropologist* 99(2): 445–46.

———. 2002. *The Otherness of Self: A Genealogy of Self in Contemporary China.* Ann Arbor: University of Michigan Press.

Lyberaki, Antigone. 2011. "Delocalization, Triangular Manufacturing, and Windows of Opportunity: Some Lessons from Greek Clothing Producers in a Fast-Changing Global Context." *Regional Studies* 45 (2): 205–18.

Mitrakos, Theodore. 2014. "Inequality, Poverty, and Social Welfare in Greece: Distributional effects of austerity." Working Paper 174. Athens: Bank of Greece.

Papahelas, Alexis. 2015. "Kan to opos oi Kinezoi." *E Kathimerini*, 22 March. Retrieved 3 August 2016 from http://www.kathimerini.gr/808481/opinion/epikairothta/politikh/kan-to-opws-oi-kinezoi/

Pieke, Frank, Pál Nyíri, Mette Thunø, and Antonella Ceccagno. 2004 *Transnational Chinese: Fujianese Migrants in Europe*. Stanford, CA: Stanford University Press.

Placas, Aimee. 2016. "Money Talk." Hot Spots, *Cultural Anthropology* website, April 21. Retrieved from http://www.culanth.org/fieldsights/856-money-talk.

Roitman, Janet. 2013. *Anti-Crisis*. Durham, NC: Duke University Press.

Rosen, Tracey. 2015."How 'Made in China' Is Made in Greece: Chinese Capitalism at the Gateway to Europe." Doctoral dissertation. Chicago: University of Chicago.

Sakellaropoulos, Spyros. 2010. "The Recent Economic Crisis in Greece and the Strategy of Capital." *Journal of Modern Greek Studies* 28(1) 321–48.

Smyth, Russell, Rebecca French, and Graeme Johnson, eds. 2009. *Living Outside the Walls: The Chinese in Prato*. Newcastle-upon-Tyne, UK: Cambridge Scholars.

Triandafyllidou, Anna. 2010. *Irregular Migration in Europe: Myths and Realities*. Farnham, UK: Ashgate.

Veblen, Thorstein. (1899) 2013. *The Theory of the Leisure Class*. Project Gutenberg. Retrieved from https://www.gutenberg.org/files/833/833-h/833-h.htm.

Vigh, Henrik. 2008. "Crisis and Chronicity: Anthropological Perspectives on Continuous Conflict and Decline." *Ethnos* 73(1): 5–24.

World Bank. 2012 World Databank, World Development Indicators. Retrieved 17 November 2012 from http://databank.worldbank.org/data/reports.aspx?source=world-development-indicators.

"Charistike Vole sten agora tes Prevezas dinoun oi Kinezoi emporoi." 2014. *Romainews*, 12 September. Retrieved 17 October 2017 from http://romiazirou.blogspot.com/2014/09/sprider.html.

Yousef, Kleopatra. 2013. "The Vicious Circle of Irregular Migration from Pakistan to Greece and Back to Pakistan." Governing Irregular Migration, Background Report: Migratory System 3. Athens: Hellenic Foundation for European and Social Policy (ELIAMEP).

Zhang, Li. 2001. *Strangers in the City: Reconfigurations of Space, Power, and Social Networks Within China's Floating Population*. Stanford University Press.

Zhang, Li, and Aihwa Ong, eds. 2008. *Privatizing China: Socialism from Afar*. Ithaca, NY: Cornell University Press.

Chapter 12

Disrupted and Disrupting Consumption
Transformations in Buying and Borrowing in Greece

Aimee Placas

Introduction

Consumption is one of the many spheres targeted as a problem needing reform during the "crisis" era in Greece. This identification meant that the consumer market would be subject to a restructuring through deregulation, a restructuring that has significantly changed the consumer landscape over these past years (particularly in conjunction with a contraction in the credit market and the economic downturn in general). The economic ideology behind this deregulation, however, is one that has been shaping the creation of a consumer society in Greece from the 1980s. At the same time, these "crisis" years, under the regime of austerity, have also seen consumption as a site of experimentation—in economic solidarity movements, alternative market formations, and more—arising in response both to the ideology of those reforms and to the concurrent economic recession.

This chapter considers the consumer to be a specific subjectivity, but not an all-consuming one. It can be taken up by an individual in order to trigger a set of rights, aspirations, or manner of giving meaning to identity and experience through the world of goods. It is also shaped by a history of policy and law that gives a culturally specific structure to what a consumer is and how it can and/or should function. I follow prior theorizations of a consumer society as one where a major source of identity comes through consumption practices (Miller 2001), where experience is

Notes for this chapter begin on page 342.

mediated through increasingly sophisticated expertise in marketing, advertising, and research (McCracken 1988), where consumer rights are formulated in tandem with the creation of an increasingly complex market (Trentmann 2005), and most recently where the consumer's activity and agency is considered a driving force in the economy (DeCastro 2015). I bring these understandings together into the assemblage I term "the consumer" in Greece in a way far more particularistic and subject to intervention than the consumer generally referred to in economic indicators, policy, or consumer research.

By giving a brief overview of the most significant changes to occur in consumption in Greece from the postwar period until today, I hope to give a general shape to what austerity has changed and instigated for the people who seek to keep themselves fed, clothed, and entertained during this economic depression. This topic is much larger than one chapter can deal with, and thus this story is necessarily incomplete.

The Creation of a Consumer Society

It has been argued that what we have come to call "consumer society" began to develop first in England in the 1700s, with an increase in the world of goods, the frequency of purchasing, and the beginning of understanding the consumer as a target that can be manipulated through marketing (McCracken 1988). Life in urban centers in Greece's early history and period of industrialization would have shared these features, but the majority of the country's population was for the most part excluded. This changed significantly in the period following the civil war in Greece, which saw a massive restructuring in Greek economy and society; rapid urbanization and economic development were only one part of the social changes under way. The Greek economy saw continuing growth from the 1950s onward in the retail and consumer spheres, coinciding with increased monetization and a concern in Greece's post-peasantry with appearing modern and thus emulating their urban counterparts, often doing so through participation in material culture (Friedl 1962, 1964; Karapostolis 1983).

Dimitris Karapostolis, in his analysis of consumer behavior through the 1960s and mid-1970s, argues that there was a marked decrease during this period in the social tolerance of deprivation: a naturalized acceptance of exclusion from the market and its goods among the economically marginalized sectors of society (farmers, workers, etc.; Karapostolis 1983). Ascending in its place was the anticipation of social inclusion, fueled and realized by the social mobility that marked the immediate postwar period.

When that social mobility began to slow and then stagnate by the early 1970s, he argues, consumerism allowed for a type of mobility that made up for the lack of movement in employment or economic circumstance for many. The ideology of inclusion and mobility persisted, even after the aspirations for achieving a higher social position through an economically better job (better in a material sense, if not prestige sense) became less and less likely for most. Karapostolis posits that the proliferation of mass-produced consumer goods created a new avenue for those aspirations to be expressed. The cars, leisure goods, and services conspicuously consumed signified the continued upward-looking intent of the individual. Consumption practices here are understood as an attempt—tangible, immediate, and public—to overcome the inequality and discrimination created in the economic and social field. Karapostolis argues that they are not meant as a display of economic power, as in Veblen's theory of conspicuous consumption (1973[1899]), but rather to assert equality and an orientation toward mobility. It is this era that brings the Greek urban and rural areas toward greater convergence in relation to consumption, as rural inhabitants turned their funds toward the consumption of goods associated with urban values and lifestyles, to a greater degree than toward increasing agricultural productivity, investment, or savings. Ernestine Friedl's ethnographic work describes this same phenomenon in rich detail (Friedl 1962, 1964). Beyond these changes in distinction enabled through consuming, consumption opportunities also offered new practices that would shape identities. Studies have identified, for example, how broader access to mass-produced toys shaped childhoods (Gkougkouli 2000), how mass tourism brought new forms of bodily enjoyment and pleasure (Nikolakakis 2016), and how emergent sexual identities were articulated through consumption practices (Yannakopoulos 2016).

I would identify this era discussed above as the first phase of the development of the consumer in Greece—a very specific orientation toward goods that assert both distinction and levelling, depending on which direction one faces. However, the increase in actual shops and goods during this period was more a matter of degree, and less a matter of diversification. In other words, the country saw tremendous growth in the number of stores, but they were mostly of the same type: small shops each owned and run by one person or family, with a clientele based on personal relationships, and wholesale and distribution networks unchanging in structure (Bennison and Boutsouki 1995). Multiple factors contributed to creating and maintaining this landscape, such as a preference for self-employment and family ventures, the availability of credit from distributors combined with a lack of credit extended from banks (Pagoulatos 2003), rapid urbanization, and government regulation protecting microenterprises through limiting shop hours, classifying what could be sold in different types of shops, and the like (Bennison and Boutsouki 1995). It was joining the European Economic Community (EEC), however, that marked the beginning of structural changes in consumption through the 1980s, some of which became dramatic in the early 1990s. These changes clearly distinguish this second phase of consumer society in Greece from the first.

The Deregulation Era

The 1980s and 1990s have a strong association with the expansion of conspicuous consumption in Greece, and are inextricably linked to both joining the European Economic Community (EEC), and the policies of Panhellenic Socialist Movement (PASOK) that expanded job prospects and wages for an emerging and expanding middle class. (I oversimplify here the economic complexity of this period, but its cultural linking as the start of a consumerist era is consistent.) Thus, though a consumer society in Greece really begins to take hold in the postwar era, what might be called consumer culture in Greece symbolically and practically is brought to a new level in the 1980s. Yes, foreign goods had for previous generations been treated as objects of status and expressions of identity (e.g., imported goods facing high import duties that are thus rare, or proudly displayed tokens of travel brought back by family members in the merchant marines). Shopping as well would sometimes have been a source of entertainment in itself, and was not just provisioning, in years past. But scale, speed, accessibility, diversity—these all increased dramatically at the same time that a host of other cultural changes also emerged as tokens of a new era, not just in urban centers but in the countryside as well. Examples of other cultural changes are the spread of the *kafeteria* (coffee/bar establishments) as a public consumption space frequented by both men and women in contrast to the traditional *kafeneio,* a consumption space limited to men, signifying changing gender relations; the position of women in the public sphere; and the expansion of consumption spaces for youths in both rural and urban areas (Cowan 1990). The shift toward suburbanization after decades of urbanization, a new geography practically and symbolically linked with new consumer lifestyles, facilitated a dramatic rise in associated consumption (Dimitriou-Kotsoni 2006; Economou 2014; Zestanakis 2015), and set the stage for another consumption space innovation: large *emporika kentra* (commercial centers) or malls. The first were built in the early 1980s in the upper-class Athenian suburbs of Glyfada and Kifissia, with a steady proliferation culminating in the lavish examples built in the post-2004 Olympic Village spaces of Marousi (Lallas 2010); these spaces symbolically stand as the paradigmatic temples to consumption.[1] Those same Olympics would turn Athens itself into a cosmopolitan city to be consumed (Chatzidakis 2014).

Alongside of these new geographies, the deregulation of mass media brought an influx of new television channels and programming during this same time (see Kassaveti 2016 on the impact of VHS machines; and Hess this volume), and the concurrent rapid growth and foreign penetration of the advertising industry correlates with this influx: the 1980s and early 1990s are called the golden era of Greek advertising (Tsakarestou 2002). Lifestyle magazines flourished (Zestanakis 2017). Additionally, increasing numbers of women in the workforce affected consumption and consumption possibilities (Costa 2005; Stratigaki 1996). Foreign chain stores and global brands proliferated as import restrictions relaxed, fully integrating Greece into the global consumer landscape (Kouremenos and Avlonitis 1995).

Joining the EEC brought with it a host of structural changes to Greece's economic structure. In terms of the transformation of consumption, the deregulation of the retail sphere was a major part of this, particularly changes instituted by New Democracy (ND) when that party came into power in 1990. The extension of shop hours, removal of price controls in many areas, and further deregulations in both retail and associated labor laws were all enacted in alignment with the EEC economic commitment to the creation of an open market (Bennison and Boutsouki 1995; Law 1892/1990 art. 42). This created a context in which many new types of stores entered the market and flourished: supermarket and do-it-yourself store chains, foreign franchises for clothing and cosmetics, fast food chains, cash and carry stores. Much of this activity was from foreign companies entering the market with their own chains or cooperating with domestic establishments (Bennison and Boutsouki 1995; Kouremenos and Avlonitis 1995; Priporas 2003).

It is significant to note that Greece's development as a consumer culture is directly linked to Europeanization, literally; these are market reforms required externally as part of belonging to the EEC (most of which carry the same structural economic goals as the later Memorandums of Understanding of the International Monetary Fund, European Central Bank, and EU, known as the Troika). They result from a general shift in policy regarding the degree to which various local sectors would be protected from foreign competition, which began with the aforementioned sudden and rapid deregulations, and continued with ongoing reforms through the intervening years. In certain cases, however, these reforms faced successful resistance, such as the persistent rejection of Sunday shop hours, or the protections around pharmacies, which held until the state of exception of "crisis" Greece.

This progression, with the proliferation of goods and thus of choices, is a fundamental feature of the development of a consumer society; it is not just that there is more to consume (an increase in activity), but also that the consumer's work is to make consumption choices, and that making ever-more-educated choices creates a better (more innovative, higher quality, competitively priced, etc.) market. Consumer rights in the dominant EU economic ideology must be developed in conjunction with market deregulations, embedding consumer protection in the legal person of the consumer instead of in market interventions by the state. That point is clear in the EU directive on consumer protection as well as in the scholarship analyzing the development of consumer protection law in general. Laws protecting the consumer in Greece (Law 2251/1994) form in response to EEC directives: Council Directive 87/102/EEC in 1986 was the first of several, and the directives continue to evolve through the most recent in 2014. These laws created the legal framework for consumer protection (which existed prior to this law only in the form of contract law) and for consumer protection groups to form and represent consumer interests in court. Prior to this point, there were few consumer cooperatives, and those few operated within a negative political and legal environment (Karantaki and Tsentekidou 1996). The General Secretariat for Consumers, located in the Ministry of Development, was established in 1997 as a source of information for consumers and an advocate for their rights; the Consumer's Ombudsman was added in 2004 as an additional administrative agency (Law 3297/2004). As a result of these legislative changes, it is not only that goods, transactions, and advertising would all be affected, but it is also that the creation of these various organizations also creates a source of information concerning what gets framed as a consumer issue. This in turn works to create a further public understanding of what a consumer is, and what this consumer cares about. Additionally, these agencies provide the legislative advocacy and the resources of expertise required for creating informed consumers: consumers who make good choices based on need, quality, and price, rewarding good products and services and punishing the bad ones; thus consumers shape the market in a positive way through their activity. All of these are necessary in the creation of the consumer who can do the work that the free market needs him or her to do, and develop most visibly in the 1990s and early 2000s as a new form of neoliberal governmentality (Giesler and Veresiu 2014).

The Impact of the Euro

What it might mean to be a European consumer came under intense public debate and concern particularly after Greece's adoption in 2002 of the

euro. The first months were marked by an excitement and careful mon-
ey-handling, something Thomas Malaby (2003) argues suggested a concern with demonstrating a competency at Europeanness and modernity.
There had always been voices speaking against the adoption of the euro,
though, such as the position consistently expressed by the main communist party the Communist Party of Greece (KKE), who have been consistent in their opposition to EU membership. Quickly, however, the sharp
rise in small consumer good prices during the first six months of 2002 provoked widespread consternation. Comparing pre- and post-euro prices
became a mainstay of conversation, while graphics or charts comparing
the prices of goods in Athens versus other major European cities were
a frequent presence in the news (Placas 2016). The removal of informal
price controls between the state and producers/distributors in certain sectors, at the exact moment of the currency changeover, certainly contributed; these so-called gentlemen's agreements were a method of limiting
price increases in order to meet Maastricht inflation criterion set by the
EU (Organisation for Economic Co-operation and Development [OECD]
2001). By summer the government was trying to reinstate these informal
controls due to popular pressure—including a buy-nothing day boycott
on September 3, 2002, organized by consumer associations but also encouraged by the government (Chee 2002). Without the legislative ability
to actually create price controls (an anathema to the free market model),
however, there was little effect. Greece is not alone in the experience of
price inflation after the introduction of the euro, a consumer concern expressed in many of the countries that switched to the euro. However, I use
that word "experience" to point to the everyday practice of understanding
prices, not to an actual increase in inflation as an economic index. In fact,
the EU has strongly argued that it was perceived but not actual inflation,
and the euro had no effect on price increases, other than providing the
opportunity for price gouging in certain sectors like the service industry (Sturm et al. 2009). My interviews with informants (nonexperts) at the
time demonstrated a popular interpretation that economic indexes related
to their consumption—inflation, the consumer price index, and so on—
were politicized and manipulated to downplay the increased cost of living they were experiencing (reflecting also a more general attitude toward
state-produced numbers and statistics).

An interpretation of these price increases as a natural market correction
after artificial suppression surfaced as one explanation appropriate to the
dominant economic ideology (Arghyrou 2007), but at the time the government was also directly blaming retailers, in a move of popular appeal.
My interviews with actors in the consumer protection arena had an additional explanation: there was ongoing problem with informal price fixing
in the Greek market, a structural feature very difficult to pursue through

legal channels, even with fairly definitive proof. The saga of price fixing in the dairy market in Greece is one particularly fraught example, a case successfully prosecuted only because of a discovered smoking-gun memo detailing meeting dates and topics discussed (Harontakis 2007). The development of the Hellenic Competition Commission as an agency independent from the state in 2000 was another move meant to address such issues. Like the consumer protection agency, it was designed to serve as a balancer of power in the consumer-retailer relationship of the free market, and to be autonomous from state and market in its ability to levy fines and decisions. Its successes in Greece have been perceived as mixed, with some industries ignoring some of its assessments; bank fees for consumers, for instance, have been an ongoing battle from the early 2000s. At the level of the everyday, in my interviews with average Athenians consuming in Greece, price-fixing was taken as a given. One example was a favorite: the same Greek yogurt was cheaper in a supermarket in Germany than it was in Greece. What the fact of this price difference might signify as a piece of evidence for something greater was a fertile ground for conversation and argument about rising Greek prices, and the failure of eurozone-belonging to match the popular imaginings of what it might bring. I discuss these issues here because after 2009 these concerns intensify and eventually become the focus of politicized consumer intervention.

Consumer Credit

Another important industry for consumption—often framed as absolutely necessary to a growth model that relies on consumer spending—also grew during the turn of the twenty-first century: consumer credit. Deregulation of the banking industry in Greece in the 1980s was the first step in the creation of a consumer credit market, something actively discouraged within the banking system in the decades prior when the state required lending priorities to focus mainly on industry and development (Pagoulatos 2003). Credit card use grew very slowly in the 1980s, when laws were still in place limiting the amount of credit banks could extend to consumers, meaning that plastic money was not a major factor in the retail growth of that era, or even of the early 1990s. But significant further deregulations occurred in 1994–95, allowing for an immediate phase of credit growth caused by an increase in the number of people gaining access to bank credit; in addition, the lessening (in 2001) and removal (in 2003) of credit ceilings gave even more strength to that growth. Consumer credit usage grew more 30 percent a year during the late 1990s, stabilizing somewhat in the 2000s but maintaining constant growth up until the credit contraction of 2008. These plastic tokens of consumerism went hand in hand with the ongoing expansion of the retail sphere, with shops everywhere offering *atokes doseis* (interest-free payments) on larger purchases, from cosmetics to furniture. Marketing for credit products was aggressive; urban and semi-urban areas were blanketed with ads for holiday loans (an unsecured consumer loan usually up to around €3,000), special credit card offers, open credit lines, and (after 2004) consolidation loans for those who had already acquired too many credit products in those few years to successfully manage their payments (Placas 2008; see also Sakellaropoulos 2010 for a critique of portraying this era as one of hyper-consumerism). Heavily advertised installment payment plans from retailers were also prominent during these years, again facilitated through the expansion of bank lending, and interest rates fell to historic lows with intense competition between lenders (Mitrakos and Simigiannis 2009).

The creation of a consumer credit market goes hand in hand with the economic growth of the first half of the 2000s, with strong consumption and housing investment facilitated by the availability and use of new credit products (Athanassiou 2006; Mitrakos, Simigiannis, and Tzamourani 2005). The Bank of Greece commissioned a research survey in 2002–3 to determine whether this new market was creating any significant problems with over-indebtedness (Bank of Greece 2003). Almost half of the households surveyed at that time reported no outstanding bank debt; debt was concentrated among the middle- and upper-income households, with those at the lowest income levels almost entirely excluded from bank borrowing. Without prior data points for comparison, the analysis is dependent on comparing Greece to other markets, but the study concludes that household borrowing is "limited in relation to their annual income and wealth," with 75 percent of all households having monthly debt payments totaling less than 30 percent of their monthly income (although this percentage could be less feasible for those with lower incomes), 4 percent of all households with debt payments exceeding their income (meaning that they could not service their loans), and concludes by pointing to room in the market for continued growth (Bank of Greece 2003: 92). The Greek household debt–to-GDP ratio was 22.6 percent at the time of that survey, compared to the euro area average of 46.9 percent.

A second survey, this one conducted in 2005, showed marked increases in average outstanding debt, and a significantly increased debt burden among the lowest income levels, but also reported a decline in the percentage of households with debt payments exceeding their income, which they attributed to declining interest rates and increased management of risk by the banks.[2] This survey also included questions on difficulty experienced in regularly servicing debt obligations; more than half of households said it was difficult or rather difficult to do so, with the average significantly higher among lower-income groups.[3] Again the survey concludes that financial stress is at reasonable levels, and that the expansion of the Tiresias database should lead to fewer cases of over-indebtedness, which the Bank of Greece attributes to inadequate knowledge on the banks' part of their customers' financial condition, and lack of caution on the part of the indebted. My own ethnographic observations would highlight the difficulty in making educated decisions about borrowing in the face of new financial technologies and aggressive advertising. Greece's household debt–to-GDP was at 36.3 percent, compared to the euro area's 52.6 percent.

A third survey, this one conducted in 2007, again reaches similar conclusions, although with warnings that at the lowest income levels debt loads can easily lead to financial precarity. It is significant to note that there are no legal protections for overindebted consumers established during this period of credit deregulation and expansion. An individual who fell into arrears could be taken to court by his creditors and had his assets seized toward the repayment of the debt. Consumer associations often assisted members who had difficulty servicing their bank loans (most often because of sudden changes in their economic circumstances) in working out repayment plans with their banks. With imperfect information on which to base their lending, banks relied heavily on the presence of real estate or steady income (civil servants being treated as a particularly credit-worthy group) on which to base their lending decisions.[4]

I am taking the time to highlight the state of indebtedness before 2008 because there has sometimes been a conflation of a "profligate Greece" and "profligate Greeks" in the popular discussion of the spending patterns that lead up to the sovereign debt crisis. There is little practical relationship between the finances of states and the finances of households in how they function; there are many connections made, however, at the levels of the symbolic and the moral. People in Greece were encouraged to spend and borrow toward a future of increased growth and alignment with stronger European economies; these are economies dependent on consumers who behave in a very specific way, and it was the work of both government and the market to shape the Greek consumer into this likeness during this era. This ideal was simply not realizable in the domestic market described above, with price collusion and notable gaps between the movement of wages and the costs of living. Some of this gap was covered through credit. In the dramatic economic downturn that followed 2008, the tremendous amount of defaulted debt comes not from so-called irresponsible borrowing preceding that downturn, but rather from suddenly changed economic circumstances that made previously manageable debt loads suddenly unmanageable.

The End of the Growth Era

As one might expect, the new geographies of consumption created by all of the above were ambivalently received. As legislative changes made small Greek shop owners more and more vulnerable to large chains and foreign companies, pushback also occurred that continued to limit their exposure. Sunday shop hours are just one example, debated and resisted for over a decade, with polls showing general popular opinion against more types of stores being open on Sundays (Genike Synomospondia Epaggelmation Viotechnon Emporon Elladas [GSEVEE] 2013). Religion and tradition are not adequate explanatory factors; the consumer in Greece is not alienated from her labor enough to contemplate store hours through the lens of consumer convenience rather than that of work. And yet part of the promise of the European Union (EU) was that in Greece one would shop, borrow, and buy like other Europeans; consumer credit combined with mortgages and with new IKEA stores and their kin were able to make a particular lifestyle available to a larger segment of the population, even at euro prices (see Rosen this volume on fashion consumption during this era). This harks back to the consumer behavior of the 1960s and 1970s described by Karapostolis: joining the eurozone did not bring the increases in wages and work opportunities that were imagined, but it did bring the opportunity to secure a European identity through consumption. This gap, however, did not go unnoticed. The critiques about consumption and value in Greece developed during this era provide the foundation for the consumer interventions that occur after 2008.

The Effects of 2008

As a result of the global financial crisis of 2008, credit markets everywhere contracted, and Greece was no exception. I interviewed employees of two Greek banks in the summer of 2008 who were being retrained from the telephone sales department to the telephone collections department, and who identified this as a new shift in their workplace. The Greek government pushed for a controversial bank bailout plan in the fall of 2008, despite resistance from some banks and criticism from various quarters, reportedly as a way to cause the banks to loosen their credit restrictions and allow business and households greater access to credit money toward the anticipated economic downturn of 2009–10; all this happened before the Greek sovereign debt crisis itself (Kontogiannis 2008). Credit growth to households (and in general) decelerated sharply in the last quarter of 2008, and marked the beginning of a continuing downturn that by 2010 had turned into negative growth (Bank of Greece 2009, 2011). In other words, access to consumer credit was set to become more difficult even before the Greek depression began.

Changes in consumer habits were also already being noted in research on consumption. Low wages and high prices were taking their toll, and consumer spending behavior showed an increase in sensitivity to price and caution toward larger expenses (see Baltas 2008). The city of Athens became seemingly overnight pockmarked with gold-buying stores and new pawn shops. The introduction of secondhand clothing stores and market stalls, a circulation of used clothing that had disappeared with the introduction of cheaper and less-durable goods, resurfaced with vigor (see Pipyrou 2014 for a discussion of similar circumstances in Italy).

The economic difficulties that arose for households during Greece's austerity years were in many ways an intensification of the circumstances that were already building, not a sudden reversal of wealth and prosperity or of high living financed by credit. The rhetoric of "crisis" that sought to locate blame for the current situation, however, found the increased consumerism of the past decades an easy target. Consumerism comes with a ready set of criticisms that are rather global in nature, a morality regarding its emptiness and its lack of productivity. Theodossopoulos finds such criticisms expressed among Greek migrants in Panama, who view protest against austerity in Greece as an "orchestrated attempt to maintain a wasteful lifestyle of consumption," and who criticize what they see as a lack of hard work or will to labor at all (Theodossopoulos 2013: 204). The neoliberal consumer, however, must indeed work: the market requires of them education, evaluative skills, economic discernment, and more. They are consumer entrepreneurs, entrepreneurs of the self, producing the self through consumption, where the skills required of the flexible body required in the changed labor market overlap with those required in the realm of consumption: Foucault's *homo œconomicus* (Foucault 2008). The economy of the growth years, Greece's years of looking forward toward increased prosperity with increased EU integration, required a consumer who spent money with the expectation of that future—that is, a consumer who aimed to bring the anticipated good life into the present through credit spending and the like. The consumer created by austerity governmentality is quite different.

Consumption under Austerity

The economic effects following Greece's sovereign debt crisis, through the subsequent restructuring of the country through austerity under the

Troika, and the depression that followed, have been widely recorded and reported on. Wage cuts (both state-prescribed and those that followed through the devaluation of labor), pension cuts, business closings, and high unemployment: all of these dramatically affected household finances. A restructuring of the retail sphere happened through legislation: the liberalization of closed-shop professions, increases in shop hours and days, greater attention to receipts given upon purchase, and so on, as well as through the disproportionate closing of smaller shops that were unable to weather the downturn because of a lack of capital or access to credit (in comparison to larger chains). The liberalization and deregulation were not new issues, however, as I have briefly discussed above; rather, these were part of the restructuring of the Greek economy that had been part of future roadmap from Greece's entry to the EEC—a roadmap not consistently followed, but ever present in external pressure nonetheless. But the state of exception enabled through Greece's crisis mode gave these changes new authority.

Theoretically, the drop in labor costs should have led to a concurrent drop in prices for goods and services. However, the structural problems affecting prices, so clearly demonstrated after the euro changeover, remained a strong feature of the consumption landscape. Prices did not fall. In fact, food prices in most categories rose faster than the EU average between 2008 and 2012; the prices themselves were higher than the EU average as well (OECD 2014). Food has been a particularly laden symbol regarding the crisis; for example, Daniel Knight has analyzed the ways in which memories of hunger, starvation, and famine during World War II become a panic-inducing interpretative frame for contemplating food scarcity under austerity (Knight 2012).

Who to blame for price stickiness was obviously a contentious issue. The Hellenic Federation of Enterprises (Greece's largest association of employers, SEV) explained high prices as a result of high costs in energy, transport, raw materials, and credit, as well as poor infrastructure, bureaucracy and red tape, and tax increases, in their 2012 memo to the Ministry of Development, placing the fault squarely at the feet of the government. At the same time, the National Federation of Greek Commerce (ESEE) blamed the multinationals and their lack of transparency in transfer-pricing (something the Greek state indeed tried to rectify the following year with new Tax Law 4110/2013). Others pointed again to pricing cartels, calling for further liberalization of the market to eliminate legislation protecting certain sectors. That is a claim also implicit in SEV's list; there is evidence that regulation imposing price ceilings can also create a locus for price collusion (Katsoulacos, Genakos, and Houpis 2015). By December 2012 the General Secretariat of Commerce, the Competition Committee,

and the OECD began a research project to investigate the pricing problems in the Greek market (OECD 2014), with results that focused in the
main on infrastructure development and further market liberalizations,
with the identification of some rent-seeking practices within the market.

Consumer Interventions

It was not, however, only industry groups and government ministries
who were seeking interventions on the problem of consumer prices. In the
framing above we have a market that is functioning improperly because
of its structure, within which the consumer has little agency other than
consuming less. In practice, several innovations arose on the part of individuals in the consumer position, functionally and ideologically challenging the shape of the market, as well as in several instances the orthodox
concept of the market itself.

Andreas Chatzidakis (2013) writes of various resistances, experiments,
and alternatives to capitalist consumption and its relationships that could
be found in the Athenian neighborhood of Exarchia following the 2008
December uprisings.[5] He points out that each of these alternatives—cooperatives, trading with producers through a framework of ethics or
solidarity, anticonsumerist bazaars, and anticonsumerist leisure spaces—
rapidly expanded beyond that neighborhood in the following years to become mainstream expressions of coping with the economics of austerity.
Although these originate as activities with explicit counter-hegemonic
positions on economy, when later taken up by individuals who did not
approach consumption from an explicit position of critique, consumption
practices under austerity de facto became practices of critique of consumerism and its related ideologies. The new forms of commercial enterprise
that Zavos describes in this volume too reflect similar consumer concerns,
regarding the ethics of production, and toward consumption spaces organized through shared ideological critiques.

The so-called Potato Movement is a particularly oft-cited example of
a grassroots innovation that mainstreams several economic solidarity
ideals. In February of 2012, as a response to the vast difference between
wholesale potato and retail potato prices, a local community organization
of Pieria (in the Macedonian region of northern Greece) organized a group
order of potatoes for its members from nearby potato producers (who had
been in the news protesting Egyptian potato imports) at wholesale prices.
The direct-from-producer practice almost immediately spread to other
communities, organized either through community groups, economic solidarity organizations, or local governments, and to other commodities as

well. It seems to have had a significant effect in pricing beyond the movement itself; by that summer average potato prices were almost 25 percent cheaper than they had been the year before (Psaropoulos 2012). Also sometimes called social markets, or *horis mesazontes* (without middlemen), these occasional markets also transformed into open markets held regularly, and there are a sizeable number that continue to function biweekly or monthly around the country (see Rakopoulos's ethnography [2014] of the anti-middleman group RA.ME. for a more explicit discussion of its development and ideals, as well as data regarding the size and impact of the middleman movement). Four years later these markets continue to play an important role in provisioning practices, additionally making the bulk buying of commodities a more significant feature in purchasing patterns (Fotiadi 2016).[6]

The practice of buying directly from producers should bring to mind the *laiki agora* (farmers' market) that is a historical staple of weekly fruit and vegetable provisioning throughout much of Greece, and where the longstanding preferences for buying local direct from the farmer are the very foundation of the institution. Olive oil, tsipouro (an alcohol often homemade), and wine have also circulated widely from time immemorial in a direct-from-producer gray market enabled through personal relationships. But these markets do not share the same moment of politicized formation that the direct-from-producers movement does, and prices in the farmers' market were seen by many to be influenced by the presence of middlemen stalls present there as well. Participants in the markets without-middlemen come primed to this new formation through the previous years' attention to high prices after introduction of the euro, an issue not created by austerity, but certainly exacerbated and newly politicized by it.

Exchange networks and alternative currency systems (formally called local exchange trading systems, or LETS) and other economic solidarity activities have also flourished after 2009, with an ideology explicitly opposed to exchange that both functions on a profit-oriented logic and is alienated from local interpersonal relationships. With the exception of one LETS operating from 2006, and another older system that exclusively exchanges agricultural goods, every other LETS currently functioning in Greece was established after 2008; in 2012 there were thirty-nine of them (Sotiropoulou 2012). It is not surprising to find increased interest in these systems during an economic depression. In fact, we find a similar era of local currency experimentation around the world during the global depression of the 1930s, most of which were wiped out by state governments when that earlier crisis abated (Lietaer and Dunne 2013). Meant to fight the social exclusion of poverty and unemployment, to encourage local consumption, to revalue undervalued (particularly gendered) labor, to eliminate the maximizing logic of profit from transactions, and to embed economic transactions in social relationships, LETS function as both a coping mechanism for reduced economic resources and as an anti-capitalist expression (see Hart 2000 for more on LETS). Free bazaars and free distribution systems that arose during this period contain a further anticonsumerist and environmental message, creating systems for giving away or requesting objects without cost or exchange at all. The bazaars are harder to calculate in number, because many of them are occasional; there were six permanent bazaars in 2010. Sotiropoulou (2012) gives a thorough accounting of the many local exchange systems that existed at that time.[7]

Austerity creates a space for counter-ideologies of consumption to flourish, in that it creates an absolute need to seek new tactics for economic survival, and makes the economic system's functioning/malfunctioning visible and thinkable in new ways. The problems that these new types of markets and exchanges seek to solve existed prior to austerity, as did examples of these types of markets themselves. The mainstreaming of these practices under austerity indicates that the anticapitalist critique they express has also become a more significant part of normative political-economic ideology in Greece. During a period where many expressed disillusionment with politics, choices about consumption in the face of scarcity are a place where political ideologies can be enacted. This is more obvious in terms of exchange systems that have an ideological intent to begin with; in the next section I will excavate consumer behavior studies of nonalternative consumption practices with the same aim in mind.

Austerities in Consumer Behavior

Reflecting some of the concerns about locality reflected in social markets and in LETS, consumer studies in the period following 2008 detect an increased preference for products identified as "Greek." Although there has been a longstanding preference in the Greek market for locally produced fruits, vegetables, and meats (even with local meat prices often higher than imports), in other product categories "Made in the EU" had historically been preferred.[8] However, the Department of Marketing and Communication at the University of Athens, which began yearly consumer behavior surveys in 2005, found for the first time in 2011 that Greekness was indicated as more desirable even in these other realms of goods (Harontakis 2011). This is reflected in changes in advertising (BIC, for instance, began to heavily advertise that their razors are made in Greece), as well as organized efforts to change consumer behavior toward purposefully choosing Greek products. The "Citizens' Movement—We Consume What We Produce," is one such example. It began in 2010 in a coordination of government officials, industry representatives, and professional associations with the slogan, "I dress . . . eat . . . vacation Greek!," with the participation of six supermarket chains. This movement, in the clear politicization of consumption even within the title, recognizes the consumer as an agent that can be activated through banal nationalism toward an economic activity beneficial to the economy. The preference signals multiple expressions: links with perceived quality (see the discussion by Rosen this volume), protection of national production (informal boycotts against German goods have also circulated concurrently, mostly at the social media level), and an explicit linking of consumption practices with the health of the economy and the nation, summoning the consumer citizen (Jubas 2007). Politicized consumption was low in Greece in comparison to other EU countries prior to the crisis (Yates 2011); these new patterns suggest an increase in that mode. This citizen consumer marks a type of neoliberal nationalism, where consumers ensure Greece's success in the free market through their consumption choices, in place of the state's failure to develop the economy (Özkan and Foster 2005).

The yearly surveys mentioned above, during the period of austerity, report yearly increases in those responding that they are buying cheaper products and that they are buying fewer products. Store brands and private label brands (as opposed to name brands) showed consistent growth, as consumers sought cheaper goods. Significantly, they also lost their stigma, as did shopping specifically to seek out sales and special offers. In 2011 Boston Consulting Group's yearly global consumer survey focused on a worldwide shift in behaviors, related to the economic downturn. The report's section "New Values: From Conspicuous to 'Conscientious' Consumption," gives Greece a special profile. "It's not just a question of having less money—cautious spending has become a habit. We've become accustomed to thinking twice before buying anything" (Roche, Ducasse, and Laio 2011: 26). Other consumer research has suggested that downwardly mobile consumers were not reporting feelings of alienation or exclusion as a result of their economic circumstances, which would have been the expected findings in consumer research for groups in poverty, but rather framed their suffering as a shared experience, equal to what others were going through (Karanika and Hogg 2016). Solidarity in austerity supplants the competitive nature of conspicuous consumption.

This austerity consumer is making choices in a manner far different from the consumers of the 1960s to 1970s whom Karapostolis described (with their ambition toward mobility and status) and the ethos of the conspicuous consumption that is commonly understood to mark the 1980s to 1990s as well, and stands in moralistic terms as a criticism of that era of excess, symbolized by luxury goods like Rolex watches and Porsche Cayennes (as austerity itself is positioned in moral terms as both corrective and critique). A competency in negotiating austerity-circumstances, signaled through the attention to price/value and necessity, rises to the fore in its place. When historic luxury clothing retailer Carouzos went into bankruptcy, it was reported as the end of an era, one that had belonged to "homo Catanaloticus" but whose fate was sealed when Greece's debt crisis began (Harontakis 2012). In symbolic contrast, the do-it-yourself retail sector managed to develop (Fragouli and Kouli 2016). In reporting the results of the 2015 consumer survey of the University of Athens (the survey mentioned above), the era of the *chouvarntades* (big spenders) was declared over, and Greeks had become Northern European in their consumption of necessities (Manifava 2015). Prestige goods, symbols of the consumerism of the prior era, shifted symbolism toward signaling excess and irresponsibility.[9] The consumer created by austerity is thrifty and careful. The ambition of status and expectations of automatic economic growth are replaced, and are supplanted by a set of practices that seek to control the uncertain future through careful management of finances.[10]

The Citizen/Consumer Connection

Another significant change in consumer behavior regards method of payment: plastic money. Although the amount of total household consumer credit declined during this period, the number of transactions on credit cards started to increase (i.e., not total debt, but the frequency with which the cards were being used) (Foundation for Economic & Industrial Research 2015). Some of this increase is related to attempts to maximize limited economic resources: special offers like loyalty programs and interest-free payment programs offered through cards (now extended to purchases like heating oil and payments to the state) increased significantly, and any stigma toward practices that explicitly sought to save money declined. With the imposition of capital controls in the summer of 2015, after which individuals could withdraw only €60 a day from the ATM but where there was no limit on the use of cards within national boundaries, the use of plastic money jumped. In fact, around 1 million cash cards were issued during July and August 2015 (Koutantou 2015), and the use of payment cards more than doubled from June to July (Foundation for Economic & Industrial Research 2015). Again, this brings Greece more in line with the use of plastic cards in many other European countries, and changes the valence of card use in Greece toward the banal and everyday.

Economic rationales and restrictions on cash, however, are not the only significant force driving the economy toward plastic money in both credit and cashless payment forms. With tax evasion marked as a special problem under the austerity regime, controlling said evasion is another realm where consumption becomes a point of intervention. Limiting consumption to taxable transactions—accountable transactions under government authority—is a main concern. Some attempts involved the enforcement of issuing legal receipts for all transactions. From 2010 a certain amount of expenses demonstrated through receipts had to be submitted with one's income tax declaration (a tactic also used in the past), with required signs placed at cash registers declaring that a receipt must be produced or the consumer has no obligation to pay, thus incentivizing the consumer to enforce and report. Encouraging the use of plastic money arrives as another obvious solution. The vice president of Visa Europe in Greece is quoted in *To Vima* in 2011 in an article concerning the increase of credit card use, that "cash transactions are the ones that feed the underground economy," suggesting that the government should lead the way by accepting cards for taxes, fees, and fines ("Ftena Psonia me Plastiko Chrema" 2011). By 2016 credit and debit cards were accepted for each of those and more, with special programs breaking the amounts into interest-free monthly payments.

Furthermore, the Ministry of Finance announced in 2016 that only those transactions conducted with credit and debit cards, or through electronic bank transfer, would be counted toward general expenses for personal income tax forms; this announcement was made by the same deputy minister of Finance who also publicly criticized high bank fees and commissions.[11] Spending a specific percentage of one's income through these forms is required to qualify for tax exemptions, and falling short of that percentage brings a fine. Additionally, legislation in 2017 began requiring that certain types of businesses are required to have point-of-sale (POS) terminals for electronic payment (plastic or mobile money); legislation plans to expand that list of business types in 2018. All shops must display a sign visible from the street as to whether they accept POS transactions, creating a visible geography of plastic money's spread, and vastly increasing the potential for everyday plastic money use. I conducted a preliminary research survey in 2017 with small shop owners regarding the new POS rules. My survey produced various interpretations: all shop owners had seen a significant increase in plastic money use or the request to use plastic money,[12] resulting from (they theorized) both the new tax law and people's increased need for credit. At the same time, the shop owners had wide variation in how they saw it affecting their businesses, and various amounts of cynicism on the plan's efficacy and fairness; they spent considerable time spent elaborating on how the nation's biggest tax evasion offenders would be unaffected by these rules. The result of this tax enforcement through encouraging plastic money consumption is, in effect, the privatization of accountability: credit card companies and banks track transactions for the state, taking their not-insignificant percentage for doing so with fees or percentages taken on credit card use, debit card use, many electronic bill payments, and intrabank electronic transfers.

The result is a sharp and dramatic increase in the number of electronic money transactions, the expansion of the retail geography where consumers can use plastic money, and the increased ease of transactions when they do so. Contactless payments, though technologically available from 2012, swiftly became widely available for amounts under €25 after 2016. The average amount spent in each credit and debit transaction has also dropped considerably over these past two years, signifying that plastic money is now being used for smaller, everyday consumption in a way it was not before. The transaction fees for plastic money (including mobile phone monies, which currently are Visa Europe products) can be quite onerous for smaller shops, with many reporting that they are also paying transaction fees on the 24 percent value added tax (VAT) added to sales (Athens Chamber of Tradesmen 2015). The long-term influence on consumer practices is unclear, but the state's encouragement toward consumption through electronic money has had demonstrable effects.[13]

Conclusion: Austerity as Pedagogy

I return here to the consumer who is a neoliberal subject, the one necessary for the functioning of the type of market the EU has attempted to create. The practices of governing that I describe above work specifically toward the creation of that consumer: one who purchases from state-approved actors in the market (after all, only those transactions are protected under consumer protection law), one whose transactions are appropriately taxed (thus properly linking state and economy), and one who does the work of making sure the market functions smoothly by exercising care and economic maximization in their consumption habits. The digitization of transactions through plastic money and electronic transfer is a form of securitization, creating a new category of authorized and accountable consumption.

I have tried to describe in this chapter multiple pedagogies of austerity. While austerity seems to offer a moral critique of the era of rampant consumerism, I argue that it is a governmentality that shifts consumer behaviors toward the immediate necessity of the economy, through rhetorics like banal nationalism. It has consumers taking it on themselves to create their own markets when normative markets are found lacking. It creates economic subjects responsible for their own security in times of extreme economic uncertainty. Pre-austerity, these consumers were encouraged to see the future through the growth ideology of that era, using their credit to bring an EU economy into being in Greece through the force of their consumption. During austerity, the economic ideology changes, but the responsibility of the consumer remains: to spend in a way that best benefits the Greek economy, making up for the state's failures. In this way, the growth consumer and the austerity consumer are two sides of the same coin.

Aside from austerity's explicit purpose in economic restructuring, it is also clear that austerity is meant to be a process that teaches a lesson—both through the reshaping of behavior and through discomfort—in its punitiveness. It is rather easy to see the lessons against profligacy, where suffering must occur so that one does not return to bad debtor behaviors, and neighbors learn what pain awaits them if they, too, stray (a lesson referred to as moral hazard in credit discourse). Austerity teaches the lesson of how to survive without the welfare state, as many other chapters in this volume have described.

At the same time, however, austerity has made the economy explicit, through public discussion of its ideologies, methods, and effects, and as such it becomes a clearer target for critique and intervention. Some activities that can be framed above as pedagogies of austerity could also be understood as the creation of alternatives, and as marks of austerity's failures. It is clear that austerity has created structural changes in both the market and in consumer habits, some of which we can expect to be long lasting past economic recovery.

Aimee Placas is a faculty member at the International Center for Hellenic and Mediterranean Studies (ΔΙΚΕΜΕΣ), College Year in Athens. She holds a PhD in Anthropology from Rice University and has published and presented on consumer debt and bankruptcy, the effect of the Greek crisis on overindebted households, and everyday economic life in Greece. She is currently writing an ethnography on the story of consumer credit in Greece in the 21st century.

Notes

1. Given the scandal involving the illegalities in the construction of the mall in Marousi (an accelerated building process that skipped normal stages of impact studies and the like), it is worth considering how being a symbol of consumption (excess) heightens the moral tale of the appropriation of public land, crony capitalism, and political corruption (see Aretaki 2013 for the backstory, written before the courts indeed declared the construction illegal). The consumption spaces seem now to be moving away from this traditional mall structure towards "open malls," not just in Greece.
2. Greece's first consumer credit reporting agency, Tiresias, did not become fully operational until 2003. Objections on the part of the Hellenic Data Protection Authority, and oligarchic banking practices where the larger banks with big internal consumer data sets were at an advantage if no external credit reporting existed, both contributed to this delay.
3. The Hellenic Statistical Authority (ELSTAT) Household Budget survey of 2004–5 reports 77.3 percent of households responding that they have difficulties meeting their financial obligations (Mitrakos, Simigiannis, and Tzamourani 2005).
4. There were no bankruptcy protections for Greek consumers until 2010, when the primary home also became (potentially) protected by the new Katseli law. Before that time a creditor bank's recourse on failed loans and mortgages to consumers would be to take the individual to court and receive compensation in seized goods and property.
5. These countrywide protests, sparked by the police shooting of a Greek teen, came to encompass a broad set of political concerns and mobilizations, including a strong anti-consumerist one.
6. Consumer cooperatives with collective-purchasing methods have existed in Greece from the postwar era, and in general cooperative organizational forms have a long history. They have been limited in size and scope, however (Ntountoumis and Siotos 2000).
7. The website Antallaktiki Oikonomia (exchange economy) keeps an up-to-date calendar of exchange bazaars and systems at http://antallaktiki.gr/.
8. This goes back farther than the EU, obviously. There's an old slang term, *megla*, meaning something good or of high quality, that most likely derives from the phrase "Made in England."
9. One would assume, however, that there are pockets of the population among whom prestige goods continue to hold their value as markers of distinction: not every shop in Kolonaki or the Golden Hall mall have gone out of business—far from it. It would be intriguing to explore whether practices and geographies of display regarding those goods have changed. Additionally, there might be a performance of these new values in answering surveys that is not represented in day-to-day consumption choices.
10. I am taking care to point to this consumer research as circulating data, rather than simply citing their findings, to indicate the significance of the studies themselves in the construction of the "Greek consumer." These are profiles of consumption which may be utilized by producers, distributors, advertisers, mass media, and the like, in a cycle that shapes the market and the same data they report.
11. Individuals over the age of seventy are exempt.
12. Cardlink, Greece's largest provider of POS terminals, reported a 145 percent increase in transactions on their network between June 2015 and June 2016 (Cardlink 2016).
13. A recent survey commissioned by the Hellenic Confederation of Commerce and Entrepreneurship in early 2017 found that 68 percent of respondents were using plastic money for their consumption (61 percent using debit cards and 21 percent credit cards), but that 52 percent would prefer to use cash over 39 percent who prefer cards (Public Issue 2017). The debit card increase is significant, because Greece's debit card use has

traditionally been low compared to credit cards (in 2013 debit cards accounted to 11.8 percent of all cashless transactions in Greece, compared to 34.2 percent in the eurozone) (Foundation for Economic & Industrial Research 2015).

References

Aretaki, Myrto. 2013. "The Mall Athens: Skandalo opos kai an to Deis." *The Press Project*, 5 April. Retrieved 15 June 2016 from https://www.thepressproject.gr/article/41284/ The-Mall-Athens-Skandalo-opos-kai-an-to-deis.

Arghyrou, Michael G. 2007. "The Price Effects of Joining the Euro: Modelling the Greek Experience Using Non-Linear Price-Adjustment Models." *Applied Economics* 39(4): 493–503.

Athanassiou, Ersi. 2006. "Prospects of Household Borrowing in Greece and Their Importance for Growth." Discussion Paper 84. Athens: Centre of Planning and Economic Research.

Athens Chamber of Tradesmen. 2015. "Erevna tou E.E.A.: Ypervolikes oi Chreoseis ton Pistotikon Karton." Epaggelmatiko Epimeleterio Athenon. Retrieved 8 June 2016 from http:// www.eea.gr/gr/el/articles/ereyna-toy-eea-ypervolikes-oi-xreoseis-ton-pistotikon-karton.

Baltas, Georgios. 2008. "Erchontai Semantines Allages Sten Katanalotike Symperiphora." *To Vima*, October 12. Retrieved 24 February 2016. http://www.tovima.gr/relatedarticles/ article/?aid=18651.

Bank of Greece. 2003. *Report on Monetary Policy 2002–2003*. Athens: Bank of Greece.

———. 2009. *Annual Report 2008*. Athens: Bank of Greece.

———. 2011. *Annual Report 2010*. Athens: Bank of Greece.

Bennison, David, and Christina Boutsouki. 1995. "Greek Retailing in Transition." *International Journal of Retail & Distribution Management* 23(1): 24–31.

Brekke, Jaya, Dimitris Dalakoglou, Christos Filippidis, and Antonis Vradis, eds. 2014. *Crisis-Scapes: Athens and Beyond*. Athens: Synthesi.

Cardlink. 2016. "Press Release: More than 10,000,000 Transactions Processed in the Network of Cardlink for the Month of June." July 4. Retrieved 6 June 2017 from http://www.card link.gr/sites/default/files/20160704_cardlink_pr_10_million_transactions.pdf.

Chatzidakis, Andreas. 2013. "Commodity Fights in Post-2008 Athens: Zapatistas Coffee, Kropotkinian Drinks and Fascist Rice." *Ephemera* 13(2): 459–68. http://www.ephemera journal.org/contribution/commodity-fights-post-2008-athens-zapatistas-coffee-kropot kinian-drinks-and-fascist.

———. 2014. "Athens as a Failed City for Consumption." In Brekke et al., *Crisis-Scapes*, 33–41.

Chee, Foo Yun. 2002. "Consumers Cry Foul over Excessive Price Increases." *Kathimerini English Edition*, 3 September. Retried 24 February 2016 from http://www.ekathimerini .com/8215/article/ekathimerini/business/consumers-cry-foul-over-excessive-price-increases.

Costa, Janeen Arnold. 2005. "Empowerment and Exploitation: Gendered Production and Consumption in Rural Greece." *Consumption, Markets and Culture* 8(3): 313–23.

Cowan, Jane K. 1990. *Dance and the Body Politic in Northern Greece*. Princeton Modern Greek Studies. Princeton, NJ: Princeton University Press.

DeCastro, Julio Cesar Lemes. 2015. "The Consumer as Agent in Neoliberalism." *MATRIZes* 9(2): 283–88.

Dimitriou-Kotsoni, Syvilla. 2006. "Katanalotikes Praktikes kai Syllogikes Tautotetes." In *Eautos kai "Allos": Ennoiologeseis, Tautotetes kai Praktikes sten Ellada kai ten Kypro*, ed Dimitra Gefou-Madianou, 305–42. Athens: Gutenberg.

Economou, Leonidas. 2014. "Political and Cultural Implications of the Suburban Transformation of Athens." In Brekke et al., *Crisis-Scapes*, 13–17.

Fotiadi, Ioanna. 2016. "To kinema tes Patatas Paramenei Zontano kai Gigantonetai." *E Kathimerini*, 3 May. Retrieved 6 June 2017 from http://www.kathimerini.gr/852050/article/epikairothta/ellada/to-kinhma-ths-patatas-paramenei-zwntano-kai-gigantwnetai.

Foucault, Michel. 2008. *The Birth of Biopolitics: Lectures at the Collège de France, 1978–1979*, translated by Graham Burchell. New York: Palgrave Macmillan.

Foundation for Economic & Industrial Research. 2015. "Digital Payments and Tax Revenues in Greece." Athens: Foundation for Economic & Industrial Research. Retrieved 24 February 2016 from http://iobe.gr/docs/research/en/RES_05_F_21102015_REP_EN.pdf.

Fragouli, Evangelia, and Panagiota Kouli. 2016. "Retail Commerce & Big Retail Chains in Greece." *International Journal of Information, Business and Management* 8(2): 286–304.

Friedl, Ernestine. 1962. *Vasilika: A Village in Modern Greece*. New York: Holt, Rinehart, and Winston.

———. 1964. "Lagging Emulation in Post-Peasant Society." *American Anthropologist* 66(3): 569–86.

"Ftena Psonia me Plastiko Chrema." 2011. *To Vima*, 3 April. Retrieved 19 June 2016 from http://www.tovima.gr/finance/article/?aid=393485.

Genike Synomospondia Epaggelmation Viotechnon Emporon Elladas (GSEVEE). 2013. "Ereuna IME GSEVEE—Apeleutherose Orariou Leitourgias Tis Kyriakes. *GSEVEE—Genike Synomospondia Epaggelmation Viotechnon Emporon Elladas*. Retrieved 24 February 2016 from http://www.gsevee.gr/meletes-2/252-2013-02-14-10-11-53.

Giesler, Markus, and Ela Veresiu. 2014. "Creating the Responsible Consumer: Moralistic Governance Regimes and Consumer Subjectivity." *Journal of Consumer Research* 41(3): 840–57.

Gkougkouli, Kleio. 2000. "Paido kai Viomechaniko Paichnidi: Chreseis kai Chrestes, Mia Anthropologike Proseggise." In *Paidi kai Paichnidi sten Neoellenike Koinonia: 19os - 20os Aionas*, edited by Kleio Gkougkouli and Aphroditi Kouria, 371–415. Athens: Kastaniotis.

Harontakis, Dimitris. 2007. "Pos Stetheke To Elleniko 'Kartel Tou Galaktos.'" *To Vima*, November 3. Retrieved 24 February 2016 from http://www.tovima.gr/finance/article/?aid=179611.

———. 2011. "Oi Katanalotes Anakalyptoun Kai Pali Ta Ellenika Proinonta." *To Vima*, May 8. Retrieved 24 February 2016 from http://www.tovima.gr/finance/article/?aid=399607.

———. 2012. "Pikro to Telos tes Eumareias Gia Ten Carouzos." *To Vima*, July 8. Retrieved 24 February 2016 from http://www.tovima.gr/finance/article/?aid=465899.

Hart, Keith. 2000. *The Memory Bank: Money in an Unequal World*. London: Profile.

Jubas, Kaela. 2007. "Conceptual Con/Fusion in Democratic Societies: Understandings and Limitations of Consumer-Citizenship." *Journal of Consumer Culture* 7(2): 231–54.

Karanika, Katerina, and Margaret Hogg. 2016. "Being Kind to Ourselves: Self-Compassion, Coping, and Consumption." *Journal of Business Research* 69(2): 760–69.

Karantaki, Magdalini, and Anna Tsentekidou. 1996. *Oi Katanalotikoi Synetairismoi Sten Ellada Kai sten Europe*. Dissertation. Kavala, Greece: T.E.I. Kavalas.

Karapostolis, Vassilis. 1983. "Consumption Patterns in Greek Rural Communities: A Socioeconomic Approach." *Ekistics* 50(303): 442–48.

Kassaveti, Ursula-Helen. 2016. "Audio-visual Consumption in the Greek VHS Era: Social Mobility, Privatization and the VCR Audiences in the 1980s." In Kornetis, Kotsovili, and Papadogiannis, *Consumption and Gender*, 241–256.

Katsoulacos, Yannis, Christos Genakos, and George Houpis. 2015. "Product Market Regulation and Competitiveness: Towards a National Competition and Competitiveness Policy in Greece." In *Reforming the Greek Economy*, ED Costas Meghir, Christopher Pissarides, Dimitry Vayanos and Nikolaos Vettas. Cambridge: MIT Press.

Knight, Daniel. 2012. "Cultural Proximity: Crisis, Time and Social Memory in Central Greece." *History and Anthropology* 23(3): 349–74.

Kontogiannis, Dimitris. 2008. "Gov't Insistence on Bank Bailout Package Raises Control Questions." *Kathimerini English Edition*, 10 November. Retrieved 24 February 2016 from http://www.ekathimerini.com/60515/article/ekathimerini/business/govt-insisten ce-on-bank-bailout-package-raises-control-questions.

Kornetis, Kostis, Eirini Kotsovili, and Nikolaos Papadogiannis. 2016. *Consumption and Gender in Southern Europe since the Long 1960s*. London: Bloomsbury.

Kouremenos, Athanassios, and George Avlonitis. 1995. "The Changing Consumer in Greece." *International Journal of Research in Marketing* 12(5): 435–48.

Koutantou, Angeliki. 2015. "Greeks Fall in Love with Plastic after Cash Controls." *Kathimerini English Edition*, October 13. Retrieved 24 February 2016 from http://www.ekath imerini.com/202466/article/ekathimerini/business/greeks-fall-in-love-with-plastic-after-cash-controls.

Lallas, Dimitrios. 2010. "Katanalose Kai Koinonikes Anaparastaseis Stous Sygchronous Emporikous Polychorous: To Paradeigma Tou The Mall Athens." PhD dissertation. Athens: Panteion University of Social and Political Sciences.

Lietaer, Bernard, and Jacqui Dunne. 2013. *Rethinking Money: How New Currencies Turn Scarcity into Prosperity*. Oakland, CA: Berrett-Koehler Publishers.

Malaby, T. M. 2003. "The Currency of Proof: Euro Competence and the Refiguring of Value in Greece." *Social Analysis* 47(1): 42–52.

Manifava, Dimitra. 2015. "E Krise ekane Voreioeuropaious tous Ellenes Katanalotes." *E Kathimerini*, April 19. Retrieved 24 February 2016 from http://www.kathimerini.gr/811902/article/oikonomia/ellhnikh-oikonomia/h-krish-ekane-boreioeyrwpai

McCracken, Grant. 1988. *Culture and Consumption: New Approaches to the Symbolic Character of Consumer Goods and Activities*. Bloomington: Indiana University Press.

Miller, Daniel. 2001. *Consumption*, Vol 4, *Objects, Subjects and Mediations in Consumption*. London: Routledge.

Mitrakos, Theodoros, and Simigiannis, George. 2009. "The Determinants of Greek Household Indebtedness and Financial Stress." *Economic Bulletin* 32: 7–26. Athens: Bank of Greece.

Mitrakos, Theodoros, George Simigiannis, and Panagiota Tzamourani. 2005. "Indebtedness of Greek Households: Evidence from a Survey." *Economic Bulletin* 25: 13–35. Athens: Bank of Greece.

Nikolakakis, Michalis. 2016. "Tourism, Body, and Seaside Recreational Practices in Postwar Greek Society until 1974." In Kornetis, Kotsovili, and Papadogiannis, *Consumption and Gender*, 103–17.

Ntountoumis, Anastasios, and Ioannis Siotos. 2000. *Consumer Cooperatives in the Period 1946–1969*. Dissertation. Mesolloggi, Greece: T.E.I. Mesolloggiou.

Organisation for Economic Co-operation and Development (OECD). 2001. *OECD Economic Surveys: Greece 2001*. Paris: Organisation for Economic Co-operation and Development.

———. 2014. *OECD Competition Assessment Reviews: Greece*. Paris: Organisation for Economic Co-operation and Development.

Özkan, Derya, and Robert John Foster. 2005. "Consumer Citizenship, Nationalism, and Neoliberal Globalization in Turkey: The Advertising Launch of Cola Turka." *Advertising & Society Review* 6(3): n.p. Retrieved 24 February 2016 from https://doi.org/10.1353/asr.2006.0001.

Pagoulatos, George. 2003. *Greece's New Political Economy: State, Finance, and Growth from Postwar to E.M.U.* New York: Palgrave Macmillan.

Pipyrou, Stavroula. 2014. "Cutting Bella Figura: Irony, Crisis, and Secondhand Clothes in South Italy." *American Ethnologist* 41(3): 532–46.

Placas, Aimee Jessica. 2008. "The Emergence of Consumer Credit in Greece: An Ethnography of Indebtedness." PhD dissertation. Houston, TX: Rice University.

————. 2016. "Money Talk." Hot Spots, *Cultural Anthropology.* April 21. Retrieved 6 June 2017 from http://www.culanth.org/fieldsights/856-money-talk.

Priporas, Constantinos. 2003. "The Impact of Foreign Retailers on Structure and Competition in the Greek Supermarket Sector." *Journal of Business & Society* 16(2): 212–22.

Psaropoulos, John. 2012. "Greece's 'Potato Movement' Grows in Power." *Al Jazeera,* June 11. Retrieved 24 February 2016 from http://www.aljazeera.com/indepth/features/2012/06/2012611102126662269.html.

Public Issue. 2017. "Ereuna Koines Gnomes gia tis Staseis ton Ellenon Katanaloton apenanti sto Plastiko Chrema." Athens: The Hellenic Confederation of Commerce and Entrepreneurship. Retrieved 6 June 2017 from http://www.publicissue.gr/wp-content/uploads/2017/03/2017002_Graphs_POS.pdf.

Rakopoulos, Theodoros. 2014. "The Crisis Seen from Below, Within, and Against: From Solidarity Economy to Food Distribution Cooperatives in Greece." *Dialectical Anthropology* 38(2): 189–207.

Roche, Catherine, Patrick Ducasse, and Carol Laio. 2011. "Navigating the New Consumer Realities: Consumer Sentiment 2011." Boston: Boston Consulting Group. Retrieved 24 February 2016 from https://www.bcg.com/documents/file79398.pdf.

Sakellaropoulos, Spyros. 2010. "The Recent Economic Crisis in Greece and the Strategy of Capital." *Journal of Modern Greek Studies* 28(2): 321–48.

Sotiropoulou, Irene. 2012. "Exchange Networks and Parallel Currencies: Theoretical Approaches and the Case of Greece." PhD dissertation. Rethymnon, Greece: University of Crete.

Stratigaki, Maria. 1996. *Phylo Ergasia Technologia.* Athens: Politis.

Sturm, Jan-Egbert, Ulrich Fritsche, Michael Graff, Michael Lamla, Sarah Lein, Volker Nitsch, David Liechti, and Daniel Triet. 2009. *The Euro and Prices Changeover-Related Inflation and Price Convergence in the Euro Area.* Brussels: European Commission, Directorate-General for Economic and Financial Affairs. Retrieved 24 February 2016 from http://ec.europa.eu/economy_finance/publications/publication15287_en.pdf.

Theodossopoulos, Dimitrios. 2013. "Infuriated with the Infuriated?: Blaming Tactics and Discontent about the Greek Financial Crisis." *Current Anthropology* 54(2): 200–21.

Trentmann, Frank. 2005. "Knowing Consumers–Histories, Identities, Practices: An Introduction. In *The Making of the Consumer: Knowledge, Power and Identity in the Modern World,* edited by Frank Trentmann, 1–27. Oxford: Berg Publishers.

Tsakarestou, Betty. 2002. "Advertising in Greece." In *More Advertising Worldwide,* edited by Ingomar Kloss, 64–79. Berlin: Springer.

Veblen, Thorstein. 1973 [1899]. *The Theory of the Leisure Class: An Economic Study in the Evolution of Institutions.* Boston: Houghton Mifflin.

Yannakopoulos, Kostas. 2016. "'Naked Piazza': Male (Homo)Sexualities, Masculinities and Consumer Culture in Greece since the 1960s." In Kornetis, Kotsovili, and Papadogiannis, *Consumption and Gender,* 173–89.

Yates, Luke S. 2011. "Critical Consumption: Boycotting and Buycotting in Europe." *European Societies* 13(2): 191–217.

Zestanakis, Panagiotis. 2017. "Gender and Sexuality in Three Late-1980s Greek Lifestyle Magazines: *Playboy, Status* and *Click.*" *Journal of Greek Media & Culture* 3(1): 95–115.

Conclusion

Aimee Placas and Evdoxios Doxiadis

W hen we first conceived this volume in 2014 there was some slight optimism in Greece that the worst of the crisis was nearing its end. The economy seemed to be picking up, the world markets seemed to have stabilized, many of Europe's economies were growing again, and a new party—untainted by the old political establishment—seemed poised to take power, promising a new beginning. Those hopes however were soon dashed by a return to recession, a new memorandum of understanding (MoU) with the International Monetary Fund, European Central Bank, and European Union (together known as the Troika), and new austerity measures. The cautious optimism of 2014 has given way to pessimism as many of the chapters in this volume show.

Our purpose in putting together this volume was to avoid the common explorations for causes and remedies for the Greek sovereign debt crisis that have amply been discussed by a series of volumes by influential scholars,[1] and look at the effects along a broad spectrum of Greek society, trying to identify continuities and ruptures, seeking a better understanding of the impact of prolonged economic crises on previously prosperous and developed economies and societies. Our contributors, as the reader will have noticed, cover a great political and ideological spectrum and quite clearly disagree as to the forces implicated in the crisis, as do the editors. Some assign culpability to the effects of neoliberalism and processes of Europeanization, while others point to domestic factors, primarily to a political system mired in patronage and unable to reform (not that these are in any way mutually exclusive). But that was, as we discuss in the introduction, not the primary concern of the chapters of this volume. What interested us was what happened to Greece once people started talking about "crisis," and what lessons one could draw from Greek responses to

Notes for this chapter begin on page 352.

the austerity policies implemented. The common threads and agreements between these chapters on the results of austerity are perhaps thus more significant, given the disparate vantage points from which the authors start.

One evident result had been the deterioration of the living standards of people in Greece, an expected outcome of course considering the prolonged recession that removed nearly a quarter of the precrisis GDP of Greece, the collapse of employment especially in the private sector, and cuts in social services across the board. This deterioration, however, has not been uniform; because of the structure of the Greek economy and the Greek welfare state the effects of the deterioration have had a particularly deleterious effect on women, immigrants, and the young. As scholars have shown, Greece and much of Europe's south had developed a social welfare state that relied substantially on the family for many aspects that are the responsibility of social services elsewhere such as daycare, care for the elderly, and so on. As Greece became wealthier, foreign migrants (particularly female) were used in increasing numbers to compensate for the inadequacies of the state services while allowing Greeks and in particular Greek women to be employed, parallel to changes both economic and social that made two-income households all the more necessary (see Ireland 2011). The collapse of Greek incomes has made this fragile model unsustainable and has exacerbated the effects of the cuts in the funding of social services. This is a crucial social context for all of the chapters of this volume, because the background of economic difficulty (from discomfort to complete destitution, and the creation of a nouveau poor) intersects both with the creation of coping mechanisms, and with increasing political dissatisfaction.

One clear and very important conclusion that arises from these chapters is that while actions taken in the name of debt reduction (i.e., spending cuts, revenue raising, and economic reorganization) have acquired a new urgency and political legitimacy under austerity, they are but the latest chapters of a much longer story. The dramatic defunding of health care described by Burgi follows a model of commodification already ascendant elsewhere. Hess shows that the defunding of public media is only the most recent event in a long history of political shaping of Greece's mediascape; efforts to better capture tax revenue through consumer expenditures are argued by Placas to be a continuation of the financialization of everyday life. Although these actions do not introduce new ideas, however, the chapters are consistent in the evidence they provide concerning austerity's deleterious effects; they happen abruptly, in a moment when the populace is least able to absorb or manage them. The harshness of austerity in Greece is pointed to by Bremer and Vidal to distinguish its effects in Greece in comparison to other European contexts, significant in understanding its political effects.

In this respect, although the crisis of the political system in Greece is well explored elsewhere, it could not be absent from this volume. Although the traditional parties of the center left (Panhellenic Socialist Movement, or PASOK) and center right (New Democracy, or ND) were punished by the electorate, the political system did not find a new equilibrium but continued to remain unreformed and unstable. New parties were created but proved unable to get much traction (Potami; Popular Unity, or LAE), antisystemic parties that profited from the crisis quickly became arguably indistinguishable from the earlier systemic ones (Coalition of the Radical Left, or SYRIZA; Independent Greeks, or ANEL), and parties at the very opposite ends of the political spectrum experienced considerable success (Golden Dawn, and more recently the Communist Party of Greece, or KKE). To a certain degree the fundamental structure of Greek politics—which some scholars have described as rent-based (Pappas 2013: 39–40)—arguably continues, now with a new disheartening debate about whether any political party or democratic process can successfully challenge the form of austerity reforms. Clearly this volume shows that the political effects of austerity have deeper roots than just expressions of dissatisfaction with the MoUs or the mishandling of the crisis, and that prior political structures have shaped critical aspects of political life in Greece—from the historically longstanding discourses suspicious of foreign debt Doxiadis discusses, to the recent succession problems within the major parties Mylonas describes, to the ongoing place of parties and unions in organizing protest that Kanellopoulos and Kousis find.

And yet another clear conclusion from this volume is that new political subjectivities, separate from the party identification crucial to traditional party clientelism, have found strong expression these past years. Whereas political activity in later-twentieth-century Greece was nearly subsumed by party politics, a tendency away from this was already visible at the century's turn, and these past years have seen this tendency continue to develop with austerity reforms and effects as its focal point. For example, although political parties and trade unions were major sources of protest organization, there were other additional protests that marked themselves as distinct from such groups (as with the Greek Indignados, and in the summer of 2011). Activism independent of party support, and often positioned against it, drove the creation of grassroots initiatives in the realms of health care, refugee support, and economic exchange, as these chapters have outlined. Although often created to cope with the withdrawal of welfare provisions, these new social formations have sometimes been seen as hallmarks of neoliberal subjectivity, in the sense that they train citizens to "do for themselves." However, this volume also identifies formations that are explicit ideological experiments in opposition to this idea. (See Rozakou 2011 for a consideration of the tension between these two subject positions.) These are only a few of the places where people in Greece today are acting politically in ways that escape traditional political structures.

In fact, these types of bottom-up initiatives emerge in this volume as one of the most hopeful realms in Greece, where we see the subjects of austerity as more than just its victims. One common theme that emerges from these articles is that despite the severe effects of austerity and the true hardship of Greek society, change has been slow, incremental, and frequently more cosmetic than substantive. The lack of funds has certainly eroded social services, undermined the political system, and dealt a severe blow to the mediascape, let alone the banks, companies, and education in Greece. The more-promising changes have not come from the state but rather from the people themselves who used new technologies, formed new types of support organizations, businesses, and exchange forms, and created new political actors and voices, as Zavos, Hess, Placas, and Cabot show in this volume.

Another one of the crucial conclusions of this volume has to do with the complex question of immigration, a problem that far exceeds the confines of Greece. However, as Cabot and Rosen show in their chapters, immigration has long been a topic of concern for the Greek electorate; however, through the 1990s and early 2000s the economic benefits of immigration in agriculture, construction, and as a substitute for absent social services soothed the nationalist and racist fears for many Greeks. The crisis transformed the tentative equilibrium and gave the opportunity to a fringe party, Golden Dawn, to seize the issue and catapult itself into the Parliament as a major political force, affecting perhaps the most dramatic transformation in the Greek political establishment since 1974. Golden Dawn is not the product of the crisis, as Karpozilos shows, having a long history in Greece, but the party's ability to seize on the existing powerful nationalist fears of the Greek electorate (Macedonia, immigration) explain its recent successes.

At the same time, this volume also challenges the simplistic linking between xenophobia and economic difficulty found often in popular and academic discussion, where the rise of suspicion, negative attitudes, and even violence are treated as if they rise spontaneously out of the emotions of financial anxiety. The work by Doxiadis, Karpozilos, and Cheliotis and Xenaki show that these antagonistic orientations toward foreigners (both internal foreigners and external foreigners) have been systematically developed and fostered by political elites. We see the process by which xenophobia is not just manipulated, but actually created. This is a useful point of comparison toward looking at what is happening outside Greece, with Brexit and with recent election results in EU countries and the US.

It is fitting to discuss what we have not managed to achieve in this volume. We were hoping to cover several other aspects of Greek society that have seen significant transformations in recent years under the impact of the crisis and austerity policies such as secondary and tertiary education, a perennial issue in the news for over a decade, as well as questions regarding gender identity and rights related to lesbian, gay, bisexual, transgender, and other sexualities (LGBTQI+) that have been dramatically reformed for the better through recent legislation (e.g., rights to same-sex civil unions, reduced restrictions on legal gender changes) though, unfortunately, this transformation was accompanied by increased violence toward those who identify themselves outside the traditional gender binary. For a variety of reasons we were not able to include these topics (and many other relevant topics) in our volume, and we hope that these issues will be given the serious concern they deserve in future publications.

As this volume goes to press we realize that our contributors, even though they generally refrain from speculating about the future, exude a sense of pessimism about Greek society, at least as far as the short term is concerned. With the exception of individual efforts there appears to be little positive agency from the Greek state, political parties, or society at large that would give hope for an eventual recovery. Greek society, the political establishment, even business, seems to have survived the crisis thus far by hankering down and waiting for the gale to pass rather than proactively seeking to find solutions to its structural problems. It is perhaps worth noting, as Zavos does in her chapter, that most of the authors here write from within the experience of austerity themselves, whether located in Greece or abroad, as academic and research contexts have been reshaped and defunded. One of austerity's effects is that the production of knowledge about such effects becomes ever more difficult.

It is our hope that this pessimism is misplaced, but as these chapters indicate, there has been little in the past decade to give us grounds for optimism. Perhaps one final direction we can take from the discussion in these chapters is to point away from the nation-state as the source of solution to these problems, and to direct attention either upward toward the structures and institutions outside of Greece shaping austerity's implementation, and/or downward toward further exploration of the productive resistances and coping mechanisms created in Greece on the ground during these past years.

Aimee Placas is a faculty member at the International Center for Hellenic and Mediterranean Studies (ΔΙΚΕΜΕΣ), College Year in Athens. She holds a PhD in

Anthropology from Rice University and has published and presented on consumer debt and bankruptcy, the effect of the Greek crisis on overindebted households, and everyday economic life in Greece. She is currently writing an ethnography on the story of consumer credit in Greece in the 21st century.

Evdoxios Doxiadis is an Associate Professor at the Department of History at Simon Fraser University. His research is on Greek, Balkan, and Mediterranean history with a focus in the 18th and 19th centuries and a particular interest in questions of gender, law, state formation, and minorities. His publications include *The Shackles of Modernity: Women, Property, and the Transition from the Ottoman Empire to the Modern Greek State 1750–1850* (2011) and *State, Nationalism, and the Jewish Communities of Modern Greece* (2018).

Note

1. See, for a small example of disparate opinions, Kalyvas, Pagoulatos and Tsoukas (2012); Lapavitsas (2014); Pappas (2017); Varoufakis (2016).

References

Ireland, Patrick R. 2011. "Female Migrant Domestic Workers in Southern Europe and the Levant: Towards an Expanded Mediterranean Model?" *Mediterranean Politics* 16(3): 343–63.
Kalyvas, Stathis, George Pagoulatos, and Haridimos Tsoukas, eds. 2012. *From Stagnation to Forced Adjustment Reforms in Greece, 1974–2010*. London: Hurst & Company.
Lapavitsas, Kostas. 2014. *Lexi pros Lexi: Keimena yia tin Elliniki Krisi, 2010–2013*. Athens: Topos.
Pappas, Takis S. 2013. "Why Greece Failed." *Journal of Democracy* 24(2): 31–45.
———. 2017. *Se Tentomeno Skoini Ethnikes Kriseis aki Politikoi Akrovatismoi apo ton Trikoupi eos ton Tsipra*. Athens: Ikaros.
Rozakou, Katerina. 2011. "The Pitfalls of Volunteerism: The Production of the New, European Citizen in Greece." *European Institute for Progressive Cultural Policies*. Retrieved 25 January 2017 from http://eipcp.net/policies/rozakou/en.
Varoufakis, Yanis. 2016. "Greek Debt Denial: A Modest Debt Restructuring Proposal and Why It Was Ignored." In *Too Little Too Late: The Quest to Resolve Sovereign Debt Crises*, edited by Martin Guzman, José Antonio Ocampo, and Joseph E. Stiglitz, 84–105. New York: Columbia University Press.

Index

9 781789 208320